INDEX
TO
LOUDOUN COUNTY
VIRGINIA

Wills

1757–1850

Louisa Skinner Hutchison

HERITAGE BOOKS
2012

HERITAGE BOOKS
AN IMPRINT OF HERITAGE BOOKS, INC.

Books, CDs, and more—Worldwide

For our listing of thousands of titles see our website
at
www.HeritageBooks.com

Published 2012 by
HERITAGE BOOKS, INC.
Publishing Division
100 Railroad Ave. #104
Westminster, Maryland 21157

Copyright © 1997 Louisa Skinner Hutchison

Other Heritage Books by the author:
Apprentices, Poor Children and Bastards, Loudoun County, Virginia, 1757–1850

All rights reserved. No part of this book may be reproduced or transmitted in any form or by any means, electronic or mechanical, including photocopying, recording or by any information storage and retrieval system without written permission from the author, except for the inclusion of brief quotations in a review.

International Standard Book Numbers
Paperbound: 978-1-888265-11-8
Clothbound: 978-0-7884-9374-4

INTRODUCTION

In the 1960s while I was employed in the Clerk's Office of Loudoun County, some attorneys searching titles to real estate inquired for the devisee index to wills. Apparently some jurisdictions had them, but there was none for Loudoun. I realized what a help it would be in tracing the chain of ownership, so I embarked on the project of making such an index. Other duties in the office prevented me from spending much time on this, so it was soon abandoned.

After I retired I resumed the project. By this time I had become more interested in genealogy and realized that not only the names of devisees but of administrators, executors, and others mentioned would be of interest, and perhaps assistance in locating the section of the county in which the testator lived. By 1990 I had listed the names in the wills recorded from 1757 to 1843. I found the list useful and mentioned it to several others by offering to check it for a name for which they were looking. Then in 1995, it was suggested that the list could be published. It was decided to include the names of witnesses and to extend the list to include wills recorded through 1850.

This book is the result of that work. Spellings may vary, but an attempt has been made to follow the spelling in the will books. I hope this book will be of help to those who seek ancestors in Loudoun County, Virginia.

Louisa S. Hutchison
Leesburg, Virginia
May 1997

Abbreviations

< age	under age
Admr.	Administrator
[c], [cl], [c2]	codicil, first codicil, second codicil
Dau.	Daughter
dec'd.	Deceased
Exor.	Executor
Gr-	Grand
[GS]	German Script Name
Wit.	Witness
W/o	wife of

How to use this book

This book lists the names of persons mentioned in Loudoun County, Virginia wills between 1757 and 1850. A testator's entry is bold. It consists of the name of the individual, the will book and page, and a series of dates. The first year is the year the will was written. The last date is the year the will was probated. If there are more then two years shown, the middle years are the years of the codicils. Additional information about the testator may be included, such as occupation or place of residence. A name entry consists of the name of the individual, the relationship to the testator, and further identifying information. If only a name is listed this means that a relationship was not identified in the will.

Persons interested in obtaining copies of the wills identified in this book may contact the publisher for further information.

INDEX TO LOUDOUN COUNTY WILLS, 1757 - 1850

Thomas, Evan, A:1, 1757
Potts, Jonas, Son-in-law
Thomas, James, Son
Thomas, David, Son
Thomas, Ann, Wife
Langley, John, Wit.
Burson, Benjamin, Wit.
Burson, Sarah, Wit.
Davis, Thomas, A:3, 1758
Davis, Margaret, Mother
Davis, John, Brother
Vernon, Ruth, Wit.
Mobley, Mary, Wit.
Marcy, Charles, A:10, 1757/59
Noding, Sarah, Cousin
Noding, W., Wit.
McPherson, Wm., Wit.
Brown, Benjamin, Wit.
Simond, Thomas, Wit.
Poultney, John, A:12, 1759
Poultney, Mary, Dau.
Poultney, Sarah, Dau.
Poultney, Anthony, Son
Poultney, Elenor, Wife
Davis, Sarah, A:14, 1759
Plackney, Sarah, Niece
Davis, John, Brother
Davis, Rachell, Niece, married Pritchet
Thomas, Elizabeth, Sister
Wright, Mary, Sister
Kelly, Thomas, Wit.
Owsley, Wm., Wit.
Davis, Jonathan, Wit.
Hollingsworth, Isaac, A:21, 1758/59
Hollingsworth, Ann, Dau.
Hollingsworth, Jonah, Son
Hollingsworth, Unborn child
Hollingsworth, Lydia, Dau.
Hollingsworth, Phebe, Dau.
Hollingsworth, Rachel, Wife
Hough, John, Exor.
Janney, Abel, Wit.
Poultney, John, Wit.
Norton, Edward, Wit.
Janney, Joseph, Wit.
Jackson, Alexis, Renter
Jackson, Heneritta, Renter, husband & wife
Maccoy, Wm., Wit.
Jackson, Henry, Wit.
Booth, Robert, A:24, 1759/60
Chambers, Viallator, Gr-Dau.
Stump, Jane, Dau., w/o Thomas
Stump, Elizabeth, Gr-Dau.
Booth, James, Son
Booth, John, Son
Chambers, Ann, Dau., w/o William
Jenning, Mary, A:25, 1760
Foutch, Mary, Dau.
Sinkler, Sarah, Dau.
Jenning, Rebeccah, Dau.
Donohow, Margrate, Dau.
McDowell, Ann, Dau.
McDowell, Jean, Dau.
Campbell, Aens., Wit.
McCarty, John, Wit.
Davis, Elizabeth, Wit.
[Note: the will is signed by her mark and is written Jenney, indexed as Janney, Order Book A:342 says Jenning, inventory says Jennings; Mary married Thomas McDowell, then Alexander Jennings (Chancery M2797)]
Spurr, James, A:29, 1759/60
Spurr, Judath, Wife
Spurr, Richard, Son
Spurr, Judath, Dau.
Owens, John, Wit.
Williams, Original, Wit.
Hancocke, Wm., Wit.
Adams, Gabriel, A:35, 1761
Adams, Philip, Son
Adams, Elizabeth, Wife
Adams, William, Brother
Adams, —, Son
Adams, —, Son
Stark, William, Wit.
Littleton, William, Wit.
Dement, Benoni, Wit.

Megeach, Joseph, A:36, 1761
  Megeach, —, Unborn child
  Megeach, Mary, Wife
  Megeach, Anne, Dau.
  Megeach, John, Son
  Megeach, Elizabeth, Dau.
  Megeach, Joseph, Son
  Megeach, Jane, Dau.
  Megeach, James, Son
  Megeach, Thomas, Son
  McIlheney, John, Wit.
  Yates, Joseph, Wit.
  Lynham, Phil., Wit.
Insle, Henry, A:37, 1761
  Baty, Jean, Sister-in-law
  Insle, Mary, Wife
  Insle, William, Son
  Foster, Isabel
  Mead, William, Wit.
  Ross, William, Wit.
  Wildman, Jacob, Wit.
Yates, Joseph, A:43, 1761
  Yates, Alice, Wife
  Yates, Robert, Son
  Yates, Benjamin, Son
  Yates, Isaac, Son
  Yates, Alice, Dau.
  Yates, Jane, Dau.
  Yates, Providence's children, Dau.
  Yates, Joseph, Son
  Yates, Hannah, Dau.
  Yates, William, Son
Roberts, Richard, A:56, 1762
  Green, Ruth, Dau.
  Roberts, Joseph, Son
  Roberts, Ann, Wife
  Roberts, Ann, Dau.
  Roberts, Richard, Son
  Roberts, John, Son
  Roberts, William, Son
  Roberts, Mary, Dau.
  Roberts, Susanna, Dau.
  Jones, William, Exor.
  Massey, Lee, Wit.
  Steere, James, Wit.
Read, Joseph, A:57, 1761/62
  Read, Barbary, Wife
  Read, Joseph, Son
  Read, William, Son
  Read, Thadeus, Son, son of former wife
  Read, John, Son
  Read, Reuben, Son
  Read, Andrew, Son
  Read, Elizabeth, Dau.
  Read, Frances, Dau.
  Read, Lettice, Dau.
  Read, Ann, Dau.
  Read, Ruth, Mother
  Hutchison, Jeremiah, Exor.
  Porter, Edward, Wit.
  Johnson, Jeffrey, Wit.
  Porter, Mary, Wit.
Sinckler, Wayman Sr., A:59, 1762
  Sinckler, Alexander, Son
  Sinckler, Isaac, Son
  Sinckler, Mary, Dau.
  Sinckler, George, Son
  Sinckler, Wayman, Son
  Sinckler, Elizabeth, Dau.
  Sinckler, Hester, Wife
  Sinckler, John, Brother
  Sinckler, Robert, Son
  Haynie, Bridgar, Exor.
  Wilson, Russel, Wit.
  Jordan, George, Wit.
  Jordan, Ann, Wit.
West, William Jr., A:73, 1762/63
  West, Charles, Son
  West, Mary, Wife
  West, Cato, Son
  West, W., Wit.
  Hall, John, Wit.
  Atterbury, William, Wit.
Shreve (or Shrieve), William, A:76, 1758/63
  Shrieve, Catherine, Wife
  Shrieve, David, Son, <21
  Shrieve, Mary, Dau., <18
  Shrieve, Elizabeth, Dau., <18,
  Shrieve, Sarah, Dau., <18
  Shrieve, Benjamin, Brother
  Shrieve, Elizabeth (Hulls), Sister
  Shrieve, Mary, Sister
  Shrieve, James, Brother
  Hulls, Elizabeth, Sister

Russell, Capt. Anthony, Exor.
Holmes, William, Wit.
Wildman, Jacob, Wit.
Seward, Nicholas, A:78, 1762/63
Seward, Anne, Wife
Sorrell, Thomas, Father-in-law
Chilton, Steerman, Wit.
Chilton, Elisabeth, Wit.
Sorrell, Martha, Wit.
O'Mehundro, Ann, A:95, 1752/63
Remey, William, Son
Grove, William, Wit.
Headen, Richd., Wit.
Grove, Elizabeth, Wit.
Champe, John, A:96, 1763
Champe, John, Son
Champe, Thomas, Son
Jones, Elizabeth, Dau.
Champe, Ann, Dau.
Champe, Susy, Dau.
Champe, John, Gr-Son
Peyton, Henry, Admr. w.w.a.
Hogan, Thomas, Wit.
Leech, George, Wit.
Coleman, Richard, A:98, 1763/64
Brewer, Elizabeth, Dau.
Coleman, James, Son
Hurst, Jemimah, Dau.
Coleman, Elenor, Wife
Masterson, Mary, Dau.
Evans, Griffith, Wit.
Gess, John, Wit.
Goteley, Elizabeth, Wit.
Harris, Samuel, A:103, 1757/64
Harris, Samuel, Son
Harris, Joseph, Son
Harris, Ann, Dau.
Harris, David, Son
Harris, William, Son
West, W., Wit.
West, Wm. Jr., Wit.
Gardner, Elender, Wit.
West, Ann, Wit.
Redmond, Andrew, A:111, 1764
Redmond, Mary, Wife
Redmond, William, Son
Redmond, Elizabeth, Dau.
Redmond, Ann, Dau.
Redmond, Margaret, Dau.
Redmond, John, Son

Redmond, Sarah, Dau.
Philips, Edmond, Son-in-law
Redmond, Andrew, Son
Crague, Margaret, Wit.
Thompson, Israel, Wit.
Arnet, Thomas, Wit.
Santclar, Margaret, A:115, 1764
Richardson, Mary, Dau.
Hamby, John, Friend
Santclar, John, Son
Morris, Samuel, Gr-Son
Hawling, John, Gr-Son
Hampton, Elizabeth, Dau.
Santclar, Margaret, Gr-Dau.
Morris, Benjamin, Gr-Son
Morris, Rebecka, Gr-Dau.
Vines, Ann, Friend
Luckett, Wm., Wit.
Luckett, Charity, Wit.
Luckett, Wm. Jr., Wit.
Vandiver, George, A:120, 1764
Vandiver, Amenthia, Dau.
Vandiver, Tobitha, Dau.
Vandiver, Sarah, Dau.
Vandiver, Edward, Son
Vandiver, Ann, Wife
Lane, James, Admr.
West, W., Wit.
Smith, William, Wit.
Tyler, John, Wit.
Field, John, Wit.
Spencer, Jno., Wit.
Hall, Jas., Wit.
Long, Thomas, A:122, 1764/65
Long, James, Friend
Massey, Lee, Wit.
Weisel, Frederick, Wit.
Stroud Sr., Samuel, A:124, 1765
Beeson, Phebe, Dau.
Stroud, James, Exor.
Redmond (alias Stroud),
  George, Wife's son
Stroud, Samuel, Son
Stroud, Susanah, Dau., < age
Stroud, Ann, Dau., <18
Stroud, Ann, Wife
Potts, Samuel, Exor.
Potts, Jonas, Son-in-law
Potts, Mary, Dau.
Pitts, Martha, Dau.

Hatfield, Thomas, Wit.
Potts, Ezekiel, Wit.
Dillon, Wm., Wit.
Willcoxson (alias Winser) John, A:125, 1765
Hawling, John Wilcoxsen, Wife's son
Willcoxson, Agnes, Mother
Willcoxson, Mary, Wife
Willcoxson, Elizabeth, Dau., <16
Luckett, William Sr., Friend
Luckett, William Jr., Wit.
Hanby, John, Wit.
Cole, Mary, Wit.
McGrew, Charles of Pa., A:134, 1764/65
McGrew, James, Son
McGrew, John, Son
McGrew, Charles, Son
McGrew, Elizabeth, Dau.
McGrew, Robert, Son, <17
Switser, Jacob, Wit.
Wanger, Abraham, Wit.
Millard, Jos., Wit.
Ethel (or Ethell), John, A:137, 1766
Ethel, Winefred, Wife
Lewis, Thomas, Wit.
Simpson, Gilbert, Wit.
O'Neal, Ferdinando, Wit.
Dyel, William, A:138, 1765/66
Dyel, Tibithe, Dau.
Dyel, Elizabeth, Wife
Dyel, James, Son
Dyel, Leonard, Son
Dyer, Ann, Dau., w/o James
Dyel, Sarah
Dyel, Stasey
Dyel, Littes
Dyel, Rebecca
Dyel, William George Josius, Son
Stephens, Joseph, Exor.
Sotherd, William, Exor.
Sothard, Larance, Wit.
Griffith, Charles, Wit.
Sotherd, Sarah, Wit.
Grimes Sr., Nicholas, A:144, 1765/66
Grimes, Nicholas, Son
Grimes, Philip, Son

Grimes, Edward, Son
Grimes, William, Gr-Son, son of William
Lay, Sarah, Dau.
Trammel, Jemima
Donaldson, James, Wit.
Lay, Silvester, Wit.
Payne, Sanford, Wit.
Hopewell, John, A:146, 1766
Hopewell, six children
Hopewell, Hannah, Wife
Hopewell, Thomas, Brother
King, John, Father-in-law
King, Osborn, Wit.
King, John, Wit.
Donaldson, James, Wit.
Wiggington, James, A:148, 1766
Botts, Aaron, Brother-in-law
Botts, Sibacah, Mother-in-law
Botts, Seth, Father-in-law
Wiggington, all children, boys <18, girls <16
Wiggington, Benjamin, Eldest Son
Wiggington, John, Brother
Wiggington, Sarah, Wife
Wiggington, Sarah, Mother
Clage, Joseph, Wit.
Campbell, Aens., Wit.
Ellis, Robert, A:152, 1766
Hews, Edward, Admr.
Ellis, Marget, Dau.
Ellis, Nancy, Dau.
Ellis, Ruth, Dau.
Ellis, Mary, Dau., <16
Ellis, Samuel, Son, <16
Ellis, Robert, Son, <16
Ellis, Mary, Wife
Ellis, Jassa, Son
Ellis, Elias, Son
Jones, William, Wit.
George, Thomas, Wit.
Dehaven, Abrm., Wit.
Phillips, Thomas Sr., A:155, 1766
Phillips, Jenkin, Son
Phillips, Thomas, Son
Phillips, Jenkin, Brother
Phillips, Joana, Wife
Phillips, Milford, Son
Phillips, John, Son

Phillips, Cathrone, Dau.
Potts, Jonas, Wit. blacksmith
Phillips, Thomas, Wit. wagoner
Phillips, Mary, Wit.
Hague, John, A:167, 1767
Hague, Ann, Wife
Hague, Francis, Son, <14
Hague, Samuel, Son, <14
Hague, Jonah, Son, <14
Mead, William Jr., Exor.
Baker, Wm., Wit.
Rhodes, Moses, Wit.
Hague, Isaac, Wit.
Mead, William Sr., Exor.
Janney, Mary, A:169, 1767
Hough, John, kinsman, Exor.
Janney, Mahlon, Son
Janney, Ruth, Dau.
Janney, Mary, Dau.
Brooke, Hannah, Dau.,
  w/o James
Hague, Francis, Wit.
Hough, Joseph, Wit.
Janney, Samuel, Wit.
Jackson, Lovell, A:174, 1752/67
Bell, William, son of Elizabeth
Bell, Elizabeth
Botts, Ann, sister of
  Elizabeth Bell
West, W., Wit.
Ethell, John, Wit.
Ethell, Winniford, Wit.
Middleton, Jane, A:175, 1767
Brown, Molly Middleton
Middleton, Lettice, Dau., <16
Middleton, Hannah, Dau., <16
Brown, Joseph, Exor.
Miller, John, Wit.
Lane, James, Wit.
Hamrick, James, Wit.
Illegible Name, Wit.
John, James, A:178, 1767
—, Mary, Step-Dau.
John, Mary, Wife
Potts, Jonas, Wit. (blacksmith)
Burson, Joseph, Wit. (mason)
Sholders, Conrod, Wit.
Evans, John, A:180, 1766/67
Evans, Elizabeth, Wife
Evans, William, Son

Evans, Mary, Dau.
Evans, Joshua, Son
Evans, David, Son
Evans, Richard, Son
Evans, Elizabeth, Dau.
Evans, Griffith, Son
Thomas, Amy, Dau.
Davis, Nathan, Wit.
Davis, John, Wit.
Marshal, Joseph, Wit.
John, Mary, A:182, 1767
Phillips, Mary, Dau.,
  w/o Thomas
Phillips, Jenkins, Wit.
Shoulders, Conrad, Wit.
Potts, Jonas, blacksmith, Wit.
Moss, John, A:190, 1767/68
Talbut, Anne, Dau.
Moss, Thomas Belford, Son
Lewis, Mary, Dau.
Moss, John Jr., Exor. & Son
Moss, Elizabeth, Dau.
Moss, Frances, Dau.
Moss, Hannah, Dau.
Moss, William, Exor. & Son
Moss, Frances, Wife
Andrews, John, Wit.
Lewis, Thos., Wit.
Field, John, Wit.
Potts, David, A:194, 1768
Potts, Ezekiel, Son
Potts, Nathan, Son
Potts, Ann, Wife
Potts, Jonas, Son
Potts, Samuel, Son
Pearson, Christian, Gr-Dau.
Potts, Jonathan, Son
Potts, David, Son
Potts, Rachel, Dau.
Potts, Susanah, Dau.
Bagus, Mary, Dau.
David, Jenkin, Wit.
Lewellin, Thomas, Wit.
Dillon, Wm., Wit.
Potts, Jonas, A:202, 1768
Potts, Mary, Wife
Potts, John, Son
Potts, David, Son
Potts, Samuel, Son
Potts, Jonas, Son

Potts, Edward, Son
Potts, Hannah, Dau., <18
Potts, Elizabeth, Dau., <18
Vestel, John, Brother-in-law
Person, Samuel, Brother-in-law
Potts, Jonathan, Brother
Potts, David, Father, dec'd.
Potts, Samuel, Wit.
Conrads, James, Wit.
Roberts, Owen, Wit.

Scatterday, George, A:206, 1768
Scatterday, Esther, Wife
Scatterday, John, Son, <14
Craig, John, Exor.
Thompson, Israel, Wit.
Nixon, George, Wit.
Dunnington, George, Wit.

McGeach, Thomas, A:208, 1768/69
Griggs, George, Exor. & Friend
McGeach, John, Sister, <21
McGeach, William, Brother
McGeach, Jane, Sister
McGeach, Elizabeth, Sister
McGeach, Ann, Sister
McGeach, James, Brother
McGeach, Joseph, Sister, <21
Cavens, William, Father-in-law
  [Note: actually Step-father]
Coutsman, Jacob, Wit.
Sands, Isaac, Wit.
Roberts, Owen, Wit.

Miller, John, A:213, 1769
Miller, Catherine, Wife
Thompson, Rev. Amos, Exor.
Miller, our children
Thompson, Amos, Wit.
Kevens (Cavens), John, Wit.
Patterson, Neil, Wit.

Tyler, Anne, A:215, 1769
Tyler, Benjamin, Son, <16
Tyler, Anne, Dau.
Tyler, Charles, Son, <16
Tyler, Susanna, Dau.
Tyler, John, Son
Tyler, Spence, Son, <16
Tyler, William, Son
West, George, Exor.
Peake, John, Exor.

Smith, William, Exor.
Whitely, William, Wit.
Taylor, John, Wit.
Moore, William, Wit.

Monroe, George, A:218, 1767/69
Conner, Margaret, Orphan child
Monroe, Sarah, Dau., <18
Monroe, Roseannah, Dau., <18
Monroe, Philis, Wife
Thompson, Rev. Mr., Exor.
Buckley, James, Exor. & Wit.
Roszel, Stephen, Wit.
Duncan, Joshua, Wit.

John, Thomas, A:220, 1769
John, Martha, Wife
John, Benjamin, Son
John, Mary, Dau., < age
John, Thomas, Son, < age
John, Sarah, Dau., < age
John, Hannah, Dau., < age
Thomas, Joseph, Friend
George, Thomas, Friend
Robinett, Allen, Wit.
Lewis, George, Wit.
Price, Jonathan, Wit.

John, Thomas, A:220, 1769
John, Dinah, Dau., < age
John, John, Son, < age
John, Daniel, Son, < age
Thomas, Joseph, Friend
George, Thomas, Friend
Robinett, Allen, Wit.
Lewis, George, Wit.
Price, Jonathan, Wit.

Burson, Benjamin, A:222, 1769
Burson, Joseph, Father
Burson, Ann, Wife
Roberts, Owen, Father-in-law
My children, Not named
Burson, —, Son
Burson, —, Son
Potts, Samuel, Exor.
Dodd, John, Wit.
Williams, John, Wit.
Illegible, Johan, Wit.

Mobley, Samuel, A:224, 1769
Fouch, Susannah, Dau.
Awbery, Mary, Dau.
Mobley, Mary, Wife

Fouch, Jacob, Wit.
Fouch, Alice, Wit.
Jacobs, Anne, Wit.
Sanders, Phillip, A:225, 1769
  Sanders, Elizabeth, Wife
  Sanders, William, Son
  Sanders, Benjamin, Son
  Lewis, John, Wit.
  Taylor, John, Wit.
West, William, A:226, 1769
  West, Charles, Gr-Son
  Peyton, Craven, Gr-Son
  West, Thomas, Son
  Peyton, Francis, Gr-Son
  West, Cato, Gr-Son
  Peyton, Margaret, Gr-Dau.
  West, John, Son
  Peyton, William, Gr-Son
  Peyton, Anne, Dau.
  West, Charles, Son
  West, Mary, Wife
  West, Elizabeth, Gr-Dau., dau.
    of Charles & Ann
  West, William, Son, dec'd.
  Hall, John, Wit.
  Hall, Bety, Wit.
  Hamilton, Robert, Wit.
  Baker, Wm., Wit.
Rhodes, Moses, A:229, 1769
  Rhodes, Ann, Dau.
  Rhodes, Elizabeth, Dau.
  Rhodes, Abigail, Dau.
  Rhodes, Mary, Dau.
  Rhodes, Hannah, Dau.
  Rhodes, Joseph, Son
  Rhodes, Thomas, Son
  Rhodes, John, Son
  Rhodes, William, Son
  Rhodes, Mary, Wife
  Baker, Wm., Wit.
Robertson, Henry, A:236, 1769
  Robertson, Jenny, Wife
  Barrot, Thomas Mattox
  Jenings, James, Wit.
  Linton, John, Wit.
  Carter, Peter, Wit.
Moren, Joseph, A:237, 1769
  Moren, Prudence, Dau.
  Moren, Nancy, Dau.
  Moren, Katy, Dau.
  Moren, Joseph
  Moren, John
  Moren, Daniel
  Moren, Peggy, Dau.
  Moren, James, Son
  Moren, Molly, Wife
  Metcalfe, John, Exor.
  Metcalfe, James, Wit.
  Pickett, William, Wit.
Arnet, Alexander, A:239, 1769/70
  Arnet, Samuel, Son
  Arnet, Ruth, Wife
  Phillips, Thomas, Wit.
  Boulton, Margaret, Wit.
  Boulton, David, Wit.
Andrews, John, A:252, 1766/70
  Turner, Fielding Major
  Turner, Anne
  Turner, Lewis Ellzey, Godson
  Groves, William
  Lane, William Carr, Exor.
  Patterson, Fleming, Exor.
  Hutchison, Jeremiah, Wit.
  Lane, Hardage, Wit.
Johnson, John, A:253, 1770
  Chaney, Mary, Dau.
  Johnson, Smith, Son
  Johnson, Mary, Wife
  Johnson, Bayley, Son
  Debell, William, Wit.
  Swain, Joseph, Wit.
  Hutchison, Jeremiah, Wit.
  Debell, John, Wit.
Chinn, Christopher, A:254, 1769/70
  Downman, William, Cousin
  Chinn, Christopher, Nephew,
    son of Charles
  Downman, Rawleigh, Cousin
  Chinn, Charles, Brother
  Downman, Rawleigh, Brother
  Chinn, John, Nephew, son of
    Charles
  Chinn, Christopher, Nephew,
    son of Elijah
  Chinn, Elijah, Brother
  Chinn, Rawleigh, Nephew, son
    of Elijah
  Chinn, Elizabeth, Niece, dau. of
    Elijah

Powell, Leven, Wit.
Chinn, Thomas, Wit.
Goodin, John, A:256, 1769/70
Pettit, —, children of
　Isaac & Margaret
Pettit, John, son of
　Isaac & Margaret
Goodin, Samuel, son of
　David & Kesiah
Goodin, Amos, Brother
Goodin, Martha, dau. of
　Amos & Sarah
Goodin, David, son of
　Amos & Sarah
Goodin, Samuel, son of
　Amos & Sarah
Goodin, Rebekah, dau. of
　Amos & Sarah
Goodin, Sarah dau. of
　Amos & Sarah
Forg, Francis, Exor.
Reed, Jonathan, Wit.
Marks, Elisha, Wit.
Oliver, Peter, Wit.
Davis, Nathan, A:259, 1770
Evans, Mary, Sister
Matthews, Anne, Sister
Davis, Mary, Wife
Davis, John, Brother
Davis, Enoch, Brother
Moss, John, Wit.
Frier, James, Wit.
Evans, John, A:260, 1770
Henderson, Amy, Dau.
Evans, Mary, Wife
Evans, William, Son, <21
Evans, Mary, Dau.
Evans, Catherine, Dau.
Evans, Sarah, Dau.
Perril, Charity, Dau.
Read, Jacob, Exor.
Bodine, Jacob, Wit.
Bodine, Isaac, Wit.
Cooper, Apollos, Wit.
Best, John, A:264, 1769/70
Best, Martha, Wife
Rattaken, Rachel, Dau.
Best, James, Son
Best, Thomas, Son
Best, John, Gr-Son,
　son of Thomas
Best, John, Son
Cannaday, James, Wit.
Jameson, Benjamin, Wit.
Roberts, Owen, Wit.
Beavers, Thomas, A:269, 1770
Carlile, David, Exor.
Beavers, William, Son
Beavers, Thomas, Son
Beavers, Robert, Son
Beavers, Martha, Wife
Beavers, Joseph, Son
Beavers, Samuel, Youngest Son
Beavers, John, Son
Beavers, James, Son
Beavers, William Sr., Exor.
Clack, Spencer, Wit.
Beaty, William, Wit.
Beaty, Andrew, Wit.
Reeder, Joseph, A:271, 1770
Reeder, Eleanor, Dau.
Reeder, David, Son
Reeder, Daniel, Son
Reeder, Joseph, Son
Reeder, William, Eldest Son
Reeder, Elizabeth, Wife
Reeder, Mary, Dau.
Reeder, Stephen, Son
Reeder, Jacob, Son
Reeder, Elijah, Son
Thomas, Evan, Stepson
Lake, Elizabeth, Dau.
Russell, Anthony, Exor.
Huff, John
Pigg, Nathaniel
Poling, Samuel, Wit.
Snedeker, Garrat, Wit.
Poling, Samuel Jr.., Wit.
Johnson, Tunes, Wit.
Poling, Peter, Wit.
Poling, John, Wit.
Price, Evan, A:272, 1762/70
Robeson, Ann, Dau.,
　w/o Sylvanus
Price, Jonathan, Son
Price, John, Son
Price, Oliver, Son
Price, Sarah, Dau.
Price, Mary, Dau.

Price, Sarah, Wife, mother of all my children
Smith, Eleanor, Dau., w/o John Jr.
Massey, Lee, Wit.
Patterson, Samuel, Wit.
Jones, William, Wit.
Lane, William Carr, A:284, 1770
Lane, Joseph, Brother
Lane, James, Brother
Lane, Sally, Dau.
Lane, Carr Wilson, Son
Lane, Presly Carr, Son
Lane, Anne, Wife
Cockerell, Thomas, Wit.
Brown, Joseph, Wit.
Clark, Charles, Wit.
John, Thomas, A:289, 1770/71
Reynolds, Rachel, Dau., of Carolina
Hogue, William, Exor.
Harris, Samuel, Son-in-law
Cox, Jane, Dau., of Carolina
Mathews, Hannah, Dau., of Maryland
Williams, Richard, Exor.
Harris, Mary, Dau., w/o Samuel
Gregg, George, Wit.
Howell, Abner, Wit.
Roberts, Owen, Wit.
Chinn, Elijah, A:290, 1771
Dent, Rhoda, child of Rhoda
Dent, Mary
Dent, William, child of Rhoda
Chinn, Elizabeth, Dau.
Chinn, Christopher, Son
Chinn, Rawleigh, Son
Harrison, Peyton, Wit.
Harrison, Burr, Wit.
Meyrick, Griffith, A:294, 1771
Meyrick, Hannah, Dau.
Meyrick, John, Son
Meyrick, James, Son
Meyrick, Hannah, Wife
Wells, Jacob, Wit.
Greenwood, Caleb, Wit.
Smith, William, Wit.
Ellis, Elias, Wit.

Porter, Edward, A:295, 1770/71
Porter, Ellender
Porter, Ann Murphy, Dau.
Porter, Edward, Son
Porter, John Brickey, Son
Porter, Elias, Son
Porter, Daniel, Son
Porter, Mary, Wife
Porter, Demsey, Brother
Porter, William, Brother
Lane, Hardage, Exor.
Carroll, Sanford, Exor.
Carroll, William Porter, Wit.
Carroll, Frances, Wit.
Clark, Susanna, Wit.
Lane, Aaron, Wit.
Thorn, Humphrey, A:297, 1771
Thompson, Israel, Son-in-law
Shreve, Samuel, Cousin
Shreve, James, Cousin
Shreve, Massey, Cousin
Russell, Wm., Wit.
Clandinen, Saml., Wit.
Dehaven, Abraham, A:298, 1770/71
Dehaven, Rebecca, Wife
Dehaven, Jesse, Son
Dehaven, Jacob, Son
Dehaven, Abraham, Son
Dehaven, Isaac, Son
Dehaven, Rebecca, Dau.
Dehaven, Elizabeth, Dau.
Dehaven, Hannah, Dau.
Dehaven, Ann, Dau.
Dehaven, Sarah, Dau.
McKinney, George, Wit.
Ellis, Elias, Wit.
Dehaven, William, Wit.
Everhard, Jacob, miller, A:300, 1771
Shover, Adam, Exor.
Everhard, —, Unborn child
Everhard, Charlotte, Dau.
Everhard, Jacob, Son
Everhard, Elizabeth, Wife
Ott, Nicholas, Exor.
Philips, Nicholas, Wit.
Crecelius, Rudolph, Wit.
Wikmen, William, Wit.
Haman, George, Wit.
Forgh, Adam, Wit.

Todhunter, John, A:303, 1770/71
Todhunter, Margaret, Wife
Todhunter, Isaac, Son
Todhunter, John, Son
Clapham, Josias, Wit.
Oxley, Henry Jr., Wit.
Sands, Isaac, Wit.

Marshall (or Martial), Joseph, A:304, 1770/71
Scott, Samuel, Exor.
Fryer (or Frier), Robert, Exor.
Marshall, Martha Hannah, Dau.
Marshall, James, Son
Marshall, Samuel, Son
Marshall, Rachael, Wife
Marshall, Joseph, Son
Marshall, Robert, Son
Marshall, Mary, Dau.
Marshall, Margaret, Dau.
Marshall, Racheal, Dau.
Moss, John, Exor.
Frier, James, Wit.
Scott, Joseph, Wit.
Fox, William, Wit.

Chilton, George, A:306, 1771
Chilton, Mary, Dau.
Chilton, Thomas John, Son
Chilton, Ann, Wife
Rozsell, Sarah, Dau.
Russell, Anthony, Exor.
Owsley, Thomas, Exor.
Lewis, Thomas, Exor.
Lewis, Ann, Wit.
Lewis, John, Wit.
Elliott, Catharine, Wit.

Jones, William, A:310, 1771
Griffith, Mary, Dau.
Jones, —, Wife
Jones, James, Son
Jones, Joshua, Son
Clapham, J., Wit.
Lewis, William, Wit.
Griffith, Sarah, Wit.

Taylor, Henry Sr., A:318, 1770/71
Williams, Walter, Son-in-law
Harden, Thomas, Son-in-law
Taylor, Susanna, Wife
Taylor, William, Son
Taylor, John, Son
Taylor, Henry, Son
Taylor, Joshua, Son
Cotton, William, Son-in-law
Williams, Notley, Son-in-law
Sutton, Mary, Wit.
Burk, John, Wit.
Burk, Rhoda, Wit.

Frier, James, A:340, 1771
Killgore, George, Exor., uncle of son Robert Frier
Muir, Robert, uncle of son Daniel Frier
Moss, John, Exor.
Frier, Daniel, Son
Frier, Robert, Son
Frier, Hannah, Dau.
Frier, Pheby, Dau.
Frier, —, Wife
Bayles, John, Wit.

Hutton, John, B:1, 1771/72
Hutton, Sarah, Wife
Edwards, Catherine
Hutton, Sarah, Gr-Dau., dau. of Thomas
Hutton, Joseph, Son
Hutton, John, Son
Purdom, Benjamin, Wit.
Edwards, John, Wit.
Purdom, Jeremiah, Wit.

Evans, Elisabeth, B:4, 1771/72
Thomas, Amet, Dau.
Gardner, Mary, Dau.
Evans, William, Son
Evans, Joshua, Son
Evans, Mary, Dau.-in-law
Coleman, James, Wit.
Fox, William, Wit.
Davis, Evan, Wit.

Stark, William, B:5, 1772
Minor, Mary, Dau.
Stark, Susanna, Wife
Stark, William, Son
Stark, John, Son
Stark, Siner, Dau.
Stark, Nancy, Dau.
Stark, Elizabeth, Dau.
Cockrell, Susannah, Dau.
Clapham, Josias, Exor.

Index to Loudoun County Wills, 1757 - 1850   11

Stanhope, William, Wit.
Littleton, William, Wit.
Harl, John, Wit.
Berkley, Elizabeth, B:9, 1772
Hancock, Alethea, Dau.
Berkley, Reubin, Son
Berkley, John, Son
Linton, Ann, Gr-Dau.
Clark, Charles, Wit.
Berkley, Scarlett, Wit.
Martin, Ralph, B:12, 1772
Homan, Ann, Dau.
Martin, Mary, Wife
Martin, William, Son
Martin, Joseph, Son
Martin, John, Son
Eaton, Mary, Dau.
Thompson, Israel, Exor.
Martin, Thomas, Son
Castleberry, Sarah, Dau.
Richardson, Joseph, Wit.
Cogswell, Joseph, Wit.
Hammon, Ephraim, Wit.
Conn, Hugh, B:14, 1771/72
Lewis, Thomas Jr., Exor.
Trammell, Garard Sr., Exor.
Conn, Coxon, Son
Conn, Mary, Wife
Conn, Hugh, Son
Conn, Ruth, Dau.
Conn, Josias, Oldest Son
Trammell, Garr, A child
Jenkins, James Sr., Wit.
Thrift, Ann, Wit.
Eliot, M—, Wit.
Wyatt, Thomas, B:21, 1772
Lynn, Mary, Dau.
Treebe, John, Exor.
Hanks, Elizabeth, Dau.
Wyatt, Margaret, Wife
Wyatt, Thomas, Son
Wyatt, Ruth, Dau.
Wyatt, Abner, Son
Wyatt, Margaret, Dau.
Wyatt, Reuben, Son
Williams, William, Exor.
Wyatt, Edward, Son
Wyatt, John, Son
Cooper, Sarah, Dau.

French, James, Wit.
Tobin, Esther, Wit.
Hauge, Isaac, Wit.
Wintzel, Adam, B:23, 1772
Wintzel, Elizabeth, Wife
Wintzel, Adam, Eldest Son
Richie, Frantz, Exor.
Daub, Henry, Exor.
Creedius, Rudolph, Wit.
Ruess, Michael, Wit.
Shoemaker, George, Wit.
Bartel, Eva, , Wit.
Gorham, Sanford, B:29, 1772/73
Triplett, Simon, Exor.
Gorham, Harving, Son
Vandiver, Sarah, Dau.
Gorham, William, Son
Gorham, Lamken, Son
Gorham, Ann, Wife
Kelsie, John, Servant
Orr, John, Wit.
Millan, Jane, Wit.
Vandiver, Sarah, Wit.
Chilton, Martha, B:31, 1772
Chilton, Sarah, Eldest Dau.
Chilton, Thomas, Son
Chilton, Mark, Son
Chilton, Nancy, Dau.
Chilton, James, Son
Chilton, John, Gr-Son,
    son of James
Chilton, Ann, Dau.-in-law,
    w/o son James
Clark, Mary, Dau.
Chilton, John, Wit.
Losson, Thomas, Wit.
Chilton, Sturman, Wit.
McIlhaney, John, B:39, 1773
McCamey, Mary, Dau.
McIlhaney, John, Son, <21
McIlhaney, Rosana, Wife
McIlhaney, James, Son
McIlhaney, Hanna, Dau.
McIlhaney, Rachel, Dau.
McIlhaney, Thomas, Son
Shore, Michael, Wit.
Nixon, James, Wit.

Jinkins, John Sr., B:46, 1772/73
Gibbs, Anne, Dau.
Gibbs, William, Exor.
Perry, Elizabeth, Dau.
Jenkins, Daniel, Wit.
Ballenger, William, Wit.
Stephens, Giles, B:47, 1772/73
Stephens, Edward, Son
Stephens, Giles, Son
Stephens, James, Son
Stephens, Ephraim, Son
Stephens, Thomas, Son
Stephens, Else, Wife
Cole, Mary, Dau.,
  widow of William
Abbett, Joseph, Wit.
Abbett, Richard, Wit.
Collings, Joseph, Wit.
Pool, Benjamin, B:49, 1773
Pool, Mary, Dau.
Pool, Martha, Dau.
Pool, Hannah, Dau.
Pool, Israel, Youngest Son
Pool, Joseph, Son
Pool, Rebecca, Wife
Pool, Benjamin, Son
Pool, Ann, Dau.
Pool, Elisath, Dau.
Pool, Sarah, Dau.
Dillon, James, Wit.
Jones, Stephen, Wit.
Dillon, William, Wit.
Fierst, John, B:72, 1773/74
Fierst, Ann, Dau.
Fierst, Peter, Son
Fierst, Christian, Eldest Son
Fierst, Elizabeth, Dau.
Fierst, Sarah, Wife
Mangold, Valentine, Wit.
Clise, John, Wit.
Osborn, Nicholas, Wit.
Thompson, Edward, B:75, 1773/74
Thompson, Israel, Son
Woodward, Jesse, Son-in-law
Woodward, Prudence, Dau.
Woodward, Sarah, Gr-Dau.
Woodward, Jane, Gr-Dau.
Woodward, Prudence, Gr-Dau.

Janney, Joseph, Exor.
Willson, David, Wit.
Clendinan, Samuel, Wit.
Chamberlin, John, Wit.
Evans, Joshua, B:77, 1773
Thomas, Emmet (Amet), Sister
Thomas, William, Sister's son
Evans, David, his widow,
  Sister-in-law
Evans, John, Nephew,
  son of William
Evans, William, Brother
Wiggenton, Roger, Exor.
Evans, Martha, Wife
Gardner, Mary, Sister
Spurr, Richard, Exor.
Fryor, Robert, Exor.
Burns, John, Servant
Robinson, Thomas, Servant
Moss, John, Wit.
Scott, Robert, Wit.
Harper, William, Wit.
Tobin, James, B:80, 1774
Tobin, George, Son
Tobin, Thomas, Son
Tobin, Mary, Dau.
Tobin, Joseph, Son
Tobin, Lydia, Dau.
Tobin, Robert, Son
Tobin, Ruth, Dau.
Tobin, Naomy, Dau.
Tobin, Esther, Wife
Masterson, Sarah, Dau.
Tobin, Rosannah, Dau.
Gregg, Samuel, Wit.
Hague, Isaac, Wit.
Williams, Thomas, Wit.
Manamy, Charles, Wit.
Kirk, William, B:83, 1774
Hughes, Mary, Dau.,
  of Pennsylvania
Hughes, Elizabeth, Gr-Dau.
Hughes, Margaret, Gr-Dau.
Hughes, Rachel, Gr-Dau.
Hughes, Mary, Gr-Dau.
Brown, Mercer
Brown, Betsey,
  w/o William Brown
Brown, Mary, dau. of
  Mercer Brown

Reynolds, Elizabeth, Gr-Dau.
Brown, Sarah,
  w/o Mercer Brown
Clapham, Josias, Exor.
Brown, Henry, Wit.
John, James, Wit.
Brown, Sarah, Wit.
Sorrell, Thomas, B:89, 1774
Watson, Thomas Weldon, Gr-Son
Moss, Frances, Dau, w/o William
Sorrell, Martha, Dau.
Stevens, Hannah, Dau.,
  w/o Robert
Sorrell, Thomas Ballard, Son,
  son of Elizabeth
Sorrell, John Spence Ariss, Son,
  son of Elizabeth
Sorrell, Elizabeth, Wife
Rogers, Richard, Wit.
Harris, John, Wit.
Combs, Andrew, B:91, 1773/74
Combs, Israel, Son
Combs, Mary, Wife
Combs, Joseph, Son
Combs, Rebecca, Dau.
Combs, Andrew, Son
Combs, John, Son
Combs, Samuel, Brother
Combs, Mailon, Son
Megeath, James, Wit.
Vansikle, Gilbert, Wit.
McKee, Joseph, Wit.
Janney, Abel, B:98, 1770/74
Hutton, Joseph, Son-in-law
Hutton, Sarah, Dau.
Hough, John, Brother-in-law
Janney, Abel, Son
Janney, Joseph, Son
Janney, Samuel, Son
Janney, Amos, Son
Janney, John, Son
Janney, Rebeccah, Dau.
Janney, Rachel, Dau.
Janney, Ruth, Dau.
Baker, William, Son-in-law
Baker, Mary, Dau.
Janney, Sarah, Wife
Janney, Ruth, Wit.
Hough, Eleanor, Wit.

Sands, Edmund, B:102, 1774/75
Roach, Hannah, Dau.
Sands, —, Wife
Sands, Gideon, Gr-Son,
  son of Sarah
Sands, Isaac, Son
Sands, Joseph, Son
Sands, Benjamin, Son
Sands, Jacob, Son
Sands, Sarah, Dau.
Harriss, Jacob, Servant,
  son of Ann Harriss
Roach, James, Wit.
Shrigley, Lawrence, Wit.
Sands, Benjamin, Wit.
Baker, Nathan, B:104, 1775
Baker, Nathan, Son
Baker, Bitty, Dau.
Baker, Rachel, Dau.
Baker, Joseph, Son
Baker, Isaac, Son
Baker, Elizabeth, Wife
Matthews, Thomas, Wit.
Janney, Abel, Wit.
Feirst, Peter, B:106, 1775
Feirst, John, Son, <14
Cunnard, Jonathan, Exor.
Feirst, —, Wife
Feirst, Christian, Brother
Miller, Christian, Exor.
Mangold, Valentine, Wit.
Jamison, Robert, Wit.
Hamilton, James, B:111, 1775
Hamilton, John, Son, <21
Hamilton, James, Son
Hamilton, Mary, Dau., <18
Hamilton, Jane, Wife
Cavins, William, Exor.
Vandevander, Isaac, Exor.
Griffith, David, Wit.
Roberts, Owen, Wit.
McClelan, William, B:115, 1775
Murpha, Martha, Dau.
McClelan, Sarah Wilson, Wife
McClelan, Robert, Son
McClelan, William, Son
Skinner, Phineas, Exor.
Skinner, Richard, Exor.
Beavers, Mary, Dau.
Linn, William, Exor.

Linn, James
  Wyckoff, Nicholas, Wit.
  Gorham, Thomas, Wit.
  Lewis, Thomas, Wit.
Fox, William Sr., B:118, 1771/75
  Scott, Susannah, Dau.,
    w/o Samuel
  Scott, Margaret, Dau.,
    w/o Robert
  Fox, William, Son
  Fox, James, Son
  Fox, Elizabeth, Wife
  Scott, Samuel, Exor.
  Evans, William, Wit.
  Jackson, Thomas, Wit.
  Davis, Evan, Wit.
Letch, Jesse, B:119, 1775
  Paxton, Sarah, Sister
  Letch, Isaac, Brother
  Letch, —, Mother
  Beans, William, Exor.
  Hurst, John, Exor.
  Janney, Joseph, Wit.
  Janney, Abel Jr., Wit.
  Janney, Jacob, Wit.
Holms, William, B:123, 1775
  Holms, Sarah, Dau.
  Taverns (Tavener), George, Exor.
  Holms, Deborah, Dau.
  Brown, William, Exor.
  Holms, Rachel, Dau.
  Holms, Mary, Dau.
  Holms, Magret, Dau.
  Harris, Elizabeth, Dau.
  Holms, Joseph, Son, <21
  Holms, Joshua, Son, <21
  Holmns [sic], William, Son, <21
  Wilks, Samuel, Wit.
  Combs, Samuel, Wit.
  Updike, John, Wit.
  Holms, Edward, Wit.
Palmer, John, B:125, 1773/75
  Palmer, David, Son
  Palmer, Samuel, Eldest Son
  Palmer, Elisbeth, Wife
  Palmer, Priscilla, Youngest Dau.
  Palmer, Abel, Son
  Palmer, —, all my children

Jared, John, Wit.
  Howel, Timothy, Wit.
  Palmer, Jonathan, Wit.
Brooke, Hannah, B:127, 1776
  Janney, Cosmelia, Cousin,
    dau. of Abel
  Brooke, Elizabeth, Dau.
  Brooke, Deborah, Dau.
  Jones, Ann, Friend, Widow
  Janney, Mahlon, Nephew,
    son of Mary
  Janney, Amos, Nephew,
    son of Mary
  Janney, Mary, Sister
  Janney, Ruth, Sister
  Janney, Mahlon, Brother
  Janney, Joseph, Wit.
Carrol, Demse, B:132, 1776
  Jackson, Ann, Dau.
  Hogen, Thomas, Gr-Son,
    son of Mary Owens, <18
  Carrol, Rebekah, Wife
  Owens, Thomas Hogen, Gr-Son,
    son of Mary Owens, <18
  Owens, Mary, Dau.
  Welch, Jamimah, Dau.
  Pinkstone, Athaliah, Dau.
  Carrol, Mary Ann Heath, Dau.
  Pinkstone, Frances, Dau.,
    w/o Henry
  Carrol, Cynthia, Dau.
  Carrol, William Porter, Son
  Carrol, Demse Jr., Son
  Carrol, Sandford, Son
  Carrol, Sarah, Dau.
  Carrol, Rachel, Dau.
  Smith, William, Son-in-law
  Welch, Silvester, Son-in-law
  Turner, William Sr., Wit.
  Turner, William, Wit.
  Porter, Mary, Wit.
  Wisheart, Henry, Wit.
Byland, David, B:134, 1776
  Ellis, Elias, Exor.
  Byland, Martha, Dau.
  Byland, Rachel, Dau.,
    to be 21 on 18 May 1781
  Byland, Jesse, Son,
    to be 21 on 14 May 1779

Byland, Samuel, Son
Byland, Elizabeth, Dau.
Ross, William, Wit.
Brown, John Alexander, Wit.
Dehaven, Rebecca, Wit.
Pitters, Abraham, Wit.
West, Thomas (Captain), B:142, 1776/77
West, Elizabeth, Niece
Peyton, Craven, Exor.
West, Ann, Niece
Peyton, Valentine, Nephew
West, Charles, Brother
West, Charles, Nephew
Peyton, Cravin, Nephew
Peyton, Francis, Nephew
Peyton, William, Nephew
Peyton, Ann, Sister
Peyton, Margaret, Niece
Hychew, Nicholas, Wit.
Hychew, Jacob, Wit.
Hychew, Sybel, Wit.
Hychew, Mary, Wit.
Elliot, John, B:144, 1776/77
Elliot, Thomasin, Wife
Lewis, John, Friend
Mason, Thomson, Wit.
Lewis, Sarah, Wit.
Lewis, Levi, Wit.
Holmes, John, B:145, 1776/77
Holmes, William, Son
Holmes, Joshua, Son
Holmes, Mary, Wife
Rattican, James, Exor.
Minor, John, Wit.
Atchley (Askley), Joshua, Wit.
Minor, Francis, Wit.
Dorris, Martha, Wit.
Willson, George, B:146, 1776/77
Willson, Elizabeth, Dau.
Willson, Joseph, Son
Willson, George, Son
Willson, Margaret, Dau.
Willson, Cathrine, Wife
Longley, Joseph, Wit.
Hanks, John, Wit.
Skilman, John, B:148, 1776/77
Skilman, children, one unborn
Skilman, Catharine, Wife
Fox, Gabriel, Exor.

Overfield, Susannah, Wit.
Fox, William, Wit.
Fox, Ann, Wit.
Scott, Joseph, B:150, 1775/77
Marshall, Samuel, Exor.
Scott, Martha, Dau.
Price, Oliver, Exor.
Scott, Hannah, Wife
Scott, William, Son
Scott, Robert, Son
Scott, Thomas, Son
Marshal, James, Wit.
Scott, Samuel, Wit.
Marshal, Rachel, Wit.
Keen, John, B:159, 1775/77
Keen, Francis, Nephew
Russell, Anthony, Exor.
Keen, Richard, Son, dec'd.
Keen, Ann, Gr-Dau.
Keen, John, Gr-Son
Keen, Mary, Dau.
Keen, James, Son, <21
Keen, Richard, Son, <21
Keen, Sarah, Wife
Hopewell, Ann, Step-Dau.
Smalley, Andrew, Wit.
Mittinger, Daniel, Wit.
Potten, Henry, Wit.
Fitzgerald, James, Wit.
Field, Thomas Jr., B:161, 1776/77
Field, Thomas, Nephew
Priest, Eleanor, Sister,
  w/o William
Field, John, Nephew
Russell, Anthony (Col.), Exor.
Field, William, Brother
Field, John, Brother
Davis, Amos, Wit.
Potten, Henry, Wit.
Taylor, John, Admr. w.w.a.
Roberts, Owen, B:169, 1777
Burson, Joseph, Gr-Son, <21
Griffith, Ann, Dau.
Roberts, William, Son
Popkin, Catharine, Dau.
Roberts, Jean, Wife
Cavins, John, Wit.
Williams, John, Wit.
Danniel, Joshua, Wit.

Lutsinger, Philip, B:174, 1777
  Quick, Gasper Casper, Exor.
  Lutsinger, Rebecka, Dau.
  Lutsinger, Philip, Son
  Lutsinger, Michal, Son
  Lutsinger, Sarah, Wife
  Thomas, John, Wit.
  Darr, Conrod, Wit.
Howell, Hugh, B:176, 1777
  Howell, Margret, Wife
  Howell, William, Son
  Howell, Andrew, Son
  Howell, Abner, Son
  Howell, John, Son
  Howell, Benjamin, Son
  Howell, Daniel, Son
  Howell, Reuben, Son
  Howell, Rachel, Dau.
  Howell, Ann, Dau.
  Hixon, Timothy, Exor.
  Haugue, Francis, Wit.
  Hixon, William, Wit.
Hough, Joseph, B:177, 1777
  Hough, Amos, Exor.
  Hough, Janny, Son
  Hough, William, Son
  Hough, Thomas, Son
  Hough, Bernard, Son
  Hough, Sarah, Dau.
  Hough, —, Wife
  Hough, John, Wit.
  Hough, William Jr., Wit.
  Hough, William, Wit.
Poston, Francis, B:178, 1776/77
  Poston, Elija, Son
  Poston, Francis, Son
  Poston, Samuel, Son
  Poston, Sarah, Wife
  Barker, John, Wit.
  Saunders, James, Wit.
  Williams, Elijah, Wit.
Lucas, Alexander, B:179, 1776/77
  Lucas, Casander, Wife
  Lucas, Lindorus, Brother
  Littleton, John, Exor.
  Spurr, Richard, Exor.
  Littleton, William, Wit.
  Littleton, Charles, Wit.
  Herring, John, Wit.

Johnston, George Col., B:180, 1776/77
  Johnston, Archibald, Brother
  Johnston, Dennis McCarty, Brother
  Johnston, Wilfrid, Brother
  Johnston, Betty, Sister
  McCarty, Dennis, Uncle, dec'd.
  Powell, Leven, Exor.
Hamilton, Robert, B:181, 1777
  Hamilton, James, Son
  Hamilton, Robert, Son
  Hamilton, Jane, Dau.
  Hamilton, Ann, Dau.
  Nepper, Margaret
  Cooper, Alesander, Exor.
  McIntyr, Alexander, Exor.
  Murrey, Samuel, Wit.
  Hammatt, George, Wit.
  Harris, Henry, Wit.
Brickell, Wright, B:185, 1777
  Armat, Thomas, Exor.
  Brickell, Elizabeth, Wife
  Murrey, Samuel, Wit.
  Respess, Thomas, Wit.
Oxley, Henry, B:188, 1776/77
  Oxley, Henry, Son
  Oxley, Jesse, Gr-Son
  Henings, Hannah, Dau.
  Sanders, Barthaney, Gr-Dau.
  Oxley, Rachel, Dau.
  Howell, Mary, Dau.
  Slocombe, Robert, Exor.
  Janney, Joseph, Exor.
  Oxley, Clear
  Fulton, Robert, Wit.
  Oxley, Ann, Wit.
  Oxley, Brittain, Wit.
David, Jenkin, B:196, 1777
  David, Mary, Dau.
  David, Margaret, Dau.
  David, Isaac, Son
  David, John, Son
  Lodge, Josabad, Wit.
  Lodge, William, Wit.
  Rich, Samuel, Wit.
Martin, James, B:201, 1776/77
  Patten, Elizabeth, Servant
  Swick, Anthony, Servant
  Martin, William, Brother

Index to Loudoun County Wills, 1757 - 1850 17

Likins, William, Nephew
Smith, William, Exor.
Martin, Uphamma, Wife
Likins, James, Nephew
Martin, James, Nephew,
    son of William
Russell, Samuel, Wit.
Patten, John, Wit.
Farnsworth, Henry, Wit.
Butcher, Samuel, B:203, 1769/78
Phillips, Hannah, Dau.
Butcher, Elizabeth, Dau.
Pierce, Elese, Dau.
Butcher, Jane, Dau.
Butcher, John, Eldest Son
Butcher, Samuel, Son, <21
Butcher, Susannah, Wife
Phillips, Jenkin, Exor.
Overfelt, Benjamin, Exor.
Grady, James, Wit.
Boulton, David, Wit.
Romine, Peter, Wit.
Yeates, Samuel, B:217, 1778
Porter, James, Gr-Son
Money, Mary, Dau.
Money, Racheal, Dau.
Yeates, Johanna, Wife
Simmonds, Frances, Dau.
Yeates, Joshua, Son
Yeates, George, Son
Yeates, Benjamin, Son
Moss, John, Wit.
Said, William, Wit.
Money, Nicholas, Wit.
Cockerill, Thomas, B:219, 1777/78
Hall, Ann Remey, Dau.
Triplett, Elizabeth, Dau.
Cockerill, John, Son
Cockerill, Jeremiah, Son
Cockerill, Sandford, Son, one of
    three younger sons
Cockerill, Thomas, Son, one of
    three younger sons
Cockerill, Benjamin, Son, one of
    three younger sons
Hutchison, Jer., Wit.
Bland, Robert, Wit.
Haddocks, John, Wit.
Hogens, Wm., Wit.

Gist, John, B:221, 1778
Gist, Constant, Dau.
Keen, Elizabeth, Gr-Dau.
Gist, Henson Lewis, Gr-Son
Keen, Elender, Gr-child
Gist, Sarah, Dau.
Keen, Mary, Dau.
Gist, Thomas, Son
Keen, Nancy, Dau.
Gist, Nathaniel, Son
Lewis, George, Exor.
Gist, William, Son
Lewis, Vilet, Dau.
Low, Elizabeth, Dau.
Gist, John, Son
Gist, Mary, Wife
Lewis, Joseph, Wit.
Paul, James, Wit.
Reiley, Robert, Wit.
Wigginton, Roger, B:223, 1778
Davis, John, Exor.
Wigginton, William, Son
Davis, Mary, Dau.
Wigginton, Benjamin, Son, <21
Wigginton, Elizabeth, Dau.
Wigginton, Roger, Son
Wigginton, Elenor, Dau.
Wigginton, Henry, Son
Wigginton, Eleanor, Wife
Donaldson, —, Wit.
Jackson, John Jr., Wit.
Bayles, John, Wit.
Muir, Robert, B:227, 1778
Muir, Phebe, Wife
Muir, John, Son
Muir, George Cato, Son
Muir, Samuel, Son
Muir, Robert, Son
Muir, James, Son
Muir, Jeremiah, Son
Baylis, John, Exor.
Kilgore, George, Exor.
Dickey, James, Wit.
Noding, John, Wit.
Marshall, James, Wit.
Sanders, James, B:236, 1778
Sanders, Barbara, Dau.
Sanders, Henry, Nephew, <21
Sanders, John, Son
Sanders, James, Son

Sanders, Sarah, Wife
Sanders, Cyrus, Son
Sanders, Aaron, Son
Sanders, Moses, Son
Sanders, Henry, Son
Sanders, Presly, Son
Sanders, Gunnel, Son
Sanders, Thomas, Wit.
Price, Sarah, Wit.
Price, Jonathan, Wit.
Battson, James, B:243, 1778
Battson, John, Eldest Son
Battson, Margery, Wife
Crupper, Richard, Wit.
Gibson, Thomas, Wit.
Lewis, Nathan, B:244, 1777/78
Thompson, Israel, Exor.
Lewis, Solomon, Brother
Lewis, Stephen, Father
Davis, John, Wit.
White, Josiah, Wit.
Rich, Samuel, Wit.
Smith, William, B:246, 1778
Eskridge, Charles Major, Exor.
Orr, John, Exor.
Smith, Daniel, Brother, son of
  William & Jean Smith of
  Ireland
Smith, James, Brother, son of
  William & Jean Smith
Smith, Mary, Sister, son of
  William & Jean Smith
Smith, Elizabeth, Sister, son of
  William & Jean Smith
Smith, Jean, Sister, son of
  William & Jean Smith
Smith, Allice, Sister, son of
  William & Jean Smith
Smith, William, son of Hanna
  Millan, <21
Eskridge, Ann, Wit.
Lane, Sally, Wit.
Willson, John, Wit.
Walker, John, Wit.
Remey, Jacob Jr., Wit.
Lies, George, B:248, 1778
Lies, Dorety, Wife
Lies, John, Son
Lies, Joseph, Youngest Son
Lies, Catrean, Dau.

Lies, Dorety, Dau.
Lies, George, Son
Lies, Bartholeme, Son
Lies, Hannah, Dau.
Green, Richard, Wit.
Dawson, Matthias, Wit.
Corneluson, Garrett, B:257, 1775/79
Corneluson, Peter, Son
Corneluson, John, Son
Corneluson, Conrod, Son
Corneluson, Cornelus, Son
Corneluson, Mary, Wife
Adams, Thomas, Wit.
Adams, Sarai, Wit.
McVay, Patrick, Wit.
Russell, Anthony, B:271, 1779
Russell, Francis, Son
Russell, Milly, Eldest Dau.
Grayson, Rev. Spence, Exor.
Hall, Amy, dau. of Mary Hall, <18
Russell, Penelope, Youngest Dau.
Lake, Mary, w/o John
Ellzey, William, Wit.
Smith, Minor, Wit.
Allen, William, Wit.
Mitinger, Daniel, Wit.
Mitinger, Reynard, Wit.
McConahue, James, B:274, 1778/79
McConahue, Mary, Wife
McConahue, John, Son, < age
McConahue, Jamie, Son, < age
McConahue, Samuel, Son, < age
McConahue, Jane, Dau., < age
McConahue, Margaret, Dau.,
  < age
Swart, John, Wit.
Cochran, Nathan, Wit.
McFarland, John, Wit.
Pursly, Thomas Sr., B:279, 1779
Osburn, Richard, Son-in-law
Osburn, Hannah, Dau.
Pursly, Deborah, Dau.
Jamison, Robert, Exor.
McIlhaney, James, Exor.
Pursly, Elizabeth, Dau., <18
McCafferty, William,
  son of Cattrehen
Pursly, Christan, Dau., <18
McCafferty, Cattrehen

Index to Loudoun County Wills, 1757 - 1850　　　　　　　　　　19

Pursly, Mary, Dau., <18
Pursly, Larence, Son
Pursly, Benjamin, Son
Pursly, Daniel, Son
Pursly, Henry, Son
Pursly, Thomas, Son
Pursly, Samuel, Son
Pursly, John, Son
White, Josiah, Wit.
McIlhaney, John, Wit.
Smith, Richard, Wit.
Mortimer, William, B:281, 1779
Mortimer, Bethlehem, Sister
Mortimer, Sarah, Mother
Mortimer, Infamous, Brother
Geesling, Ann, Wit.
Anderson, Rebecca, Wit.
Evans, Zachariah, B:282, 1778/79
Wiggington, Ellison, Dau., w/o William
Bayly, Jane, Dau., w/o Hesekiah
Evans, Alexander, Son, <20
Evans, Elisabeth, Wife
Wiggington, Spencer, Wit.
Wood, Lashley, Wit.
Gunnell, John, Wit.
Richardson, James, B:303, 1779
Cavin, William, Exor.
Richardson, —, Wife
Richardson, 2 children < age
Richardson, John, Wit.
Ratekin, James, Wit.
McVay, Patrick, Wit.
Hophpoch, Cornelius, B:307, 1779
Hophpoch, Alice Mary, Wife
Jenings, James, Wit.
Hyler, Michael, Wit.
Moore, Thomas, Wit.
Winegardner, Harbard, B:308, 1779
Winegardner, Harbard, Son
Barb, Mary, Dau.
Winegardner, Henry, Son
Houghman, Charity, Dau.
Jenings, James, Wit.
Houghman, Anthony, Wit.
Oxley, Rachel, B:313, 1779
Stevens, Hannah, Sister
Howman, Elizabeth

Oxley, Mary, Niece, dau. of sister Hannah
Oxley, Joel, Son
Oxley, Mary, Niece, dau. of brother John
Oxley, Jesse
Oxley, Jeremiah, Son
Oxley, Henry, Father, dec'd.
Stevens, James, Wit.
Stevens, Alice, Wit.
Squires, Thomas, B:319, 1777/80
Squires, Sally, Dau.
Squires, Ann, Wife
Hancocke, Mary, Dau., w/o William,
Martin, James Green, Wit.
Potten, Henry, Wit.
Tolee, Stephen, Wit.
Neale, Robert, B:321, 1779/80
Nichols, Rebeckah
Rion, Dinah, my little girl
Drane, John
Nichols, Isaac, Exor.
Neptune, John
Neptune, Ruth
Neptune, Sarah
Hewatson, Benjamin, Exor.
Sands, Benjamin, Wit.
Field, Thomas, B:323, 1778/80
Field, Jemima, Wife
Priest, Eleanor, Dau.
Field, William, Son
Field, John, Son
Hopkins, James, Wit.
Potten, Henry, Wit.
Twiddy, George, Wit.
Allen, William, B:327, 1776/77/80
Fox, Gabriel, Exor.
Allen, Elizabeth, Sister, <18
Allen, Ann, Sister
Allen, Else, Sister
Allen, Joseph, Brother, <21
Frazer, James, Wit.
Fox, William, Wit.
Coutzman, Jacob, B:348, 1780
Coutzman, Louisa, Dau.
Coutzman, Hannah, Dau.
Coutzman, Cathrine, Wife
Coutzman, —, Unborn child
Coutzman, Catherine, Dau.

Coutzman, Clarissa, Dau.
Coutzman, Jacob, Son, <21
Kirk, James, Exor.
Murray, Samuel, Exor.
Reigor, John, Exor.
Cavans, Patrick, Exor.
Taylor, William, Wit.
Rine, George, Wit.
Harris, John, Wit.
Hague, Francis, B:355, 1780
Hague, Hannah, Dau.
Janney, Jane, Gr-Dau.
Hague, Sarah, Dau.
Hague, Rebeckah, Dau.
Hague, Mary, Dau.
Hague, Ann, Dau.
Hague, Samuel, Son
Hague, Thomas, Son
Hague, Isaac, Son
Thompson, Israel, Exor.
Roberts, Jane, Wit.
Roberts, Elleanor, Wit.
Brown, Andrew, Wit.
Hough, John Jr., Wit.
Fouch, Hugh, B:357, 1780
Fouch, Jack, Son
Fouch, Mary, Gr-Dau., dau. of Jack
Fouch, Jacob, Son
Fouch, Jonathan, Son
Fouch, Abraham, Son
Fouch, Mary, Wife
Brown, William, Wit.
Morehane, Joseph, Wit.
Hetherly, Thomas, Wit.
Talbert, Anne, B:358, 1780
Wren, William, Exor.
Talbert, Anne (Nancy), Dau.
Moss, John, Brother
Talbert, Frances, Dau.
Minor, John, Exor.
Talbert, Benjamin, Son
Talbert, John, Son
Talbert, William, Son
Boydstone, Benjamin, Exor. & Friend
Boydstone, Mary, Friend
Ringo, Cornelius, Wit.
Ringo, Margaret, Wit.

Littlejohn, Monica, Wit.
Minor, Frances, Wit.
Boyd, William, B:364, 1780/81
Boyd, Nancy, Dau.
Boyd, James, Son
Boyd, Thomas, Son
Boyd, Betty, Dau.
Boyd, William, Son
Boyd, John, Son
Boyd, Jane, Wife
Minor, John, Wit.
Harrison, John, Wit.
Lucas, Ruth, Wit.
Hamilton, Elizabeth, B:365, 1780/81
Hamilton, Ann, Mother
Hamilton, Robert, Wit.
Carter, Janet, Wit.
Phillips, Benjamin, B:365, 1780/81
Phillips, Sarah, Dau.
Phillips, John, Brother
Phillips, Hume, Dau.
Phillips, Rhode, Wife
Phillips, Samuel, Son
Phillips, Jenkin, Son
Phillips, Asael, Son
Dillon, James, Wit.
Gregg, Susanna, Wit.
Buffington, James, Wit.
Self, Thomas, B:366, 1781
Self, Elizabeth, Dau.
Self, Charnock, Son
Self, Presley, Son
Self, Joseph, Son
Self, Elizabeth, Wife
Offutt, William Macbe, Wit.
Green, John, Wit.
Thomas, Leonard, Wit.
Scott, Samuel, Wit.
Hatcher, William, B:370, 1780/81
Hatcher, John, Son
Hatcher, William, Son
Hatcher, James, Son
Hatcher, George, Son
Gibson, Mary, Dau.
Russell, Sarah, Dau.
Hatcher, Thomas, Son
Hoge, Solomon, Wit.
Janney, Israel, Wit.
Janney, Joseph, Wit.

Bodine, Cornelius, B:372, 1779/81
Bodine, Idah, Wife
Bodine, Jacob, Son
Bodine, Isaac, Son
Bodine, John, Son
Bodine, Sarah, Dau.
Bodine, Mary, Dau.
Rightmire, Orrionehe, Dau.
Bodine, Elizabeth, Dau.
Carter, John, Wit.
Carter, Morris, Wit.
Taylor, John, Wit.
Thatcher, Richard, B:373, 1781
Osborn, Reany, 3rd Dau.,
  w/o Benjamin
Palmer, Lidy, 8th Dau.
Musgrove, Emy, 5th Dau.
Striplin, Mary, 7th Dau.,
  w/o William
Hoff, Joseph, Son-in-law
Forguson, Abigail, Gr-Dau.
Thatcher, Ann, Eldest Dau.
Harrison, Eliza, 2nd Dau.,
  w/o Alexander
Thatcher, Stephen, Eldest Son
Thatcher, Katharine, 4th Dau.
Thatcher, Rachel, 9th Dau.
Thatcher, John, 3rd Son
Thatcher, Richard, 4th Son
Thatcher, Bartholomew, 2nd Son
Nicholls, James, Wit.
Matheny, James, Wit.
Hurley, Hannah, Wit.
Shore, Michael, Wit. [c]
Palmer, Jonathan, Wit. [c]
Smalley, Isaac, B:376, 1781
Smalley, Andrew, Son
Heth, Haner, Dau.
Smalley, Cathrine, Dau.
Smalley, Joshua, Son
Smalley, Susannah, Wife
Smalley, Ezekiel, Son
Smalley, David, Son
Smalley, William, Son
Drum, George, Wit.
Heth, Andrew, Wit.
Peyton, Craven, B:378, 1780/81
Peyton, Francis, Brother
Peyton, Ann, Dau.
Peyton, Valentine, Son
Peyton, Craven, Son
Peyton, Francis, Son
Peyton, William, Son
Peyton, Ann, Wife
Peyton, Margaret, Dau.
Moore, Jeremiah, Wit.
French, James, Wit.
Greenup, Christopher, Wit.
Ferguson, Francis, B:391, 1781/82
Lacock, Nathan, Exor.
Polton, John, Exor.
Ferguson, Elijah, Son
Ferguson, Ruth, Dau.
Ferguson, Abner, Son
Ferguson, Samuel, Son
Ferguson, Sarah, Dau.
Ferguson, Jane, Dau.
Ferguson, Ann, Wife
Dillon, James, Wit.
Patten, William, Wit.
Lacock, Jean, Wit.
Levering, Septimus, B:395, 1781/82
Lawrason, James, Son-in-law
Lawrason, Alice, Dau.
Levering, Thomas, Son
Levering, Septimus, Son
Levering, Mary, Dau.
Levering, Griffith, Son
Levering, Mary, Wife
Kirk, James, Exor.
Greenup, Christopher, Wit.
Leonard, Noble, Wit.
Hunt, William, Wit.
Tobit, Hannah, Wit.
Campbell, Matthew, B:397, 1782
Paterson, Janney
Neilson, William, Exor.
Cavan, Patrick, Exor.
Adam, Robert, Exor.
Campbell, Marion, Mother
Kirk, James, Exor.
Curtis, Mary, dau. of Helen
Curtis, Helen, widow
Campbell, Marion, Sister
Wilson, James, Wit.
Wilson, Mary, Wit.
McCabe, Henry, Wit.

Moore, Ann, B:413, 1782
Marye, Elizabeth, Dau.
Brent, Hannah, Dau.
Neale, Thomas, Son
Orr, John, Exor.
Turley, Charles, Wit.
Turley, Ann, Wit.
Swink, Adam, B:414, 1782
Swink, Jane, Dau.
Potts, David Sr., Exor.
Swink, Rachel, Wife
Connard, Jonathan, Exor.
Potts, Ezekiel, Wit.
Chalfant, Robert, Wit.
Thomas, John, Wit.
Adams, James, Wit.
Donaldson, Daniel, B:415, 1782
Donaldson, Ann, Sister
Moore, Jeremiah, Friend
Donaldson, Stephen, Wit.
Donaldson, Sally, Wit.
Walker, Isaac, B:416, 1782
Norris, Sarah, Sister
Trahern, William, Cousin
Janney, Israel, Exor.
Smith, Hannah, Sister
Trahern, James, Cousin
Trahern, Sarah, Cousin
Trahern, Rebeccah, Sister
Lemert, Lewis, Wit.
Janney, Jacob, Wit.
Spencer, Nathan, Wit.
Robison, John, B:418, 1782
Robison, Sarah, Dau.
Robison, Nancy, Dau.
Robison, Elizabeth, Dau.
Robison, Sarah, Wife
King, Smith, Exor.
Hitch, Thomas, Exor.
Cooper, Benjamin, Exor.
Frier, Robert, Wit.
Ward, Lawrence, Wit.
Wood, Mary, Wit.
Wood, Milley, Wit.
Baker, William, B:419, 1778/82
Baker, Mary, Wife
Baker, Sarah, Dau.
Baker, Joshua, Son
Baker, Rachel, Dau.
Janney, Joseph, Exor.

Janney, Mahlon, Exor.
Janney, Samuel, Wit.
Janney, Abel, Wit.
Minor, John, B:426, 1782
Minor, Frances, Wife
Stanhope, William, Wit.
Minor, Thomas, Wit.
Benham, John a tailor, B:427, 1781/82
Mason, Benjamin, Exor.
Benham, Robert, Son
Mason, George, Wit.
Race, Joab, Wit.
Mason, Margaret, Wit.
Elgin, Francis, B:428, 1776/82
Elgin, Rebeccah, Wife
Elgin, Gustavus, Son
Elgin, Walter, Son
Elgin, Francis, Son
Elgin, Elizabeth, Dau.
Elgin, Margaret, Dau.
Elgin, Rebeccah, Dau.
Elgin, William, Son
Elgin, Nancy, Dau.
Elgin, Jessey, Son
Elgin, George, Son
Elgin, Ignatius, Son
Greenup, Christopher, Wit.
Shreve, Benjamin, Wit.
Hunt, Stephen, Wit.
Minor, Nicholas, B:432, 1782
Minor, Thomas, Son
Minor, Rebecca, Dau.
Minor, Frances, Wife
Minor, John, Son
Minor, Spence, Son
Minor, George, Son, beyond the seas
Gunnell, Elizabeth, Dau.
Moss, John Sr., Exor.
Linton, John, Wit.
Boyd, William, Wit.
Minor, Steuart, Wit.
Scott, Samuel Sr., B:441, 1782
Lindsay, Martha, Dau., w/o Thomas
Scott, Susannah, Wife
Scott, Robert, Son
Scott, Elizabeth, Dau.
Scott, Susannah, Dau.

Scott, Rachel, Dau.
Scott, Peggy, Dau.
Scott, James, Son
Scott, Samuel, Son
Fox, James, Wit.
Offutt, William M, Wit.
Graham, John, Wit.
Schooley, Samuel Sr., B:444, 1769/82
Schooley, William, Son
Schooley, Samuel, Son
Schooley, John, Son
Schooley, Sarah, Wife
Myers, Mary, Dau.
Miers, Phebe, Dau.
Hague, Ann, Dau.
Brown, William, Wit.
Taverner, George, Wit.
Pool, Thomas, C:11, 1782/83
Mason, Benjamin, Exor.
Pool, Daniel, Son
Pool, Dorothy, Dau.
Pool, Elizabeth, Wife
Pool, Frances Elliot, Dau.
Berkley, Ruben, Exor.
Browne, Elizabeth, Dau.
Gibbs, James Lewin, Exor.
Hodges, Richard, Son-in-law
Tyler, William, Wit.
Taylor, George Gray, Wit.
Douglass, William, C:15, 1780/82/83
Records, Joseph, Friend
Douglass, Sarah, Wife, died between 1780 and 1783
Douglass, Hugh, Son
Douglass, Patrick, Son
Douglass, Elizabeth, Dau., <18
Douglass, Nancy, Dau., <18
Douglass, Hannah, Dau., <14
Douglass, Peggy, Dau., <14
Neal, Kitty, Eldest Dau.
Clark, Thomas, Wit.
Sheperd, William, Wit.
Harris, Samuel, C:20, 1782/83
Harris, William, Son
Harris, Samuel, Son
Harris, Thomas, Son
Harris, Acey (Asa), Son
Harris, Mary, Wife
Danniel, Joshua, Wit.
Danniel, Jane, Wit.
Jones, John, C:23, 1781/83
Fields, Elizabeth, Dau.
Jones, Joseph <21, Youngest Son
Jones, John, Son, <21
Jones, Martha, Wife
Jones, William, Son, <21
Ritchie, John, Wit.
Power, Joseph, Wit.
Hughs, Isaac, Wit.
Byrne, Bennadic, Wit.
Jennings, Daniel, C:28, 1783
Jennings, Anne, Wife
Jennings, Daniel, Son
Jennings, Owen, Son, <14
Williams, Jeremiah, Exor.
Jennings, James, Exor.
Minor, Spence, Wit.
Linton, John, Wit.
Minor, Thomas, Wit.
Sorrell, John, C:32, 1780/83
Taylor, Patty, Sister
Sharpe, Elizabeth, Mother
Watson, Thomas Weldon
Moss, Spencer Aris
Emrey, Stephen, Wit.
Roper, Thomas, Wit.
Morehane, Joseph, Wit.
Cooper, Frederick, C:41, 1773/83
Branner, Phillip, Exor.
Shoemaker, Jacob, Exor.
Cooper, Cathariny, Wife
Shoemaker, George, Wit.
Crealius, Rudolph, Wit.
Hartman, Mathias, C:44, 1782/83
Hartman, Catherine, Wife
Slatser, Jacob, Wit.
Hallar, Peter, Wit.
Eacha, Martain, Wit.
Waltman, Emanuel, C:70, 1782/84
Waltman, Jacob, Son
Waltman, Margarita, Wife
Waltman, George, Son
Waltman, Samuel, Son
Waltman, Michael, Son
Waltman, William, Son

Stroupe, Mary Ann, Dau.,
  w/o Milcher
Botterfield, Adam, Wit.
Smithie, Matthias, Wit.
Crafe, Philip, C:72, 1784
  Boyer, George
  Bower, Barnett
  Shockheart, George, Wit.
  Peckner, Peter, Wit.
  Aldamus, William, Wit.
Farrow, Joseph, C:72, 1781/84
  Crupper, Richard, Exor.
  Cocke, William, Exor.
  Farrow, Elizabeth, Wife
  Farrow, Sarah William, Dau.
  Farrow, Thornton, Son
  Farrow, Joseph, Son
  Farrow, Thomas, Son
  Farrow, Mary Ann, Dau.
  Hutchison, Peter, Wit.
Jack, Dr. Patrick, C:73, 1784
  Hough, Samuel, Exor.
  Drean, John, Exor.
  Jack, John, Brother
  Jack, Nancy, Mother, in Ireland
  Murray, Samuel, Wit.
  Emrey, George, Wit.
  Gilbert, Joseph, Wit.
Claypole, Joseph, C:75, 1779/84
  Claypole, —, Wife
  Claypole, James, Son
  Bishop, Mary, Dau., w/o John
  Reid, Rebecca, Dau.,
    w/o Joseph
  Brown, William, Wit.
  Brown, Richard, Wit.
  Hains, Simeon, Wit.
Loyd, David, C:77, 1784
  Griffith, Rebecca, Sister,
    w/o John
  David, Joan, Sister, w/o James
  David, Elijah, Nephew,
    son of Joan
  King, John Jr., Wit.
  Chew, Joseph, Wit.
  Moxley, Daniel, Wit.

Foutt, George, C:80, 1779/84
  Connard, John, Exor.
  Foutt, Eve, Wife
  Foutt, Philip, Son
  Foutt, Hannah, Dau.
  Foutt, Eve, Dau.
  Foutt, Elizabeth, Dau.
  Foutt, George, Gr-Son,
    son of Frederick
  Wolf, John, Exor.
  Foutt, Frederick, Son
  Osborn, Nicholas, Wit.
  Vanderen, Barnard, Wit.
  Connard, Jonathan, Wit.
Clews, Thomas, C:84, 1784
  Gore, Sarah, Dau.
  Potts, Nathan
  Mead, Christian, Gr-Dau.
  Clews, Joseph, Son
  Janney, Jacob, Wit.
  Gore, Joshua, Wit.
Mead, William, C:85, 1780/84
  Potts, Elizabeth, Dau.
  Rhodes, William, Gr-Son,
    son of Mary Browne
  Rhodes, Thomas, Gr-Son,
    son of Mary Browne
  Rhodes, Joseph, Gr-Son,
    son of Mary Browne
  Thomas, Hannah, Dau.
  Thomas, Mary, Gr-Dau.
  Thomas, Martha, Gr-Dau.
  Thomas, Joseph, Gr-Son
  Mead, Ellin, Wife
  Mead, William, Son
  Mead, Ann, Dau.
  Wright, William, Gr-Son
  Wright, Martha, Dau.
  Browne, Mary, Dau.
  Greenup, Christopher, Wit.
  Binns, Charles, Wit.
  Binns, John, Wit.
Whaley, James, C:87, 1784
  Remey, Benjamin Talbot, alias
    Benjamin Whaley, Son
  Remey, Barbara,
    mother of my children
  Remey, James, Son
  Remey, Elizabeth, Dau.
  Remey, Rebecca, Dau.

Index to Loudoun County Wills, 1757 - 1850   25

Remey, Henry, Son
Remey, Elijah, Son
Remey, Jacob. alias Gilson
  Whaley, Son
Lane, Hardage, Exor.
Ellis (or Eales), Jane, Dau.
Whaley, Rebecca, Dau.
Whaley, Elizabeth, Dau.
Whaley, Charles, Gr-Son
Whaley, Elizabeth, Dau.-in-law
Whaley, James, Son
Whaley, William, Son
Whaley, Henry, Son
Whaley, Elijah, Son
Whaley, Ann, Wife
Whaley, John, Son
Whaley, Benjamin, Son
Whaley, George, Son, <21
Whaley, Gilson, Son
Sears, Charles Lee, Gr-Son
Simms, Charles, Exor.
Summers, George, Exor.
Sears, Elizabeth, Dau.,
  w/o William Bernard
Talbot, Mary, Dau.,
  w/o Benjamin
Talbot, Barbara, Dau.,
  w/o Henry
Talbot, Hannah Neale, Gr-Dau.,
  <16,
Whaley, William, Brother
Lane, William, Exor.
Thomas, Mo., Wit.
Curtis, John, Wit.
McIntosh, Thomas, Wit.
Cockerill, Benjamin, Wit.
Smith, Henry, C:96, 1782/84
Smith, Thomas, Son
Smith, Ann, Dau., <21
Smith, George, Son
Smith, John, Son
Smith, Sarah, Dau., <21
Smith, Samuel, Son
Smith, Alice, Wife
Smith, William, Son
Smith, David, Son
McIlhaney, James, Wit.
Potts, Ezekiel, Wit.
Potts, Nathan, Wit.
Osburne, William, Wit.

Wornall, Roby, C:114, 1784/85
Ecton, Drucilla, Dau.
Ecton, Theodore, Gr-Son
Ecton, Francis, Exor.
Gunnell, William, Exor.
Tucker, Mary, Gr-Dau.
Tucker, Ann, Dau.
Wornall, James, Son
Wornall, Thomas, Son
Wornall, Elizabeth Sarah, Dau.
Wornall, Edey, Wife
Moss, Gideon, Wit.
Foreman, Peter, Wit.
Neilson, William, Wit.
Hall, Jane, C:118, 1785
Gunn, John, Son-in-law
Cooper, Agnes, Dau.
Dougherty, James, Wit.
Hinksman, Samuel, Wit.
Patterson, Robert, Wit.
King, John, C:119, 1784/85
Talbutt, Hannah, Dau.
Floyd, Sarah, Dau.
Stephens, Elizabeth, Dau.,
  w/o Joseph
Whaley, Penelope, Dau., dec'd.
King, John, Son
Smith, Mary, Dau., w/o John
Carrington, Winney, Dau.
King, Smith, Son
Stephens, Eleanor, Dau.
King, Osborn, Son
King, Mary, Wife
Stephens, Ann, Dau., dec'd.
Rincker, Edward, Wit.
Rincker, Sarah, Wit.
Rincker, Henry, Wit.
Harl, Leven, Wit.
Lay, Abraham, C:121, 1784/85
Lay, Sylvanus, Son, dec'd.
Jinkins, Leana, Dau., w/o John
Lay, Sarah, Wife
Lay, Abraham Jr., Son
Lay, Emmanuel, Son
Lay, Joseph, Son
Lay, Stephen, Son
Lay, Marmaduke, Gr-Son
Jenkins, Sylvanius, Gr-Son,
  son of Amos & Athesias

Richards, Lydia, Dau.,
  w/o William
Payne, Abigail, Dau.,
  w/o Sanford
Ellzey, Lydia, Gr-Dau.
Ellzey, Lewis, Gr-Son
Self, Athesias, Dau.,
  w/o Presley
Horseman, Helena, Dau.,
  w/o William
Ellzey, Prudence, Dau.,
  w/o John
Lay, —, Gr-Dau.,
  dau. of Sylvanus
Powell, William, Wit.
Evans, Mary, Wit.
Money, Nicholas, Wit.
**Chilton, Steerman, C:126,
1784/85**
Williams, Agathy, Dau.,
  w/o Joshua
Smith, Jemima, w/o Gideon
Cockerill, Ann, w/o John
Chilton, John, Brother
Chilton, Thomas, Son
Chilton, William, Son
Chilton, Catherine, Dau.
Chilton, Sarah, Dau.
Chilton, Mary, Dau.
Chilton, John, Son
Chilton, Mary, Wife
Cockerill, Christopher, Wit.
Jewell, Jonathan, Wit.
Graham, John, Wit.
**Murphy, Michael soldier, C:128,
1777/85**
Warford, Job
Carlile, David, Wit.
Noland, Philip Jr., C:134, 1783/85
Noland, Thomas, Brother
Noland, Mary, Wife
Noland, Nancy, Dau.
Noland, Æneas, Son
Noland, Thomas, Son
Noland, Sarah (Sally), Dau., <18
Noland, Philip Nelson, Son, <21
Luckett, Molley Ann, Wit.
Jack, Patrick, Wit.
Clapham, Josias, Wit.

Awbrey, William, Wit.
Awbrey, Samuel, Wit.
Awbrey, Richard, Wit.
Lovett, Daniel, C:136, 1785
Grigg, Martha, Dau., <18
Lovett, Edmund, Son, <21
Lovett, Elias, Son, <21
Lovett, Lidia, Dau., <18
Lovett, Sarah, Dau., <18
Lovett, Letisha, Dau., <18
Lovett, Elizabeth, Dau., <18
Lovett, Sarah, Wife
Lovett, Daniel, Son, <21
Lovett, Jonathan, Son
Lovett, Joseph, Son
Lovett, David, Son, <21
Lewis, Joel, Wit.
Edwards, Amos, Wit.
Lewis, George, Wit.
Goodin, Samuel, Wit.
Goodin, David, Wit.
Lewis, Jesse, Wit.
Whitacre, George, C:147, 1785
Whitacre, Enuck, Son
Whitacre, Ruth, Dau.
Whitacre, Caleb, Brother
Whitacre, Neomy, Dau.
Whitacre, Robert, Son, <21
Whitacre, Elizabeth, Dau.
Whitacre, Joseph, Son, <14
Whitacre, Martha, Dau.
Whitacre, Benjamin, Son, <14
Whitacre, George, Son, <21
Whitacre, Caleb, Son, <21
Whitacre, Joshua, Son, <21
Whitacre, Ruth, Wife
Smith, William, Wit.
Dillon, James, Wit.
Gore, Joshua, C:150, 1785
Gore (Gorr), Thomas, Son
Gore (Gorr), Betsey, Dau.
Gore (Gorr), Joshua, Son
Gore (Gorr), Jonathan, Son
Osborne, William
Gore (Gorr), —, Wife,
  widow of Harry Rector
Osburn, Abner, Wit.
Kitchin, James, Wit.
Brown, Isaac, Wit.
Neilson, William, Wit.

Janney, Samuel, C:156, 1778/85
Baker, Mary, Sister
Hooton, Sarah, Sister
Janney, Joseph, Brother
Janney, Sarah, Mother
Janney, Rebeckah, Sister
Janney, John, Brother
Janney, Abel, Brother
Cavan, Patrick, Wit.
Moffett, Josiah, Wit.
McLaughlin, Amos, Wit.
Thornton, John, C:158, 1778/79/80/85
(of Stafford Co. in 1778)
(of Loudoun in 1780)
Love, Samuel, Exor.
Triplett, Samuel (Simon), Exor.
Tallieferro, John, Exor.,
  of King George Co.
Thornton, Seth, Exor.,
  of Caroline Co.
Thornton, William, Son, born between 15 Aug 1778 and 16 Apr 1779
Thornton, Benjamin Berryman, Son
Thornton, Anthony, Son
Thornton, Catharine, Wife
Jones, Joseph, Wit.
Bagnold (Bagnald), John, Wit.
Yates, Mary, Wit. [1c]
Miller, John Daniel, Wit. [2c]
Cavan, Patrick, Wit. [2c]
Moffett, Josiah, Wit. [2c]
Canton, Mark, C:168, 1785
Canton, Sarah, Infant Dau.
Canton, Elizabeth, Wife
Feagan, Daniel, Exor.
Cocke, William, Wit.
Combs, Stephen, Wit.
Jackson, Daniel, Wit.
Brent, George, C:175, 1785
Lewis, James, Exor.
Brent, Hugh, Son
Brent, Sarah, Dau.
Brent, Caty, Dau.
Brent, Martain, Son
Brent, Willis, Son
Brent, Thomas, Son
Brent, Joannah, Wife
Bartlett, James, Wit.
Brown, William, C:182, 1773/85
Brown, George, Nephew,
  son of Thomas
Brown, John, Nephew
Brown, Isaac, Nephew
Brown, John, Brother
Brown, Catharine, Niece,
  sister of Hannah
Brown, Hannah, Niece,
  sister of Catharine
Brown, Thomas, Brother
Brown, George, Nephew,
  son of John
Nickolls, James, Wit.
Gregg, John, Wit.
Craige, James, Wit.
Barkley, Barbary, C:184, 1785
Ward, Anne, Dau.
Reade, John, Son
Reade, William, Son
Reade, Ruben, Son
Barkly, Benjamin, Son
Payne, Edward, Wit.
Dunbar, William Jr., Wit.
Haden, Barsheba, Wit.
Haden, John, Wit.
Milland, Thomas, Wit.
Evernham, Sarah, Wit.
Stephens, Richard, C:187, 1785
Stephens, Robert, Married Son
Stephens, Richard, Married Son
Stephens, Eleanor, Gr-Dau.,
  dau. of Richard
Stephens, Eleanor, Wife
King, John Jr., Wit.
Watson, Weldon, Wit.
Watson, Susannah, Wit.
Phillips, Jenkin, C:189, 1785/86
Phillips, Hester, Wife
Phillips, John, Son, dec'd.
Phillips, Israel, Gr-Son, <21
Phillips, Sarah, Gr-Dau., <18
Phillips, Nancy, Gr-Dau., <18
Phillips, Thomas, Son
Phillips, Benjamin, Son

Phillips, Sarah, Dau.
Phillips, Samuel, Son
Phillips, Benjamin, Gr-Son, <21
Phillips, Hester, Gr-Dau.
Osborne, Abner, Exor.
Gregg, Stephen, Wit.
Jenkin, Isaac, Wit.
Shaver, Jacob, Wit.
Hough, Mary, Wit.
Oldaker, Henry Jr., C:191, 1785/86
Bartlett, Samuel, Brother-in-law
Oldaker, John, Brother
Oldaker, children by Elizabeth
Oldaker, Elizabeth, Wife
Wynn, Robert, Wit.
Booram, John, Wit.
Bartlett, Mary, Wit.
Oldaker, Henry Sr., C:192, 1773/86
Burson, Rebeckah, Dau.
Ouldaker, Abraham, Son
Ouldaker, Henry, Son
Ouldaker, Isaac, Son
Ouldaker, Eleanor, Dau.
Ouldaker, William, Son
Ouldaker, John, Son
Ouldaker, Jacob, Son
Dyer, John, Son-in-Law, husband of Hannah, now dec'd.
Lewellin, Mary, Dau.
Ouldaker, Enor, Wife
Harris, Daniel, Wit.
Sybold, James, Wit.
Smith, William, Wit.
Marks, Isaak, C:194, 1785/86
Humphrey, Mary, Sister
Humphrey, Thomas, Brother-in-law
Humphrey, John, Cousin, brother of Abner
Humphrey, Abner, Cousin, brother of John
Williams, Unce, Sister
Marks, Thomas, Brother
Marks, Elisha, Brother
Marks, John, Brother
Marks, Abel, Brother

Williams, William, C:197, 1780/86
Williams, Elizabeth, Wife
Williams, Elizabeth, 2nd Dau., <21
Williams, Hannah, Eldest Dau., <21
Williams, Abner, 2nd Son, <16
Williams, John, Eldest Son, <16
Williams, Rehoboth, Sister
Williams, —, Mother
Steer, Benjamin, Wit.
Smith, Abraham, Wit.
Lewis, Joel, Wit.
Williams, Henry, Wit.
Baker, Philip, C:201, 1786
Baker, Daniel, Eldest Son
Baker, Cathiren, Dau.
Baker, Mary, Dau.
Baker, William, Son
Baker, Hannah, Dau.
Baker, Jacob, Son
Baker, Christian, Dau.
Baker, David, Son
Baker, Ule, Wife
Baker, Barbary, Dau.
Baker, Mary Ann, Dau.
Baker, Samuel, Son
Purdom, Benjamin, Wit.
Householder, Adam, Wit.
Axline, Adam, Wit.
Hewatson, Benjamin, C:202, 1786
Thrailkill, John
Short, Robert
Anderson, Ann, Dau. of Robert Short
Short, Alice, w/o Robert
Short, Susannah, dau. of Robert
Short, Sarah, dau. of Robert
Short, Rebekah, dau. of Robert
Craven, James, Exor.
Myers, Andrew, Wit.
Henry, John Sr., Wit.
Newell, Sarah, C:218, 1786
Newill, Susanna dau. of William & Margott
Fletcher, Nancy, Dau.
Fletcher, Sarah Newell, dau. of William & Nancy Fletcher
Newill, Sibbel, dau. of Rachel Newill

Newill, John,
  son of Rachel Newill
Wattkins, James, Wit.
Jenkins, Stephen, Wit.
Jenkins, Conny, Wit.
Jenkins, Priscilla, Wit.
Janney, Jacob, C:223, 1786
Janney, —, Wife
Bennet, Phebe, Dau.
Gregg, Rebeckah, Dau.
Janney, Joseph, Son
Janney, Jacob, Gr-Son,
  son of Jacob, <21
Janney, Jacob, Son, dec'd.
Janney, Thomas, Son, <21
Janney, Hannah, Dau.
Janney, Elisha, Son
Janney, Aquila, Son
Janney, Israel, Son
Janney, Jonas, Son
Janney, Moses, Gr-Son,
  son of Jacob, <21
Janney, Blackstone, Son
Inglidieu, Margaret, Sister-in-law
Janney, Mahlon, Wit.
Lovett, Jonathan, Wit.
Kenworthy, William, Wit.
Burson, George, C:238, 1786
Cunnard, Esther, Dau.
Bradfield, Hannah, Dau.
Romine, Ruth, Dau.
Burson, Jonathan, Son
Burson, Benjamin, Son
Burson, Joseph, Son
Burson, James, Son
Burson, Sarah, Wife
Brown, Thomas, Wit.
Gregg, Joseph, Wit.
Dillon, William, Wit.
West, Charles, C:242, 1777/87
West, Thomas, Brother, dec'd.
West, Thomas, Son from my
  servant woman
West, Charles, Nephew
West, Anna Brown, Dau.
West, Elizabeth, Dau.
Peyton, Craven, Exor.
Tyler, John, Exor.
Walrond, William, Wit.

Hotton, Thomas, Wit.
Gardner, Joseph, Wit.
Tenly, Patrick, Wit.
Osbourn, John, C:244, 1786/87
Osbourn, William, Son
Gore (Gorr), Thomas, Exor.
Gore (Gorr), Ann, Dau.
Pursel, Elizabeth, Dau.
Pursel, Sarah, Dau.
Osbourn, John, Son
Osbourn, Sarah, Wife
Osbourn, Richard, Son
Osbourn, Samuel, Son
Thomas, John, Wit.
Smith, Thomas, Wit.
Potts, Nathan, Wit.
Vanderen, Barnard, Wit.
Hawling, John Wilcoxen, C:250, 1786/87
Halling (Hawling), Jemima, Wife
Halling (Hawling), —, Son by
  present wife
Halling (Hawling), John, Son,
  <21
Halling (Hawling), William, Son
Clapham, J., Wit.
Sinclair, Samuel, Wit.
Sinclair, John Jr., Wit.
Shepherd, William, Wit.
Luckett, Thomas Huxey, C:253, 1786/87
Luckett, Elizabeth, Wife
Luckett, Lawson, Son, <21
Luckett, John, Brother
Luckett, Vol, Son, <21
Luckett, —, Son, not yet
  baptized
Luckett, Otho, Oldest Son, <21
Davis, Reason of Md., Exor.
Campbell, Ens., Wit.
Luckett, Leven, Wit.
Fouch, Isaac Jr., Wit.
Williams, Daniel, Wit.
Awbrey, Thomas, C:258, 1784/87
Awbrey, Jemima, Wife
Awbrey, Samuel, Brother, dec'd.
Awbrey, John
Awbrey, Rhoda
Awbrey, Samuel, Son
Awbrey, Thomas, Son

Awbrey, Francis, Son
Awbrey, Towny, Gr-Son
Awbrey, William, Son
Awbrey, Henry, Son
Awbrey, Philip
Awbrey, William
Awbrey, Richard, Son
Awbrey, Jemima, Dau.
Smith, William, Wit.
Davis, John, Wit.
English, Susanna, Wit.
Schooley, Samuel, C:264, 1786/87
Schooley, Ann, Dau.
Schooley, Jesse, Son
Schooley, John, Brother
Schooley, Dorothy, Wife
Clapham, Josias, Wit.
Bagley, John, Wit.
Hammond, Daniel, Wit.
Mead, Ellin, C:268, 1785/87
Mead, Anne, Dau.
Potts, Elizabeth, Dau.
Potts, Ezekiel, Son-in-law
Wright, Martha, Dau.
Thomas, Hannah, Dau.
Brown, Martha, Sister
Brown, Mary, Dau.
Hammat, George, Wit.
Homan, Ralph, Wit.
Binns, Charles Jr., Wit.
Osburn, Nicholas, C:271, 1785/87
McClain, Duncan, Exor.
Osburn, Mary, Wife
Osburn, Abner, Son
Osburn, Nicholas, Gr-Son
Castleman, Massey, Dau.
Osburn, Lydia, Gr-Dau.
Moore, Jeremiah, Wit.
Peyton, Valentine, Wit.
Brown, Isaac, Wit.
Osburn, Mary, Wit.
Lane, James Hardage, C:280, 1787
Lane, William, Son
Lane, George, Son
Lane, Enoch Smith, Son
Lane, Rebekah, Dau.
Lane, James Hardage, Son
Lane, Mary, Dau.

Lane, Mary, Wife
Lane, Daniel Crosby, Son
Darrell, Sarah, Dau.
Lane, Delilah, Dau.
Lane, John, Son
Beach, Joel, Son-in-law
Beach, Elizabeth, Dau.
Tarel, William, Wit.
Hutchinson, Isaac, Wit.
Brown, Coleman, Wit.
Eskridge, Charles, Wit.
Lane, Presly C., Wit.
Morris, John, C:284, 1786/87
Morris, Nancy (Ann), Wife
Headon, Jennie, Dau. from 1st marriage
Eskridge, Charles, Exor.
Lane, James Hardage, Wit.
Orr, John, Wit.
Gooding, Anna, Wit.
Headen, Samuel, Wit.
Hutchinson, Isaac, Wit.
Remey, Jacob Sr., C:288, 1784/87
Whaley, Barbara, Dau. w/o William
Love, Samuel Jr., Exor.
Remey, Jacob, Son
Remey, Jacob (alias Gilson Whaley), Gr-Son
Cockerell, Jeremiah, Exor.
Summers, George, Wit.
Turley, Charles, Wit.
Turley, John, Wit.
Whaley, John, Wit.
Berkley, Reuben, C:301, 1787
Berkley, William, Son
Berkley, Ann (Nancy), Dau.
Berkley, Benjamin, Son
Berkley, John, Exor.
Berkley, Burgess, Son
Berkley, Moses, Son
Berkley, Catharine, Dau., <16
Berkley, Fanna Rogers, Dau., <16
Berkley, Susanna, Dau., <16
Berkley, George, Son, <16
Berkley, Catharine, Wife
Hutchison, Elizabeth, Dau., w/o George
Lewis, Joseph, Exor.

Mason, Benjamin, Wit.
Linton, John, Wit.
Gibbs, James Lewin, Wit.
Mason, George, Wit.
Pyott, John, C:304, 1787
McElroy, Rebekah, Dau.
McElroy, Daniel, Son-in-law
Myers, Jonathan, Exor.
Pyott, John, Son
Pyott, Amos, Son
Tavenner, Susannah, Dau.
Ratican, James, Wit.
Cox, Joseph, Wit.
Reamy, Sandford, C:314, 1787/88
Ramey, William, Brother
Ramey, John, Brother, dec'd.
Connally, John Donaldson
Connally, Ann Sanford, dau. of
 Sandford R. & Mary
Corder, Judith
Connally, William, son of
 Sandford & Mary
Carder, Mary, Sister
Connally, John, son of Sanford
 R. & Mary
Connally, Sanford Reamey
Spurr, Richard, Wit.
Whaley, William, Wit.
Allison, Bryan, Wit.
Pike, Jonathan, Wit.
[Ramey seems to be the
 prevalent spelling, except here]
Wilson, John, C:321, 1787/88
Wilson, Mary, Wife
Wilson, John Jefferson, Son
Wilson, Henry Lawrence, Son
Wilson, Maria, Dau.
Wilson, Kezia, Dau.
Dillon, James, Wit.
Hook, Isaac, Wit.
Hook, Mary, Wit.
Marks, John Sr., C:324, 1787/88
Marks, Uriah, Wife
Marks, Elisha, Son
Marks, John, Son
Marks, Thomas, Son
Marks, Abel, Son
Humphrey, Mary, Dau.,
 w/o Thomas

Howell, Martha, Dau.,
 w/o William
Williams, Uriah, Dau.,
 w/o Jenkin
Hatcher, John, Wit.
Thomas, Philip, Wit.
Thomas, David, Wit.
Romine, Peter, C:335, 1787/88
Romine, Sarah, Dau.
Romine, Isaack, Son
Romine, Peter, Son
Romine, John, Son
Romine, Abigail, Wife
Popkins, John, Wit.
Hutchison, Joseph, Wit.
Shipman, Stephen, Wit.
Gregg, John, C:338, 1778/88
Gregg, Amos, Eldest Son
Gregg, Mary, Dau.
Gregg, Amy, Dau.
Gregg, Rebekah, Dau.
Gregg, George, Son
Gregg, John, Son
Gregg, Richard, Son
Gregg, Levy, Gr-Son
Dixon, Hannah, Dau.
Howell, Lydda, Dau.
Adams, James, Wit.
McManimy, Charles, Wit.
McManimy, Jane, Wit.
Hague, Isaac, Wit.
Gregg, Samuel, Wit.
Cleveland, William, C:342, 1787/88
Cleveland, Darkes (Dorcas),
 Dau.
Cleveland, Marey (Mary), Wife
Cockerill, Benjamin, Wit.
Gardner, Essers, Wit.
Fox, Amos, Wit.
Cotton, William Sr., C:345, 1787/88
Ghoram, Margaret, Dau.
Spurr, Frances, Dau.
Cotton, John, Son
Cotton, William, Son
Cotton, Mary, Wife
Alexander, John, Wit.
Alexander, Richard B., Wit.
Brown, John, Wit.

Seybold, Jesper, D:2, 1788
  Seybold, James, Son
  Seybold, Isaac, Son
  Seybold, Robert, Son
  Seybold, Jesse, Son
  Seybold, Hester, Gr-Dau.,
    dau. of Hannah
  Seybold, Jesper, Son
  Seybold, Hannah, Dau.
  Seybold, Alice, Dau.
  Seybold, John, Son
  Seybold, Rebakah, Wife
  Seybold, Silas, Son
  Hirst, John, Wit.
  Hirst, Mary, Wit.
  Preston, John, Wit.
Kitchen, William, D:5, 1780/88
  Kitchen, —, Daus.
  Kitchen, Thompson, Son
  Kitchen, Margaret, Wife
  Kitchen, Daniel, Son
  DBell, William, Wit.
  DBell, Mary, Wit.
Evans, Mary, D:10, 1787/88
  Bodine, John, Son of Benjamin
    Rightmire's wife, <21
  Henderson, Samuel, Son-in-law
  Smith, Sarah, Dau.
  Peyton, Francis, Exor.
  Tyler, John, Exor.
  Evans, Charity, Dau.
  Reed, Ossee, Gr-Dau.
  Evans, Anney, Dau.
  Pearl, William
  Evans, Samuel, Gr-Son
  Evans, William, Son
  Moore, John, Wit.
  Swart, Adrein, Wit.
  Moore, Benjamin, Wit.
  Smith, Weedon, Wit.
  Ritacre, Mary, Wit.
  Pullen, Elizabeth, Wit.
Woollard, Mary, D:12, 1788
  Woollard, Isaac, Son
  Woollard, John, Son
  Woollard, Elizabeth, Gr-Dau.,
    now lives with me
  Woollard, Joseph, Son
  Woollard, Mary, Dau.
  Woollard, Elender, Dau.
  Woollard, Jean, Dau.
  Woollard, Ann, Dau.
  Woollard, William, Son
  Dulin, William, Wit.
  Dulin, Mary, Wit.
Stiffle(r), Martin, D:23, 1788/89
  Stiffle(r), Christener, Wife
  Richa, Francis, Exor.
  Flicklinger, John, Brother
  Shover, Adam, Wit.
  Purdum, Jeremiah, Wit.
  German Script Name, Wit.
McIntyre, Alexander of Leesburg, D:24, 1788/89
  McIntyre, William, Son, <21
  McIntyre, Elizabeth, Dau., <21
  McIntyre, Jane, Wife
  McIntyre, John, Son
  McIntyre, Robert, Son, <21
  McIntyre, Alexander, Son, <21
  McIntyre, Daniel, Son, <21
  McIntyre, Catherine, Dau., <21
  McIntyre, Charles, Son, <21
  McIntyre, Patrick, Son, <21
  Cavan, Patrick, Wit.
  Murdock, James, Wit.
  Hough, Barnett, Wit.
Buckley, William, D:36, 1786/89
  Harris, Elizabeth, Dau.
  Harris, Sarah, Dau.
  Harris, Catherine, Dau.
  Halbert, Rosanna, Dau.
  Buckley, Elijah, Gr-Son, son of
    William
  Buckley, William, Son, dec'd.
  Buckley, Samuel, Son
  Buckley, John, Son
  Buckley, Joshua, Son
  Blackburn, J., Wit.
  Blackburn, Richard, Wit.
  Dudley, John, Wit.
  Neale, Richard, Wit.
Taylor, William, D:89, 1782/90
  Davis, Rachel, Dau.
  Boggess, Jemima, Dau.
  Taylor, Sarah, Wife
  Whealer, Mary's three children,
    Gr-children
  Taylor, —, Son
  Taylor, William, Son

Index to Loudoun County Wills, 1757 - 1850   33

Taylor, Mandly, Wit.
Carroll, Demse, Wit.
Seybold, Jesper, Wit.
Taylor, George, D:91, 1788/89
Squires, Elizabeth, Dau.
Cotton, Frances, Dau.
Fielder, Hizziah, Dau.
Compton, Craven (alias Taylor), Son
Taylor, George, Son
Compton, Jack (alias Taylor), Son
Compton, Cynthia (alias Taylor), Dau.
Compton, Mildred, Housekeeper
Taylor, Stephen, Son
Cotton, William, Gr-Son, son of dau. Frances
Fouch, Thomas, Wit.
Fouch, Isaac Jr., Wit.
Humfrey, Hen., Wit.
Hoge, William Sr., D:98, 1789
Hoge, James, Brother, his children by 1st wife
Hoge, Morgan, Gr-Son
Hoge, James, Son
Hoge, William, Son
Hoge, Solomon Sr., Son
Hoge, Solomon, Gr-Son, son of James
Hays, Nancy, Dau., w/o William
Hoge, George, Son
Jenkins, Nancy, Gr-Dau., dau. of James
Pancoast, Sarah, Step-Dau.-in-law
Gore, Sarah, Gr-Dau.
Gore, Joshua son-in-law of Solomon Hoge, Exor.
Hoge, Zebulon, Son
Boone, Hannah, Dau.-in-law
Kenworthy, William, Wit.
Shields, Joseph, Wit.
Hoge, Rebekah, Wit.
James, Elias, D:102, 1789
Nickols, James, Son-in-law, husband of Ann
Nickols, Ann, Dau., dec'd.
Osburn, Abner, Exor.
James, Isaac, Son
James, Hannah, Dau.
James, James, Son, <20
James, Elias, Son, <20
James, Anne, Wife
Thomas, Owen, Exor.
James, Thomas, Son
Currell, James, Wit.
Humphrey, Thos. Jr., Wit.
Humphrey, Thomas, Wit.
Bayley, Joseph, D:107, 1789
Bayley, Samuel, Brother
Bayley, Mountjoy, Brother
Bayley, Pierce, Brother
Bayley, Robert, Nephew, son of William
Bayley, William, Nephew, son of William
Bayley, William, Brother
Bayley, child if wife now pregnant
Bayley, Elizabeth, Wife
Lewis, Thomas, Wit.
Taylor, William, Wit.
Rust, William, Wit.
Trussel, John, Wit.
Taylor, Elizabeth, Wit.
Holland, Eliener, Wit.
Myers, Jonathan, D:117, 1780/90
Myers, Mary, Wife
Myers, Isaiah, Oldest Son
Pierpoint, Esther, Dau.
Myers, Elijah, Youngest Son
Moore, James, Wit.
Moore, Thomas Jr., Wit.
Moore, Asa, Wit.
Gore, Thomas, D:132, 1789/90
Gore, Mark, Son, < age
Gore, Elizabeth, Dau., < age
Gore, Hannah, Dau., < age
Gore, Anne, Wife
Gore, Joshua, Son, < age
Osburn, Abner, Exor.
Gore, Joshua, Brother
Osburn, William, Wit.
McLean, Duncan, Wit.
McLean, Mary, Wit.
Wallentine, George, D:137, 1790
Moore, John, Exor.
Wallentine, Catharine, Dau.
Tyler, John, Exor.

Wallentine, Elizabeth, Dau.
Wallentine, Mary, Wife
Bayley, Pierce, Wit.
McClean, James, Wit.
Gulick, Moses, Wit.
Moore, Jacob, Wit.
Daymud, Jacob, Wit.
Moore, Benjamin, Wit.
Gibson, Ealse, D:145, 1787/90
Nickols, Rebekah, Dau.
Gibson, Jesse, Gr-Son,
　son of Moses
Gibson, Susannah, Gr-Dau.,
　dau. of Moses
Gibson, Rachel, Gr-Dau.,
　dau. of Moses
Gibson, Dinah, Gr-Dau.,
　dau. of Moses
Gibson, Aron, Gr-Son,
　son of Moses
Gibson, Jonathan, Gr-Son,
　son of Moses, <21
Gibson, Ealse, Gr-Dau.,
　dau. of Isaac, < age
Gibson, Miriam, Gr-Dau.,
　dau. of Joseph
Gibson, Ruth, Gr-Dau.,
　dau. of Moses
Gibson, Moses, Son
Gibson, James, Son
Gibson, John, Son
Gibson, Thomas, Son
Gibson, Joseph, Son
Gibson, Isaac, Son
Clerk, Ann, Dau.
Janney, Abel, Wit.
Rees, Edward, Wit.
Wilks, Samuel, Wit.
King, Mary, D:148, 1790
Talbutt, Hannah, Dau., dec'd.
Floyd, Sarah, w/o William, Dau.
Stephens, Ann, Dau., dec'd.
Whaley, William, Gr-Son
Whaley, Penelope, Dau., dec'd.
Stephens, Elizabeth, Dau.,
　w/o Joseph
King, John, Husband, dec'd.
Smith, Mary, Dau.
King, John, Son
Stephens, Joseph, Gr-Son

King, Smith, Son
King, Osborn, Son
Stephens, Eleanor, Dau., dec'd.
Carrington, Winney, Dau.,
　w/o Timothy
Powell, William, Wit.
Gordon, Mary, Wit.
Powell, Ann, Wit.
Reed, Jonathan, D:150, 1788/91
Reed, Elizabeth, Dau.
Abit, Jobe, Step-son, wife's son
Philips, Sarah, Gr-Dau.,
　dau. of Charity
Reed, Jonathan, Gr-Son,
　son of Stephen, <21
Reed, Andrew, Son
Poulton, Martha, Dau.
Reed, Susana, Wife
Reed, Naomy, Dau.
Reed, Stephen, Son
Reed, Eunus, Dau.
Philips, Nancey, Gr-Dau.,
　dau. of Charity
Philips, Benjamin, Gr-Son,
　son of Charity
Philips, Israel, Gr-Son,
　son of Charity
Philips, Charity, Dau., dec'd.
Reed, Cornelius, Son
Marks, Thomas, Wit.
Roach, Richard, Wit.
Poulton, John, Wit.
Stephens, Eleanor, D:150, 1787/90
Stephens, Richard, Son
Stephens, Robert, Son
Perfect, Robert, Wit.
Gordon, Mary, Wit.
Nickols, James, D:152, 1785/91
Hogue, Elizabeth, w/o Isaac, Dau.
Nickols, Ann, Gr-Dau.,
　dau. of a dec'd. son
Nickols, Mary, Gr-Dau.,
　dau. of a dec'd. son
Nickols, Nathan, Gr-Son,
　son of a dec'd. son
Nickols, Solomon
Nickols, Charity, Dau.
Nickols, Isaiah, Son

Nickols, George, Son
Nickols, Nathan, Son, <21
Nickols, James, Son, <22
Hogue, Isaac, Son-in-law
Thatcher, John, Wit.
Thatcher, Richard, Wit.
Bartlett, Daniel, Wit.
Robertson, William, D:155, 1790/91
Robertson, Susannah, Dau.
Dillard, John, Son-in-law
Dillard, Anne, Dau.
Freeman, Hezekiah, Son-in-law
Freeman, Mary, Dau.
Newman, Elizabeth, Dau.
Newman, George, Son-in-law
Newman, Richard, Wit.
Wigginton, James, Wit.
Newman, Joseph, Wit.
Short, John, D:157, 1787/91
Short, Catharine, Wife
Soop, John, Gr-Son, son of eldest Dau. Eve Clanke
Spoon, Elizabeth, Dau.
Short, Jacob, Son
Clanke, Eve, Eldest Dau.
Purdum, Benjamin, Wit.
Smidley, Mathias, Wit.
Hausfeltner, Adam, Wit.
Eblin, Peter, D:159, 1790/91
Eblin, John, Brother
Eblin, Jannet [probate order says Elizabeth], Wife
Eblin, Samuel, Nephew, child of John
Eblin, Mary, Niece, child of John
Eblin, John, Nephew, child of John
Eblin, Isaac, Nephew, child of John
Eblin, Sarah, Niece, child of John
Eblin, Rachel, Niece, child of John
Eblin, Elisia, Niece, child of John
Eblin, Hannah, Niece, child of John
Braden, Joseph, Exor.
Dodd, John, Wit.

Hide, Philip, Wit.
Gore, Joseph, Wit.
Chamblin, William, D:170, 1791
Botts, Sarah, Dau., w/o Moses
Botts, Margaret, Dau., w/o Archibald
Palmer, Elizabeth, Dau., w/o Abel
Chamblin, Sarah, Wife
Chamblin, John, Son
Chamblin, Charles, Son
Chamblin, William, Son
Chamblin, Jane, Dau., <18
Chamblin, Eleanor, Dau., <18
Chamblin, Ann, Dau.
Rose, James, Wit.
Metthew, Peter, Wit.
Thomas, David, Wit.
Claggett, Thomas, D:173, 1791
Claggett, Thomas, Son
Claggett, Monica, Dau.
Claggett, Mary, Dau.
Clapham, Josias, Wit.
Mackall, Benjamin, Wit.
Kelly, John, Wit.
Burson, Benjamin, D:188, 1790/91
Burson, George, Son, <21
Burson, Silas, Son, <21
Burson, Hannah, Wife
Burson, Sarah, Dau.
Burson, Esther, Dau.
Trahern, James, Exor.
Burson, James, Wit.
Burson, Thomas, Wit.
Burson, Jonathan, Wit.
White, Richard, D:190, 1791
White, Samuel, Son
White, Joseph, Son
White, Daniel, Son
White, William, Son
White, Rebekah, Wife
White, Benjamin, Son
Combs, Samuel, Wit.
Nixon, George, Wit.
Janney, Abel, Wit.
Pool, Rebekah, D:193, 1784/91
Pool, Ann, Dau.
Pool, Joseph, Son
Pool, Israel, Son

Pool, Benjamin, Son
Pool, Mary, Dau.
Pool, Sarah, Dau.
Pool, Hannah, Dau.
Pool, Elizabeth, Dau.
Pool, Martha, Dau.
Mead, Benjamin, Wit.
Whitacre, Caleb, Wit.
Fairhurst, George, Wit.
Janney, William, D:195, 1787/91
Janney, Jesse, Son
Janney, Stacey, Son
Janney, William, Son
Janney, Elizabeth, Wife
Janney, Isaac, Son
Hughes, Elizabeth, Dau.
White, Ann, Dau.
Wildman, Letitia, Dau.
Wildman, Abraham, Son-in-law
Price, Thomas, D:200, 1790/91
Price, Susannah, Wife
Luckett, John, Wit.
Clapham, Samuel, Wit.
Clapham, Josias, Wit.
Cleveland, James, D:202, 1783/91
Cleveland, Frances, Wife
Cleveland, Johnston, Son
Cleveland, Hannah, Dau.
Cleveland, George, Son
Cleveland, Alexander, Brother
Mason, Benjamin, Exor.
Adams, F. Francis, Wit.
Adams, Ann, Wit.
Humphries, Susanna, Wit.
Shreve, Benjamin, D:204, 1790/91
Moffett, Robert C., Gr-Son, <21
Moffett, Benjamin S. , Gr-Son, <21
Moffett, Nancy, Gr-Dau., <21
Mead, Mary, Dau.
Moffett, Elizabeth, Dau.
Shreve, Anne, Wife
Shreve, William, Son
Shreve, Benjamin, Son
Shreve, Joshua, Son
Shreve, Abner, Son, <21
Fouch, Thomas, Wit.
Fouch, Jonathan, Wit.
Fouch, Isaac Jr., Wit.

Perfect, Christopher, D:208, 1791
Roper, Elizabeth, Dau.
Roper, Nancey, Gr-Dau.
Perfect, Catharine, Wife
Perfect, Robert, Son
Perfect, Jane, Dau.
Murrey, Samuel, Wit.
Littlejohn, John, Wit.
Lane, James, D:209, 1790
Payne, Anne, Dau.
Remey, Betty, Dau., dec'd., w/o Jacob
Smith, Lydia, Dau.
Smith, Jane, Dau. , w/o Withers
Smith, Keren, Dau. , w/o George
Lane, Sarah, Dau.-in-law, widow of son James
Lane, Hardage, Son
Lane, Lydia, Wife
Lane, Aaron, Son
Lane, James, Son, dec'd.
Lane, William, Son
Major, Rev. Richard, Friend
Major, —, Friend, w/o Richard
Summers, Geo., Wit.
Evans, John, Wit.
Butler, Linney, Wit.
Davis, John, D:217, 1791/92
Toy, Mary housekeeper
Davis, Evan, Nephew, living in South Carolina
Davis, Margaret, Sister
Davis, Mary, Sister
Davis, Thomas, Brother
Davis, Jinkin, Brother
Thomas, David, Exor.
Osborn, William, Exor.
Poulsen, Jasper, Wit.
Reed, Elizabeth, Wit.
Randle, Jonas, Wit.
Huguley, Abraham, D:249, 1792
Tobit, Hannah, Step-Dau.
Tobit, John, Step-son
Titherex, George, Gr-Son, < age
Titherex, Polly, Gr-Dau. < age
Titherex, Catey, Dau.
Summers, George, Gr-Son, < age
Summers, Polly, Gr-Dau. < age

Index to Loudoun County Wills, 1757 - 1850　　　　　37

Summers, Margaret, Dau.
Huguley (Hughy), Charles, Son
Huguley (Hughy), George, Son
Rooney, Michael, Wit.
Huguley, Jacob, Wit.
Foreman, Peter, Wit.
Kemlar, John, D:251, 1792
Kemlar (Kimbler), Sarah, Dau.
Kemlar (Kimbler), John, Son
Kemlar (Kimbler), —, Wife
Oden, Thomas, Wit.
McKim, James, Wit.
Davis, John, Wit.
Hutchison, Jeremiah, Wit.
McKim, Alex., Wit.
Huffman, John, D:252, 1792
Huffman, Margaret, Wife
Huffman, Phillip, Son
Huffman, Peter, Son
Huffman, Henry, Son
Rightmire, James, Wit.
Harman, Peter, Wit.
Gregg, Thomas, D:254, 1792
Gregg, Josiah, Son
Gregg, Isaac, Son
Gregg, Joseph, Son
Gregg, Thomas, Son
Gregg, John, Gr-Son
Gregg, Thomas, Gr-Son
Gregg, Levi, Son
Gregg, Samuel, Son
Gregg, Dinah, Dau.
Gregg, Mary, Dau.
Gregg, Mary, Wife
White, Thomas, Wit.
McKee, Joseph, Wit.
Turley, Sarah, D:256, 1791/92
Turley, Ignatius, Son
Turley, John, Son
Veale, John, Wit.
Veale, Thomas, Wit.
Veale, Lydia, Wit.
Veale, Elizabeth, Wit.
Buchannan, Ann, Wit.
Thompson, Andrew, D:257, 1791/92
Thompson, Penelope, Wife
Thompson, Lomax, Son
Thompson, Isaac, Son
Thompson, Andrew, Son

Thomson, Thomas, Wit.
Vincell, Adam, Wit.
Purdum, Jeremiah, Wit.
Emrey, Jacob, Wit.
Moxley, Joseph, D:269, 1792
Neal, Rodham, Gr-Son
Neal, Penny, Gr-Dau.
Moxley, Joseph, Son
Moxley, Jack, mulatto boy
Moxley, Samuel, Son
Moxley, Margaret, Wife
Connoly, Cornelius, Son-in-law
Connoly, Margaret, Gr-Dau.
Danniel, Josh., Wit.
Moss, Thomas, Wit.
Moxley, Wm., Wit.
Clowes, Joseph, D:271, 1792
Clowes, —, Wife
Lovett, Nancy, Gr-Dau.,
　dau. of Jonathan
Clowes, Thomas, Son
Clowes, Joseph, Son
Clowes, Mary, Dau.
Clowes, Elizabeth, Dau.
Clowes, Hannah, Dau.
Clowes, Nancy, Dau.
Clowes, Ruth, Dau.
Clowes, Phebe, Dau.
Janney, Israel, Wit.
Gore, Joseph, Wit.
Fairhurst, John, Wit.
Roszell, Stephen, D:283, 1792
Roszell, Stephen George, Son
Roszell, Sarah, nee Chilton,
　Wife
Roszell, Sally, Dau.
Roszell, Stephen Wesley,
　Son, <21
Roszell, Stephen Chilton, Son
Roszell, Phebe, Dau.
Roszell, Nancy, Dau.
Triplett, Simon, Exor.
Vanhorn, John, Wit.
Queen, Jonah, Wit.
Haines, Simeon, Wit.
Cavins, John, D:297, 1787/93
Burton, Elizabth, Sister
Cavins, John, Gr-Son,
　son of Robert
Cavins, William, Son

Cavins, Joseph, Son
Willson, Elizabeth, Gr-Dau.
Willson, William, Gr-Son
Willson, Alexander, Gr-Son
Willson, James, Gr-Son
Daniel (Danniel), Joshua, Exor.
Willson, Elenor, alias Hixon, Dau.
Haines, Stacey, Wit.
Smith, Clator, D:301, 1792/93
Hamton, Elizabeth, Dau.
Richardson, Jamima, Dau.
Smith, Clator, Son
Smith, Charles, Son
Smith, Conner, Son
Smith, Nancy, Dau.
Smith, —, Son
Smith, Nathaniel, Son
Smith, Winifred, Wife
Smith, George, Brother
Littleton, William, Wit.
Cockerell, William, Wit.
one unreadable name
Todd, Robert, D:308, 1793
Todd, Rebeckah, Gr-Dau., <18
Todd, Mary, Wife
Todd, John, Son
Todd, Samuel, Son
Todd, Robert, Son
Davis, Abram, Wit.
Hamilton, John, Wit.
Roberts, William, Wit.
Meyer (Moyer), George, D:309, 1791/93
Schwenk, George, Son-in-law
Meyer (Moyer), Mary Barbara, Wife
Meyer (Moyer), ten children of 1st wife, [see E:183]
Cordall, Jacob, Wit.
Jenkins, William, Wit.
Lampart, Fk., Wit.
Veale, William Sr., D:314, 1792/93
Read, Sarah, Dau., [married Daniel Bishop before Accounting G:339]
Lucas, Susannah, Dau.
Veale, Lydia, Wife
Veale, William, Son
Veale, Amos, Son
Veale, Charles, Son
Veale, John, Son
Veale, Polly, Dau.
Veale, Peggy, Dau.
Veale, Thomas, Son
Parrott, John, Wit.
Collett, Wm., Wit.
Cullison, Jeremiah, Wit.
Caldwell, Joseph, D:319, 1792/93
Caldwell, Jean, Dau.
Hixson, Timothy, Exor.
Caldwell, Moses, Son
Cavin, William, Wit.
Phillips, David, Wit.
Brewer, Henry, D:324, 1789/93
Sandford, Rebekah, Dau.
Minor, Elizabeth, Gr-Dau., sister of John
Sandford, Daniel, Son-in-law
Sandford, Henry, Gr-Son
Brewer, John, Son
Minor, John, Gr-Son
Minor, Nicholas, Son-in-law
Minor, Elizabeth, Dau.
Mark, John, Wit.
Jewell, Elisha, Wit.
Graham, John, Wit.
Eblen, Jane, D:335, 1793
Marshall, William, Brother
Marshall, James, Nephew, son of Joseph
Marshall, Samuel, Nephew, son of Joseph
Marshall, Joseph, Brother
Gore, Joseph, son of John
Nutton, Mary, Sister
McCinley, Elizabeth, Sister
Braden, Joseph, Wit.
Herdy, Leannah, Wit.
Braden, Robert, Wit.
Janney, Joseph, D:341, 1789/93
Janney, Susanna, Dau.
Janney, Sarah, Dau., <21
Janney, —, Wife
Janney, Israel, Kinsman
Janney, John, Brother
Janney, Mary, Dau.
Janney, Rebecckah, Dau.
Janney, Hannah, Dau., <21
Janney, Elizabeth, Dau., <21

Janney, Joseph, Son, <21
Janney, Thomas, Son
Janney, John, Son
Janney, Mahlon, Wit.
Talbott, Joseph, Wit.
Moore, James, Wit.
Moore, Asa, Wit.
Brown, Thomas, D:344, 1791/93
Brown, Joseph, Son
Brown, Coleman, Son
Asbury, Rebecca, Dau.,
  w/o Joseph
Lewis, Rebecca, Gr-Dau.,
  dau. of John
Brown, Reed, Gr-Son,
  son of Joseph
Lewis, Betty, Dau., w/o John
Cockerill, Jeremiah, Exor.
Love, Samuel, Wit.
Eskridge, Charles, Wit.
Lane, William 3rd, Wit.
Thomas, John, E:1, 1791/93
McCabe, William (Blinstone),
  Step-son, wife's son
Hole, Mary, Dau.
Semple, Sarah, Wife's Dau.
Thomas, Leonard Taylor, Son
Blinstone, William, alias
  McCabe, Step-son, wife's
  son
Thomas, Joseph, Son
Thomas, Catherine, Wife
Blinstone, Thomas, Step-son,
  wife's son
Jackson, Martha, Dau.
Binns, Chas. Jr., Wit.
Binns, Simon, Wit.
Harding, Wm. H., Wit.
Field, Jamima, E:5, 1791/94
Read, Eleanor, Dau.
Russell, Albert, Exor.
Priest, Samuel, Gr-Son, <21
Russell, Melea [Amelia], Wit.
Huey, Mary, Wit.
Mayhue, James, E:9, 1793/4
Mayhue, Izable, Wife
Mayhue, Moses, Son
Mayhue, Alexander
Offutt, William M., Wit.
Lang, Peter, Wit.

Harden, Elihu, Wit.
Mayhue, Moses, Admr w.w.a.
Howell, Timothy, E:22, 1794
Meredith, Elizabeth, Dau.
Poole, Jane, Dau.
Nickols, Henry, Gr-Son, <21
Howell, Ann, Dau.
Howell, Thomas, Son,
  died 1795
Howell, Mahlon, Son
Howell, Samuel, Son
Howell, Phebe, Dau.
Howell, Deborah, Dau.
Howell, —, Wife
Dillon, James, Wit.
Smith, Wm., Wit.
Janney, Israel, Wit.
Gregg, Thomas, Wit. [c]
Heaton, James, Wit. [c]
Gregg, John, Exor.
Thatcher, Richard, Exor.
Cleveland, Frances, E:32, 1793/94
Coleman, Frances, Gr-Dau.
Coleman, Hannah, Dau.
Cleveland, Johnson, Son
Cleveland, George, Son
Cleveland, James, husband,
  dec'd.
Mason, Benjamin, Exor.
Hutchison, Jer. Sr., Wit.
Thomas, Benjamin, Wit.
Humphries, Susanna, Wit.
Gregg, George, E:35, 1772/94
Gregg, Elizabeth, Wife
Gregg, George, Youngest Son,
  <21
Gregg, William, Oldest Son
Gregg, Elisha, Son
Gregg, Hannah, Dau.
Gregg, Mary, Dau.
Gregg, Sarah, Dau.
Gregg, Elizabeth, Dau.
Gregg, Ruth, Dau.
Hague, Francis, Wit.
Hague, Isaac, Wit.
Hague, Thomas, Wit.
Williams, Wm., Wit.
Janney, Abel Jr., Wit.

Lease, John, E:39, 1794
  Bitzer, Doratha, Sister
  Kailer, Hannah, Sister
  Lease, George, Brother
  Lease, Catherine, Wife
  Parrott, John, Wit.
  Kailer, Barbara, Wit.
Nickols, Henry, E:41, 1794
  Nickols, unnamed children
  Nickols, Susanna, Wife
  Nickols, Isaac, Exor.
  Taylor, Stacy, Wit.
  Hatcher, Joshua, Wit.
  Hughes, Constantine, Wit.
Hanson, Gustavus, E:43, 1794
  Hanson, Sarah, Wife
  Hanson, Arryaner, Dau.
  Thomas, Robert, Wit.
  Lewis, Charles, Wit.
Thompkins, James, E:46, 1794
  Thompkins, Marcia, Wife
  Thompkins, — children
  Littlejohn, John, Wit.
  Campbell, John, Wit.
  Daily, Aaron, Wit.
Brown, Thomas, E:48, 1794
  Brown, Moses, Son
  Brown, Aaron, Son
  Brown, Rachel, Dau.
  Brown, Leah, Dau.
  Brown, Ann, Wife
  Brown, Tamar, Dau.
  Brown, —, Unborn child
  Mead, Benjamin, Exor.
  Lovett, Jonathan, Exor.
  Trahern, James, Wit.
  Baldwin, Mahlon, Wit.
  Whitacre, John, Wit.
Brown, William, E:50, 1788/94
  Brown, Sarah, Dau.
  Brown, John, Son
  Schooley, Hannah, Dau.
  Brown, William, Son
  Brown, Elizabeth, Dau.
  Brown, Jacob, Son
  Brown, —, Wife
  Brown, Richard, Son
  Janney, Israel, Wit.
  Hatcher, James, Wit.
  Claypoole, James, Wit.

Thomas, Catharine, E:54, 1794
  Blinston, William, alias McCabe, Son
  Sample, Sally, Dau., dec'd.
  Sample, Susanah, Gr-Dau., < age
  Sample, Catherine, Gr-Dau., < age
  Dorrell, John, Son
  Dorrell, Thomas, Son
  McCabe, William (Blinston), Son
  Brown, John, Exor.
  Brown, George, Exor.
  Brown, Jehue, Wit.
  Kevan, Wm., Wit.
  Sampell, Jas., Wit.
  Daily, Aaron, Wit.
Turner, Fielding, E:55, 1793/94
  Turner, Winifred, Wife
  Turner, Lewis, Son
  Turner, Major Fielding, Son
  Turner, John, Son
  Turner, —, Unborn child
  Turner, William, Son
  Hawley, John, Exor.
  Hutchison, Jeremiah, Exor.
  Lewis, Charles, Exor.
  Berkley, John, Wit.
  Davis, John, Wit.
  Dutton, James, Wit.
  Hutchison, John, Wit.
  Hawley, Abram, Wit.
Noland, Philip, E:67, 1794
  Noland, Thomas, Gr-Son, son of Philip
  Noland, Philip, Son, dec'd.
  Noland, Thomas, Son
  Noland, Awbry, Son
  Luckett, Philip, Gr-Son, son of John & Molly Ann
  Luckett, Molly Ann, Dau.
  Luckett, Elizabeth, Dau.
  Myre, Jacob, Wit.
  Elliott, James, Wit.
  Williams, Ann, Wit.
Fouch, Isaac, E:69, 1793/94
  Russell, Mary McDowell, Gr-Dau., dau. of Elizabeth
  Russell, Elizabeth, Dau.
  Fouch, George, Son

Fouch, Mary, Dau.
Fouch, Isaac, Son
Fouch, William, Son
Fouch, Daniel, Son
Fouch, Jonathan, Son
Fouch, Thomas, Son
Fouch, Mary, Wife
Elgin, George, Wit.
Elgin, Wm. Jr., Wit.
Elgin, Gustavus, Wit.
Power, Joseph, E:74, 1794
Power, Walter, Son
Power, Sarah, Wife
Canby, Samuel, Wit.
Fitzsimons, Mary, Wit.
Luke, Elizabeth, Wit.
Cocke, William, E:79, 1794
Cocke, Catesby, Father, dec'd.
Cocke, Washington, Son
Cocke, Lucy, Dau.
Powell, Leven, Wit.
Dishman, Samuel, Wit.
Taylor, Thomas, Wit.
Weeden, Josiah, Wit.
Peyton, Chandler, Wit.
Kennen, James, Wit. [c]
Moore, Jacob, Wit. [c]
Gregg, Isaac, E:81, 1794/95
Gregg, Sarah, Wife
Gregg, Stephen, Son, <21
Gregg, William, Son
Gregg, Levi, Brother
Janney, Israel, Exor.
Gregg, Josiah, Wit.
Gregg, Thomas, Wit.
White, Thomas, Wit.
Braden, Robert, E:82, 1794/95
Braden, Joseph, Son
Braden, Robert, Son
Wright, Robert, Exor.
Wright, Margaret, Dau.
Fox, Bartleson, Wit.
Climor, Christian, Wit.
Cowgill, Ralph Sr., E:85, 1794/95
Cowgill, Hannah, Dau.
Cowgill, Tamer, Dau.
Cowgill, Dorothy, Dau.
Cowgill, James, Son
Cowgill, Joseph, Son
Cowgill, Ralph, Son

Cowgill, Isaac, Son
Cowgill, Sarah, Wife
Wynn, Robert, Wit.
Carter, William, Wit.
Russel, Robert, Wit.
Thompson, Israel, E:87, 1795
Ritchardson, Joseph first wife's
  son, Step-son
Thompson, Sarah, formerly
  Hague, Wife
Thompson, Israel, Son, <18
Thompson, Jonah, Son,
  child of former wife
Thompson, Samuel, Son,
  child of former wife
Thompson, Pleasant, Dau., <18
Thompson, Sally, Dau., <18
Thompson, Betzey, Dau., <18
Thompson, Nancy, Dau., <18
Woodward, Prudence, Sister
Hough, William, Exor.
Janney, Mahlon, Wit.
Purdum, Benjamin, Wit.
Redman, John, Wit.
Mull, David, E:93, 1794/95
Mull, John, Gr-Son, who now
  lives with me, <21
Mull, David, Son
Mull, Madlain, Dau.
Mull, Rachel, Dau.
Mull, Margaret, Wife,
  mother of George
Mull, George, Son
Shomaker, Jacob, Wit.
Purdum, Jeremiah, Wit.
Mull, George, Wit.
Carr, John, E:96, 1788/95
Wade, Robert, Son-in-law
Carr, Joseph, Gr-Son,
  son of Peter
Carr, Peter, Son
Carr, William, Gr-Son,
  son of Peter
Carr, Daniel, Gr-Son, son of
  Sally
Carr, Sally, Dau.
Carr, John, Gr-Son, son of John
Carr, John, Son
Carr, Thomas, Son
Braden, Joseph, Exor.

Vanpelt, John, Wit.
Braden, Robert Jr., Wit.
Braden, Elizabeth, Wit.
[Fox when proved]

Jackson, William, E:104, 1782/95
Jackson, Martha, Eldest Dau.
Jackson, Mary, 2nd Dau.
Jackson, Abigil, Wife
Jackson, John, Son
Jackson, James, Son
Jackson, Ann, Dau.
Jackson, Febe, Dau.
Jackson, William, Son
Jackson, Sarah, Dau.
Jackson, Richard, Son
Purdum, Benjamin, Wit.
Houghton, Elijah, Wit.

Smarr, John, E:109, 1794/95
was married 3 times
Smarr, Samuel, Son, child of
  2nd marriage to Sarah
  Pearle
Smarr, Fanny, Dau.
Smarr, Robert, Son
Smarr, John, Son
Smarr, Reuben, Son,
  child of 2nd marriage
Smarr, Charles, Son,
  child of 2nd marriage
Smarr, Ann, Dau.,
  child of 2nd marriage
Smarr, Elizabeth, Dau.,
  child of 2nd marriage
Smarr, George, Son,
  child of 2nd marriage
Smarr, Andrew, Son,
  child of 2nd marriage
Smarr, Peril, Son,
  child of 2nd marriage
Williamson, Nancy, Dau.
More, Cloe, Dau.
Weadon, Jane, Dau.
Tilman, Sarah, Dau.
Hampton, Mary, Dau.
Smarr, Sarah, Wife
Galleher, William, Wit.
Powell, William, Wit.
Galleher, David, Wit.

Mason, Benjamin, E:118, 1791/95
Mason, Ann, Wife
Mason, George, Son
Mason, Burgess, Son
Mason, John, Son
Mason, William Wolverton, Son
Mason, Mary, Dau.
Mason, Margaret, Dau.
Linton, Ann, Dau.
Gist, Elizabeth, Dau.
Carter, Margaret, Dau.
Mason, Caty Linton, Dau., <15
Hutchison, Jeremiah, Wit.
Dunkin, Charles, Wit.
Beaty, William, Wit.
Edwards, Edward B., Wit.

Pagit, Francis, E:120, 1790/95
Cunningham, Rachel, Dau.
Hill, Nancy, Dau.
Pagit, Ruth, Wife in will
Pagit, Jane, Wife when
  probated
Walrund, Elizabeth, Dau.
Loins (Lyne), Thomas, Exor.
Loins (Lyne), Mary, Dau.
Miller, Sinthy, Dau.
Pagit, Frances, Dau.
Ervin, Peggy, Dau.
Pagit, Rubin, Son
Pagit, Amy, Dau.
Pagit, Timothy, Son
Eskridge, William, Wit.
Hutchison, Jeremiah, Wit.
Hardy, Joshua, Wit.
James, Jacob, Wit.

Lanham, Aaron, of Maryland, E:121, 1795
Lanham, Aquila, Son
Lanham, Hezekiah, Son
Lanham, Mercy Ann, Dau.
Lanham, Elizabeth, Dau.
Lanham, Walter, Son
Lanham, Zadock, Son
Lanham, Eleanor, Dau.
Lanham, Lethe, Dau.
Lanham, Elizabeth, Wife
Becraft, Peter, Wit.
English, King, Wit.
Magruder, Ninian, Wit.

Index to Loudoun County Wills, 1757 - 1850   43

Conrad, Jonathan, E:130, 1795
Osborn, Nicholas
Conrad, Gulielme, Wife
Conrad, three little daus.
Conrad, John, Brother
Davis, David, Step-son
Conrad, Jonathan, Nephew,
   son of John
Beal, Joseph, Exor.
Conrad, Edward, Exor.
Gregg, John (miller), Wit.
Bazell, Ezekiel, Wit.
Osborn, Nicholas, Wit.

Cambell, James, E:132, 1795
Cambell, Andrew, Brother
Cambell, Robert, Brother
Cambell, John, Brother
Cambell, William, Father
Lewis, George A, Wit.
West, John, Wit.
James, Margaret, Wit.

King, Benjamin Sr., E:146, 1794/95
Kent, Susannah, Gr-Dau.,
   dau. of John, <18
Williams, Susanna, Dau.,
   w/o John
King, Benjamin, Son
King, Daniel, Son
King, William, Son
King, John, Son
Brent, Charles, Wit.
Selfe, Nancy, Wit.

Pilcher, Edward, E:154, 1795
Pilcher, Sarah, Mother
Pilcher, Moses, Brother
Pilcher, Sarah, Sister
Bayley, Pierce, Wit.
Hutchison, Reuben, Wit.

Gregg, Stephen, E:161, 1791/95
Gregg, Susannah, Dau.
Gregg, Samuel, Son
Gregg, Nathan, Son
Gregg, Thomas, Son
Gregg, Susanna, Wife
Janney, Israel, Wit.
Janney, Jesse, Wit.
Brown, Wm., Wit.

Humphrey, Thomas Jr., E:165, 1796
Humphrey, Thomas, Father
Humphrey, Abner, Brother
Humphrey, all brothers & sisters
Thomas, Owen, Wit.
Hough, Jonah, Wit.
Marks, John, Wit.

Crumbacker, John, E:170, 1795/96
Crumbacker, Eve, Wife
Crumbacker, Elizabeth, Dau.
Crumbacker, Jacob, Son
Crumbacker, John, Son, < age
Shover, Adam, Wit.
Shaffer, Phillip, Wit.
Cost, Jacob, Wit.

Halbert, Michael, E:172, 1796
Halbert, Rosey, Wife
Halbert, Katey, Dau.
Halbert, William, Son
Halbert, Thomas, Son
Halbert, Michael, Son
Halbert, James, Son
Halbert, Lyddia, Dau.
Halbert, Ailsey, Dau.
Halbert, Sally, Dau.
Beavers, Polly, Dau.
Buckley, Joshua, Exor.
Lane, William Jr., Exor.
Asbury, Joseph, Wit.
Bush, Mary, Wit.
Gold, Ann, Wit.
Wiatt, Jacob Andrew, Wit.
Gold, Joseph, Wit.

Ellzey, William, atty, E:184, 1795/96
Harrison, Matthew,
   h/o of Catherine
Harrison, Catherine,
   w/o Matthew
Russell, Albert, h/o of Ann
Russell, Ann, w/o of Albert
Ellzey, Sarah, Dau.
Ellzey, Margaret, Dau.
Ellzey, Lucy, Dau.
Ellzey, Lewis, Son
Ellzey, —, Wife
Ellzey, William, Son

Powell, Elisha, E:190, 1796
　Fulton, Sarah H., Dau.
　Middleton, John
　Middleton, Mary, Dau.
　Powell, John, Son
　Powell, William, Son
　Powell, Elisha, Son
　Powell, Robert M., Son
　Lewis, Charles, Wit.
　Johnston, William, Wit.
　Triplett, Enoch, Wit.
Thomas, David, E:200, 1796
　Evans, George, Son-in-law,
　　husband of Sarah
　Evans, Sarah, Dau.
　Thomas, Owen, Son
　Thomas, Martha, Dau.-in-law
　Thomas, Philip, Son
　Thomas, George, Son
　Nickols, Nathan, Wit.
　Nickols, George, Wit.
　Taylor, Timothy, Wit.
　Taylor, Stacey, Wit.
Brown, Isaac, E:202, 1796
　Whitacre, Martha, Dau.
　Whitacre, Ed, Exor.
　Brown, Isaac, Son
　Brown, Abraham, Son
　Brown, John, Son
　Burson, James, Wit.
　Burson, Jonathan, Wit.
　Burson, John, Wit.
Jenkins, John, E:202, 1796
　Jenkins, Charles
　Self, Elizabeth, Sister
　Self, Presley, Nephew
　Jenkins, William,
　　father of Charles
　Moore, Francis, Wit.
　Jenkins, Sylvester, Wit.
Harl, Elizabeth, E:212, 1796
　Shreve, William, Nephew
　Shreve, William, father of
　　William, of Md.
　Gunnell, John, Friend
　Gunnell, Henry, Exor.
　Gunnell, Henry Jr., Wit.
　Stanhope, William, Wit.
　Green, John, Wit.
　Brent, Charles, Wit.

Carr, Thomas, E:234, 1796
　Carr, Mary, Wife
　Carr, John, Son
　Carr, Thomas, Son
　Carr, James, Son
　Carr, Joseph, Son
　Carr, Samuel, Son
　Carr, Elizabeth, Dau.
　Carr, Margaret, Dau.
　Campbell (Camell), Jane, Dau.,
　　w/o Andrew
　Hall, Mary, Dau., w/o William
　Carr, John, Father, dec'd.
　Binns, C. Jr., Wit.
　Mains, William, Wit.
　Hole, Levi, Wit.
Phillips, Thomas, E:235, 1794/96
　Martin, Sarah, Sister
　Martin, Elizabeth, Niece,
　　dau. of Sarah
　Martin, Thomas, Nephew,
　　son of Sarah
　Nitson, Israel, alias Philips,
　　Nephew
　Phillips, Israel, Nephew,
　　son of Sarah Martin
　Conner, Richard, Exor.
　McCarty, Jonathan, Exor.
　Climer, Christian, Wit.
　Braden, Robert, Wit.
　one unreadable name
Green, James, E:237, 1788/96
　Harding, Ann, Dau.
　Green, Frances, Wife
　Green, William, one of three
　　youngest sons
　Green, Fielding, one of three
　　youngest sons
　Green, Frances, one of three
　　youngest daus.
　Green, Thomas, Son
　Green, George (Gerrard), Son
　Shelton, Elizabeth, Dau.
　Saunder, Polly, Dau.
　Harding, Elihu, Son-in-law
　Bennett, Mary, Dau.
　Fox, William, Wit.
　Borbridge, J. R., Wit.

Brown, Benjamin, E:255, 1795/96
Brown, Winifred, Wife
Fox, Catheren, dau. of Mary
Middleton, William, Friend
Owens, John, Friend
Fox, Mary, widow of William
Moss, John Jr., Wit.
Self, Presley, Wit.
West, John, Wit.
Stanhope, William, Wit.
Douglass, Mary, Wit.
Eblin, John, E:257, 1795/97
Eblin, Samuel, Son
Eblin, Isaac, Son
Eblin, John, Son
Sloan, Rachel, Dau.
Eblin, Mary, Wife
Chapman, Thomas, Son-in-law
Carter, Hannah, Dau.
Carter, James, Son-in-law
Pyott, Mary, Dau.
Parker, Eliza, Dau.
Lovett, Jonathan, Exor.
Powell, Hopwell, Wit.
Oliham, John, Wit.
Lifolett, Usual, Wit.
Lifolett, Jeremiah, Wit.
Huppoh, Elsey, E:257, 1797
Ater, George Sr.
Ater, Abraham
Ater, Isaac
Sharp, Jacob
Creager, Elizabth
Huppoh, Cornelius, son of John
Huppoh, Peter
Huppoh, John
Stump, C., Wit.
Stump, Jacob, Wit.
Stephenson, Jane, E:279, 1797
Stephenson, William, Son
Stephenson, Thomas, Son
West, Joseph, Wit.
Vanhorne, Elizabeth, Wit.
Hough, John, E:280, 1797
Hough, William, Son
Hough, Samuel, Son
Hough, Jonah, Son
Hough, —, Wife
Hough, Mahlon, Son
Hough, Amos, Son
Hough, John, Son, dec'd.
Hough, Mary, Gr-Dau.,
  dau. of John
Hough, Rachel, Gr-Dau.,
  dau. of John
Hough, Sarah, Gr-Dau.,
  dau. of John
Hough, Samuel, Gr-Son,
  son of John
Mason, Sarah, Dau.
Mason, Abraham B. , Son-in-
  law, husband of Sarah
Canby, Benjamin Hough,
  Gr-Son
Nicklin, Sarah, Gr-Dau., dau. of
  John Hough
Janney, Mahlon, Wit.
Hollingsworth, John, Wit.
Steer, Benjamin, Wit.
Lewis, Vincent, E:287, 1786/96
Jennings, Anna, Dau.
Lewis, Ann, Wife, dec'd. by time
  of probate
Davis, Betty, w/o Jonathan,
  Dau.
Lewis, James, Son
Lewis, George, Son
Lewis, Joseph, Son
Lewis, John, Eldest Son
Lewis, Charles, Youngest Son
Gist, Nathaniel, Wit.
Gist, William, Wit.
Paul, Edward P., Wit.
Revely, John, Wit.
Spencer, John, Wit.
Williams, Richard, E:297, 1795/97
George, William, Gr-Son
Williams, Jinkin, Son
Shrieves, Mary, Dau.
Williams, Margrate, Wife
Williams, Enos, Son
Williams, James, Son
Williams, Joseph, Son
Bennett, Charles, Exor.
Taylor, Jesse, Wit.
Brown, William, Wit.
Major, Richard, E:303, 1796/97
Hutchison, Jeremiah Sr., Exor.
Hutchison, Sarah, Dau.
Bever, Rebecca, Dau.

Major, Elizabeth, Gr-Dau.
Crooks, James, Exor.
Major, Daniel, Son, dec'd.
Major, James, Son
Major, Elijah, Son
Major, Sarah, Wife
Mershon, Joseph, Wit.
Hutchison, Joshua, Wit.
Mershon, Thomas B., Wit.
Sanders, John, E:315, 1797
Sanders, Aron, Brother
Sanders, Presley, Brother
Sanders, Unnamed infant Dau.
Sanders, Bethany, Dau., <21
Sanders, Nancy, Dau., <21
Sanders, Patience, Dau., <21
Sanders, Mary, Dau., <21
Sanders, Barbary, Dau., <21
Sanders, Elizabeth, Dau., <21
Sanders, Sarah, Dau., <21
Sanders, John, Son, <21
Sanders, James, Son, <21
Sanders, Mary, Wife, deceased
  by time of probate
Sanders, Henry, Wit.
Sanders, Moses, Wit.
Browner, William, Wit.
Taylor, Thomas, E:317, 1797
Taylor, Thomas, Son
Canby, Benjamin Hough,
  Son-in-law
Sutherland, Anne, Dau.,
  w/o Alexander
Taylor, Jessey, Son
Taylor, Mary, Dau.
Taylor, Rachel, Dau.
Taylor, Sarah, Dau.
Taylor, Henry, Son
Taylor, Joseph, Son
Baer, George Jr., Wit.
Bowman, George, Wit.
Metzger, Jacob, Wit.
Grigsby, James, E:321, 1797
Stump, Peter, Exor.
Field, William, Exor.
Reed, Nathaniel Grigsby, Son
Reed, Ann Grigsby, Dau.
Reed, Ludwell Grigsby, Son

Reed, John Grigsby, Son
Reed, Mary, housekeeper
Reed, Lewis Grigsby, Son
Musgrove, Gilbert, Wit.
Wilkinson, George, Wit.
Huguley, Charles, E:327, 1797
Huguley, Mary, Wife
Huguley, George, Son
Huguley, John, Son
Huguley, Job, Son
Huguley, —, Dau.
Rooney, Michael, Wit.
Dorsett, Samuel, Wit.
McCarty, James, Wit.
Botts, Joshua, E:328, 1797
Botts, Moses, Son
Botts, Judah, Wife
Overfield, Martin, Son-in-law
Overfield, Nancy, Gr-Dau., <21
Overfield, Hutson, Gr-Son, <21
Overfield, Elizabeth, Dau.
Warford, John, Wit.
Lewis, George, Wit.
Grady, James, Wit.
Scatterday, John, Wit.
Redman, John, E:330, 1797
Thomson, Jonah, Exor.
McKinley, Sarah, Sister
McKinley, Willam Jr., Nephew
Redman, Mary, Mother
Redman, Andrew, Brother
Nicklin, John, Wit.
Brown, James, Wit.
Ball, Stephen, Wit.
Pullen, Charles, E:332, 1796/97
Ritaker, Catharine, Dau.
Lacey, Israel, Exor.
Pullin, William, Eldest Son
Pullin, Robert, 2nd Son
Skinner, Peggy, Dau.
Schlacht, Rhody, Dau.
McMachin, Zilpah, Dau.
Pullin, Asher, Youngest Son
Swart, Mary, Dau.
Bodine, Elizabeth, Dau.
Taylor, John, Exor.
Lacey, Israel, Wit.
Lacey, Elias, Wit.
Rogers, William A., Wit.

Ellis, Ellis, F:8, 1792/97
 Davis, Ellis, Nephew
 Davis, Hannah, Sister,
  w/o Abraham
 Huffty, Benjamin, Wit.
 Maginnis, Edward, Wit.
 Maginnis, Jean, Wit.
Janney, Elizabeth, F:11, 1797/98
 Janney, Cosmelia, Dau.
 Janney, Mahlon, Wit.
 Moore, James, Wit.
 Moore, Asa, Wit.
Smith, Mary, F:21, 1798
 Adomas, Rachel, Dau.
 Jacoby, Jacob, Son-in-law
 Jacoby, Ann, Dau.
 Smith, John, Son
 Derry, Catherine, Dau.
 Fitchcharles, Philipina, Dau.
 Smith, Sybilla, Dau.
 Smith, Catharine, Dau.-in-law
 Smith, Sally, Dau., becomes
  Sarah Hogue
 Smith, Susanna, Dau.-in-law
 Smith, Frederick, Wit.
 Smitley, Mathias, Wit.
 Betts, Andrew, Wit.
Grymes, Nicholas, F:30, 1798
 King, Sarah, Dau.
 Grymes, Jain, Wife
 Grymes, Nicholas, Son
 Grymes, William, Son
 Grymes, Silvester, Son
 Grymes, John, Son
 Grymes, Edward, Son
 Grymes, Sandford, Son
 Grymes, Jain, Dau.
 Grymes, Anna, Dau.
 Jenkins, Alice, Dau.
 Donaldson, William, Wit.
 Lay, Stephen, Wit.
 Payne, George, Wit.
 Brent, Charles, Wit.
Stevens, James, F:36, 1798
 Ward, Elizabeth, Dau.
 Stephens, George, Son
 Stephens, William, Son
 Stephens, Benjamin, Son
 Stephens, Zachariah, Son
 Stephens, Henry, Son
 Stephens, Hezekiah, Son
 Stephens, James, Son
 Stephens, Hannah, Wife
 Fouch, Ann, Dau.
 Brooks, Alice, Dau., w/o Aaron
 Homan, Mark, child of Elizabeth
  Homan
 Homan, Matthew, child of
  Elizabeth Homan
 Homan, Mary, child of Elizabeth
  Homan
 Homan, Hannah, child of
  Elizabeth Homan
 Homan, Reuben Stevens, child
  of Elizabeth Homan
 Littleton, Solomon, Wit.
 Oxley, Jenkin, Wit.
 Lester, Hugh, Wit.
Tillett, Samuel Sr., F:40, 1798
 Bennett, Sally, Gr-Dau.,
  child of Ann
 Hammett, Sarah, Dau.
 Barnett, Margaret, Dau.
 Tillett, Elizabeth, Dau.
 Stone, Jane, Dau.
 Tillett, James, Son
 Sangster, Mary, Dau.
 Tillett, Edward, Son
 Bennett, Duhanna, Gr-Dau.,
  child of Ann
 Tillett, Samuel, Son
 Bennett, Patty, Gr-Dau.,
  child of Ann
 Tillett, Giles, Son
 Bennett, Polly, Gr-Dau.,
  child of Ann
 Bennett, Joseph, Gr-Son, child
  of Ann
 Bennett, Ann, Dau.
 Bennett, Samuel, Gr-Son, child
  of Ann
 Perfect, Robert, Wit.
 Littlejohn, John, Wit.
 Perfect, Erasmus, Wit.
Wirts, Peter Sr., F:44, 1798
 Wirts, Peter, Son
 Wirts, Anna Mary, Dau.
 Wirts, Jacob, Son
 Wirts, William, Son
 Wirts, Catharine, Dau.

Wirts, Michael, Son
Wirts, Christina, Wife
Wirts, John, Son
Wirts, Christina, Dau.
Smith, Frederick, Wit.
Sheark, Michael, Wit.
Richie, Isaac, Wit.
Ansley, William, F:49, 1798
Ansley, Ann, Wife
Rhodes, William, Wit.
Milner, John, Wit.
Rhodes, George, Wit.
Ashton, Joseph, Wit.
George, Thomas, F:52, 1787/98
George, William, Son
Steer, Joseph, Son-in-law
Steer, John, Son-in-law
Steer, Isaac, Son-in-law
Clapham, Josias, Wit.
Ansell, Leonard, Wit.
Kunkel, Malcohor [GS], Wit.
Fulton, Robert, F:54, 1792/98
Fulton, David, Son
Fulton, Leanah, Dau.
Fulton, Milly (Nelly), Dau.
Fulton, James, Son
Fulton, —, Wife
Fulton, Robert, Son
Binns, John, Wit.
Sanders, Aaron, Wit.
Swart, John, F:56, 1798
Batson, James, Exor.
Swart, Elizabeth, Wife
Powell, Leven, Wit.
Batson, John, Wit.
Hagarman, Adrian, Wit.
Talbott, Joseph, F:63, 1798
Talbott, Rebekah, Dau.
Talbott, John, Son
Talbott, Susannah, Dau.
Talbott, Elizabeth, Dau.
Talbott, Anne, Dau.
Talbott, Jesse, Son
Talbott, Elisha, Son
Talbott, Mary, Dau.
Talbott, Sarah, Dau.
Talbott, Joseph, Son
Talbott, Samuel, Son
Talbott, Rebekah, Wife
Rattikin, James, Exor.

Moore, James, Exor.
Moore, Asa, Exor.
Griffith, Richard, Wit.
Williams, J., Wit.
Thompson, Israel, Wit.
Penquite, Ester, F:71, 1791/99
Penquite, John & Jain's children
Vance, Agnes
Walton (Watton), Sarah,
 sister of Mary
Taylor, Bernard
Vance, children of Samuel &
 Agnes
Walton (Watton), Mary,
 sister of Sarah
Martin, Mary, dau. of
 Daniel & Jane
Walton (Watton), Nicholas,
 son of Isaiah
Martin, Ann, dau. of
 Daniel & Jane
Martin, Ambrose, son of
 Daniel & Jane
Davis, Joannah
Davis, Agnes, dau. of
 David and Joannah
Richardson, Daniel Jr., Wit.
Taylor, William, Wit.
Patterson, Margaret, Wit.
Taylor, Jonathan, Wit.
Fine, Peter, F:83, 1798/99
Fine, Catharine, Wife
Sinkins, Elizabeth, Gr-Dau.
Richey, Isaac, Exor.
Shover, Adam, Wit.
Ritchie, Jacob, Wit.
Compher, John, Wit.
Cowgill, James, F:88, 1799
Cowgill, —, Mother
Cowgill, —, Brothers & Sisters
Cowgill, Ralph, Exor.
Massey, Samuel, Exor.
Wynn, Robert, Wit.
Carter, William, Wit.
Russell, Robert, Wit.
Allen, William, F:112, 1796/99
Allen, James, Son
Allen, David, Son
Allen, Joseph, Son
Allen, David, Brother, dec'd.

Allen, —, other daus.
Allen, Elizabeth, Dau.-in-law,
  w/o James
Furman, Elizabeth, Dau.
Harrison, M. Jr., Wit.
Skillman, John, Wit.
McPherson, Stephen Sr., F:121, 1799
Boyce, Rachel, Dau.
Merrill, Ruth, Dau.
McPherson, James, Son
McPherson, Jesse, Son
McPherson, William, Son
McPherson, Daniel, Son
McPherson, Joseph, Son
McPherson, Stephen, Son
McPherson, John, Son
McPherson, Ann, Wife
McKinney, George, Wit.
Carr, Joseph, Wit.
Gibson, George, Wit.
Hains, Thomas, F:122, 1799
Hains, Mary, Dau.
Hains, Sarah, Dau.
Hains, Simeon, Son
Hains, Thomas, Son
Hains, Stacy, Son
Hains, Hephzidah William, Son
Hains, Mary, Wife
Pierpoint, Obed, Wit.
Braden, Joseph, Wit.
Eblin, John, Wit.
Fearst, Christien, F:132, 1799/1800
Fearst, Hannah, Wife
Fearst, Cunrod, Son
Fearst, all my children
Johnson, Mary, F:143, 1795/1800
Turner, Betty, Dau.
Ashford, Sarah, Dau.
Hadducks, Barbara, Dau.
Debell, William, Son
Debell, John, Son
Debell, Dorcus, Dau.
Oden, Richard A., Wit.
Heath, Isaac, Wit.
Hutchison, Jer. Sr., Wit.

Daniel, William, F:144, 1799/1800
Daniel, Esther, Wife
Daniel, James, Son
Daniel, William, Son
Daniel, Joseph, Son
Daniel, Benjamin, Son
Daniel, Samuel, Son
Richards, Esther, Dau.
Lewis, Sarah, Dau.
Sinclear, Rachel, Dau.
Smith, Alice, Gr-Dau.
Dillon, Mary, Dau.
Rhodes, Martha, Dau.
Cadwallader, Jane, Dau.
Taylor, Stacy, Wit.
Head, John, Wit.
Ewers, William, Wit.
Gregg, Jacob, Wit.
Whaley, James Sr., F:149, 1785
Whaley, Vincent, Son
More, Ann, Dau.
Robertson, Hannah, Gr-Dau.,
  dau. of Elizabeth
Robertson, Elizabeth, Dau.
Whaley, Amelia, Dau.
Carter, Hannah, Dau.
Whaley, Winnafred, Dau.
Whaley, Levy, Son
Whaley, Mereman, Son
Whaley, Sarah, Dau.
Whaley, William, Son
Waggoner, Mary, Dau.
Whaley, James, Son
Whaley, Penelope, Dau.
Jenings, James, Wit.
Berkley, Scarlett, Wit.
Cross, Joseph, F:153, 1779/80
Cross, John, Brother
Cross, William, Brother
Cross, Robert, Brother
Cross, —, Wife
Cross, Joseph, Son
Cross, John, Son
Jennings, James, Exor.
Lane, Hardage, Exor.
Lane, William Jr., Exor.
Berkley, Scarlett, Wit.
Linton, John, Wit.
Middleton, Letty, Wit.
Lane, Susanna, Wit.

Bronaugh, William, F:154, 1796/1800
Bronaugh, William, Son
Bronaugh, Rebecca, Wife
Bronaugh, John William, Son
Bronaugh, Jeremiah William, Son
Bronaugh, James Craine, Son
Bronaugh, Rebecca, Dau.
Bronaugh, Sally, Dau.
Peyton, Elizabeth, Dau.
Bronaugh, Rosa, Dau.
Hale, Peggy, Dau.
Grayson, Nancy, Dau.
Fowke, Mary Mason, Dau.

Wilkinson, Joseph, F:155, 1795/1800
Hague, Hiram, Gr-Son
Wilkinson, Jesse, Son
Wilkinson, Joseph, Son
Wilkinson, Rachel, Wife
Hixon, Reuben, Wit.
Hixon, Timothy, Wit.
Purdum, Jeremiah, Wit.

Gregg, Thomas, F:174, 1799/1800
Nichols, Hannah, Dau.
Janney, Jonas, Exor.
Gregg, Thomas, Son
Trayhern, Dinah, Dau.
Ewers, Amy, Dau.
Gregg, Israel, Son
Taylor, Bernard, Exor.
Gregg, Jacob, Son
Gregg, Samuel, Son
Gregg, Rebeckah, Wife
Smith, William, Wit.
Head, John, Wit.
Spencer, Nathan, Wit.

Thomas, Owen, F:184, 1800
Thomas, Martha, Wife
Thomas, David, Son
Thomas, Joseph, Son
Thomas, Philip, Son
Thomas, Jesse, Son
Thomas, Sarah, Dau.
Thomas, Ruth, Dau.
Thomas, Elizabeth, Dau.
Thomas, Susannah, Dau.
Thomas, Matilda, Dau.
Harrison, George, Wit.
Chew, John, Wit.
Osburn, Abner, Wit.

Leith, James, F:186, 1800
Powell, Betty, Dau.
Leith, James, Son
Leith, Mary, Wife
Leith, William, Son
Powell, Ann, Dau.
Leith, Wheatman, Son
Lacy, Elias, Wit.
Guy, Samuel, Wit.
Boggess, Samuel, Wit.
Triplett, Simon, Wit.

Tomlinson, William, F:190, 1800
Vernon, John, Exor.
Tomlinson, Sarah, Dau.
Tomlinson, Mary, Dau.
Taylor, Bernard, Exor.
Tomlinson, Elizabeth, Dau.
Tomlinson, William, Son
Tomlinson, Thomas, Son
Tomlinson, Mary, Wife
Hook, Isaac, Wit.
Mudd, John, Wit.
Combs, Mahlon, Wit.

Jones, Ann, F:191, 1800
Janney, Mahlon, Friend
Moore, James, Friend
Larrick, Margaret, Niece
Williams, Abner, Exor.
Barrow, Thomas, Gr-nephew, son of William
Williams, Eleazer, Brother
Barrow, Margaret, Gr-niece, dau. of William
Barrow, Elizabeth, Gr-niece, dau. of John
Speaker, Ann, Niece
Barrow, Thomas, Gr-nephew, son of John
Barrow, John, Nephew
Barrow, William, Nephew
Williams, J., Wit.
Steer, Isaac, Wit.

Bayly, Pierce, F:194, 1799/1800
Bayly, Mary, Wife
Bayly, Susannah, Dau.
Bayly, Pierce, Son

Index to Loudoun County Wills, 1757 - 1850   51

Bayly, Albert, Son
Bayly, John, Son
Bayly, George, Son
Bayly, Robert, Son, <21
Bayly, Samuel, Son, <21
Bayly, William Pierce, Son
Bayly, Mountjoy, Son, <21
Bayly, Polly, Dau.
Bayly, Leah, Dau.
Drake, Anna, Dau.
Lacey, Alexander, Gr-Son,
  son of Israel
Lacey, Meriah, Gr-Dau.,
  dau. of Israel
Lacey, Mitilda, Gr-Dau.,
  dau. of Israel
Shaftoe, James, F:197, 1792/1800
Ellzey, William Jr., Friend
Harrison, Matthew Jr., Wit.
Tyler, John, Wit.
Idon, Samuel, F:199, 1797/1800
Hoge, Mary, Dau.
Hoge, Ann, Gr-Dau.,
  child of Mary
Hoge, Samuel, Gr-Son,
  child of Mary
Idon, Catheron, Wife
Idon, Samuel, Son, Exor.
Idon, John, Son
Jolly, Hanna, Dau.
Idon, Jacob, Son
Milburn, Elizabeth, Dau.
Hoge, Abner, Gr-Son,
  child of Mary
Claypole, Sabilla, Dau.
Bishop, Cathrun, Dau.
Taylor, Benjamin, Wit.
Craven, Giles, Wit.
Dillon, James, Wit.
Chinn, Richard, F:200, 1800
Shearman, Susan, Sister
Upp, Sarah, Sister
Murray, Catharine, Sister
Chinn, Thomas, Brother
Chinn, Judy, Sister
Chinn, Robert, Brother
Chinn, Hugh, Brother
Powell, Burr, Exor.

Lacey, Elias, Wit.
McVeigh, Jesse, Wit.
Lewis, John H., Wit.
Scott, Elizabeth, F:207, 1797/1800
Scott, Stephen, Son
Scott, Hannah, Dau.
Scott, Merab, Dau.
Roberts, Rebecca, Dau.
Roberts, John, Son-in-law, of
  Frederick Co., Md.
Wilson, Martha, Dau.
Williams, John, Wit.
Williams, Abner, Wit.
Dnisor, John, Wit.
Thomas, Griffith, F:209, 1800
Thomas, Phineas, Brother
Thomas, Evan, Brother
Thomas, Joseph, Son
Thomas, Phineas, Youngest
  Son
Thomas, Jacob, Brother
Thomas, Elizabeth, Wife
Carr, Joseph Jr., Wit.
Wynn, Robert, Wit.
Winder, William, Wit.
Lacey, Joseph, F:220, 1800/1801
Beard, Orpah, Dau.
Lacey, Tacey, Dau.
Lacey, Euphama, Dau.
Lacey, Matilda, Wife
Lacey, Elias, Son
Lacey, Israel, Son
Lacey, Mesheck, Son
Lacey, Niomy, Dau.
Lacey, Ruth, Dau.
Lacey, Huldah, Dau.
Tyler, John, Wit.
Wildman, Jair, Wit.
Greenlees, James, Wit.
Nixon, George, F:221, 1797/1801
Nixon, Rebekah, Dau.
White, Sarah, Dau.
Tavender, Patty, Dau.
Tavender, George, Son-in-law
Nixon, Hannah, Dau.
White, Joseph, Son-in-law
White, Elizabeth, Dau.
Nixon, John, Son, <21
Myers, Ann, Dau.
Harris, Peggy, Dau.

Nixon, Ruth, Gr-Dau.,
  dau. of Jonah, <21
Nixon, Joanner, Gr-Dau.,
  dau. of Jonah, <21
Nixon, Nancy, Gr-Dau.,
  dau. of Jonah, <21
Nixon, Jonah, Gr-Son,
  son of Jonah, <21
Nixon, George, Gr-Son,
  son of Jonah, <21
Nixon, Jonah, Son, dec'd.
Nixon, George, Son
Nixon, Mary, Wife
Fouch, Thomas, Wit.
Caruthis, James, Wit.
Hall, William, Wit.
White, Daniel, Wit.

Ball, Burgess, F:226, 1800
Ball, Frances, Wife, niece of
  George Washington
Ball, Mildred Thornton, Dau.
Ball, George Washington, Son
Ball, Fayette, Son
Ball, Charles Burgess, Son
Ball, Martha Dandrige, Dau.
Lee, Thomas Ludwell, Exor.
Washington, Mildred,
  Mother-in-law
Ball, Frances Washington, Dau.
Long, Elizabeth, Dau.
Washington, Dorothia,
  Sister-in-law
Sim, Dr. Thomas L., Friend
Payne, Jane, Mother-in-law
Washington, Bushrod, Exor.
Hammond, Thomas, Exor.
Hammond, Mildred Gregory,
  Sister-in-law
Sim, Catharine L., Wit.

Carter, Peter, F:228, 1794/1801
Carter, Hannah, Wife
Whaley, James, Son-in-law
Whaley, Lettice, Dau.
Moss, Thomas, Son-in-law
Carter, Molly, Dau.
Moss, Milia, Dau.
Carter, Elam, Son
Carter, Ephriam, Son
Carter, Morris Veale, Son
Carter, Edward, Son

Carter, John, Son
Carter, Fanny, Dau., born after
  will made
Carter, Ann, Youngest Dau.
Carter, Elizabeth, Dau.
Carter, James, Son
Carter, Elihu, Son
Parrott, John, Wit.
Jennings, James, Wit.
Shadburn, Amos, Wit.
Jennings, Charles, Wit.

Myers, William, F:230, 1801
Myers, —, other children
Myers, Sally, Dau.
Myers, Jonathan, Son
Myers, Lambert, Son
Myers, Sarah, Wife
Moore, James, Wit.
Braden, Joseph, Wit.
Fox, William, Wit.
Wright, Samuel, Wit.
Harris, Asa, Wit.

Updike, John, F:231, 1791/1801
More, James, Exor.
Updike, Samuel, Eldest Son
Updike, Amon, Son
Updike, Rufus, Son
Updike, Daniel, Son
Updike, Jane, Dau.
Updike, Sarah, Dau.
Updike, Phebe, Dau.
Updike, Elizabeth, Eldest Dau.
Gore, Joshua, Exor.
Updike, John, Son
McClain, James, Wit.
Craven, James Jr., Wit.
Short, Robert, Wit.

Neece, Devault, F:244, 1800/1801
Baker, Dorothy, Dau.
Neece, Gertrout, Wife
Fawley, Barbara, Dau.
Fawley, Jacob, Son-in-law
Smith, Frederick, Wit.
Tushtimer, Jacob, Wit.
Gleasor, Jacob, [GS] Wit.

Overfield, Peter, F:246, 1797/1801
Divers, Margaret, Gr-Dau., <16
Divers, Mary, Gr-Dau., <16
Divers, John, Son-in-law
Divers, Catherine, Dau.

Bronaugh, William Jr., Wit.
Gill, Cornalas, Wit.
Burson, Joseph, Wit.
Lovett, Joseph, Exor.
Marshall, Thomas, F:254, 1801
Starks, Elizabeth <16, Gr-Dau.
Kean, Molly, Dau.
Marshall, John, Son
Marshall, William, Son
Marshall, Frances, Dau.
Marshall, Jacob, Brother
Jones, Thomas T., Wit.
Stonestreet, Basil, Wit.
Grymes, John, Wit.
Howell, Samuel, F:268, 1801
Humphrey, Abner, Exor.
Howell, Rebecah, Dau.
Howell, Mary, Wife
Carr, Joseph, Wit.
Bird, Derrick, Wit.
Howell, Mahlon, Wit.
Goodin, Amos, F:270, 1798/1801
Goodin, David, Son
Goodin, Samuel, Son
Goodin, Martha, Dau.
Goodin, Rebekah, Dau.
Goodin, Sarah, Dau.
Goodin, Jean, Dau.
Goodin, Mary, Dau.
Goodin, John, Son
Love, James Jr., Wit.
Hughes, Thomas, Wit.
Stevens, Ezekiah, F:271, 1801
Stevens, James, Father, dec'd.
Stevens, Ann, Wife
Stevens, Rebecky, Dau.
Stevens, Fanny, Dau.
Stevens, Margaritt, Dau.
Stevens, Joseph, Son, <21
Stevens, Henry, Wit.
Stevens, James, Wit.
Humphrey, Jane, Wit.
Note: Stephens is used throughout
Potts, Samuel, F:277, 1800/1801
Potts, Elizabeth, Wife
Potts, Nathan, Wit.
Smith, William, Wit.
Potts, Jane, Wit.

Millholland, Patrick, F:278, 1800/1801
Millholland, Thomas, Son
Millholland, Jonathan, Son
Millholland, Hetty, Dau.
Millholland, Mary, Wife
Millholland, John, Son
Millholland, Patrick, Son
Grant, Mary, Dau.
Brewer, Nancy, Dau.
Millholland, Esther, Dau.
Jones, Sarah, Dau.
Hough, William, Wit.
Moore, Asa, Wit.
Griffith, Richard, Wit.
Williams, J., Wit.
Schooley, Reuben, Wit. [c]
Watts, Thomas, Wit. [c]
Taylor, Joseph, F:281, 1801
Sutherland, Nancy, Sister
Sutherland, Thomas Jr., Nephew, son of Alexander & Nancy
Stouseberger, John, Wit.
Prince, Levy, Wit.
Steer, Ann, F:282, 1801
Steer, Benjamin, Son
Gregg, Hannah, Dau.
Whitacre, Ann, Dau.
Purdom, Benjamin, Wit.
Siddall, Isaac, Wit.
Steer, John, F:289, 1801
Steer, Thomas, Son
Steer, Joseph, Son
Steer, Hannah, Dau.
Steer, Isaac, Son
Steer, Mary, Wife
Roach, Edmund, Wit.
Ball, William, Wit.
Williams, Enos, Wit.
Brown, Henry, F:300, 1796/1802
Brown, John, Son
Brown, Esther, Wife
Brown, Henry, Son
Brown, William, Son
Sands, Esther, Dau.
Brown, Hannah, Dau.
Roach, Edmund, Wit.
Ball, William, Wit.
Williams, Enos, Wit.

**Matthew, Simon, F:314,
1793/1801**
Matthew, William, Youngest Son
Matthew, Jonathan, Son
Matthew, Rachel, Dau.
Matthew, Martha, Dau.
Matthew, Hannah, Dau.
Matthew, Ley, Son
Matthew, Jesse, Son
Matthew, John, Eldest Son
Potts, Ezekiel, Wit.
Potts, Nathan, Wit.
Beans, Timothy, F:316, 1797/1801
Done (Dunn), Mary, Dau.
Beans, Rebecca, Wife
Cooper, Sarah, Dau.
Beans, William, Son
Beans, James, Son
Beans, Amos, Son
Beans, Matthew, Son
Beans, Jacob, Son
McIlhaney, James, Wit.
Tribbey, Thomas, Wit.
Alder, George, Wit.
Allder, James, Wit.
Binns, Charles, F:317, 1800/1801
Durham, Catherine A., Dau.,
  w/o Lee Durham
Harding, Ann Alexander, Dau.,
  w/o William H. Harding
Binns, John Alexander, Son
Waugh, Susannah Pearson,
  Dau., w/o Alexander
Binns, Thomas Neilson, Son
Adams, Elizabeth Alexander
Lawer, Gr-Dau., dau. of my
  dau. Elizabeth Alexander,
  w/o Wesley Adams
Binns, Anne, Wife
Binns, William Alexander, Son
Binns, Simon Alexander, Son
Binns, Charles, Son
Blincoe, Sampson, Wit.
Shreve, Benjamin, Wit.
Taylor, William R., Wit.
Boyd, Samuel, F:415, 1802
Boyd, Elizabeth, Wife
Johnson, George, Wit.

Ferguson, James, Wit.
Lovett, Joseph, Wit.
Martin, John, Wit.
**Boggess, Vincent, F:424,
1791/1802**
Boggess, other children
Boggess, Hanly, Son
Boggess, Samuel, Son
Boggess, —, Wife
Taylor, William R., Wit.
Rust, George, Wit.
Singleton, Joshua Jr., Wit.
Elgin, William, F:438, 1801/02
Elgin, Sarah, Dau., <16
Elgin, Frederick, Brother
Turley, John, Wit.
Edelen, Robert, Wit.
Elgin, Francis, Wit.
Cravan, James, F:441, 1802
Shorts, Alice, Dau.
Brown, Hannah, Dau.
Bolon, Elizabeth, Dau.
Vansickle, Philip, Exor.
McCrony, Sarah, Dau.
Vansickle, Esther, Dau.
Cravan, John, Son
Gore, Joshua, Exor.
Neifus, Margaret, Dau.
Nixon, Ann, Dau.
Cravan, Giles, Son
Cravan, James, Son
Beale, David, Wit.
Hughs, Constantine, Wit.
Taylor, Bernard, Wit.
Palmer, Jonathan, F:443, 1802
Orendorf, Martha, Dau.
Nichols, James, Exor.
Palmer, Jonathan, Gr-Son
Payne, Catharina, Dau.
Palmer, John, Son
Pain, Jonathan, Gr-Son
Palmer, Cornelius, Son
Bonhem, Jonathan, Gr-Son
Bonam, Sarah, Dau.
Williams, Jude(y), Dau.
Brown, George, Wit.
Nickols, George, Wit.
Nickols, Nathan, Wit.

**Summers, Francis, F:448,
1793/1802**
Winlock, Effy, Gr-Dau.,
w/o Joseph
Night, Mary, Dau., w/o Dr. John
Stevenson, Betsy, Gr-Dau.
Summers, George, Son
Lane, Sarah, Dau.,
w/o Presley Carr
Beall, Elizabeth, Dau.
Coleman, Sarah, Gr-Dau.,
w/o Thomas
Debell, Wm., Wit.
Cockerill, Benja., Wit.
Littleton, Thomas, Wit.
Littleton, Solomon, Wit.
Shively, Jacob, Wit.
Lane, William, Wit.
Towner, John, F:449, 1802
Towner, Benjamin, Son, <21
Towner, Fanny, Wife
Littlejohn, John, Wit.
Harris, Isaac, Wit.
Hamilton, Jas., Wit.
Lewis, Abraham, F:456, 1802
Lewis, Rebekah, Wife
Butcher, John, Exor.
Guy, Mary, Dau.
Lewis, Isaac, Son
Butcher, Susan, Dau.
Beck, Martha, Dau.
Guy, Nancy, Dau.
Lewis, Abraham, Son
Lewis, Joseph, Son
Lewis, James, Son
Lewis, Jacob, Son
McKinny, George, Wit.
Harper, Thomas, Wit.
Harper, John, Wit.
**Roler, John Andrew David, F:457,
1802**
Snyder, Elizabeth, Dau., dec'd.
Stetz, Margaret, Dau.
Smitley, Mathias, Exor.
Roler, Conrod, Son
Preeht, Magdalen, Dau.
Roler, John, Son
Able, Catharine, Dau.
Burnhouse, Rosina, Dau.

Burnhouse, Christian,
Son-in-law
Smith, Frederick, Wit.
Wine, Christian, Wit.
Steere, John, Wit.
Long, Jacob, Wit.
Gunn, John, F:459, 1801/1802
Gunn, Jane, Wife
Gunn, James, Son
Patterson, Joseph, Wife's
Gr-Son
Hinksman, Jane, Wife's Gr-Dau.
Sinclair, John, Wit.
Sealock, Thomas, Wit.
McCarty, William R., Wit.
Simpson, John, F:461, 1796/1802
Simpson, Mary, Wife
Simpson, William, Son
Simpson, —, all my children
Feild [sic], William, Wit.
Beveridge, John, Wit.
**Warford, Abraham, F:470,
1796/1802**
Warford, Catharine, Dau.
Warford, Sarah, Dau.
Warford, William, Son
Warford, Hannah, Wife
Hutchison, Joseph, Exor.
Warford, Theodocia, Dau.
Crooks, James, Exor.
Ellgin, Frederick, Wit.
Ellgin, William, Wit.
Crooks, Mary, Wit.
Ralls, George, F:474, 1780/99
Tebbs, Captain Willoughby,
Exor.
Ralls, John Damey, Son, <20
Ralls, Jenny, Wife
Scott, William, Wit.
Elliott, Peter, Wit.
Ralls, Charles, Wit.
Calvert, George, Admr. w.w.a.
Osborne, Abner, G:1, 1796/1802
Heaton, James, Son-in-law
Osborne, Nicholas, Son, <21
Osborne, Mary, Dau., <18
Heaton, Lydia, Dau.
Osborne, Patience, Wife
Osborne, Abner, Son, <21
Osborne, William, Exor.

Taylor, Stacy, Exor.
Lindsey, James, Wit.
Dillon, Daniel, Wit.
Pursell, Samuel, Wit.
Carr, William, Wit.
Taylor, John, G:6, 1802/03
Taylor, Henry, Son
Taylor, Matthew, Son
Taylor, Elizabeth, Dau.
Taylor, Margaret, Dau.
Taylor, John, Son
Taylor, Susannah, Dau.
Taylor, Nicholas, Son
Taylor, Walter, Son
Taylor, Molly, Wife
Cotton, William Jr., Wit.
Wycoff, Cornelius, Wit.
Swart, Simon, Wit.
Reece, Lewis, G:11, 1802/03
Reece, David, Son
Reece, Esther, Wife
Reece, Polly, Dau.
Beans, Matthew, Wit.
Nicklin, John, Wit.
Beans, Aaron, Wit.
Nickols, Isaac, G:27, 1800/02/03
Pancoast, John, Son-in-law
Hatcher, Rebekah, Dau.
Pancoast, Ann, Gr-Dau.
Hatcher, Catherine, Dau.
Pancoast, Ruth, Dau., dec'd.
Hoge, Mary, Dau., w/o Solomon
Pancoast, Lydia, Gr-Dau.
Nickols, Sarah, Dau.-in-law, widow of William
Pancoast, John, Gr-Son
Nickols, William, Gr-Son, youngest son of William
Pancoast, Joshua, Gr-Son
Nickols, Samuel, Gr-Son, son of William
Nickols, Isaac, Gr-Son, son of William
Nickols, Isaac, Son
Nickols, Samuel, Son
Nickols, Lydia, deranged Dau.
Nickols, William, Eldest Son, dec'd. by 13 Dec 1802
Nickols, Margery, Wife
Hatcher, Isaac, Wit.

Wyer, Uriah, Wit.
McCulloh, Mary, Wit.
Hatcher, Edith, Wit.
Spencer, Nathan, Wit. [c]
Nichols, Isaac, Wit. [c]
McCulloh, Robert, Wit. [c]
Ewers, Jonathan, G:51, 1803
Gerrard, Susannah, Dau.
Jury, Mary, Dau.
Ewers, Thomas, Son
Moore, Nancy, Dau.
Ewers, Helen, Gr-Dau.
Moore, Hannah, Dau.
Ewers, Hannah, Dau.-in-law, w/o Thomas
Ewers, Jonathan, Son
Ewers, Barton, Son
Powell, William, Wit.
Gregg, Joseph, Wit.
Hope, Christian, Wit.
Mason, Stephens Thomas, G:58, 1803
Ellzey, Fanny, w/o Col. William Mason
Mason, —, Daus.
Mason, Stephens Thomson Jr., Son
Mason, John Thomson Jr., Son
Mason, Armstead Thomson, Son
Mason, John Thomson, Brother
Mason, Mary, Wife
Hurst, Ann, w/o Thomas
Settle, Reuben, G:65, 1803
Settle, Henry, Son
Harmon, Susanna, Dau.
Settle, Susannah, Wife
Settle, Daniel, Son
Settle, Mary, Dau.
Settle, Dorcas, Dau.
Settle, Newman, Son
Settle, Elizabeth, Dau.
Settle, Reuben, Son
Cunningham, Ann, Dau
Debell, John, Exor.
Lewis, Charles, Exor.
Buckner, Ariss, Wit.
Sim, Thomas, Wit.
Oden, Hezekiah, Wit.
James, Abel, Wit.
James, Moses, Wit.

Davis, Benjamin, G:68, 1799/1803
Davis, Ann, Dau.
Orison, Martha, Gr-Dau.
Davis, Abel, Son
Davis, Sarah, Dau.
Davis, Rachel, Dau.
Davis, Elizabeth, Dau.
Davis, Howell, Son
Davis, Hannah, Wife
White, Joseph, Wit.
Licky, Conrod, Wit.
White, Daniel, Wit.

Pool, Elizabeth, G:86, 1801/03
Bennett, Charles, Exor.
Williams, Enos, Exor.
Williams, Hannah, Niece
Sands, Jacob, Wit.
Brown, William, Wit.

Vandevanter, Isaac, G:89, 1803
Henry, Matilda, Gr-Dau., <18
Vandevanter, Mary, Dau., <21
Vandevanter, Sarah, Dau., <21
Vandevanter, Cornelius, Son, <21
Vandevanter, John, Son
Vandevanter, Joseph, Son
Vandevanter, Isaac, Son
Hamilton, John, Exor.
Braden, Robert, Exor.
Daniel, Joshua, Wit.
Daniel, Joseph, Wit.
Hospital, Andrew, Wit.

Clapham, Josias, G:92, 1803
Sanders, Aaron, Exor.
Clapham, Samuel, Nephew, son of Joseph
Price, Sarah, Dau.
Price, Benjamin, Son-in-law
Clapham, Joseph, Brother
Clapham, Rebeckah, Dau.
Clapham, Samuel, Son
Clapham, —, Wife
Dulin, William, Wit.
Chilton, Thomas, Wit.
Steere, Isaac, Wit.

Moul, George, G:96, 1803
Moul, —, Wife
Moul, Daniel, Son
Moul, Susannah, Dau.
Moul, Catharine, Dau.
Moul, Peggy, Dau.
Moul, Philip, Son
Moul, Mary, Dau.
Larrowe, Isaac, Exor.
Sanders, Aaron, Wit.
Sanders, Presley, Wit.
Sanders, Moses, Wit.

DeGras, Joseph C., G:99, 1803
Tutt, Charles, merchant
Spoont, —, widow
Williams, Richard

Conrad, John, G:100, 1803
Conrad, Joseph, Son
Conrad, Elizabeth, Dau.
Conrad, —, Wife
Conrad, Anthony, Son
Conrad, John, Son
Conrad, Ann, Dau.
Conrad, Sarah, Dau.
Conrad, Nathan, Son
Conrad, Samuel, Son
Conrad, Jonathan, Son
Towberman, Peter, Wit.
Osborne, Anthony, Wit.
Gray, Samuel, Wit.

Evans, William, G:102, 1803
Swarts, Mary, Dau.
Lacey, Israel, Exor.
Roberts, Henry, Exor.
Roberts, Charles, Exor.
Evans, Martha, Dau.
Evans, Ann, Dau.
Evans, Martha, Wife
Evans, Catharine, Dau.
Evans, William, Son
Evans, Henry, Son
Evans, John, Son
Beveridge, John, Wit.
Gheen, James, Wit.
Cochrane, Richard, Wit.
Riticor, Elijah, Wit.

Hiler, Henry, G:117, 1803
Hiler, Sarah, Wife
Hiler, Sally, Dau.
Hiler, Peggy, Dau.
Streets, Margaret, Dau.
Oden, Thomas, Wit.
Heath, Isaac, Wit.
Janny, Abel, Wit.

Dawson, Mathias, G:118, 1803
Dawson, Charles, Son
Dawson, Ann, Wife
Hawley, Absolom, Wit.
Carter, Hannah, Wit.
Poston, Leonard, G:118, 1802/03
Frye (Foye), Elizabeth,
 Niece, <18
Frye (Foye), Lewis,
 Nephew, <21
Frye (Foye), John, Nephew, <21
Poston, Elizabeth, Dau.
Poston, Joseph, Son
Poston, Wilsey, Son
Frye (Foye), Terence
Poston, James, Son
Clapham, J., Wit.
Shover, Adam, Wit.
Sanbower, John, Wit.
German Script Name, Wit.
Evans, William, farmer, G:124, 1775/1803
Davis, Nathan, Wife's Brother
Evans, Mary, Wife
Evans, John, Son, <21
Hanne (Hannah), Thomas wife's son, Step-son
Hanne (Hannah), John
Davis, John, Exor.
Harper, Nicholas, Exor.
Steel, John, Wit., resident of Ky. by Feb 1802
Jenkin, Samuel, Wit.
Hanna, John, Wit., resident of Tenn. by Feb 1802
Wildman, Jacob, G:135, 1795/1804
Wildman, Grace, Dau., [married but no name given]
Wildman, James, Son
Wildman, John, Son
Wildman, Joseph, Son
Wildman, Mary, Dau. [married but no name given]
Wildman, Elizabeth, Dau.
Wildman, Marcy, Dau.
Wildman, Sarah, Dau.
Wildman, Elizabeth, Wife
Wildman, Rachel, Dau.

Ellgin, Gustavus, Wit.
Ellgin, Francis, Wit.
Fouch, Thomas, Wit.
Cochran, Andrew, G:137, 1803/04
Fort, Andrew, son of Polly
Fort, Polly's children
Cochran, William's children
Cochran, James' children
Cochran, Richard
Beveridge, Noble, Wit.
Lacy, Mesheck, Wit.
Souder, Anthony, G:137, 1803/04
Crumrine, Philip, Gr-Son
Crumrine, Catherine, Gr-Dau.
Crumrine, Michael, Gr-Son
Statzer (Slater), John, Son-in-law
Souder, Jacob, Son
Statzer (Slater), Catherine, Dau.
Souder, Michael, Son
Souder, Susana, Gr-Dau.
Souder, Philip, Son
Souder, Margaret, Wife
Smith, Frederick, Wit.
Compher, John, Wit.
Stoneburner, John, Wit.
Armistead, Mary, G:144, 1803/04
Mason, Mary, Dau.
Lacey, Elizabeth, Dau.
Armistead, Robert, Son
Long, Armistead, Wit.
English, David, Wit.
Losh, Daniel, G:149, 1800/04
Speckt, Peggy, Gr-Dau.
Speckt, Rosanna C., Gr-Dau.
Losh, Elizabeth, Wife
Losh, Sebastian, Son
Headman, Mary, Dau.
Calihan, Catharine, wife's Dau., formerly Catharine Coutsman, w/o Dr. Jacob Coutsman, afterwards, w/o Andrew Speckt
Hough, Rosannah, wife's dau., Step-Dau.
Binns, Charles Jr., Exor.
Mains, William, Exor.
Spoond, Joseph, Wit.
Binns, John, Wit.
Binns, Simon A., Wit.

Sullivan, Murtho, Wit.
Moffett, Josiah, Wit.
Thrift, William, Wit.
Moffett, Charles, Wit.
Gregg, Samuel, G:159, 1803/04
  Nicols, Elizabeth, Dau.,
    w/o Vallentine
  Gregg, Aaron, Son
  Gregg, Nancy, Dau.,
    w/o Richard Gregg
  Gregg, Israel's children, Son
  Gregg, Rebeckah, Dau.,
    w/o William Gregg
  Gregg, John, Son, dec'd.
  Gregg, Persillah, Dau.,
    w/o Amos Gregg
  Gregg, Thomas, Son
  Gregg, Easther, Wife
  Tobin, James, Wife's former
    husband
  McIlhaney, James, Exor.
  Roach, James, Wit.
  Williams, Uriah, Wit.
  Roach, Richard, Wit.
  Roach, George, Wit.
  Roach, John, Wit.
Ashford, Michael, G:177, 1804
  Lewis, Captain Charles, Exor.
  Moxley, Sary, Dau.
  Rightmire, Anna, Dau.
  Ashford, Jane, Gr-child,
    dau. of William
  Ashford, Anna, Gr-child,
    dau. of William
  Ashford, Michael, Gr-child,
    son of William
  Ashford, John, Son
  Ashford, Jane, Dau.
  Ashford, Dilla, Dau.
  Ashford, Rebeckah, Dau.
  Ashford, Elizabeth, Dau.
  Ashford, William, Son
  Shivelley, George, Wit.
  Horseman, Esaias, Wit.
  Fox, Elisha, Wit.
  Wooleard, William, Wit.
  McAtee, Colmore, Wit.
  Settle, Henry, Exor.
  Moxley, John, Exor.

Fred, Joseph, G:195, 1804
  Fred, Rebeckah, Dau.
  Fred, Joshua, Son
  Fred, Thomas, Son
  Cogel, Joseph, Gr-Son
  Gibson, Rachel, Dau.
  Cogel, Amey, Gr-Dau.
  Fred, Joseph, Son
  Hall, William, Wit.
  French, George, Wit.
Blare, John, G:235, 1794/1804
  Blare, James, Brother
  Blare, Charles, Nephew,
    son of James
  Blare, Jean, Wife
  McBride, James, Wit.
  Grubb, William, Wit.
  Mathew, John, Wit.
  White, Robert, Wit.
Dow, Peter, G:237, 1802/04
  Peacock, Mary, reputed
    natural Dau.
  Dow, Janet, Wife
  Dow, Alexander, Son
  Dow, Anna, Dau.
Thatcher, Richard, G:245, 1804
  Thatcher, Mary, Wife
  Thatcher, William, Son
  Thatcher, Jonah, Son
  Thatcher, Calvin, Son
  Thatcher, Nancy, Dau.
  Thatcher, Albine, Dau.
  Taylor, Stacy, Exor.
  Brown, George, Wit.
  Palmer, William E., Wit.
  Chamblin, John, Wit.
Pegg, Nathaniel, G:247, 1801/04
  Pegg, Catherine, Wife
  Polin (Poland), Nathaniel,
    Nephew
  Polin (Poland), William, Nephew
  Pegg, Elias, Brother
  Pegg, Samuel, Brother
  Pegg, William, Brother
  Pegg, Daniel, Brother
  Pegg, Joseph, Brother
  Pegg, Isaac, Brother

Lacey, Israel, Wit.
Cooke, William, Wit.
Beveridge, Thomas, Wit.
Carr, Joseph Jr., G:249, 1804
  Campbell, Jane, Sister
  Carr, Mary, Mother
  Carr, Elizabeth, Sister
  Carr, Margaret, Sister
  Carr, Samuel, Brother
  Carr, James, Brother
  Carr, Mary, Sister
  Carr, Thomas, Brother
  Carr, John, Brother
  Woodford, William Jr., Wit.
  Moore, Peter, Wit.
Hughes, Theophilus, G:250, 1802/04
  Settle, Ishmael
  Hughes (Huse), Ann, Dau.
  Hughes (Huse), Theophilus, Son
  Hughes (Huse), Lezy, Wife
  Huffman, John, Wit.
  Holding, John leaving the state May 1804, Wit.
  Settle, Ishmael, Wit.
  James, Benjamin, Exor.
  Settle, Reuben Sr., Exor.
Durham, Lee, G:253, 1804
  Durham, Catherine Alexander, Wife
  Durham, Nancy, Dau.
  Durham, Lee, Son
  Binns, C., Wit.
  Sim, Thomas L., Wit.
Bartlett, William, G:261, 1804
  Bartlett, Samuel, Son
  Bartlett, Thomas, Son
  Bartlett, John, Son
  Bartlett, William, Son
  Bartlett, Gardner, Son
  Bartlett, Mary, Wife
  Bartlett, Daniel, Son
  Bartlett, Alley Theary Althea
  Hieronimus, Betsey, Dau.
  Bartlett, Stacey, Son
  Gore, John's wife, Dau.
  Fowke, William, Wit.
  Squires, Asa, Wit.
  Jones, Ignatious, Wit.

Steers, Joseph, G:261, 1804
  Steers, Isaac, Brother
  Steers, Hannah, Sister
  Steers, Thomas, Brother
  Steers, Isaac Jr., Wit.
  Steers, Mary, Wit.
Cockrell, Joseph M., G:264, 1804
  Cockrell, Francis M.
  Cockrell, —, Wife
  Cockrell, rest of my children
  Cockrell, Thebea M., Dau.
  Eskeridge, William, Wit.
  Hummer, Michael, Wit.
  Harper, Walter, Wit.
Juray, Abner, G:265, 1804
  Juray, Mary otherwise Ewers, Wife
  Juray, Rachel, Dau.
  Juray, Rees, Son
  Juray, Jesse, Son
  Juray, George, Son
  Juray, Lewis, Son
  Ewers, Rachel, Dau.
  Juray, Abner, Son
  Ewers, Barton, Son-in-law
  Innes, Alexander, Wit.
  Rhodes, John, Wit.
Whelan, Timothy, G:266, 1804
  Whelan, James, Brother
  Whelan, Margaret, Sister
  Whelan, Judith, Sister
  Whelan, Winnifred, Sister
  Whelan, Catherine, Sister
  Dulany, Morris, Exor.
  Cuddy, Michael, Exor.
  Hamilton, James, Wit.
  Figh, Terrence, Wit.
  Ritchie, Isaac, Wit.
  Kern, Jacob, Wit.
Butcher, John, G:269, 1804
  Butcher, Samuel, Brother
  Butcher, Susannah, Wife
  Butcher, John, Nephew, Samuel's son
  Overfield, Mary, Sister
  Hickman, Joseph, son of John
  Hickman, Jane, Sister
  Pierce, Eales, Sister
  Phillips, Hannah, Sister
  Lewis, Susannah, dau. of Isaac

Index to Loudoun County Wills, 1757 - 1850   61

Grady, Edward
Grady, Susannah, Sister
Lewis, Jacob, Wife's Brother
Humphrey, Abner, Exor.
Newlon, James, Wit.
Lewis, James, Wit.
McMorris, Sarah, Wit.
Paxon, James, G:273, 1803/04
Paxon, Sarah, Wife
Paxon, Joseph, Son
Paxon, Elizabeth, Dau.
Paxon, James, Son
Paxon, William, Son
Siddle, Sarah, Dau.
Paxon, Amos, Son
Siddle, William, Son-in-law
Moore, James, Wit.
Moore, Asa, Wit.
Phillips, Thomas, Wit.
Derflinger, Henry, G:274, 1804
Evans, Elizabeth, w/o Isaac, Eldest Dau.
Derflinger, Frederick, Son
Derflinger, Eve, Dau.
Derflinger, Mary, Dau.
Derflinger, Catherine, Dau.
Derflinger, Daniel, Son
Derflinger, Thomas, Son
Jacob, Peter, Wit.
Miller, George, Wit.
Smallwood, Bayn, Wit.
Ross, John, G:284, 1804
Ross, Nancy, Dau.
Ross, Armstrong, Son
Ross, Mary, Wife
Ross, Sarah, Dau.
Ross, Mary, Dau.
Ross, William, Son
Ross, David, Son
Ross, Jane, Dau.
Ross, Joshua, Son
Ross, Joseph, Son
Ross, Rebeckah, Dau.
Ross, John, Son
Ross, Elizabeth, Dau.
Moffett, Josiah, Wit.
Thrift, William, Wit.
Hetherley, Thomas, Wit.

Smith, Joseph, G:292, 1804
Smith, —, my children
Potts, Jonas, Wit.
Merrick, Patrick, Wit.
Craven, Abner, Wit.
Mcgaha, Benjamin, Wit.
Baugh, Jacob, Exor.
Dillon, James, G:293, 1804/05
Stalcup, Rebecca, Dau.
Dillon, Moses, Son
Love, Susanna, Dau.
Dillon, Mary, Dau.
Dillon, Abdon, Son
Dillon, Mary, Wife
Taylor, Stacy, Wit.
Pursel, Samuel, Wit.
Pancoast, John, Wit.
Thompson, Rev. Amos, G:296, 1776/1805
Thompson, Jane, Wife
Clapman, Josias, Exor.
Poling, Samuel, Exor.
Reider, Joseph, Wit.
Fox, Gabriel, Wit.
Lewis, Samuel, Wit.
Lee, George, of Farmwell, G:301, 1802/05
Lee, Thomas L., Brother, of Coton
Lee, Evelyn Byrd, Wife
Lee, William A., Brother, dec'd.
Lee, Maria Carter, Dau., <16
Lee, George, Son, < 7
Jenkins, Henry, G:304, u.d./1805
Jenkins, Henry Hamilton, Son
Jenkins, Elizabeth, Admr.
Smith, James, Wit.
Lafaver, Henry Sr., Wit.
Lafaver, Henry Jr., Wit.
Moffet, Mary, G:305, 1802/05
Stadley, Elizabeth, Dau.
McFarlin, James
McFarlin, Nancy, Dau.
McFarlin, Polly, Dau.
Cockerill, Thomas, Wit.
Lewis, Charles, Wit.
Oden, Thomas, Wit.

Thompson, Amos, G:316, 1787/05
  Meade, Sarah, Sister
  Payne, Mary, Sister
  King, Rebecca, Sister
  Thompson, Jane, Wife
  Thompson, Mary, Niece,
    dau. of Asa
  Thompson, Sarah, Niece,
    dau. of Asa
  Thompson, Rebecca, Niece,
    dau. of Asa
  Thompson, Amos, Nephew,
    son of Asa
  Thompson, Asa, Nephew,
    son of Asa
  Thompson, Phoebe, Niece,
    dau. of Asa
  Thompson, Eunice, Niece,
    dau. of Asa
  Thompson, John, Nephew,
    son of Asa
  Thompson, Asa, Brother
  Thompson, Asa, Nephew
  Thompson, Jane, Wife
  Forbes, Samuel, Exor.
  Burrel, Jonathan, Exor.
  Adam, John, Exor.
  Clapman, Josias, Exor.
  Wells, Samuel, Wit.,
    resident of Conn.
  Wells, Noah, Wit.,
    resident of Conn.
  Wells, Sally, Wit.,
    resident of Conn.
  Lewis, Charles, Admr. w.w.a.
Smith, Jacob, G:350, 1805
  Smith, Elizabeth, Dau.
  Smith, Jacob, Son
  Smith, Susannah, Dau.
  Smith, Rachel, Dau.
  Smith, Lydia, Dau., <18
  Smith, Samuel, Son, <16
  Smith, Susannah, Wife
  Smith, Catherine, Dau.
  Smith, Mary, Dau.
  Smith, George, Son
  Smith, Sarah, Dau.
  Smitley, Matthias, Wit.
  States, Frederick, Wit.
  McPherson, Samuel, Wit.

Shumaker, Jacob, G:351, 1804/05
  Holtsman, Margeret, Dau.
  Shumaker, Simon, Son
  Shumaker, George, Son
  Smith, Susannah, Dau.
  Shumaker, Simon, Gr-Son
  Shumaker, Elizabeth, Wife
  Shults, Elizabeth, Dau.
  Beltz, Catharine, Dau.
  Hamilton, James, Wit.
  Shumaker, George, Wit.
Gregg, John, G:352, 1804/05
  Hoge, Ruth, Dau.
  Smith, Sarah, Dau.
  Cookus, Lydia, Dau.
  Gregg, Abner, Son,
    now lives on Ohio
  Gregg, Stephen, Son
  Gregg, John, Son
  Gregg, Caleb, Son
  Gregg, Joshua, Son
  Gregg, Mahlon, Son
  Gregg, John, Gr-Son,
    child of son Thomas
  Gregg, Susanna, Gr-Dau.,
    child of son Thomas
  Gregg, Betsey, Gr-Dau.,
    child of son Thomas, <18
  Gregg, Joshua, Gr-Son,
    child of son Thomas, <21
  Taylor, Bernard, Wit.
  Brown, George, Wit.
  Brown, William, Wit.
Wren, William, G:355, 1805
  Wren, Margaret, Sister
  Wren, James, Brother
  Wren, Travis, Admr. w.w.a.
  Wren, —, Father & Mother
  Wren, Jane, Sister
  Love, Augustine, Wit.
  Harris, Amos, Wit.
Rowan, George, G:369, 1805
  Rowan, —, Unborn child
  Rowan, Jane, Dau.
  Rowan, Emeley, Dau.
  Rowan, Sarah, Wife
  McCormack, John, Exor.
  Mains, Archibald, Wit.
  Littlejohn, John, Wit.

Index to Loudoun County Wills, 1757 - 1850   63

Harris, Isaac, Wit.
Mains, William, Wit.
Jones, William, G:377, 1805
  Jones, Ignatius, Brother
  Jones, Mary, Wife
  Arden, Aaron, Wit.
  Barkley, Thomas, Wit.
  Keene, George, Wit.
Queen, John, G:379, 1803/05
  Queen, Zilpha, dau. of
    Elizabeth, Gr-Dau.
  Queen, Mary, Dau.
  Queen, Martha, Dau.
  Queen, Elijah, Son
  Queen, Jonah, Son
  Queen, Elizabeth, Dau.
  Queen, John, Son
  Martin, Jane, Dau.
  Hatten, Rosanna, Dau.
  Queen, Abner
  Mead, Benjamin, Exor.
  Janney, Blackstone, Exor.
  Janney, Israel, Wit.
  Janney, David, Wit.
  Janney, Jonathan, Wit.
Fairhurst, Jeremiah, G:381, 1801/05
  Fairhurst, George, Son
  Fairhurst, John, Son
  Ellis, Ruth, w/o Evan, Dau.
  Smith, Hannah, Dau.
  Fairhurst, Eliza, Dau.
  Brown, Phebe, Dau.
  Bowlin (Bolin), Jane, Dau.
  Mead, Benjamin, Exor.
  Mead, Samuel, Wit.
  Janney, Blackstone, Wit.
  Shields, Joseph, Wit.
  Janney, Israel, Wit.
McKim, Alexander, G:382, 1800/05
  McKim, Jeannet, Wife
  McKim, John, Son
  McKim, Andrew, Son
  McKim, William, Son
  McKim, Robert, Son
  McKim, Alexander, Son
  McKim, Joseph, Son
  McKim, Samuel, Son
  McKim, Agnes, Dau.

  McKim, James, Son
  Pagit, Timothy, Wit.
  James, Jacob, Wit.
  Beatty, John, Wit.
  Dutton, James, Wit.
  Hutchison, John, Wit.
Hutchison, Joseph, G:394, 1804/05
  Hutchison, Nathan, Son
  Hutchison, Sampson, Son
  Hutchison, William, Son
  Hutchison, Elijah, Son
  Hutchison, John, Son
  Hutchison, Reuben, Son
  Helm, Elizabeth, Dau.
  Hutchison, James, Son
  Hutchison, Thomas, Son
  Bayley, John, Wit.
  Daymud (Daymeed), Jacob, Wit.
  Perry, William, Wit.
Reed, Naomi, G:399, 1805
  Marks, Kitty, dau. of Thomas, <18
  Marks, Sarah, w/o Elisha
  Dillon, Betsey, dau. of Thomas
  Marks, w/o David
  Marks, Thomas, Exor.
  Powell, William, Wit.
  Silcott, Jesse, Wit.
  Hughes, Constantine, Wit.
Marks, Elisha, G:421, 1805
  Peugh, Uree, w/o Samuel, Dau.
  Watkins, Christian, Dau., w/o Ebenezer
  Ewers, Hannah, Dau., w/o Thomas
  Marks, Milly, Dau.
  Marks, Sarah, Dau.
  Ewers, Mary, Dau., w/o Jonathan
  Marks, Anna, Dau.
  Marks, Thomas, Son, <21
  Marks, George, Son
  Marks, Mariah, Gr-Dau., dau. of Milly
  Marks, Isaiah, Son
  Marks, John, Eldest Son
  Marks, Sarah, Wife
  Grayson, Benjamin, Wit.

Boggess, Samuel, Wit.
Grayson, William, Wit.
Grayson, Robert A., Wit.
Rust, George, Wit.
Phelps, Eli, G:432, u.d./1805
  Woodard, Jamima, Sister
  Phelps, Lucy, Wife
  Phelps, Elisha, Brother, of
    Frederick Co., Va.
  Phelps, Polly, Dau., <21
  Harlan, Mary, Mother
  Lee, Robert, Step-son,
    wife's son, <21
  Lee, James, Step-son,
    wife's son
  Lee, John, Step-son,
    wife's son
  Lee, Daniel, Step-son,
    wife's son
  Gante, Daniel, Wit.
  Hill, James, Wit.
  Adam, Matthew, Wit.
  Lucas, Lindous, Wit.
Jones, Joseph, G:437, 1795/1806
  Dawson, John, Exor.
  Jones, Joseph, Son
  Tyler, Dr. James, Exor.
  Tyler, Esther, Sister, dec'd.
  Monroe, Andrew, Exor.
  Monroe, Col. James, Nephew
  Monroe, Elizabeth, Sister, dec'd.
Osborn, William, G:438, 1805/06
  Lessley, Ann, Dau.
  Worthington, Elizabeth, Dau.
  Osborn, Hannah, Wife
  Osborn, Joshua, Son
  Osborn, Craven, Son
  Osborn, —, all my children
  Taylor, Stacey, Wit.
  Heskett, William, Wit.
  Phillips, Sarah, Wit.
  Hamilton, Robert, Wit.
Cavens, William, G:440, 1804/1806
  McGeath, Polley
  McGeath, Jane
  Hixson, Samuel, Nephew
  Hixson, Eleanor, Sister
  Hixson, Timothy, Exor.
  Henry, James

  Danniel, Jane
  Anderson, Sarah
  Larowe, Isaac, Exor.
  Cavens, Joseph, Brother
  Vandevanter, John, Wit.
  McFadian, Patrick, Wit.
  McGeath, Joshua, Wit.
Guy, Samuel, G:449, 1799/1806
  Guy, Mary, Wife
  Guy, Kesanders, Dau.
  Guy, Sampson, Son
  Guy, Tase, Dau.
  Guy, Kesiar, Dau.
  Guy, Rhoda, Dau.
  Henderson, William, Wit.
  Gardner, Jeremiah, Wit.
Lowry, David, G:466, 1806
  Lowry, Catharine, Wife
  Lowry, Jacob, Son
  Lowry, Thomas, Son
  Lowry, Sophiah, Dau.
  Lowry, Mary, Dau.
  Lowry, Frederick, Son
  Lowry, Lydia, Dau.
  Lowry, Catharine, Dau.
  Lowry, David, Son
  Lowry, Mariah, Dau.
  Wenner, William, Wit.
  Short, Henry Sr., Wit.
  Peirpoint, Sam, Wit.
Harding, Joseph, G:470, 1805/06
  Harding, Elizabeth, Wife
  Harding, Frances, Dau.
  Harding, William, Son
  Harding, Pressley, Son
  Harding, Lewis, Son
  Harding, Henry, Son
  Triplett, Simon, Wit.
  Rose, Silas, Wit.
  Triplett, Martha, Wit.
Williams, Israel, G:474, 1804/06
  Williams, Elizabeth, Dau.,
    18 on 3 July 1815
  Williams, Hannah, Wife
  Humphrey, Abner, Exor.
  Smith, William, Exor.
  Natt, Jonathan, Wit.
  Farnsworth, John, Wit.
  Humphrey, Thomas, Wit.

Gregg, Esther, H:14, u.d./1806
Gregg, Mary, Dau.
Gregg, Ruth, Dau.
Mote, Anna, Dau.
Smith, Sarah, Dau.
Gregg, Joseph, Gr-Son,
  son of Ruth
Hough, Isaac, Wit.
Morison, Jane, Wit.
Fulton, John, Wit.

Milhollen, Esther, H:15, 1806
Milhollen, Joseph,
  Eldest Son, <21
Milhollen, John,
  Youngest Son, <21
Milhollen, Patrick, Brother
Schooley, Reuben, Exor.
Neale, W. S., Wit.
Inglish, John, Wit.
Burgoyne, Joseph, Wit.
Coldwell, Moses, Wit.

McClusky, Daniel, H:17, 1806
McClusky, Rebecah, Wife
McClusky, William, Son
McClusky, Reuben,
  Admr. w.w.a.
Roots, Nancy, Dau.
Roach, Richard, Wit.
Braden, Joseph Jr., Wit.

Russell, Samuel, H:19, 1799/06
Cummings, Rebecka, Dau.
Russell, William, Son
Campbell, James, Exor.
Russell, Sarah, Wife
Russell, Robert, Son
Carlile, David, Wit.
Carter, Richard, Wit.
Dillon, Samuel, Wit.

Miley, Jacob, H:23, 1806
Miley, Chrishannah, Wife
Miley, Chrisley, Son
Miley, John, Son
Miley, Jacob, Son
Miley, Nancey, Dau.
Miley, Chrisshanna, Dau.
Miley, Catherine, Dau.
Miley, Elizabeth, Dau.
Lyons, James, Wit.
Tucker, Christopher, Wit.
Niswanger, Christopher, Wit.

Moore, John, H:31, 1806
Stump, Beckey, Gr-Dau.
Stump, Peter, Gr-Son
Moore, Sally, Gr-Dau.,
  dau. of Benjamin
Reid, Polly, Dau.
Moore, Peggy, Gr-Dau.,
  dau. of Benjamin
Riticor, Nancy, Dau.
Moore, Henry, Son
Bussell, Sally, Dau.
Moore, Samuel, Son
Moore, Joseph, Son
Moore, Jacob, Son
Stump, Polly, Gr-Dau.
Peyton, Francis, Exor.
Tyler, John, Exor.
Lacey, Elias, Wit.
Kelley, Edward, Wit.
Schofield, Jonathan H., Wit.
Ish, Jacob, Wit.

Davisson, Nathaniel, H:39, 1806
McIlhaney, James,
  Brother-in-law
Davisson, Margaret Rosannah,
  Dau.
Davisson, Frederick
  Augustus M., Son
Davisson, Theodore, Son
Davisson, Lemuel, Brother
Davisson, Nancy, Wife

Thompson, Israel H., H:43, 1806
Thompson, Sally, Sister
Thompson, Nancy, Sister
Thompson, Betsy, Sister
Thompson, Pleasant, Sister
Thompson, Jonah, Brother
Thompson, Eleanor, infant Dau.
Neale, W. S., Wit.
Bond, Joseph, Wit.
Phillips, Thomas, Wit.

Hamilton, James, H:46, 1806
Hamilton, —, girls
Hamilton, —, boys
Hamilton, John, Exor.
Bennett, Charles, Exor.
Hough, Isaac, Wit.
Hough, Robert B., Wit.
McGeath, John, Wit.

Coop, George, Wit.
Peyton, Francis H., Wit.
Demery, John, H:47, 1806
Demery, John, Son
Demery, Elizabeth, Dau.
Demery, Peter, Son
Demery, Margaret, Wife
Near, John Sr., Wit.
Smith, George, Wit.
McPhersen, Samuel, Wit.
Mason, Ann, H:72, 1806/07
Hole, Levi
Hole, Ruth, Gr-Dau.
Hole, Ann, Gr-Dau.
Mead, William, Wit.
Rhodes, William, Wit.
Rhodes, Mary, Wit.
Smith, Alice, widow of Henry, H:78, u.d./1807
Smith, Ann, Dau.
Smith, Sarah, Dau.
Smith, William, Son
Smith, David, Son
Smith, Thomas
Smith, Martha
Beal, Joseph, Exor.
Beal, Hannah Sr., Wit., in Ohio 29 Nov 1806
Beal, Hannah Jr., Wit., in Ohio 29 Nov 1806
Beal, Thomas, Wit., in Ohio 29 Nov 1806
Taylor, Bernard, Admr. w.w.a.
Beaty, William, H:80, 1806/07
Beaty, Elizabeth, Dau.
Beaty, George, Son
Beard, Joseph, Wit.
McNealidge, James, Wit.
Stokey, Nehemiah, Wit.
Hixon, Benjamin, H:82, 1806/07
Raecner (Reasonor), Susannah, Dau.
Hixon, David, Brother
Hixon, Elizabeth, Wife
Hixon, William, Son
Mains, Archibald, Wit.
Lacey, David, Wit.
Reasnor, Leonard, Wit.

Copeland, Andrew, H:83, 1807
Newhouse, Mary, Oldest Dau.
Copeland, Bennet, Son
Copeland, Sally, Dau.
Copeland, Jonathan, Oldest Son
Coe, Elizabeth, 2nd Dau.
Copeland, Nancy, Dau.
Copeland, Andrew, Son
Copeland, David, Son
Copeland, James, Wit.
Love, Thomas, Wit.
Pancoast, Israel, H:93, 1795
Pancoast, Joseph, Son
Pancoast, Elizabeth, Wife
Pancoast, Ame, Dau.
Pancoast, Simeon, Son
Pancoast, Hannah, Dau.
Pancoast, Elizabeth, Dau.
Lacy, Mary, w/o Samuel, Dau.
Pancoast, Priscillah, Dau.
Lacy, Sarah, w/o David, Dau.
Claypoole, James, Wit.
Burson, Joseph, Wit.
Gregg, Samuel, Wit.
Woofter, Sebastian, H:94, 1807
Hyde, Elizabeth, Gr-Dau., dau. of Elizabeth Windgrove
Costalow, Jane, Gr-Dau., dau. of Elizabeth Windgrove
Phillips, Elizabeth, Gr-Dau.
Windgrove, Nancy, Gr-Dau.
Bronaugh, William, Exor.
Phillips, William, Gr-Son
Woofter, Mary, Wife
Starkey, Elizabeth, Gr-Dau.
Phillips, Mary, Gr-Dau.
Windgrove, John, Gr-Son
Starkey, Jacob, Gr-Son
Phillips, Mary, Dau., w/o Jenkin
Windgrove, Elizabeth, Dau., dec'd.
Starkey, Jane, Dau., w/o Isaac
Woofter, —, Gr-Dau., dau. of John
Starkey, Eppha, Gr-Dau.
Woofter, James, Gr-Son, son of John

Starkey, John, Gr-Son
Woofter, Jonathan, Gr-Son,
 son of John
Woofter, John, Gr-Son,
 son of John
Woofter, Priscilla, Gr-Dau.,
 dau. of John
Woofter, Susanna, Gr-Dau.,
 dau. of John
Woofter, John, Son
Brown, Moses, Wit.
Reed, James, Wit.
Spencer, Nathan, H:95, 1802/06
Spencer, Sarah, Dau.
Spencer, Mary, Dau.
Spencer, Rachel, Dau.
Spencer, Hannah, Dau.
Spencer, Samuel, Son
Spencer, John, Son
Spencer, William, Son
Spencer, Nathan, Son
Spencer, Margaret, Dau.
Hirst, John, Wit.
Janney, Israel, Wit.
Bradfield, Benjamin, Wit.
Merchant, Philip, H:103, 1807
Harris, John A., Exor.
Merchant, Mary Ann, Wife
Hancock, Elizabeth, H:106, 1802/07
Ellzey, William, Brother, dec'd.
Ellzey, Elizabeth, Niece,
 dau. of William
Ellzey, Mary, Niece,
 dau. of William
Ellzey, William, Exor.
Hough, Joseph of Waterford, H:108, 1807
Hough, Washington, Son, <21
Stone, Daniel, Brother-in-law
Hough, Peyton, Son, <21
Hough, Nancy, Dau., <21
Hough, William, Brother
Moore, Asa, Wit.
Smith, Ralph, Wit.
Smallwood, Leaven, Wit.
Templar, William, Wit.
Tillett, Edward, H:108, 1807
Tillett, Elizabeth, Wife

Willson, Ebenezer, H:112, 1803/07
Fierce, Elizabeth, Dau.
Phillips, Mary, Dau.
Phillips, Sarah, Dau.
Willson, Hannah Jr., Dau.
Green, Margaret, Dau.
Willson, Asa, Son
Willson, Samuel, Son
Willson, Nancy, Dau.
Willson, Jane, Dau.
Willson, John, Son
Willson, Thomas, Eldest Son
Willson, Hannah, Wife
Yoe, William, Wit.
Cunard, Edward Jr., Wit.
Cunard, Edward Sr., Wit.
Thompson, Jane, H:113, 1805/07
Evans, Robert, Brother
—, my sister and her heirs
Thompson, Asa
Lewis, Charles, Exor.
Lewis, James, Wit.
Lewis, Catharine, Wit.
Lewis, George, H:114, 1800/07/07
Brown, George, Exor.
James, Thomas, Step-son,
 wife's son
Evans, Mary, Dau.
Lewis, Keziah, Gr-Dau., natural
 Dau. of Lewis Lewis
Marks, Elisha, Exor., dec'd.
 according to 1807 codicil
Lewis, Mary, Wife
Lewis, Rachel, Dau.
Lewis, Lewis only son, Son
Lewis, Sarah, Dau.
West, John, Wit.
Sandford, Jeremiah, Wit.
Hesser, Andrew, Wit.
Lunsford, Lewis, Wit. [c]
Hesser, Betty, Wit. [c]
Brown, John, Wit. [c]
Tarbert, Samuel of Montgomery Co., Pa., H:118, 1791/1807
Tarbert, Thomas, Brother
Tarbert, Elizabeth, Mother
Tarbert, Thomas, Father
Tarbert, all my brothers and
 sisters

Tarbert, James, Brother
Taylor, Jonathan, Wit.
Morewine, Andrew, Wit.
Bockins, Godfrey, Wit.
Thompson, Sally W., H:125, 1807
Hamilton, Betsey, Sister
Thompson, Sarah, Mother
Vandevanter, Pleasant, Sister
Moore, James, Exor.
Thompson, Israel, Father, dec'd.
Griffith, Nancy, Sister
Thompson, Sally Eleanor,
   Niece, dau. of dec'd. brother
   Israel H.
Moore, Asa, Wit.
Bond, Joseph, Wit.
Phillips, Thomas, Wit.
Taylor, Jesse, H:127, 1807
Sapington, Mary, Dau.
Hixson, Timothy, Exor.
Taylor, John, Son, <21
Moore, James, Exor.
Taylor, Samuel, Son, <21
Danniel, Joshua, Wit.
Wright, William, Wit.
Wright, Samuel, Wit.
Williams, Thomas, H:128, 1803/07
Williams, Jane, Wife
Lee, Thomas Ludwell, H:151, 1806/07
Lee, Thomas Ludwell, Son, dec'd.
Lee, Francis Lightfoot, Uncle, dec'd.
Lee, Fanny, Wife
Lee, —, Daus.
Carter, George, Exor.
Helm, John, H:170, 1800/07
Harbourt, Peggy, Dau.
Milborn, John, Gr-Son,
   son of Ann, <21
Milborn, Ann, Dau.
Helm, John Jr., Son
Helm, Charles, Son
Helm, Meredith, Son
Helm, Mary Ann, Gr-Dau.,
   dau. of Merideth, <16
Helm, Sarah, Wife
Riley, Lettice, Housekeeper
Berkley, George, Wit.

Berkley, John L, .Wit.
Timms, John, Wit.
Dunkin, Charles, H:172, 1807
Dunkin, George, Son
Dunkin, Nancy, Dau.
Dunkin, Susanna, Wife
Dunkin, Susanna, Dau.
Dunkin, William, Son
Dunkin, Charles, Son
Dunkin, Henry, Son
Dunkin, Benjamin, Son, <15
Dunkin, Mason, Son, <15
Dunkin, Catharine, Dau.
Dunkin, Coleman, Son
Lacey, Israel, Wit.
Athey, Hezekiah W., Wit.
Hicks, Thomas, Wit.
Turley, John, Wit.
Crooks, James, Wit.
Castle, Rebekah, Wit.
Lafaber, Henry, H:176, 1807
Wildman, Polly, Dau.
Schoolley, Onnes, Dau.
Howser, Peggy, Dau.
Lafaber, Sookey, Dau.
Lafaber, Henry, Son
Lafaber, Rachel, Dau.
Lafaber, Beckey, Dau.
Lafaber, Fanne, Dau.
Lafaber, Rosanna, Dau.
Lafaber, Zilphy, lame Dau.
Lafaber, William, Son
Lafaber, Onnes, Wife
Francis, Enoch, Wit.
Howser, John, Wit.
Porter, Mary, H:184, 1806/07
Porter, John B. (or R.), Son
Porter, Elias
Porter, Daniel
Grant, William, Wit.
MacDanniel, William, Wit.
Buckner, Thornton, Wit.
Bartlett, James, Wit.
Milton, John, H:188, 1807/08
Milton, Henry, Brother
Milton, —, Mother
Milton, Sarah, Wife
Milton, Peggy, Sister
Milton, Alexander, Brother
Smith, Weeden, Wit.

Pullen, Asher, Wit.
Kelley, Edward, Wit.
Boswell, Ann, H:196, 1808
Inglish, Nancy
Donaldson, Stephen F.
Donaldson, James W.
Donaldson, Betsey
Donaldson, Mary Jane
Inglish, John, Exor.
Donaldson, Susannah, Wit.
Donaldson, Stephen, Wit.
McVicker, John, H:215, 1808
McVicker, Esther, Dau.
McVicker, Ann, Wife
Thomson, Mary, Dau.
Triplett, Simon, Wit.
Rose, Christopher, Wit.
Lewis, William, Wit.
Taylor, Thomas, Wit.
Carruthers, James, H:216, 1807/08
Gore, Joshua, Exor.
Carruthers, James, Son
Carruthers, Ann, Dau.
Carruthers, Rachel, Dau.
Carruthers, Phebe, Dau.
Carruthers, Christian, Dau.
Carruthers, Hannah, Dau.
Carruthers, Thomas, Son, <21
Clowes, Joseph, Wit.
Clowes, Thomas, Wit.
Gore, Thomas, Wit.
Griffith, Richard, H:240, 1808
Griffith, Sarah Pleasant, Dau.
Griffith, Nancy, Wife
Griffith, Israel Thompson, Son
Thompson, Jonah, Exor.
Neale, W. S., Wit.
Phillips, Thomas, Wit.
Janney, David, Wit.
McIlhaney, John Jr., H:243, 1808
McIlhany, Harriott, Wife
McIlhany, Talliferro Milton, Son
McIlhany, James, Brother
McIlhany, Mortimer, Brother
McIlhany, Nancy (White), Sister
McIlhany, Rosanna, Sister
McIlhany, Elizabeth, Sister
McIlhany, Mary, Sister
McIlhany, Cecelia, Sister
McIlhany, Louisa, Sister
McIlhany, —, Mother
McIlhany, Hannah, Aunt
McIlhany, Rosannah, Niece
McIlhaney, John Sr., Friend
Milton, John, Father-in-law
White, Polly, Cousin
White, John, Friend
Heaton, Dr. James, Friend
Davis, Solomon, Friend
Ellzey, Lewis, Friend
Tribby, Joseph, Friend
Grant, Mary, H:248, 1808
Grant, Esther, Dau.
Lacey, Sally, Dau., w/o William
Johnson, Patty, Dau.
Reed, Mary, Dau.
Mount, Charity, Dau.
Johnson, John, Exor.
Moore, James, Exor.
Schooley, Reuben, Exor.
Neale, W. S., Wit.
Milhollen, Patrick, Wit.
Stone, Daniel, Wit.
Gulick, John, H:260, 1807/08
Gulick, Leanor, Wife
Gulick, Aaron, Gr-Son, <21
Gulick, Fardinan, Son
Gulick, Moses, Son, son of Leanor
Johnson, Sarah, Dau.
Gulick, Elizabeth, Dau.
Gulick, Leanor, Dau.
Gulick, Francis, Son
Daniel, Joseph, Wit.
Sheid, James, Wit.
Rose, Christopher, Wit.
Shoemaker, George, H:275, 1808
Bottonfield, Elisabeth, Dau.
Winner (Vinner), John, Gr-Son
Shoemaker, George, Son
Warner, Sarah, Dau.
Shoemaker, John, Son
Vinner (Winner), John, Gr-Son
Shoemaker, Sollomon, Son
Shoemaker, Christiana, Dau.
Shoemaker, Daniel, Son
Shoemaker, Anna Mary Barbara, Wife
Shoemaker, Joseph, Son

Shoemaker, Judith, Dau.
Shoemaker, Simon, Nephew
Shoemaker, Sarah (Warner), Dau.
Fry, Henry Joseph, Exor.
Tribbey, Joseph, Wit.
Baker, Samuel, Wit.
McCormick, Robert, H:295, 1808
McCormick, John, Brother
McCormick, Robert, Nephew, son of John
McCormick, Nancy, Niece, dau. of James
McCormick, James, Brother
McCormick, Martha, Sister
Lovett, Joseph, Exor.
Smith, Samuel, Exor.
Smith, Seth, Wit.
Dunkin, Anna, Wit.
Hill, George, Wit.
Smith, W., Wit.
Peyton, Francis H., H:296, 1807/08
Hale, George, Nephew, eldest son of William
Luckett, Francis W., Nephew, eldest, son of Leven
Peyton, Richard, Nephew, oldest son of Townshend
Peyton, Frances, Wife
Luckett, Leven, Exor.
Heaton, Dr. James, Exor.
Dodd, John Jr., Wit.
Heaton, Jonathan, Wit.
George, John, H:298, 1808
George, Elizabeth, Wife
George, John, Son
Shover, Adam, Wit.
Smitly, Mathias, Wit.
Shover, John, Wit.
Derry, Baltzer, H:324, 1808
Watkins, Benjamin
Murch, Adam
Derry, Jacob
Derry, Barbara, Wife
Derry, Philip, Son
Harding, J., Wit.
Conard, John, Wit.
Demery, Peter, Wit.

Wykoff, Nicholas, H:329, 1796/1809
Wykoff, Isaac, Son
Wykoff, Peter, Son
Wykoff, Abraham, Son
Wykoff, Cornelius, Son
Wykoff, Margaret, Wife
Wykoff, Nicholas, Son
Skinner, Richard, Wit.
Skinner, Cornelius Jr., Wit.
Lacey, Elias, Wit.
Taylor, John, Wit.
Marmaduke, Samson, I:1, 1809
Marmaduke, Olee (Alee), Dau., <18
Marmaduke, Silas, Son
Marmaduke, Pressley, Son
Marmaduke, John A., Son
Marmaduke, William, Son
Demit, Jane, Dau., dec'd.
Ogelvee, Betsey, Dau.
Marmaduke, Jesse, Son
Demit, Sinclear, Gr-Son, son of Jane
Waters, Patty, Dau.
Bonsall, Jane, Wit.
Lewis, Rachel, Wit.
Brown, George Sr., Wit.
Brown, Brown Jon., Wit.
Johnston, George, I:9, 1809
McKenny, Jane, Dau.
Johnston, Hugh, Son
Johnston, George, Son
Johnston, Robert, Son
Johnston, John, Son
Johnston, William, Son
Johnston, James, Son
Johnston, Peggy, Dau.
Johnston, Margery, Dau.
Johnston, Polly, Dau.
Bronaugh, William, Wit.
Martin, John, Wit.
Redmond, Andrew, I:12, 1807
Redmond, Hariot, Dau., <18
Redmond, Hannah, Dau.
Redmond, Benjamin, Son
Redmond, Stephen, Son, <21
Redmond, John, Son, <21
Redmond, Israel, Son, <21
Redmond, Nancy, Dau., <18

Index to Loudoun County Wills, 1757 - 1850   71

Redmond, Ann, Wife, married
  about 1805
Buckner, Aris, Wit.
James, Benjamin, Wit.
Shepherd, Charles, I:22,
  1805/1809
  Shepherd, Leven, Son
  Shepherd, Kitty, Dau.
  Shepherd, Fanny, Dau.
  Shepherd, Elizabeth, Dau.
  Shepherd, Nancy, Dau.
  Shepherd, John, Son
  Shepherd, Polly, Dau.
  Shepherd, Charles, Son
  Shepherd, James, Son
  Shepherd, Eleanor, Wife
  Luckett, Samuel, Wit.
  Wilson, Levi, Wit.
  Wollard, Joseph, Wit.
  Burns, William, Wit.
Clifford, Obediah, I:26, 1809/09
  Cooper, Alexander Jr.
  Smith, Fleet
  Binns, Charles
  Clifford, —, Wife
  Clifford, —, Children
  Littlejohn, John, Wit.
  McCormick, John, Wit.
  Potts, Jonas, Wit.
Oxley, John, I:38, 1809
  Oxley, Amey, Dau.
  Wollard, Mary, Dau.
  Stevins, Eleanor, Dau.
  Oxley, John, Son
  Warner, Caty, Dau.
  Oxley, Lewis, Gr-Son,
    son of Henry
  Oxley, Scintha, Gr-Dau.,
    dau. of Henry
  Oxley, Mary, Gr-Dau.,
    dau. of Henry
  Oxley, Enoch, Gr-Son,
    son of Henry
  Oxley, Francis, Gr-Son,
    son of Henry
  Oxley, Aaron, Gr-Son,
    son of Henry
  Oxley, Aaron, Son
  Oxley, Jane, Dau.-in-law,
    widow of Henry

  Oxley, Henry, Son, dec'd.
  Sanders, Aaron, Exor.
  Rose, John, Wit.
  Littleton, Solomon, Wit.
  Littleton, John, Wit.
Oxley, Henry, I:40, 1809
  Oxley, Jane, Wife
  Oxley, Aaron, Oldest Son
  Littleton, Solomon, Wit.
  Stevens, Henry, Wit.
Jenkins, Leanna, I:77, 1809
  Vaugh, Kizziah, Dau.
  Jenkins, Elizabeth, Dau.
  Legg, Hellen, Dau.
  Turner, Mimy, Dau.
  Kent, Elizabeth, Gr-Dau.
  Jenkins, John, Son
  Jenkins, Leanna, Dau.
  Shively, George, Friend
  Cleveland, Johnston, Exor.
  Wolcard, William, Wit.
  Legg, Elijah, Wit.
Helm, Sarah, I:82, 1809
  Shanks, Susannah, Dau., dec'd.
  Neale, Lettitia, Dau., dec'd.
  Lewis, Charles, Exor.
  Lewis, James, Exor.
  Lewis, James M., Jr., Wit.
  Lewis, Catherine, Wit.
  Lewis, Elizabeth, Wit.
Presgraves, William, I:96, 1809/10
  Giles, Sally, Dau.
  Presgraves, Elizabeth, Dau.
  Timms, Joseph, Son-in-law
  Summers, Mary, Dau.
  Presgraves, George, Son
  Timms, Milly, Dau.
  Summers, George, Son-in-law
  Presgraves, John, Son
  Presgraves, Richard, Son
  Presgraves, William, Son
  Presgraves, Catherine, Dau.
  Presgraves, Nancy, Dau.
  Humphries, Samuel, Wit.
  Shively, George, Wit.
  Morgan, Reuben, Wit.
Smith, George Sr., I:112, 1809/10
  Coonce, Mary
  Smith, George, Son
  Coonce, Nicholas

Smith, David, Son
Coonce, Adam
Smith, Barbarah, Dau.
Coonce, Henry
Smith, Mary, Wife
Smith, Catherine, Dau.
Smith, Sarah, Dau.
Smith, Ann, Dau.
Smith, Jacob, Son
Shaver, John, Wit.
Demory, John, Wit.
Potts, John, Wit.
Fox, William, I:121, 1809/10
Fox, Bushrod M., Son, <21
Fox, Mary, Dau., <21
Fox, Frances, Dau., <21
Fox, Elizabeth, Dau., <21
Fox, Mary, Wife
Fox, Alfred B., Son, <21
Braden, Robert, Exor.
Baltzer, Conrad, Exor.
Braden, Joseph Jr., Wit.
Fox, Cephus, Wit.
Bennett, Charles Jr., Wit.
Braden, John, Wit.
Arnett, Samuel, I:128, 1809/10
Arnett, Samuel, Nephew, son of Thomas
Williams, Samuel, Nephew
Jackson, Sarah
Arnett, Thomas, Nephew, son of Alexander
Williams, Levi, Nephew
Jones, Sarah, w/o Thomas
Jackson, Benjamin
Jones, Alford, son of Thomas & Sarah
Jones, Thomas
Evans, Barten, Wit.
Marks, George, Wit.
Gregg, John, Wit.
Carr, Mary, I:148, 1810
Hall, Mary, Dau.
Carr, Thomas, Son
Carr, Joseph, Gr-Son, son of Thomas
Carr, Elizabeth, Dau.
Cline, Margaret, Dau., w/o William

Campbell, Jane's children, Gr-child
Campbell, Jane, Dau.
Carr, Samuel, Son
Carr, James, Son
Mines, John, Wit.
Hole, Meriam, Wit.
McKamy, John, I:156, 1810
McKamy, James, Father
White, Thomas 3rd, Exor.
Peacock, Samuel, Wit.
White, Rachel, Wit.
White, Josiah, Wit.
Mead, Benjamin, I:157, 1810
Mead, Louisa, Gr-Dau., dau. of Margaret
Mead, Joseph, Son
Mead, Aquilla, Son
Mead, John, Son
Mead, Samuel, Son
Mead, Asenath, Dau.
Mead, Christian, Dau.
Mead, Margaret, Dau.
Mead, Ann, Wife
Taylor, Bernard, Exor.
Janney, Eli, Wit.
Gardner, Joseph, Wit.
Janney, Thomas, Wit.
Richcreek, Philip Jacob, I:159, 1805/10
Clip, Mary, Dau.
Clip, John, Exor.
Richcreek, John, Son
Richcreek, Gisbert, Son
Richcreek, Philip, Son
Hatcher, Jane, Dau.
Redd, Elizabeth, Dau.
Humphrey, Thomas, Exor.
Williams, Notley C., Wit.
Frits, George, Wit.
Jackson, Stiles, I:169, 1810
Jackson, Elizabeth, Wife
Jackson, —, Son
Jenners, Abiel, Exor.
McTiney, Francis, Exor.
Frey, Henry Joseph, Wit.
Casey, Leven, Wit.
Jackson, John, Wit.

Triplett, Simon, I:180, 1806/10
Triplett, Philip, Son
Triplett, James Lane, Son
Triplett, William H., Son
Triplett, Lucinda, Dau.
Triplett, Katharine, Dau.
Triplett, Simon Jr., Son
Triplett, Martha, Wife
Triplett, Reuben, Brother
Taylor, Polly, Gr-Dau.
Adam, Susanah, Dau.
Taylor, Alice, Gr-Dau.
Powell, Burr, Exor.
Hurrford, Francis, Exor.
Bronaugh, William, Wit.
Roszell, Stephen C., Wit.
Brabham, Thomas, Wit.

McIlhany, John, I:204, 1809
Russell, Mahlon, son of Sarah
McIlhany, Hannah, Sister
Davis, Morris
Russell, Sarah,
　now w/o Morris Davis
Tribby, Josiah, Exor.
Russell, Samuel, Exor.
Scott, Thomas C., Wit.
White, James, Wit.
Hereford, Francis, Wit.

McIlhany, John, I:204, 1809
Gregory, Louiza,
　child of Ann Gregory
Gregory, Evelina,
　child of Ann Gregory
Gregory, James Mandiville,
　child of Ann Gregory

McManamy, Charles, I:208, 1807/10
McCrea, Janey, Gr-Dau.
Farrhouse (Fairhurst), George, Exor.
McManamy, Sarah, Dau.
McManamy, Elizabeth, Dau.
McManamy, Ann, Dau.
McManamy, Catherine, Dau.
McManamy, Isabel, Dau.
McManamy, Margaret, Dau.
McManamy, Rebekah, Dau.
McManamy, Jane, Wife
McManamy, George, Son
McManamy, William, Son
McManamy, James, Son
Martin, David, Wit.
Oram, Mary, Wit.
King, Edward, Wit.
Nixon, Joel, Wit.
White, Benjamin, Wit.

Braden, Joseph, I:216, 1810
Lacy, Sally, Dau.
White, Margaret, Dau.
Braden, Sarah, Wife
Fox, Mary, Dau.
Braden, John, Son
Fox, Elizabeth, Dau.
Bennett, Charles Jr., Exor.
Braden, Joseph, Son
Braden, Robert, Son
Hough, Fanny, Dau.
Neale, William S., Wit.
Talbott, Joseph, Wit.
Vandevanter, Isaac, Wit.
Vandevanter, John, Wit.

Rasor, George, I:226, 1805/10
Comber, Peggy, Dau.
Long, Adam, Father-in-law, dec'd.
Shaver, Polly, Dau.
Rasor, David, Gr-Son, <16
Stoneburner, Betsey, Dau.
Rasor, Barbery, Dau.
Rasor, Molly (Mary), Wife,
　dau. of Adam Long
Rasor, Catherine, Dau.
Rasor, Christianor, Dau.
Rasor, Hannah, Dau.
Rasor, Jacob, Son, <16
Rasor, Philip, Son
Rasor, George, Son
Rasor, John, Son
Steere, Isaac Jr., Exor.
Clapham, Samuel, Wit.
Elliott, David, Wit.
Elliott, Samuel, Wit.

Edwards, Jonathan Sr., I:230, 1808/10
Moran, Mary, Dau.,
　w/o John Myvert Moran
Lewis, Elizabeth, Dau.,
　w/o John
Edwards, Sarah, Wife
Edwards, Rebecca, Dau.

Edwards, Joseph, Son
Edwards, Jonathan, Son, dec'd.
Edwards, Edward, Son
Edwards, Sarah, Dau.
Stovin, Charles, Wit.
Casidy, Thomas, Wit.
Casidy, John, Wit.
Powell, Leven, I:250, 1809/10
Chilton, Sarah Harrison, Dau.
Powell, Leven Mynn, Gr-Son,
son of Alfred
Powell, Alfred, Gr-Son,
son of Leven
Powell, John Leven, Gr-Son,
son of Leven
Powell, Cuthbert, Gr-Son,
son of Leven
Powell, Alexander, Gr-Son,
son of Leven
Powell, Levin D., Gr-Son
Powell, Sally, Gr-Dau.,
dau. of William H.
Powell, Emily, Gr-Dau.,
dau. of William H.
Powell, Burr, Gr-Son,
son of William H.
Powell, Thomas W., Gr-Son,
son of William H.
Powell, Leven, Son, dec'd.
Powell, Alfred, Son
Powell, Cuthbert, Son
Powell, Sarah, Wife
Powell, William H., Son, dec'd.
Powell, Burr, Son
Powell, Maria, Gr-Dau.,
dau. of William H.
Smith, William, I:271, 1810
Dulin, William, Father-in-law
Smith, Hannah, Wife
Smith, Mary Dulin, Dau.
Smith, Catharine Wren, Dau.
Smith, George Dulin, Son, <21
Smith, Sarah Ann, Dau.
Noland, William, Wit.
Williams, William, Wit.
Sinclair, George, Wit.
Danniell, Joshua, I:287, 1810
Danniell, Stephen, Son
Danniell, Jane, Wife
Danniell, Elizabeth, Dau.

Talbott, Jane, Dau.
Danniell, Nancy, Dau.
Moore, James, Exor.
Williams, John, Wit.
James, Levi, Wit.
Elgin, Charles, Wit.
Divine, Bonham, Wit.
Beatey, David, I:305, 1806/11
Beatey, Elizabeth, Wife
Beatey, John, Son
Beatey, David, Son
Beatey, William, Son
Elliot, Mary, Dau., w/o George
Beatey, Robert, Son
Steer, Jane, Dau., w/o John
Chilton, William, Wit.
Chilton, Sarah H., Wit.
Thomas, Lloyd, Wit.
Miner, John, Wit.
Myres, Sarah, I:314, 1801/06/11
Myres, Lambert, Gr-Son,
son of William
Myres, William, Son
Myres, Sally, Dau.
Myres, William, Husband, dec'd.
Fox, William, Exor.
Braden, Joseph Sr., Wit.
Braden, John, Wit.
Mull, John, I:316, 1810/11
Mull, David, Uncle
Mull, George, Uncle
Ball, Isaac, Wit.
Shumaker, Simon, Wit.
Shumaker, Daniel, Wit.
Hoge, Solomon, I:343, 1810/11
Kenworthy, Rebecca, Dau.
Hoge, Jesse, Son
Nichols, Mary, Dau.
Gore, Joshua, Son-in-law
Hoge, William, Son
Nichols, Ann, Dau.
Gregg, Lydia, Dau.
Gore, Sarah, Dau.
Hoge, David, Son
Hoge, Solomon, Son
Hoge, Joshua, Son
Hoge, Margery, Dau.
Hoge, Isaac, Son
Hoge, Mary, Wife
Taylor, Mahlon, Exor.

Index to Loudoun County Wills, 1757 - 1850   75

Gore, Thomas, Wit.
Janney, Jonathan, Wit.
Janney, Daniel, Wit.
Tribby, Joseph, I:360, 1810/11
Tribby, Louisa, Dau.
Tribby, Asahel, Eldest Son
Tribby, Sarah, Dau.
Tribby, Jonathan, Son
Tribby, George, Son
Tribby, Elizabeth, Dau.
Tribby, Ruth, Wife
Nixon, William, Wit.
White, John, Wit.
McCarty, Charles, Wit.
Roach, Mahlon, Wit.
Johnson, John, I:363, 1811
Clapham, Samuel, Exor.
Clapham, Elizabeth, Dau.
Lacey, Elias, Wit.
Jackson, John, Wit.
Scandrett, Jacob, Wit.
Griffith, Nancy, I:371, 1811
Thompson, Sally, Sister, dec'd.
Thompson, Samuel, Brother, dec'd.
Griffith, Israel Thompson, Son, <16
Williams, John, Friend, husband of Lydia
Griffith, Sarah Pleasant, Dau. <10
Williams, Lydia, Friend
Thompson, Jonah, Brother
Neale, William S., Wit.
Paxson, William, Wit.
Goodwin, William, Wit.
Stonestreet, Basil, I:373, 1810/11
Stonestreet, Elizabeth, Wife
Stonestreet, Sarah, Dau.
Stonestreet, Benjamin Asa, Son
Stonestreet, Augustus, Son
Blincoe, Elizabeth, Dau.
Jones, Henry, Friend
Jones, Ann, Dau.
Cleveland, Johnston, Wit.
Horseman, William, Wit.
DBell, George, Wit.
Noland, Thomas, I:377, 1811
Noland, Francis, Gr-Dau.
Love, Jane, Dau.
Noland, William, Son

Noland, Lloyd, Son
Noland, Thomas, Son
Noland, Samuel, Son
Noland, Dade, Son
Noland, Betsy, Dau.
Noland, Eleanor, Wife
Luckett, Catharine, Niece
Douglas, Hugh, Wit.
Henderson, Richard H., Wit.
Dawson, Samuel, Wit.
Ball, George Washington, Wit.
Cost, Catarine, I:387, 1808/11
Dorsthimer, Charles, Son-in-law
Pickins, Robert, Son-in-law
Gross, Henry, Son-in-law
Yeco, Simon, Son-in-law
Cost, Francis, Husband, dec'd.
Wolf, Mary's son, Gr-Son, supposed to be son George
Cost's son
Cost, Jacob, Son
Cost, Barbara, Dau.
Cost, Elisabeth, Dau.
Cost, Beckey, Dau.
—, Jonathan, Gr-Son
Cost, George, Son
Cost, John, Son
Cost, Beator (Peter), Son
Stousenberger, John, Wit.
Amour, Laurence, Wit.
Fawley, Jacob, Wit.
McMullan, Alexander, I:388, 1803/11
Richards, Rosanah, Dau.
McMullan, Elizabeth, Wife
McMullan, Alexander, Son
McMullan, William, Son
McMullan, Daniel, Son
McMullan, Andrew, Son, <21
McMullan, Rachel, Dau.
McMullan, Elizabeth, Dau.
McMullan, Archibald, Son
Swarts, Mary, Dau.
Moffet, Margaret, Dau.
Johnson, Nancy, Dau.
Gregg, Thomas, Wit.
James, David, Wit.
Vernon, John, Wit.
McKnight, Margaret, K:10, 1811
Larrow, Elizabeth, Dau.

Brown, Hannah, Dau.
Bradfield, Nancy, Gr-Dau.
Alexander, Mary, Dau.
Cunnard, Edward Jr., Exor.
Brown, Margaret, Gr-Dau.
McKnight, Uriah, Son
Jenkins, Margaret, Dau.
McKnight, Eli, Son
McKnight, Peninna, Gr-Dau.
McKnight, Nimrod, Gr-Son
McKnight, John, Son
McKnight, Benjamin, Son
McKnight, Deliah, Gr-Dau.
McKnight, Deborah, Dau.
Thomas, John, Wit.
Harrison, Alexander, Wit.
McKnight, William, Wit.
Young, Archibald, Wit.
McDaniel, Edward, K:14, 1810/11
McDaniel, Ann, Wife
McDaniel, Mary Ann, Dau.
McDaniel, Sarah, Dau.
McDaniel, Senior, Dau.
McDaniel, James, Son
McDaniel, Archibald, Son
McDaniel, Matilda, Dau.
McDaniel, Fanny, Dau.
Garret, Elizabeth, Dau., dec'd.
Garret, Barton, Gr-Son
Garret, Archabald, Gr-Son
Braden, Robert, Wit.
Stevens, John B., Wit.
Stevens, Thomas Jr., Wit.
Ellzey, Alice, K:23, 1808/11
Ellzey, Alice Ann, Gr-Dau.
Ellzey, William, Son
Ellzey, Elizabeth, Dau.
Ellzey, Sally, Dau.
Ellzey, Mary, Dau.
Tyler, John, Wit.
Brown Sr., John, K:26, 1811
Brown, Susanna, Dau.
Brown, Hyram, Step-Son,
  wife's son
Brown, Isaac, Son
Brown, John, Son
Brown, Sally, Dau.
Brown, Nimrod, Son
Brown, Sarah, Wife
Brown, George, Son

Brown, Harmon, Gr-Son,
  son of George
Brown, Hannah, Dau.
Brown, Catharine, Dau.
Cunard, Edward Jr., Exor.
Thomas, Philip Sr., Exor.
Gregg, Mahlon, Wit.
Jones, George H., Wit.
Cochran, James Jr., Wit.
White, Thomas, Wit.
Gray, Daniel, Wit.
Drake, Thomas, K:45, 1804/11
Richards, Deborah, Dau.
Hopkins, Susannah, Dau.,
  now Leonard
Hopkins, David, Son-in-law,
  Susanah's 1st husband
Hopkins, Susannah's children
Glasscock, Uree, Dau.,
  w/o Daniel
Glasscock, Uree's children
Combs, Tacy, Dau.
Drake, Jacob, Son
Drake, Uriee, Wife
Drake, James Heaton, Gr-Son
Drake, Thomas, Son
Butcher, Hannah, Dau.
Grayson, Benjamin, Wit.
Humphrey, Abner, Wit.
Lynn, Benson, Wit.
McCullah, Robert, K:51, 1810/11
McCullah, Mary, Wife
McCullah, George, Brother
Alexander, Susanna
McCullah, Jesse's widow,
  Sister-in-law, brother's wife
Janney, James, Exor.
Janney, Jesse, Exor.
Nichols, Isaac, Wit.
Taylor, Bernard, Wit.
Nichols, Samuel, Wit.
Janney, Abijah, Wit.
Beazer, John, K:56, 1797/1811
Beazer, —, Wife
Carter, Edith, Eldest Dau.
Campbell, John, Son-in-law
Campbell, Elizabeth, Dau.
Painter, Guluhnah, Dau.
Shively, Sarah, Dau.

Clandenning, Samuel, Exor.
White, James, Wit.
Beal, Thomas, Wit.
White, Robert, Wit.
Whitacre, Benjamin, K:65, 1811/13
Whitacre, Amos, Son
Whitacre, John, Son
Whitacre, Alice, Wife
Whitacre, Abner, Son
—, Mary Ann, Gr-Dau., dau. of Hannah
—, Hannah, Dau.
Gore, Joshua, Exor.
Gore, Joseph, Exor.
Janney, Abijah, Exor.
Gore, William, Wit.
Taylor, Bernard, Wit.
Curtis, James, K:66, 1812
Curtis, Mary, Wife
Smith, Fleet, Wit.
Holiday, James W., Wit.
Craig, James, K:73, 1808/12
Craig, Samuel, Son
Craig, James, Son
Craig, Rebecca, Dau.-in-law, w/o James
Craig, James, Gr-Son, son of William
Craig, William, Son, dec'd.
Craig, Isaac, Gr-Son, son of William
Craig, Robert, Son
Combs, John, Son-in-law
Huddleston, Izabel, Dau.
Cavens, Edward, Son-in-law
Redman, Agnes, Dau.
Janney, Israel, Wit.
Brown, John, Wit.
Brown, James (or Jacob), Wit.
Kline, Elizabeth, K:81, 1812
Dorsey, Patty, Sister
Dorsey, Edward, Brother-in-law
James, Levi, Wit.
Talbott, Joseph, Wit.
Hough, Isaac, Wit.
Hixon, Timothy, K:89, 1811/12
Gregg, Margaret, Dau.
Hixon, Noah, Gr-Son, son of Reuben
Davis, Rachel, Dau.
Hixon, Timothy, Son
King, Mary, Dau.
Hixon, Benjamin, Son
Hixon, Mary, Gr-Dau., dau. of Reuben
Hixon, William, Son
Hixon, John, Son
Hixon, Catherine, Gr-Dau., dau. of Reuben
Hixon, Rachel, Gr-Dau., dau. of Reuben
Hixon, Jean, Gr-Dau., dau. of Reuben
Hixon, Timothy, Gr-Son, son of Elijah
Hixon, Elijah, Son
Hixon, Reuben, Son
Hixon, Elonar, Dau., <21
Hixon, Flemon, Son, <21
Hixon, Andrew, Son
Hixon, Stephen, Gr-Son, son of Reuben
Hixon, Samuel, Son
Hixon, Sarah, Dau.
Hixon, Margaret, Wife
Clapham, Samuel, Wit.
Sanders, Aaron, Wit.
Hamilton, John, Wit.
Lyne, Mary, K:94, 1812
Lyne, William, Son
Lyne, Sanford, Son
Lyne, Robert, Son
Hutchison, Joshua, Wit.
Settle, Ann, Wit.
Hutchison, Jemima, Wit.
Settle, Jane, Wit.
Orr, Susannah, K:95, 1810/12
Orr, Alexander D., Son
Orr, John D., Son
Powell, Betsy, Dau.
Orr, William Grayson, Son
Stuart, Anne, Dau.
Peake, Humphrey, Wit.
Blackburn, J., Wit.
Carr, Peter, K:96, 1810/12
Rickmyers, Sally, former wife's niece, <16
McMackin, Mary, Dau.
Wilson, Henry, Step-son

Wilson, Maria, Step-Dau.
Carr, Jane, Dau.
Carr, Mary, Wife
Carr, Peter, Son
Carr, William, Son
Carr, Joseph, Son
Carr, John, Son
McCormick, John, Wit.
McCowat, Thomas, Wit.
Cranwell, John L., Wit.
Warford, John, K:98, 1812
Warford, Mary, Wife
Warford, John, Son, dec'd.
Warford, James, Son
Warford, Elijah, Son
Warford, Lydia, Dau.
Warford, Samuel, Gr-Son,
  son of John
Warford, Mary, Dau.
Miles, Rhody, formerly Warford
Flitter, Sarah, Dau.
Palmer, Ann, Dau.
Gregg, Hannah, Dau.
Cunard, Edward Jr., Wit.
Brown, John, Wit.
Barton, Thomas, Wit.
Janney, Mahlon, K:119, 1809/12
Janney, Mary, Niece, dau. of
  John Gibson
Chandlee, George, niece's
  husband
Gibson, Amos, Nephew,
  son of John
Janney, Sarah, Wife
Chandlee, Deborah, Niece,
  George's former wife
Gover, Elizabeth, one of
  Samuel's two eldest Daus.
Janney, Sarah, Niece
Chandlee, Mahlon, Gr-nephew,
  child of George & Deborah
Gover, Mary, one of Samuel's
  eldest Daus.
Janney, Cosmelia, Cousin
Chandlee, Hannah, Gr-niece,
  child of George & Deborah
Talbott, Elizabeth,
  dau. of Joseph
Elliott, Elizabeth, Niece
Janney, Lightfoot, Nephew

Elliott, Elizabeth's twin Daus.,
  Gr-niece
Janney, Richard, Nephew,
  son fo Abel
Janney, Mahlon, Nephew,
  son of Abel
Moore, James, Exor.
Moore, Asa, Exor.
Williams, John, Exor.
Braden, Robert, Wit.
Phillips, Thomas, Wit.
Dorsey, Edward, Wit.
Gover, Samuel, Wit.
Lacey, Joseph, Wit.
Carr, Elizabeth, K:141, 1812
Kline, Margaret, Sister
Campbell, Jane, Sister
Carr, James, Brother
Carr, Thomas, Brother
Carr, Samuel, Brother
Carr, Eliza Ann, Niece
Hall, Mary, Sister
Carr, Mary Ann, Niece
McCormick, John, Exor.
Waid (Wade), Robert, Wit.
Mines, John, Wit.
Poston, Wilse, K:142, 1812
Poston, Elizabeth, Dau., < age
Furr, Minor, Exor.
Poston, Leonard, Son, < age
Lewis, Lewis, Wit.
Clarke, Richard, Wit.
Miley, Chrisley, Wit.
Dulin, William, K:153, n.d./1812
Dulin, John, Brother
Smith, George, Gr-Son
Wren, Mary, Gr-Dau.
Dulin, Mary, Wife
Smith, Hannah, Dau.
Wren, Sanford
Dulin, Edward, Son
Wren, William, Gr-Son
Minor, William, Wit.
Weagley, George, Wit.
Summers, William A., Wit.
Battson, James, K:155, 1811/12
Tolles, Marey, Sister
Dennis, Margaret, child of
  Thomas A. Dennis
West, Elenor, Sister

—, Elizabeth's children, Sister
Dennis, Thomas A.
Battson, William, Brother
Downs, Walter, bound to
  Battson
Battson, James, Nephew, born
  after 22 Nov 1811
Dennis, Matilda, child of
  Thomas A. Dennis
Battson, Elizabeth, Niece,
  child of Thomas
Downs, Nancy, bound to
  Battson
Battson, Mehaley, Niece,
  child of Thomas
Downs, Henry, Nephew,
  son of Nancy
Battson, Nancy, Niece,
  child of Thomas
Dennis, Lettes
Battson, Thomas, Brother
Downs, William, bound to
  Battson
Battson, Polly, Niece, James
  sister
Downs, Nancy, Sister
Battson, James, Nephew,
  son of John
Dennis, James Battson,
  child of Thomas A. Dennis
Battson, Hannah, Wife
Boyde, Elizabeth
Battson, John, Brother
Weatherley, Jane, Wit.
Dennis, William, Wit.
Powell, Burr, Wit.
Cochran, Richard, Wit.
McVeigh, Jesse, Exor.
Carter, James, K:157, 1812
Carter, Hannah, Wife
Yates, Sarah, Dau.
Carter, Dempey, Son
Newton, Ruth, Dau.
Carter, John, Son
Carter, Henry, Son
Carter, Asa, Son
Carter, Mahlon, Son
Carter, Edon, Son
Carter, James, Son
Humphrey, Abner, Wit.

Barton, Thomas, Wit.
Cowgill, Isaac, Wit.
Smith, Seth, Wit.
Yeaca, Martin, K:174, 1808/12
Davis, Catharine, Dau.
Yeaca, Mary, Dau.
Yeaca, Peter, Son
Yeaca, Martin, Son
Yeaca, Jacob, Son
Yeaca, Simon, Son
Yeaca, Elizabeth, Dau.
Yeaca, Catharine, Wife
Hamilton, John, Wit.
Stouseberger, John, Wit.
Spring, Andrew, Wit.
McCarty, Thadues, K:190, 1812
Russell, Sarah C., Dau.
McCarty, Dennis, Son
McCarty, Sarah Elizabeth, Wife
McCarty, William R., Son
McCarty, George Washington,
  Son
McCarty, Mary, Dau.
McCarty, Mahala, Gr-Dau.,
  dau. of Mary
Powell, Burr, Wit.
Rogers, Hugh, Wit.
Simpson, Henson, Wit.
Lodge, Jozabed, K:195, 1801/08
Grubb, three children of Hester
  & Ebenezer, Gr-children
Grubb, Ebenezer, Son-in-law
Grubb, Hester, Dau., dec'd.
White, Susanna, Dau.
Lodge, Abel, Son
Lodge, Caterene, Wife
Lodge, Jonathan, Son
Lodge, Jozabed, Son
Lodge, William, Son
Lodge, Nancy, Dau.
Lodge, Jacob, Son
Bradfield, Jonathan, Exor.
Sanford, Jeremiah, Wit.
Mercer, Henry, Wit.
Bradfield, Jonathan Jr., Wit.
Housley (Owsley), Points, K:205, 1811/13
Housley (Owsley), Ann, Wife
Housley (Owsley), Moses, Son
Housley (Owsley), Ann, Dau.

Rees, Elizabeth, Dau.
Rees, Linney, Dau.
Gallaher, Feabey, Dau.
Owsley (Housley), Ann, Dau.
Owsley (Housley), Moses, Son
Owsley (Housley), Ann, Wife
Love, Augustine, Wit.
Mount, Ezekiel, Wit.
Lynn, Fielding, Wit.
Mason, Abraham Barnes Thomson, K:207, 1812/13
Mason, Mary Barnes, Dau., <20
Mason, Sarah Ann, Dau., < 20
Mason, Abraham Barnes Thomson, Youngest Son
Mason, John Hough, Son
Mason, Richard Barnes, Son
Mason, Thomson, Oldest Son
Mason, Armistead T., Wit.
Luckett, Samuel, Wit.
Watson, Thomas, Wit.
Piggott, John, K:229, 1810/13
Piggott, Ebenezer, Son
Piggott, William, Son
Piggott, Nathan, Son
Piggott, Phebe, Wife
Piggott, John, Son
Taylor, Mahlon, Wit.
Wynn, Jesse, Wit.
Losh, Elizabeth, K:235, 1813
Speck, Catherine
Speck, Margaret
Losh, Daniel, Husband, dec'd.
Payne, John, Wit.
Hough, Mary, Wit.
Drish, Susanna, Wit.
Crupper, Richard, K:237, 1812/13
Crupper, William, Son
Crupper, Elisha, Son
Crupper, Leven, Son
Crupper, Ann, Dau.
Crupper, John, Son
Crupper, Richard, Son
Crupper, Benjamin, Gr-child, child of Richard
Crupper, John, Gr-child, child of Richard
Crupper, Serepta, Gr-child, child of Richard
Crupper, Thomas, Son
Crupper, Kitty, Gr-child, dau. of Thomas
Cameron, Mary, Dau.
Crupper, —, Wife
Toll, Emily, Dau.
Lynn, Elizabeth, Dau.
Gibson, David, Exor.
Luckett, Leven, Wit.
McCarty, William R., Wit.
Simpson, Henson, Wit.
Purdum, Benjamin, K:246, 1812/13
Purdum, Jeremiah, Son
Purdum, John, Son
Jeans, Lydia, Sister-in-law, former wife's sister
Jenners, Abiel, Wit.
Wood, Joseph, Wit.
Talbott, Joseph, Wit.
Williams, Rebecca, niece of John
Williams, Abner, Step-son, last wife's son
Williams, John, Step-son, last wife's son
Lambourn, Hannah, Step-Dau., last wife's Dau.
Bradock, Deborah, Sister-in-law, former wife's sister
Brown, William, K:256, 1813
Brown, Hannah, Wife
Brown, James, Son
Brown, Margaret, Dau.
Brown, Vincent, Son
Brown, Elizabeth, Dau.
Brown, Uriah, Son
Brown, William, Son
Brown, Mason, Son
McKnight, Charles, Step-son
Harrison, Alexander, Wit.
Thomas, Philip, Wit.
Hart, Thomas, Wit.
Russell, William, K:260, 1813
Russell, Edith, Wife
Russell, Henry, Son
Russell, Joseph, Son
Russell, Mary, Dau.
Russell, Aaron, Son
Russell, Rachel, Dau.
Russell, James, Son

Russell, Emla, Dau.
Russell, John, Son,
  not son of Edith
Russell, William, Son,
  not of this part of the country
Russell, Thomas, Son
Russell, Ann, Dau.
Russell, Mahlon, Son
Russell, Robert, Son
Clendenen, Ruth, Dau.
Russell, Samuel, Son
Harvy, Elizabeth, Dau.
Love, Thomas, Wit.
Purcel, Joseph, Wit.
Emry, Adam, K:295, 1813
Vinsel, George, Exor.
Emry, Mary, Wife
Emry, Elizabeth, Dau.
Tribbey, Asahel, Wit.
Arnold, Jacob, Wit.
Frey, Henry Joseph, Wit.
Rinker, Edward, K:297, 1808/13
Rinker, our children
Rinker, my 1st set of children
Rinker, Sarah, Wife
Rinker, —, her 1st set of
  children
Binns, Charles, Wit.
Campbell, John, Wit.
Brown, Richard, K:302, 1811/13
Brown, Richard, Son, <21
Brown, Joseph, Son
Brown, William, Son
Brown, Samuel, Son, <21
Brown, Sarah, Dau.
Brown, Betsy, Dau.
Brown, Hannah, Dau.
Brown, Sarah, Wife
Braden, Robert, Exor.
Murry, John, Wit.
Dodd, William, Wit.
Tavender (Tavenner), Richard,
  Wit.
Derry, Peter, K:325, 1813
Smith, John, Gr-Son, son of
  Catherine Kindle, dec'd.
Smith, George, Gr-Son, son of
  Catherine Kindle, dec'd.
Smith, William, Gr-Son, son of
  Catherine Kindle, dec'd.

Kindle, Catherine, Dau., dec'd.
Kindle, Sarah, Gr-Dau.,
  child of Catherine
Rymer, Elizabeth, Dau., if living
Rymer, John, Gr-Son,
  son of Elizabeth
Rymer, Jacob, Gr-Son,
  son of Elizabeth
Derry, Jacob, Son
Kindle, Adam, Gr-Son,
  son of Catherine
Wiatt, Mary Elizabeth, Dau.,
  w/o Jacob
Derry, Andrew, Son
Smitly, Mathias, Wit.
Potterfield, Jacob, Wit.
McCabe, George, Wit.
Binns, John Alexander, K:343, 1813
Harding, Betsey, Niece
Harding, Susannah, Niece
Harding, Nancy, Niece
Harding, Caty, Niece
Harding, Nancy, Sister
Binns, Charles, Brother
Binns, Simon A., Brother
Binns, Mary Ann, Niece,
  dau. of Simon A.
Binns, Betsey, Niece, one of
  eldest daus. of Thomas N.
Binns, Luisa, Niece, one of
  eldest daus. of Thomas N.
Binns, Elizabeth, Niece,
  dau. of Charles
Binns, Nancy, Niece,
  dau. of Charles
Binns, Thomas Nelson, Brother
Durham, Nancy, Niece
Binns, Dewanner, Wife
Durham, Caty, Sister
Curtis, Levi, Wit.
Robertson, John, Wit.
Robertson, Elizabeth, Wit.
Sands, Jacob, Wit.
Sands, Elizabeth, Wit.
Sands, Stephen, Wit.
Stocks, William, Wit.
Mitinger, Rynart, K:346, 1813
Mitinger, Jacob, Brother
Vanpelt, Richard, Exor.

Adams, Samuel, Wit.
Elliss, Thomas, Wit.
Kelly, Edward, Wit.
Palmer, Thomas, K:347, 1812/13
Blunt, Susan, Dau.
Low, Thomas, Gr-Son
Chichester, Daniel McCarty, Exor.
Low, John, Gr-Son
Palmer, William, Son
Payne, Edmond, Wit.
Chichester, George, Wit.
Mills, John, Wit.
Gregg, John, K:348, 1813
Gregg, Thomas, Son
Gregg, John, Son
Gregg, Hannah, Dau.
Ewers, Martha, Dau.
Ewers, Gregg, Gr-Son, < age
Ewers, Eden, Gr-Son, < age
Ewers, Hannah, Gr-Dau., < age
Grigsby, Lewis, Wit.
Pancoast, John, Wit.
Beall, David T., Wit.
Gregg, Stephen, Wit.
Leath, William, K:351, 1812/13
Carter, Edward, Exor.
Leath, Elizabeth Elenor, Dau.
Leath, Theodorick, Son, < age
Leath, Jemimah, Dau.
Leath, Joannah, Dau.
Leath, Polly, Dau.
Leath, Peggy, Dau.
Leath, James, Son, < age
Leath, William, Son, < age
Leath, Elenor, Wife
Leath, Patsey, Dau.
Beveridge, Noble, Wit.
Skinner, Samuel, Wit.
Johnston, James, Wit.
Noland, Pierce, Wit.
Ridenbaugh, Margaret, K:359, 1813/14
Ridenbaugh, Margaret, Dau.
Ridenbaugh, Mary, Dau.
Ridenbaugh, George, Son, <16
Ridenbaugh, Mahala, Dau.
Roofe, John, Son
Ridenbaugh, Sarah, Dau.
Roofe, Elizabeth, Dau.
Ridenbaugh, Peter, Husband, dec'd.
Waltman, Jacob Jr., Wit.
Beaver, Bazil, Wit.
McCabe, George, Wit.
Douglas, Catherine, K:371, 1800/14
Douglas, Hugh, Husband
Nasmith, Margaret, Aunt, sister of Robert
Nasmith, Robert, Father, dec'd.
Binns, C. Jr., Wit.
Douglas, Patrick H., Wit.
Sullivan, Murtho, K:378, 1813/14
Sullivan, Samuel, Son
Sullivan, William, Son
Sullivan, Elizabeth, Wife
Sullivan, John Lewis, Son
Larowe, Isaac, Exor.
Talbott, Joseph, Wit.
Cavins, John, Wit.
McCabe, John H., Wit.
Hammat, George, K:383, 1814
Hammat, Sarah, Wife
Thomas, Nancy, Dau.
Hammat, Samuel, Son
Hammat, John, Son
Hammat, William, Son
Hammat, Polly, Dau.
Hammat, George, Son
Hammat, Giles, Son
Hammat, James, Son
Hammat, Edward, Son
Henderson, Richard H., Wit.
Edwards, Samuel M., Wit.
Hammerly, John, Wit.
Martin, William, K:428, 1812/14
Martin, James, Son
Martin, William, Son
Martin, John, Son
Martin, Edward, Son
Martin, Robert, Son
Martin, Andrew, Son
Martin, Elizabeth, Dau.
Martin, Mary, Dau.
Garrett, Sarah, Gr-Dau.
Bronaugh, William, Wit.
Kile, Nicholas, Wit.

Index to Loudoun County Wills, 1757 - 1850 83

Sword, John, K:436, 1814
Henning, Persiller, Sister,
  w/o Thomas
Sword, Urriah, Brother
Sword, John, Nephew,
  son of Urriah & Ann
Wheatly, Margaret, Sister
Henning, Ignatious, Nephew,
  son of Persiller, <21
Shermindine, Ann, Sister,
  w/o James
Lowe, Samuel P., Exor.
Matthias, John, Wit.
Wilson, John T., Wit.
Currlane, Robert, Wit.
Hyde, Philip, K:438, 1814
Mount, John, Friend
Marks, John, Friend
Lloyd, George E., Exor.
Woofter, Betsey, Dau.
Marks, George, Exor.
Plaster, Susanna, Wit.
Plaster, Jane, Wit.
Plaster, James, Wit.
Simpson, Mary, K:439, 1814
Jones, John, Gr-Son
Simpson, John, Son
Jones, William, Gr-Son
Simpson, Hendley, Son
Jones, John, Son-in-law
Jones, Elizabeth, Dau.
Simpson, William, Son, dec'd.
Skilman, Violinda, Dau.
Simpson, Henson, Gr-Son,
  eldest son of Henson
Simpson, Henson, Son
Simpson, Samuel,
  Youngest Son
Simpson, French, Son
Simpson, James, Son
Simpson, John, Husband,
  dec'd.
Davis, Howel, Wit.
Coe, Edward M, Wit.
Coe, Menan, Wit.
Coe, Edward, Wit.
Perfect, Robert, L:7, 1814
Newton, Nancy, Dau.
McGirth, Elizabeth, Dau.
Perfect, Harriett, Dau.

Giles, Sally, Dau.
Perfect, Jane, Dau.
Perfect, William, Son
Perfect, Robert, Son
Perfect, Jane, Wife
Perfect, John, Son
Cordell, Presley, Wit.
Saunders, Evritt, Wit.
Fadeley, Jacob, Wit.
Potter, Ebenezer, L:8, 1807/14
Potter, John, Brother
Potter, —, Unborn child
Potter, Mary, Dau.
Potter, Elizabeth, Wife
Potter, Lucy, Dau.
Mines, John, Wit.
McCormick, John, Wit.
Smith, Sarah, L:9, 1808/13
Tyler, Letty, Dau.
Smith, Weedon, Son
Lacey, Israel, Exor., of Goshen
Smith, George, Son
Gorham, Priscilla, Dau.
George, Jesse, Dau.
Boggess, Susannah, Dau.
Cavan, James Jr., L:11, 1809/14
Kirk, Merab, mother of his
  children
Kirk, Malcom, Son
Kirk, Elizabeth, Dau.
Littlejohn, John, Wit.
Swann, Thomas, Wit.
McIntyre, Patrick, Wit.
Lacey, Matilda, L:11, 1809/14
Lacey, Joseph, Husband, dec'd.
Lacey, Euphama, Dau.
Lacey, Naomi, Dau.
Lacey, Ruth, Dau.
Lacey, Hulda, Dau.
Lacey, Tacey, Dau.
Tyler, John, Wit.
Ish, Jacob, Wit.
Smith, Charles, Wit.
Jordan, Ann, L:18, 1814
Minear, Jamima, Dau.
Hiler, Jane, Dau.
Jordan, Caty, Dau.
Jordan, William, Son
Davis, Ann, Dau.
Hoskinson, Andrew J., Wit.

French, Mason, Wit.
Lafaver, William, Wit.
Violet, John, L:19, 1814
　Violett, Jemima, Wife
　Violett, James, Son
　Violett, John of Ohio, Son
　Violett, Sampson, Son
　Violett, Elijah, Son
　Violett, Benjamin, Son, dec'd.
　Violett, John, Gr-Son,
　　son of Benjamin
　Violett, Juliet, Gr-Dau.,
　　dau. of Benjamin
　Turner, Thomas, Gr-Son,
　　son of Sally
　Turner, James, Gr-Son,
　　son of Sally
　Turner, Sally, Dau., second
　　marriage to Fouch
　Leith, Patty, Gr-Dau.
　Fouch, —, Gr-Son,
　　son of dau. Sally
　Martin, Betsey, Dau.
　Finety, Jemimah, Dau.
　Leith, James, Gr-Son
　Carr, Joseph, Wit.
　Gibbs, James L., Wit.
　Reid, Alfred, Wit.
　Bailey, Sydner, Wit.
Boggess, Samuel, L:24, 1809/14
　Boggess, Ann, Mother
　Boggess, Henley, Brother
　Taylor, Agnes, Wit.
　Taylor, Alice T., Wit.
　Reid, Alfred, Wit.
Hamilton, Elizabeth, L:25, 1811/14
　Hamilton, Ann B., Dau.
　Bennett, Charles, Father
　Hamilton, Jane, Dau.
　Hamilton, Charles, Son
　Schooley, John Jr., Wit.
　Bennett, Elizabeth, Wit.
Dulin, Mary, L:26, 1814
　Dulin, Edward, Son
　Smith, Hannah, Dau.
　Dulin, Rebecka
　Smith, Sarah Ann
　Wren, Mary, Gr-Dau.
　Smith, George, Gr-Son

　Dulin, Mary Ann, Gr-Dau.
　Smith, Mary, Gr-Dau.
　Wren, William, Gr-Son
　Saunders, Aaron, Wit.
　Frank, Samuel, Wit.
Green, Cloe, L:34, 1811/14
　Woodey, Elizabeth, Dau.
　Jacobs, Matilda, Gr-Dau.,
　　dau. of Sally
　Green, William, Gr-Son, son of
　　dau. Elizabeth Woodey
　Jacobs, Thomas, Exor.
　Jacobs, Sally, Dau.
　Littlejohn, John, Wit.
　Littlejohn, John Jr., Wit.
Schooley, John, L:46, 1814/15
　Hewes, Sarah, Dau.
　Schooley, Ruben, Son
　Schooley, William, Son
　Schooley, Elisha, Son
　Schooley, Mary, Wife
　Moore, James, Wit.
　Bond, Joseph, Wit.
　Griffith, Richard, Wit.
Jones, William, L:47, 1812/15
　Long, Jane, Sister
　Reynolds, Henry, adopted
　　Nephew
　Rhodes, Randolph, Exor.
　Reynolds, Elizabeth, Exor.
　Firth, George, Wit.
　Wilson, Henry, Wit.
　Hicks, Kimble, Wit.
Violett, Jamimah, L:49, 1814/15
　Patterson, Eleanor, w/o Elijah
　Violett, Jamimah, Dau.
　Violett, John, Husband, dec'd.
　Martin, Elizabeth, Dau.
　Leith, Betsey, Gr-Dau.
　Martin, Sarah, Gr-Dau.
　Silcott, William, Wit.
　Seaton, Hiram, Wit.
　Glascock, Enoch, Wit.
　Ramey, Sanford, Admr. w.w.a.
Stephens, Thomas Darnal, L:52, 1811/14
　Campbell, Elizabeth, Mother-in-
　　law, wife's mother
　Stephens, Leven, Son
　Braden, Elizabeth, Dau.

Braden, Mary D., Dau.
Braden, Mary Eleanor, Gr-Dau.
Braden, Robert, Exor.
Stephens, Mary Eleanor, Gr-Dau.
Stephens, Thomas, Son
Stephens, John B., Son
Braden, Joseph, Wit.
McDaniel, James, Wit.
McDaniel, Archibald, Wit.
Suddith, William, L:65, 1811/15
Atwell, Peggy Thomson, Dau.
Fox, Malinda, Gr-Dau.,
   dau. of Grace
Atwell, Thompson, Gr-Son
Atwell, Jesse, Son-in-law
Green, Elizabeth, companion
Geen (Gheen), Narcissa, Dau.
Atwell, William, Gr-Son
Fox, Grace Minton, Dau.
Vansickler, Philip, Exor.
Brown, John, Wit.
Brown, Nathan, Wit.
Combs, Israel, Wit.
Nichols, Margery, L:72, 1806/15
Tate, Edith, w/o Levi, Gr-Dau.
Piggott, Mary, Gr-Dau.
Pancoast, Joshua, Gr-Son
Gregg, Lydia, Gr-Dau.
Hoge, Jesse, Gr-Son
Hatcher, Rebecca, Dau.
Hoge, Lydia, Dau.
Hatcher, Catherine, Dau.
Hatcher, Margery, Gr-Dau.,
   only daugther of Rebecca
Hoge, Margary, Gr-Dau.
Hatcher, Isaac, Gr-Son
Hoge, Joshua, Son-in-law
Hoge, William, Gr-Son
Hoge, Joshua, Gr-Son
Hatcher, Samuel, Gr-Son
Hatcher, Joseph, Gr-Son
Hatcher, Thomas, Gr-Son
Hatcher, Isaac, Gr-Son
Hatcher, James, Gr-Son
Hatcher, Edith, Gr-Dau.
Hoge, Mary, Dau.
Nickols, Isaac, Eldest Son
Nickols, Samuel, Son

Nickols, Margary, Gr-Dau.,
   w/o Jacob
Nickols, Isaac, Gr-Son
Nickols, Samuel, Gr-Son
Nickols, William, Gr-Son
Nickols, Rebecca, Gr-Dau.
Pancoast, John, Gr-Son
Young, Elizabeth, Gr-Dau.
Spencer, Sarah, Gr-Dau.
Gibson, Jonathan, Wit.
Young, John, Wit.
Hatcher, Thomas, Wit.
Horseman, William, L:74, 1814/15
Neale, Signey, Dau.
Carter, Mima, Dau.
Horseman, George, Gr-Son,
   son of Stephen
Horseman, William, Son
Horseman, Elender, Wife
Horseman, Stephen, Son
Horseman, Joseph, Son
Horseman, Eaisas, Son
Horseman, James, Son
Horseman, Esaias, Gr-Son,
   son of Stephen
Horseman, Sally, Gr-Dau.,
   dau. of Stephen
Horseman, Elizabeth, Gr-Dau.,
   dau. of Stephen
Horseman, Julia, Gr-Dau.,
   dau. of Stephen
Horseman, Kitty, Gr-Dau.,
   dau. of Stephen
Veale, Linny, Dau.
Latimer, Jacob, Wit.
Harris, John A., Wit.
Summers, Henry, Wit.
Turley, Lawson, Wit.
Wilcoxan, Levi, Wit.
Kline, Mary, L:104, 1812/15
Kline, Lewis, Son
Bruner (Brooner), Margaret,
   Eldest Dau.
Dorsey, Mary, Dau.
Dorsey, Edward, Son-in-law
Kline, John, Son
Williams, J., Wit.
Wilkinson, Thomas, Wit.
Morgan, J., Wit.

Hawley, John, L:105, 1815
  Hawley, Mary, Dau.
  Davis, Mary, Gr-Dau.
  Hawley, Barton, Son
  Davis, Thomas, Gr-Son
  McKim, James, Exor.
  Latham, Robert, Exor.
  Hutchison, Lewis, Wit.
  James, William, Wit.
  Ambler, Lewis, Wit.
  Lyne, Sanford, Wit.
Lacey, Thomas, L:108, 1815
  Lacey, Sarah, Wife
  Lacey, Margarett, Step-Mother
  Lacey, Thomas, Nephew,
    son of William
  Lacey, William, Brother
  Braden, Robert, Exor.
  Williams, John, Exor.
  Moore, James, Wit.
  Dorsey, Edward, Wit.
  Schooley, Aaron, Wit.
Coe, Edward, L:116, 1814/15
  Coe, Menan, Son
  Coe, Edward Milstead, Son
  Coe, John Wilson, Son
  Coe, David Jameson, Son
  Coe, Catherine, Dau.,
    w/o William
  Coe, Robert, Son
  Smith, Winifred, Gr-mother of
    his Gr-Daus.
  Smith, Emala, Gr-Dau., <21
  Smith, Ann, Gr-Dau., <21
  Smith, Charles
  Blincoe, Sampson, Wit.
  Curtis, Thomas, Wit.
  Gulick, Moses, Wit.
  Daniel, Joseph, Wit.
  Rogers, Hamilton, Wit.
  White, Levi, Wit.
  Curtis, Samuel, Wit. [1c]
  Fouch, Thompson, Wit. [1c]
  Carter, G., Wit. [2c]
  Jameson, John, Wit. [2c]
Janney, Sarah, L:127, 1814/15
  Lambag, Rachel
  Phillips, Thomas, Exor.
  Talbott, Ann, Sister, dec'd.
  Ballenger, Casandria, Sister

  Plummer, Ursla, Sister
  Poultney, Susannah, Sister,
    dec'd.
  Talbott, Elizabeth, Niece,
    dau. of Ann
  Harven, Ann
  Williams, John, Exor.
  Vietch, Jemimah
  Hanes, Rachel, Sister
  Williams, Lydia, Friend
  Hough, Elizabeth, dau. of niece
    Sarah Gover
  Gover, Abinah, dau. of Samuel
  Janney, Sarah, late husband's
    niece
  Head, Mary, dau. of niece Sarah
    Gover
  Yates, Sarah
  Janney, Jacob, son of niece
    Sarah Gover
  Janney, Moses, son of niece
    Sarah Gover
  Gover, Rachel, dau. of Samuel
  Gover, Hannah, dau. of Samuel
  Gover, Ann, dau. of Samuel
  Gover, Samuel, son of Samuel
  Gover, Jesse, son of Samuel
  Gover, Robert, son of Samuel
  Gover, Anthony, son of Samuel
  Gover, Samuel
  Gover, Jesse, son of Sarah,
  Gover, Sarah, Niece
  McCabe, John H., Wit.
  Mendenhall, Jacob, Wit.
  Thomas, Joseph P., Wit.
Hough, William, L:129, 1813/15
  Stone, Sarah, Dau., w/o Daniel
  Thompson, Sarah Eleanor,
    Gr-Dau., only dau. of Israel
    and Nancy, <18
  Schooley, Elizabeth, Dau.,
    w/o John
  Thompson, Nancy, Dau., dec'd.
  Schooley, John, Son-in-law
  Stone, Daniel, Son-in-law
  Hough, Peyton, Gr-Son,
    son of Joseph
  Hough, Samuel, Son
  Hough, Thomas, Son
  Hough, William, Son

Hough, Amasa, unmarried Son
Hough, John, Son
Hough, Eleanor, Wife
Hough, Washington, Gr-Son,
    son of Joseph
Hough, Joseph, Son, dec'd.
Hough, Benjamin, Son
Hough, Eleanor, Dau.
Hough, Nancy, Gr-Dau.,
    dau of Joseph
Moore, Asa, Wit.
Hough, Samuel, Wit.
James, Levi, Wit.
Steer, Joseph, Wit.
Williams, John, Wit.
White, Daniel, L:138, 1815
White, Ann, Wife
Tavender, Ann, Dau.
White, Levi, Son
White, Elizabeth, Dau.
White, William, Son
Kerrick, Stephen, Wit.
Hall, Josiah, Wit.
White, Benjamin, Wit.
Tillett, Giles, L:141, 1815
Tillett, Effey, Dau.
Davis, Mary, Dau.
Tillett, Nancy, Dau.
Tillett, Margarett, Dau.
Tillett, Mahala, Dau.
Tillett, Sarah, Dau.
Tillett, Samuel, Son
Tillett, Giles, Son, <21
Tillett, Honour, Wife
Murrey, Samuel, Wit.
Harris, Isaac, Wit.
Janney, Amos, L:143, 1815
Janney, Grace, Wife
Janney, John, Son
Janney, Amos, Son
Simpson, Henson, L:148, 1815
Simpson, —, five children
Simpson, —, Wife
Simpson, James, Brother
McCarty, Daniel, Wit.
McCarty, William, Wit.
Chinn, Thomas Jr., Wit.
Richards, Richard, L:149, 1803/15
Barton, Rachel, Dau.,
    w/o Joseph

Barton, Joseph, Son-in-law
Richards, Samuel, Son
Richards, Hannah, Dau.
Richards, Pheby, Dau.
Richards, Ann, Dau.
Richards, Isaac, Son
Richards, John, Son
Richards, William, Son
Richards, Sarah, Dau.
Richards, Mary, Wife
Richards, Elizabeth, Dau.
Arden, Aaron, Wit.
Grayson, Benjamin, Wit.
Grayson, Nancy, Wit.
Mudd, John, L:155, 1810/15
Doudle, Trecey, Sister-in-law
Mudd, Walter, Brother
Mudd, John, Nephew, son of
    Walter
Mudd, Patty, Wife
Gregg, Capt. Thomas, Exor.
Janney, Abijah, Wit.
Cummings, John, Wit.
Megeath, Gabriel, Wit.
Miller, Peter Sr., L:158, 1815
Delaplane, Catharine, Dau.
Miller, Jesse, Son
Miller, Adam, Son
Miller, Daniel, Son
Miller, Aaron, Son
Miller, William
Miller, Peggy, Gr-Dau.,
    dau. of William
Miller, Mary, girl we raised
Miller, Jacob, Son
Miller, Moses, Son
Miller, John, Son
Miller, Peter, Son
Miller, Catharine, Wife
Shoemaker, Peggy, Dau.
Hatcher, Hannah, Dau.
Frye, Philip, Wit.
Fry, John, Wit.
Janney, John, Wit.
Cooper, Michael, L:169, 1813/15
Shoemaker, Charlotta, Dau.
Cooper, Peter, Son
Cooper, Michael, Son
Cooper, John, Son
Cooper, Daniel, Son

Cooper, Frederick, Son
Cooper, Philip, Son
Cooper, Jacob, Son
Cooper, George, Son
Cooper, Catharine, Wife
Huff (Hough), George, Wit.
Compher, Peter, Wit.
Cooper, John, Wit.
Thatcher, Stephen, L:186, 1815
Thatcher, Alice, Wife
Ferguson, Urias
Cunnard, Adah, Dau.
Cunnard, Edward Jr., Exor.
Cunnard, Luther Calvin, Gr-Son
Chamblin, John, Exor.
Chamblin, Mary, Dau.
Elliott, Henson, Wit.
Thomas, Philip, Wit.
Thatcher, Calvin, Surety for Exors
Humphries, Susannah, L:199, 1814/15
Deliforce, Catharine
Hutchison, Hannah, Dau.
Humphries, Samuel, Son
Cleveland, Johnson, Wit.
Jones, Henry, Wit.
Jones, Ann, Wit.
Hutchison, Nathan, Admr. w.w.a.
Coleman, James Jr., L:200, 1815
Coleman, Johnson James, Son
Coleman, James Richard, Son
Coleman, Sarah, Dau.
Cleveland, Johnston, Exor.
Coleman, Ann, Dau.
Coleman, Hannah, Wife
Coleman, John James, Son, <21
Coleman, Frances, Dau.
Coleman, John, Brother
Shiveley, George, Wit.
Shiveley, Rebeccah, Wit.
Marshall, William, Wit.
Coleman, Ann M., Wit.
Hobbs, Richard, L:212, 1815
Daniel, William, Brother-in-law
Moore, Asa, Wit.
Moore, James, Wit.
McCabe, John H., Wit.

Cooke, Stephen, L:216, 1815
Cooke, H. S., Son
Dawson, Matilda, Niece
Doubleday, Sally
Cooke, John E., Son
Cooke, John R., Son
Cooke, Catharine, Wife
Cooke, Edward E., Son
Blincoe, Sampson, Wit.
Weedon, James, Wit.
Beale, Charles, Wit.
Weldon, W. S., Wit.
Osburne, Landon, L:222, 1815
Jones, Nancy, alias Bond
Jackson, Farendo Osburne, Eldest Dau. of Ellen Jackson, an iligetimate child
Osburne, Joshua, Brother
Osburne, Craven, Brother
Osburne, Turner, Brother
Osburne, Herod, Brother
Osburne, Heaton, Brother
Osburne, Norvel, Brother
Leslie, Thomas, Brother-in-law
Worthington, Elizabeth, Sister
Taylor, Stacy, Wit.
Young, Samuel W., Wit.
Heaton, Jonathan, Wit.
Reese, Edward, L:230, 1815
Reese, Joseph, Son
Reese, Sarah, Wife
Bradfield, Benjamin, Exor.
Brooke, Benjamin, Wit.
Bradfield, James, Wit.
Fitch, James, Wit.
Lacey, Eyrphemia, L:244, 1815
Lacey, Tacey, Sister
Tyler, John, Wit.
Lewis, William, Wit.
Ish, William K., Wit.
Riticor, Elijah, Wit.
Trayhorn, James, L:247, 1815
Trayhorn, Thomas, Son
Trayhorn, Asa, Son
Trayhorn, Isaac, Son
Trayhorn, Jesse, Son
Trayhorn, James, Son
Trayhorn, Samuel, Son
Trayhorn, Enos, Son
Trayhorn, Israel, Son

Janney, Abel, Exor.
Nichols, Isaac, Exor.
Janney, Jonas, Wit.
Moore, Hannah, Wit.
Smith, Seth, Wit.
Myres, Mary, L:249, 1811/15
Myres, Elijah, Son
Pairpoint, Elizabeth, Gr-Dau.
Pairpoint, Ann, Gr-Dau.
Pairpoint, Esther, Dau.
Moore, James, Wit.
Pierpoint, Obed, Wit.
Douglas, Hugh, L:257, 1812/15
Binns, Charles, Brother-in-law
Douglass, Margaret, Sister
Douglass, Charles, Son, <21
Douglass, Lewis Fordice, Son, <21
Douglass, Louisa Anne, Dau., <21
Douglass, Archibald Nasmith, Son, <21
Mason, Armistead T., Exor.
McCabe, John H., Wit.
Talbott, Joseph, Wit.
Hamilton, John, Wit.
Clapham, Samuel, Wit.
Walters, George, L:259, 1815
Walters, Dinah, Wife
Walters, Mahlon, Son
Walters, James, Son
Nixon, Nancy, Dau.
Nichols, Lydia, Dau., dec'd.
Nichols, Betsy, Gr-Dau., dau. of Lydia
Nichols, Thomas, Gr-Son, son of Lydia
Brown, Judith, Dau.
Brown, Sarah, Dau.
Walters, Isaac, Son
Taylor, Bernard, Exor.
Moore, James, Wit.
Moore, James Jr., Wit.
Rhorbaugh, Adam, L:284, 1812/15
Rhorbaugh, Hannah, Wife
Rhorbaugh, George, Son
—, Clara Polly, Gr-Dau., dau. of Ann Catherine

—, Margaret, Gr-Dau., dau. of Ann Catherine
Rhorbaugh, Ann Catharine, Dau.
—, Elizabeth, Gr-Dau., dau. of Ann Catherine
Waltman, Jacob, Exor.
Canby, John H., Wit.
Kern, Jacob, Wit.
Mann, John, Wit.
German Script Name, Wit.
Burson, James, L:286, 1814/15
Burson, Ruth, Dau.
Burson, Lydia, Dau.
Burson, Laban, Gr-Son
Burson, Aaron, Son
Burson, Isaiah, Son
Burson, John, Son
Burson, Joseph, Son
Burson, Rebecca, Dau.
Burson, Anne, Dau.
Burson, Sarah, Dau.
Burson, Susannah, Dau.
Smith, Samuel, Exor.
Smith, Seth, Wit.
Burson, Jonathan, Wit.
Burson, Moses, Wit.
Race, Job, L:288, 1815
Race, Elizabeth, Wife
Race, my children
Adams, Samuel, Wit.
Lewis, James, Wit.
Lewis, Charles, Wit.
Patterson, Flemon Wilson, L:289, 1815
Hixon, Flemon, son of Timothy
Hixon, Margaret, Admr.
Morgan, John
Rogers, Flemon, son of James, in Ky.
Carnahan, George
Templer, John, son of William
Williams, John, Exor.
Phillips, Thomas, Exor.
Neale, W. S., Wit.
Potts, Jonas, Wit.
Schooley, John, Wit.
Cain, Mary, L:290, 1815
Kirk, Elizabeth, Gr-Dau.
Kirk, Malcom, Gr-Son, <21

Kirk, Mareb, Dau.
Kirk, Charles, Son
Wilkinson, Macha, Dau.
Wilkinson, Israel, Exor.
Jones, Jane, Dau.
Fichter, John, Wit.
Kline, John Nicholas, Wit.
Gregg, Aaron, L:305, 1815
Gregg, Margaret, Wife
Gregg, William, Father
Gregg, George, Brother
Hixson, Samuel, Brother-in-law
Gregg, —, all my children
Neale, W. S., Wit.
Hobson, John, Wit.
Steer, Isaac, Wit.
Thomas, George, L:307, 1815/16
Thomas, Herod, alias Nichols, Son, illegitmate son of Charity Nichols
Baily, Sydnor, Exor.
Boggess, Henley, Exor.
Littleton, Thomas Jr., Wit.
Duty, Simpson, Wit.
Emary, Jacob, L:308, 1815
Potterfield, Elizabeth, Dau., w/o Jacob
Arnold, Mary, w/o Jacob, Dau.
Bumcrots, Christianna, Dau., w/o John
Shoemaker, Catharine, Dau., w/o Simon
Emary, Catharine, Wife
Emary, Elizabeth, Gr-Dau., <18
Axline, David, Exor.
Cooper, George, Wit.
Jackson, John, Wit.
Grubb, John, Wit.
Mason, Stephen T., L:324, 1815
Howard, Mary, Sister, dec'd.
Mason, Emily, Sister
Mason, Catharine, Sister
Mason, John T. Jr., Brother
Mason, John T., Uncle, dec'd.
Mason, Armistead T., Brother
Mason, —, Mother
Canby, John H., Wit.
Monroe, A. G., Wit.
Mason, Thomson, Wit.

Peyton, Francis, L:333, 1810/16
Luckett, Leven, Son-in-law
Luckett, Lettice, Dau.
Hale, Elizabeth, Dau.
Peyton, Townsend D., Son
Hale, William, Son-in-law
Peyton, Ann, Dau.
Waugh, Mary P., Gr-Dau.
Murphy, John, Gr-Son-in-law
White, Robert, L:334, 1813/16
Keys, Robert
Potts, Joseph
Cockeril, Joseph
White, Agnes, Wife
White, Agnes, Dau.
White, Josiah, Son
White, Thomas, Son
White, John, Son
White, Joseph, Son
White, James, Son
Gardner, Arthur, Wit.
Jacobs, Jacob, Wit.
Chilton, Susanna, M:1, 1815/16
Rose, John, Exor.
Mullikin, William, Son-in-law
Chilton, Sally, Dau., < age
Mullikin, Ann Eliza, Gr-Dau.
Mullikin, Nancy, Dau., of Prince Georges Co., Maryland
Chilton, Charles William, Son, < age
Chilton, Thomas, Husband, dec'd.
Chilton, Susannah Ann Rebeckah, Dau., < age
Chilton, Charles, Exor.
Clapham, Samuel, Exor.
Blincoe, Sampson, Wit.
Birkby, Thomas, Wit.
Rieley, Joshua, Wit.
Skinner, Samuel, M:18, 1815/16
Skinner, Gabriel, Son
Skinner, Elizabeth, Dau.
Skinner, Ann, Dau.
Skinner, Sarah, Dau.
Skinner, Mary, Dau.
Skinner, Francis, Dau.
Skinner, Robert, Son
Skinner, Samuel, Son
Skinner, Alexander, Son

Skinner, Rebecah, Dau.
Skinner, Jane, Dau.
Skinner, Phoeby, Wife
Beveridge, William, Wit.
Chinn, Thomas, Wit.
Chinn, Samuel, Wit.
Frey, Philip, Wit.
Beveridge, Noble, Wit.
Love, Thomas, M:19, 1816
Love, Sarah, Wife
Love, John Perpoint, Son
Love, Eli Alfred, Son
Love, Thomas, Son
Taylor, Bernard, Exor.
Smith, David, Exor.
Pierpoint, Eli, Exor.
Hirst, Jesse, Wit.
Love, Thomas B., Wit.
Pierpoint, Samuel, Wit.
Mead, William, M:31, 1806/u.d./16
Mead, —, Wife
Mead, William, Son
Mead, Ellen, Dau.
Mead, Elizabeth, Dau.
Mead, Ann, Dau.
Mead, Thomas, Son
Mead, Mary, Dau.
Mead, Joseph, Son
Mead, Hannah, Dau., cripple
Mead, Martha, Dau.
Rhodes, William, Wit.
Rhodes, Joseph, Wit.
Anderson, Robert, Wit.
Carr, Mary, M:42, 1815/16
Mocaboy, Emily
Wilson, Maria Susanna, Dau.
Wilson, Henry L., Son
Taylor, Bernard, Exor.
Boggess, Henly, Exor.
Taylor, Stacey, Wit.
Carr, John, Wit.
Batson, John, M:43, 1816
Culverhouse, Franky, Dau.
Batson, William, Exor.
Culverhouse, James, Exor.
Batson, Hannah, Dau.
Rawlings, Sally, Dau.
McConnekey, Nancy, Dau.
Batson, Polly, Dau.
Batson, Betsey, Dau.

Batson, Susanna, Dau.
Batson, James, Son
Batson, Elizabeth, Wife
Jones, Thornton, Wit.
Powell, Burr, Wit.
Rogers, Hugh, Wit.
Swart, William, Wit.
Pottenfield, Jacob, M:44, 1815/16
Pottenfield, Catharine, Dau.
Pottenfield, Elizabeth, Dau.
Pottenfield, Mary, Dau.
Pottenfield, Jacob, Son, <21
Pottenfield, Adam, Son
Pottenfield, Samuel, Son
Pottenfield, Henry, Brother
Pottenfield, Elizabeth, Wife
Pottenfield, Leah, Dau.
McCabe, George, Wit.
Derry, Jacob, Wit.
Kalb, John, Wit.
Chinn, Rawleigh, M:45, 1815/16
Wilson, Elizabeth, Dau.
Chinn, Elizabeth, Wife
Chinn, Samuel, Son
Beveridge, William
Beveridge, Lucy, Dau.
Johnson, Amos, Wit.
Cochran, Richard, Wit.
Denham, Oliver, Wit.
Hatcher, Thomas, Jr., M:45, 1816
Seaton, William <21, Nephew
Hatcher, Rebeckah, Mother
Hatcher, Thomas, Father
Hatcher, Joseph, Brother
Hatcher, Samuel, Brother
Tavenner, Joseph, Wit.
Nichols, Isaiah, Wit.
Hoge, James, Wit.
Walker, George W., Wit.
Wornall, William, M:47, 1798/1802/16
McVay, Margret, Gr-Dau.
Wornall, James, Son
Wornall, Mary, Wife
Davis, Ann, Dau.
Carter, Richard, Wit.
Carter, Jonathan, Wit.
Megeath, James, Wit.

Lacey, Israel, M:51, 1816
  Bell, Mrs. Elizabeth, lives with
    Dau.
  Briscoe, Matilda, Dau.
  Cooke, William, Exor.
  Lacey, Elias, Wit.
  Mason, Armistead T., Wit.
  Lacey, Misheck, Wit.
Beatty, Thomas of Frederick Co.,
** Md., M:55, 1810/15/16**
  Beatty, Thomas Jr., Son
  Parkinson, Rev. William,
    Son-in-law
  Ritchie, Thomas, Gr-Son
  Parkinson, Henrietta, Dau.,
    of N.Y.
  Ritchie, Catharine, Dau., dec'd.
  Ritchie, Mary (Polly), Gr-Dau.
  Ritchie, John, Son-in-law,
    husband of Catherine
  Beatty, Anna, Dau.-in-law,
    widow of Thomas Jr. [c]
  Beatty, Thomas Alexander
    Contee, Gr-Son, son of
    Thomas Jr. [c]
  Beatty, Eleanor Harrison, Gr-Dau.,
    dau. of Thomas, Jr. [c]
  Beatty, Jane Contee, Gr-Dau.,
    dau. of Thomas Jr. [c]
  Beatty, John, Gr-Son, son of
    Thomas Jr. [c]
  Ridge, Cornelius, Wit.
  Beckenbaugh, Jacob, Wit.
  Hase, Frederick C., Wit.
  Scott, Samuel, Wit.
  Grimes, Samuel, Wit.
Locker, Thomas, M:57, 1808/16
  Green, Nancy, Dau.
  Locker, Mary, Gr-Dau.,
    sister of George
  Locker, William, Son
  Locker, Alexander, Son
  Locker, George Lowry, Gr-Son,
    brother of Mary
  Locker, Eleanor, Wife
  Locker, Walter, Son
  Latimer, Wm. Jr., Wit.
  Huguely, James, Wit.
  Farr, Nicholas, Wit.

Berkley, George, M:62, 1816
  Berkley, George William, Son
  Berkley, —, Wife
  Berkley, —, Daus.
  Lewis, Charles, Exor.
  Berkley, John L., Exor.
  Douglas, Patrick H., Wit.
  Lewis, James, Wit.
  Linton, John H., Wit.
Vanhorn, George, M:65, 1816
  Walker, Garret, Cousin
  Vanhorn, Ann, Sister
  Vanhorn, Sarah, Step-Mother
  Vanhorn, Chilton, Son, <21
  Sutton, Elijah, Wit.
  Walker, Benjamin, Wit.
  Walker, William, Wit.
Hatcher, James, M:66, 1816
  Young, David, Son-in-law
  Hatcher, James, Son
  Hatcher, Edith, Dau.
  Hatcher, Mary, Dau.
  Hatcher, Catharine, Wife
  Hatcher, my nine children
  Hatcher, Samuel, Exor.
  Hatcher, Thomas, Wit.
  Tavenner, George, Wit.
  Brown, Henry, Wit.
Carter, John, M:67, 1816
  Carter, James, Half-Brother
  Carter, Morris, Brother
  Carter, Efraim, Half-Brother
  Carter, Fanny, Half-Sister
  Gunnell, Henry Jr., Exor.
  Veale, William, Wit.
  Douglas, Patrick H., Wit.
  Lafaver, William, Wit.
  Houser, Philip, Wit.
Hatcher, William, M:89, 1816
  Hatcher, John, Brother, dec'd.
  Hatcher, James, Brother, dec'd.
  Hatcher, George, Brother,
    dec'd.
  Hatcher, Thomas, Brother
  Russell (Roszel), Sarah, Sister
  Ingledue, Anne, housekeeper
  Gibson, Mary, Sister, dec'd.
  Hatcher, Samuel, Exor.
  Smith, David, Exor.
  Taylor, Bernard, Exor.

Index to Loudoun County Wills, 1757 - 1850　　　　93

Taylor, Yardly, Wit.
Fairhurst, George, Wit.
Summers, Richard, Wit.
Braden, Sarah, M:90, 1816
Fox, Mary, Dau.
Fox, Cemelio, Gr-Dau.,
　dau. of Elizabeth
White, Margaret, Dau.
White, Sarah Anne,
　Gr-Dau., <21
White, John Randolph
Lacey, Sarah, Dau.
Braden, Robert, Son
Fox, Elizabeth, Dau.
White, Theodore Braden,
　son of Jozabed, <21
Hough, Francis, Dau.
Hough, Annie, Gr-Dau.,
　dau. of Francis
Dulaney, Zachariah, Wit.
Braden, Noble S., Wit.
Evans, William, M:91, 1816
Evans, Catharine, Wife
Humphrey, Charles, Wit.
Nutt, Joseph Jr., Wit.
Nutt, Joseph Sr., Wit.
Minor, Rebekah, M:98, 1811/17
Minor, Rebecca
Minor, Nancy, Sister-in-law,
　w/o Thomas
Minor, Thomas, Brother
Binns, Simon A., Wit.
Longley, George, Wit.
Garner, Mahlon, Wit.
Braden, Joseph, M:100, 1814/17
Braden, Mary, Wife
Braden, Flavious, Son, <21
Braden, Robert, Brother
Braden, John, Brother
Poll, Sarah, Sister-in-law,
　wife's sister
Poll, Elizabeth, Sister-in-law,
　wife's sister
Poll, Mildred, Sister-in-law,
　wife's sister
Williams, John, Wit.
Hough, Samuel, Wit.
Hough, Amasa, Wit.
Eaches, Joseph, Wit.

**Janney, Blackstone, M:107,
　1812/16/17**
Janney, Eli, Son
Janney, Thomas, Son, dec'd.
Janney, —, Gr-Son,
　son of Thomas
Janney, Lydia, Eldest Dau.
Janney, Mary, Wife
Nichols, Mary, 3rd Dau.
Brown, —, daus. of William and
　Hannah
Brown, William, Son-in-law
Brown, Hannah, 2nd Dau.
Watters, Mahlon, Exor.
Schooley, Isaac, Wit.
Schooley, William, Wit.
Ingledue, Ann, Wit.
Nichols, Isaac, Wit. [c]
Taylor, Jonathan Jr., Wit. [c]
Sands, Stephen, Wit. [c]
Peugh, Spencer, M:112, 1816/17
Watkins, Sarah, Dau.
Hann, John, Exor.
Hann, Nancy, Dau.
Peugh, William, Son
Peugh, Samuel, Son
Peugh, David Levi, Son
Peugh, Mary, Wife
Powell, William, Wit.
Chamblain, John, Wit.
Jenkins, John, Wit.
Powell, Nancy H., Wit.
Clayton, William, M:113, 1813/17
Galloway, Polly, Dau.
Galloway, Amos, Gr-Son, <21
Galloway, Israel, Gr-Son, <21
Hooffman, Phebe, Dau.
Clayton, William, Son
Clayton, Sally, Dau.
Clayton, Martha, Dau.
Clayton, Nancy, Dau.
Clayton, Israel, Son
Clayton, Amos, Son
Glasgow, Catharine, Wife
Parker, Parker, Exor.
Janney, Jonas, Exor.
Grady, Edward B., Wit.
Allder, George H., Wit.
Dagg, John L., Wit.
Parker, Sally, Wit. [c]

Hough, John, M:127, 1816/17
  Hough, Jane, Wife
  Hough, —, all my children
  Hough, Amasa, Exor.
  Daily, John, Exor.
  Stone, Daniel, Wit.
  Hough, William H., Wit.
Muse, Edward, M:140, 1808/09
  Muse, —, Wife
  Muse, Thomas Harbot, Nephew
  Muse, Robert, Brother
  Muse, Nancy, Sister
  Lee, George, son of George
    Lee, dec'd.
  Muse, Betsey, Sister
  Armstrong, Susanna Franklin,
    Sister
  Douglas, Patrick H., Wit.
  Douglas, Evelyn B., Wit.
Fortney, George, M:141, 1817
  Fortney, Henry, Brother
  Fortney, John, Brother
  Fortney, Susan, Wife
  Robbins, Isaac, Exor.
  Deagon, Henry B., Exor.
  Monroe, A. G., Wit.
  Fulton, Thomas, Wit.
  Benedum, Peter, Wit.
Davis, Joseph, M:145, 1812/17
  Davis, Jason, Brother
  Davis, William, Nephew,
    son of James
  Davis, Polly, Sister
  Davis, William, Father
  Davis, Sarah, Niece, sister of
    William, dau. of James, <21
  Moore, James, Exor.
  Sappington, John F., Wit.
  Connard, Anthony, Wit.
Glasgow, Henry, M:175, 1817
  Glasgow, —, all my children
  Cartnail, Susan, Mother-in-law
  Cartnail, John, Father-in-law
  Littlejohn, John, Exor.
  Cordell, Presly, Exor.
  Edwards, Samuel M., Wit.
  Carney, John, Wit.
**Passmore, Ellis of St. Mary's Co.,
  Md., M:206, 1817**
  Kirk, Phebe, Dau.
  Hall, M. wife's Dau., Step-Dau.
  Passmore, Sarah, Wife
  Passmore, Ellis P., Son
  Passmore, Ruth M., Dau.
  Passmore, Andrew, Son
  Passmore, John W., Son
  Passmore, George P., Son
  Passmore, Benjamin James,
    Son
  Passmore, William Wallace,
    Son
  Jones, Benjamin, Exor.
  Irwin, Samuel, Exor.
  Kirk, Josiah, Exor.
  Taylor, Stacy, Wit.
  Heaton, James, Wit.
  Bradfield, Benjamin, Wit.
Slater, Elizabeth, M:208, 1816/17
  Stoutseberger, John, Exor.
  Ullem, Andrew, Son, dec'd.
  Slater, Elizabeth, Dau.,
    now in Ohio
  Ullem, John, Son
  Ullem, Peggy, Gr-Dau.
  Ullem, Jacob, Gr-Son
  Huff, Henry, Wit.
  Fanner, Mealy, Wit.
Davis, Thomas, M:209, 1817
  Fohley, John, Exor.
  Davis, Abraham, Son
  Householder, Adam, Exor.
  Davis, Solomon, Son
  Davis, Jacob, Son
  Davis, Joseph, Son
  Davis, Samuel, Son
  —, dau. of Elizabeth, Step-Dau.
  Davis, Elizabeth, Wife
  Davis, Daniel, Son
  Davis, John, Son
  Davis, Thomas, Son
  Williams, Presly, Wit.
  Hixon, Stephenson, Wit.
  Hixon, Noah, Wit.
  Troutman, Peter, Wit.
Janney, Jesse, M:218, 1816/17
  Hughs, children, Sister
  Cimmings, Ann, girl now living
    with family
  Taylor, Bernard, Exor.
  Janney, Stacey, Brother

Nichols, William, Exor.
Wildman, Leatitia's children,
   Sister
White, Ann's children, Sister
Janney, Isaac's children,
   Brother
Janney, Hannah, Niece,
   dau. of Stacey
Janney, William, Brother
Taylor, Yardly, Wit.
Taylor, Henry S., Wit.
Piggott, William, Wit.
Reece, David, Wit.
Chichester, Anne Thompson, M:220, 1817
Chichester, Richard, Son
Chichester, George Mason, Son
Tutt, Ann Mason, Dau.
Mason, John T., Brother
Tutt, Charles P., Son-in-law
Mason, Mary, Wit.
Mason, Ann, Wit.
Wilson, John T., Wit.
Lacey, Sarah, M:224, 1817
White, Sarah, Niece, dau. of
   Margaret
White, Josibed, Brother-in-law,
   millwright
White, John, Nephew,
   son of Margaret
Hough, Frances, Sister
Hough, Matlida, Niece,
   of George Town
Fox, Frances, Niece,
   dau. of Mary
Fox, Betsey, Niece,
   of Georgetown
Fox, Betsey, Niece,
   of Waterford
Fox, Mary, Sister
White, Margaret, Sister
Fox, Elizabeth, Sister
Hough, Amasa, Wit.
Hough, Washington, Wit.
Williams, John, Wit.
Gregg, Elisha, M:225, 1815/17
Ekart, Ann, Dau., w/o Casper
Gregg, Martha Lovett, Gr-Dau.,
   dau. of George
Gregg, Sarah Ann, Gr-Dau.,
   dau. of George
Gregg, George, Son, dec'd.
Gregg, Martha, Wife
Ekart, Caspar, Son-in-law
Stevens, Henry, Wit.
Stevens, Eleanor, Wit.
Steere, Isaac, Wit.
Sanders, Aaron, Wit.
Luckett, L—, Wit.
Neale, W. S., Wit.
Gourley, Joseph, M:231, 1816/18
Gourley, Grace, Wife
Gourley, William, Son
Gourley, Absalom, Son
Gourley, Hannah, Dau.
Gourley, Joseph B., Son, <16
Gourley, Johnathan, Son, <16
Gourley, Thomas, Son
Gourley, Susannah, Dau.
Heskett, Mary, Dau.
Massey, Lewis, M:231, 1817/18
Wilson, Mahlon, wife's Gr-Son
Massey, Mary, Wife
Vandevanter, Joseph, Wit.
White, Benjamin, Wit.
Beales, Amos, Wit.
Beans, William, M:236, 1817/18
Newhouse, Hannah, Dau.,
   w/o David, in Ohio
Beans, William, Son, in
   Culpepper Co.
Taylor, Ruth, Dau.
Taylor, Lydia, Gr-Dau.,
   w/o Joseph
Beans, Isaiah, Son
Beans, Samuel, Son
Beans, Levi, Son
Beans, John, Son
Beans, Rachael, Dau.
Beans, Timothy, Son, in Ohio
Beans, Rebecca, Dau.
Beans, Absalam, Son
Beans, Rebecca, Wife
Taylor, Mahlon, Exor.
Smith, Seth, Wit.
Taylor, Joseph, Wit.
Goodin, David, Wit.

Hatcher, Thomas, M:236, 1818
Nichols, Isaac, Father-in-law, dec'd.
Nichols, Isaac, Brother-in-law
Nichols, Samuel, Brother-in-law
Beatty, Elizabeth, M:241, 1816/18
Bitzer, Polly, Dau.
Biscoe, Sarah, Dau.
Beatty, Silas, Son
Beveridge, Noble, Wit.
Harris, John, Wit.
Hampton, Jeremiah, Wit.
Heath, Andrew, M:246, 1817/18
James, Sarah, Dau.
Heath, Lydia, Dau.
McKim, James, Son-in-law
McKim, Reuhannah, Dau.
Halley, Barton D.
Halley, Catharine's seven children, Gr-children
Heath, Isaac, Son
Heath, Andrew, Son
James, William, Wit.
Davis, Thomas, Wit.
Pagit, Timothy, Wit.
Heath, Andrew Shelton, Wit.
Smalley, William, M:247, 1818
Heath, Andrew, Exor.
Crowe, Hiland, Wit.
Beard, Stephen, Wit.
Braves, Joseph, Wit.
Mullen, Daniel, M:248, 1812/17
Binns, Thomas N., Friend
—, John, Wit.
Langley, Alexander, Wit.
Norris, Ignatius, Wit.
Gulick, Leannah, M:268, 1813/18
Mount, Charity, Dau.
Reed, Mary, Dau.
Johnson, Martha, Dau.
Johnson, Sarah, Dau.
Johnson, Casper, Son-in-law
Gulick, Leannah, Dau.
Gulick, Ferdinando, Son
Gulick, Francis, Son
Gulick, Moses, Son
Gulick, George, Son
Sinclair, John, Wit.
Alexander, David, Wit.
Lewis, William, Wit.

Boss, Peter, M:275, 1818
Boss, —, all my children and Gr-children
Boss, Samuel, Son
Boss, Mary, Wife
Littlejohn, John, Wit.
Beard, Joseph, Wit.
Bover, R. H., Wit.
Field, William of Mason Co., Ky., M:276, 1817/18
Field, —, all my children
Field, Thomas, Son
Field, Elizabeth, Wife
Field, John, Son
Field, George, Son
Fenton, Michael, Wit.
Leachman, George, Wit.
Wright, Anthony, M:281, 1818
Stone, Daniel, Exor.
Wright, Elizabeth, Wife
Wright, Anthony, Son
Harris, Elizabeth, Dau.
Wright, Daniel, Son
Wright, Robert, Son
Wright, John, Son
Wright, William, Son
Wright, Samuel, Son
Wright, Moses, Son
Wright, Patterson, Son
Neale, W. S., Wit.
Mageth, John, Wit.
White, Joseph, Wit.
Stone, William, Wit.
Peacock, Benjamin, M:306, 1808/18
Peacock, —, Wife
Peacock, John, Son
Peacock, Samuel, Son
Peacock, William, Son
Peacock, Susannah, Dau.
Peacock, Ann, Dau.
Peacock, Hezekiah, Son
Love, Thomas, Wit.
Love, Samuel, Wit.
Hatcher, Thomas, M:307, 1818
Seaton, Hiram, Son-in-law
Seaton, Margary, Dau., dec'd.
Seaton, William, Gr-Son
Hatcher, Samuel, Eldest Son
Hatcher, Rebecca, Wife

Hatcher, William, Brother, dec'd.
Hatcher, William, Father, dec'd.
Hatcher, Joseph, 2nd Son
Hatcher, Mahlon B., Gr-Son,
  son of Anne Bishop, dec'd.
Nicholls, Samuel, Wit.
Tavenor, George, Wit.
Hoge, James, Wit.
Gill, Ann, M:314, 1818
Hatcher, Joseph, Exor.
Keller, Gourley, Exor.
Gill, Uriah, Son, <21
Gill, Levi, Son, <21
Gill, Daniel, Husband, dec'd.
Hart, William, Wit.
Jones, Edmund, Wit.
Steer, Benjamin, M:318, 1811/18
Pierpoint, Ann, Dau.
Steer, Elizabeth, Dau.
Steer, William, Son
Birdsall, Hannah, Dau.
Steer, Isaac E., Son
Phillips, Thomas, Wit.
Schooley, Reuben, Wit.
Wheeler, Elizabeth, N:1, 1818
McCabe, Mary, Friend,
  w/o Dr. McCabe
Powell, Elen, Cousin
Powell, Fethy, Cousin
Hervey, Ann, Friend
Conn, Henrietta, Exor.
Conn, Hamilton, Friend
Willis, Rev. Nicholas, Friend
Conn, Leanna, Friend
Edwards, Dr. Charles, Cousin
Adams, Esther, w/o William
Adams, Kerid, Friend
Broden, Robert, Exor.
Adams, William, Wit.
Adams, Abraham, Wit.
Lane, James B., N:25, 1818
Swearingen, Julia, Sister
Edwards, Elvira, Sister
Lane, Harvey, Brother
Lane, Hardage, Brother
Coleman, Lydia, Sister
Coleman, William,
  Brother-in-law
Darne, William, Wit.
West, Norman, Wit.

Doud, John, Wit.
Boswell, William, Wit.
Coleman, J. W., Wit.
Coleman, Thomas W., Wit.
Wildman, Rebecca, N:31, 1818
Tillett, Eliza, Dau.
Binns, Sarah, Dau.
Wildman, —, all of my Daus.
Huff, Catharine, Wit.
Binns, William A., Admr. w.w.a.
Norton, Nathaniel, N:35, 1818
Norton, Barbara, Wife
Norton, Hamilton, Son, <21
Norton, Hiram, Son, <21
Norton, Franklin, Son, <21
Norton, Benedict, Son, <21
Norton, Metildia, Dau.
Norton, Mahala, Dau.
Norton, Elvira, Dau.
Norton, Carolina, Dau.
Vernon, Daniel, Exor.
Grady, Edward B., Wit.
Johnson, James, Wit.
Reese, Daniel O., Wit.
Lacey, David, N:42, 1809/18
Lacey, Thirza, Dau.
Lacey, Castilinia, Dau.
Lacey, Diadema, Dau.
Lacey, Sarah, Wife
Phillips, Thomas, Exor.
Manning, Euphemia, Dau.
Schooley, Reuben C., Exor.
Williams, John, Wit.
Janney, Mahlon Jr., Wit.
Steer, Joseph, Wit.
Manning, Nathaniel, Wit.
Casady, alias Megeath, Nancy,
  N:48, 1816/18
Casady, John James,
  Infant Son
Casady, John H., Husband
Megeath, William, Father, dec'd.
Caldwell, Joseph, Wit.
McCabe, John H., Wit.
Edwards, Charles G., Wit.
Steer, Joseph, Wit.
Henderson, Samuel, N:60,
  1815/19
Murrey, Catharine, Dau.
Crider, Peggy, Dau.

Toll, Betsey, Dau.,
  w/o Jonathan, went to Ky.
Jackson, Sarah, Dau.
Jackson, Alfred, Gr-Son
Jackson, Jane, Gr-Dau.
Henderson, Amy, Wife
Henderson, Amy, Dau.
Henderson, Molly, Dau.
Henderson, John, Son
Henderson, Henry, Son
Henderson, William, Son
Gibson, Abner, Exor.
Henderson, Samuel, Son
Powell, Burr, Wit.
Cochrane, Richard, Wit.
Smith, Hugh, Wit.
Kilgore, George, N:70, 1817/19
Sheid, Martinah B., Gr-Dau.
Fox, George K., Gr-Son
Sheid, Sarah G., Gr-Dau.
Fox, Anna H., Gr-Dau.
Sheid, James W., Gr-Son
Fox, Elizabeth F., Gr-Dau.
Sheid, John H., Gr-Son
Sheid, William, Exor.
Sheid, Rebecca, Dau.
Sheid, George, Son-in-law
Gunnell, H., Wit.
Bell, George D., Wit.
Hossman, James, Wit.
Rose, Capt. John, Admr. w.w.a.
Noland, Mary Eleanor, N:93, 1819
Simpson, Catharine, Niece
Luckett, Leven, Brother
Love, Jane, Dau.
Noland, Mary Eleanor,
  Gr-Dau., <18
Noland, Dade P., Son
Noland, Mary Louisa,
  Gr-Dau. <18
Noland, Samuel, Son
Luckett, Lettice, Sister-in-law,
  w/o Leven
Noland, William, Wit.
Livingston, Pleasant, N:106, 1819
Livingston, Mary, Dau.
Livingston, —, four sons
Reeder, Gourley, Exor.
Reeder, William, Wit.
Martin, William, Wit.
Silcott, Jacob, Wit.
O'Neil, John, N:110, 1819
Burson, Aaron, Exor.
Thompson, Margaret, Dau.
Marks, Mahala, Dau.
Marks, George, Exor.
O'Neil (O'Neal), Daniel, Son
Curtis, Nancy, Gr-Dau.
O'Neil (O'Neal), John, Son
French, Mason, N:111, 1817/19
Henderson, Jane, Dau.
French, Margaret Burgess, Dau.
French, Lewis, Son
French, Reuben, Son
French, Ann (Francis Ann), Dau.
French, James Burgess, Son
French, Ann, Wife
Blincoe, S., Wit.
Berry, Fielding, Wit.
French, Mason, N:111, 1817/19
Butler, Mary, Dau., w/o John
Brown, Sarah, Dau.,
  w/o Alexander
Lloyd, George E. Jr., Wit.
Dunkin, Samuel, Wit.
Dunkin, John, Wit.
Gill, John L., Wit.
Evans, John, N:128, 1819
Evans, Elizabeth, Dau.
Evans, Nancy, Dau.
Evans, Sarah, Dau.
Evans, Asahel, Son
Evans, Susanna, Dau.
Evans, Rachel, Dau.
Evans, John, Son
Evans, Eleazer, Son
Evans, Deborah, Wife
Cummings, Robert, Exor.
Grady, Edward B., Wit.
Griffith, Thomas, Wit.
Lewis, Joseph, N:189, 1820
Barrington, Elizabeth,
  dau. of Barbara
Barrington, Barbara
Lewis, Charles, Exor.
Lewis, Joseph, Son
Lewis, Hannah, Dau.
Lewis, William, Son
Lewis, James, Exor.

Lewis, Susannah, Dau.
Lewis, John, Son
Davis, Mary, Dau.
Oden, Nathaniel S., Wit.
Lyne, William, Wit.
Edwards, Thomas G., Wit.
Field, Luke, N:230, 1819/20
Field, Margaret, Wife
Rees, Daniel, Wit.
Burson, Jesse, Wit.
Joice, George W., Wit.
Gregg, John, N:230, 1818/20
Gregg, Esther, Wife
Gregg, Abner, Son, <21
Gregg, Abner, Brother
Gregg, Joshua, Brother
Walker, Ruth, Cousin
Walker, Garrett, Exor.
Taylor, Yardley Trustee
Brown, Samuel, Step-son, <21
Smith, William, Brother-in-law
Brown, James, Step-son, <21
McPherson, Stephen Jr., Wit.
Walker, Benjamin, Wit.
McGeath, Gabriel, Wit.
Stump, Eleanor, N:246, 1820
Hibbs, Jane, Sister
Stump, Thomas, Nephew
Stump, Joseph, Nephew
Stump, Sarah, Niece
McCabe, George, Wit.
George, John, Wit.
Mull, David, Wit.
Marsh, James, N:256, 1816/20
Hains, Mary, Dau.
Vernon, John, Son-in-law
Marsh, Ruth, Wife
Hains, Daniel, Son-in-law
Vernon, Phebe, Dau.
Rand, Ruth, Dau.
Vernon, James, Gr-Son
Love, Augt., Wit.
Downs, John, Wit.
McMullin, Andrew B., Wit.
Hesser, Hannah, N:258, 1820
James, Thomas
Davis, Elizabeth, Dau.,
 w/o John
Hesser, Emiline, Dau., <18
Hesser, John, Son

Hesser, Cornelia, Dau., <18
Hesser, Sarah, Dau.
Hesser, Lucinda, Dau.
Hesser, Mary, Dau.
Hesser, Nancy, Dau.
Hesser, Andrew, Son
Hesser, David, Son
Nichols, Thomas, Wit.
Moore, Samuel, Wit.
Hollingsworth, Jehu, Wit.
Shawen, Cornelius, N:259, 1820
Paxon, Nancy, Dau.
Ogden, Elizabeth, Dau.
Shawen, Mary, Wife
Shawen, George, Son
Shawen, Mary Catharine, Dau.
Shawen, David, Son
Jenners, Abiel, Wit.
Hamilton, John, Wit.
Edwards, Charles G., Wit.
Weist, John, N:260, 1820
Copeland, John, Exor.
Wiest, Catharine, Wife
Loy, Sophia, Dau.
Fawley, John, Exor.
Long, Barbara, Dau.
Minor, Spence, Wit.
Hamilton, John, Wit.
Firth, George A., Wit.
Leslie, Thomas, N:261, 1814/20
Leslie, Nancy, Wife
Leslie, Amanda Osburn,
 Eldest Dau.
Leslie, Mary, Mother
Leslie, Benjamin, Brother
Leslie, Joseph, Brother
Leslie, Samuel D., Brother
Leslie, Caroline Frances, Dau.
Osburn, Craven, Exor.
Hough, Thomas, Wit.
White, Josiah, Wit.
White, John, Wit.
Clendening, Samuel, Wit.
Cook, Samuel, Wit.
Potts, Edward, Wit.
Ellzey, L., Wit. [c]
Heaton, James, Wit. [c]
Heaton, Jonathan, Wit. [c]
Taylor, Timothy, Wit. [c]

Frazer, Catharine, N:265, 1820
  Taylor, Mary Ann
  Frazer, Dinah, Sister
  Frazer, Nancy, Sister
  Frazer, Margaret, Sister
  Frazer, James, Father
  Lewis, Charles, Wit.
  Latimer, Thomas, Wit.
  Moran, John M., Wit.
Sanders, Benjamin, N:270, 1820
  Milbourn, Mary, Dau.
  Masseh, Mary
  Milbourn, Sarah, Dau.
  Puller, Mary, Niece
  Sanders, William, Nephew
  Sanders, Benjamin, Brother
  Sanders, Washington, Exor.,
    son of Benjamin
  Sanders, William, Exor.,
    son of Benjamin
  Sanders, James, Nephew,
    son of James
  Sanders, Philip, Nephew,
    son of James
  Sanders, Elizabeth, Niece,
    dau. of James
  Sanders, Washington, Nephew,
    son of James
  Sanders, James, Brother
  Sanders, Hannah, Niece,
    dau. of Philip, Niece
  Sanders, Benjamin, Nephew
  Burgoyne, Joseph, Wit.
  Strother, James, Wit.
Shaffer, Conrad, N:280, 1818/21
  Shaffer, Elizabeth, Wife
  Shaffer, William, Son
  Shaffer, Conrad, Son
  Shaffer, Jacob, Gr-Son,
    son of John
  Stoutseberger, John, Exor.
  Shaffer, Magdelena, Dau.
  Shaffer, John, Gr-Son,
    son of Magdelena
  Shaffer, Jacob, Gr-Son,
    son of Suana Rasor
  Marlow, Edward, Exor.
  Wissinger, Peggy, Dau.
  Hosholder, Frederick, Gr-Son
  Adams, Mary, Dau.
  Rasor, Susana, Dau.
  Rasor, John, Son-in-law
  Askin, John & his wife,
    Son-in-law & Dau.
  Askin, John's children,
    Gr-children
  Huff, Henry, Wit.
  Hickman, John, Wit.
  Hickman, Peter, Wit.
Jenkins, William, N:281, 1821
  Jenkins, Job, Brother
  Marlow, Edward, Exor.
  Marlow, George, Wit.
  Cole, William, Wit.
  Ball, Henry, Wit.
Gover, Samuel of Waterford,
  N:284, 1820
  Head, Mary, Dau.
  Huff, Elizabeth, Dau.
  Gover, Rachel, Dau.
  Gover, Hannah, Dau.
  Gover, Anthony P., Son
  Gover, Robert, Son
  Gover, Jesse, Son
  Gover, Samuel, Son
  Gover, Anna, Dau.
  Gover, Albina, Dau.
  Moore, Asa, Wit.
  Phillips, Thomas, Wit.
Bennett, Charles, N:285, 1817/21
  Hamilton, Ann B.
  Wildman, Enos, Friend
  Wildman, Jane D.
  Barnett, Mary, Sister
  Sanders, Thomas, Wit.
  Ball, Charles B., Wit.
Waltman, Emanuel, N:309, 1821
  Dever, Abraham, Nephew,
    child of Ann
  Dever, Margarate, Niece,
    child of Ann
  Dever, Daniel, Nephew,
    child of Ann
  Dever, Ann, Sister
  Dever, Deley, Niece,
    child of Ann
  Everhart, Jacob, Nephew, sister
    Ann's child, Ann now Dever
  Everhart, John, Nephew, sister
    Ann's child, Ann now Dever

Everhart, Joseph, Nephew,
 sister Ann's child, Ann now
 Dever
Everhart, Sarah, Niece, sister
 Ann's child, Ann now Dever
Wenner, Elsebeth, Sister
Waltman, David, Nephew,
 son of John
Waltman, Joseph, Nephew
Waltman, Jacob, Brother
Waltman, —, Step-Mother
Waltman, Samuel, Nephew,
 son of John
Waltman, Elisebeth, Niece,
 dau. of John
Waltman, Mereah, Niece,
 dau. of John
Wenner, Emanuel, Nephew
Waltman, —, Father
Waltman, John, Brother
Wenner, John, Exor.
Moore, John, Wit.
Thomas, John, Wit.
States, Frederick, Wit.
Carter, Cassius, N:315, 1820/22
Carter, Charles S. (Shirly),
 Brother
Carter, Edward E., Brother
Carter, Mary, Sister
Carter, John Hill, Brother
Edwards, Gilbert, Wit.
Spencer, Jasper, Wit.
Hixon, Margaret, N:338, 1818/21
Rodgers, Flemon, Nephew,
 son of Jane
Rodgers, Jane, Sister
Rodgers, Jane, Niece
Rodgers, other children, nieces
 & nephews
Hixon, Timothy, Husband, dec'd.
Rodgers, Esibel, Niece
Hixson, Flemon, Son, <21
Braden, Robert, Exor.
Phillips, Thomas, Exor.
McCabe, John H., Wit.
Balch, L. P. W., Wit.
Wathen, Isaac, Wit.
**Jackson, John Sr., N:344,
 1820/21**
Houser, Abigail, Dau.

Grubb, John, son of William,
 Exor.
Campbell, Mary, Dau.
Lowry, Martha, Dau.
Knight, Priscilla, Dau.
Saunders, Ann, Dau.
Jackson, John, son of Styles,
 <21, Gr-Son
Jackson, Styles, Son, dec'd.
Jenkins, Sarah, Dau.
Jackson, Samuel, Son
Jackson, John, Son
McKimmie, Elizabeth, Dau.
Shoemaker, Daniel, Wit.
Grubb, Adam, Wit.
McIntyre, Patrick, N:346, 1821
McIntyre, all my children, <21
Newton, Joseph T., Exor.
McIntyre, Christopher, Son, <21
McIntyre, Mary, Wife
Cordell, Presley, Wit.
Wilson, John T., Wit.
Moore, John, Wit.
**Vandevanter, Joseph, N:347,
 1821**
Vandevanter, —, children
Vandevanter, —, Wife
Janney, Eli, Wit.
Mains, Archibald, Wit.
**Gillmeyer, Francis of Frederick
 Co., Md., N:348, 1816**
Jenkins, Catharine, Dau.
Gillmeyer, Taresa, Dau.
Gillmeyer, Sarah, Dau.
Gillmeyer, Elizabeth, Dau.
Gillmeyer, Jacob, Son
Gillmeyer, Francis, Son
Gillmeyer, Joseph, Son
Gillmeyer, John, Son
Gillmeyer, George, Son
Gillmeyer, Catharine, Wife
Miller, Mary, Dau.
Emmit, William, Wit.
Radford, Thomas, Wit.
Moore, Daniel M., Wit.
Besicks, Priscilla, N:357, 1821
Cooms, David, Brother
Vollmer, Margaret, Servant
Bisicks, Hindley, Son
Bisicks, Jesse, Son

Butler, Matilda servant
Bisicks, James, Husband
Simpson, John, Exor.
Johnson, Casper, Wit.
Stonestreet, Thomas, Wit.
Mendenhall, Ruth, N:359, 1821
Janney, Rebekah, Dau.
Janney, William, son of Aquilla, Son
Janney, Israel, Son
Howell, Hannah, Dau.
Janney, Mary Ann, Dau.
Howell, Samuel, Son-in-law
Edwards, Charles G., Wit.
Williams, John, Wit.
Ruse, Christian, N:360, 1821
Sager, Nancy, Gr-Dau.
Ruse, Henry, Son
Ruse, Frederick, Son
Ruse, Jacob, Son
Ruse, Michael, Son
Ruse, Solomon, Son
Ruse, Christeana, Dau.
Ruse, Christian, Son
Ruse, John, Son
Ruse, Rachel, Dau.
Fisher, Catherine, Dau.
States, Elizabeth, Dau.
Doring, Polly, Dau.
Moore, John, Wit.
Mann, John, Wit.
Bogar, Michael, Wit.
Murry, Samuel, N:362, 1819/21
Donohoe, Samuel, Wife's Brother
Harris, Isaac, Nephew
Murry, Sarah, Dau.
Murry, Betsey, Wife
Harris, Samuel, Nephew
Nichols, Isaac, N:369, 1821
Bennett, Judith, Sister
Tavenner, Thomas
Janney, Mary, Sister
Farro, Ann
Heald, Rachel, Sister
Hamilton, James, a boy I raised
Walters, Mahlon, Nephew
Nichols, Thomas, Nephew
Walters, Isaac
Walters, Dinah, Sister

Nichols, Daniel, Brother
Nichols, Amos, Brother
Nichols, Henry, Brother
Nichols, Eli, Brother
Nichols, Isaac, Nephew
Nichols, Rebecca, Wife
Taylor, Bernard, Wit.
Shoemaker, Abraham, Wit.
McGeth, Betsina, Wit.
McGeath, John, O:14, 1821/22
Walker, Suyntha, Dau.
Burgoine, Ann, Dau.
Burgoine, Joseph
Scott, Elizabeth, Dau.
McGeath, Thomas, Son
McGeath, Josenah, Dau.
McDermot, Stephen, Gr-Son
Miller, Margaret, Dau.
Jenners, Abiel, Exor.
Dowell, Mary, Dau.
Russell, Euphamy, Dau.
Shawen, David, Wit.
Dorsey, Edward, Wit.
Virtz, Conrad, O:15, 1821/22
Virtz, Peter, Son
Virtz, John, Son
Virtz, William, Son
Virtz, Adam, Son
Virtz, Henry, Son, dec'd.
Virtz, Elizabeth, Dau.
Virtz, Caty, Dau.
Virtz, Barbary, Dau.
Virtz, Christiana, Dau.
Virtz, William, Gr-Son, son of Henry
Virtz, Betey, Gr-Dau., dau. of Henry
Braden, R., Wit.
Walker, Isaac, Wit.
Conard, David, Wit.
Stone, William H., Wit.
Weatherby, Matthew, O:16, 1821/22
Fadeley, Jacob
Carr, Samuel, Wit.
McCormick, John, Wit.
Hough, Robert R., Wit.
McKim, William H., O:53, 1822
McKim, Reuhannah, Mother
Coleman, Richard, Wit.

Index to Loudoun County Wills, 1757 - 1850   103

Little, R. H., Wit.
James, Dean, Wit.
Heath, Andrew, Wit.
Davis, Thomas, O:89, 1819/22
  Brown, Margaret, Dau.
  Davis, John, Son
  Davis, Rebecca, Wife
  Brown, John, Son-in-law,
    Margaret's husband
  White, Benniah, Wit.
  Slater, Samuel, Wit.
  Darr, Leonard, Wit.
**Evans, Robert of Cecil Co., Md.,
  O:95, 1821/22**
  Oldham, Eleanor, Dau.
  Mitchell, Jane T., Dau.
  Oldham, Cyrus, Son-in-law
  Evans, James, Son
  Evans, Robert, Son
  Evans, John, Son
  Evans, Margaret, Dau.
  Evans, Isabella Sophia, Dau.
  Evans, Rebekah Hannah, Dau.
  Evans, Mary Eliza, Dau.
  Evans, Isabella, Wife
  Foster, Edward, Wit.
  White, Eli, Wit.
  Holliday, Urban, Wit.
Rice, Bethany, O:116, 1821/22
  Oxley, Evrett, Brother
  Morris, Ede, Sister
  Saunders, Evrett, Nephew
  Saunders, Thomas, Nephew
  Saunders, John, Wit.
  Saunders, Presley, Wit.
  Saunders, Mary, Wit.
Humphrey, Thomas, O:117, 1822
  Humphrey, Thomas, Gr-child,
    child of Jesse
  Humphrey, Letty, Gr-child,
    child of Jesse
  Humphrey, Marcus, Son
  Humphrey, Mary, Wife
  Humphrey, Abner, Son
  Humphrey, Jesse, Son
  Humphrey, Rachel, Gr-child,
    child of Jesse
  Humphrey, Martha, Gr-child,
    child of Jesse

  Humphrey, Mary, Gr-child,
    child of Jesse
  Humphrey, Morris, Gr-child,
    child of Jesse
  Humphrey, Ute's children, child
    of Jesse, Gr-Gr-children
  Humphrey, Jonah, Son
  Humphrey, Thomas, Gr-Son,
    son of Jacob
  Humphrey, Margaret, Dau.-in-
    law
  Humphrey, Urie, Gr-Dau., dau.
    of Margaret
  Humphrey, Mary Ann, Gr-Dau.,
    dau. of Margaret
  Humphrey, Charles
  Jonson, Nancy, Dau.
  Osburn, Mary, Dau.
  Young, Effee, Dau.
  Danniel, Tracy, Dau.
  Crowe, Martha, Dau.
  West, Uree, Dau., dec'd.
  Bedom, Hannah, Dau.
  Humphrey, John, Gr-Son
  Osburn, Nicholas, Wit.
  Ervin, James, Wit.
  Heaton, Jonathan, Wit.
  Cochran, James Sr., Wit.
Veale, William, O:118, 1806/22
  Cullison, Nancy, dau. of Amelia
    Darnes
  Darne (Veale), Thomas, Son
  Veale (a.k.a. Darne), Thomas,
    Son
  Veale (a.k.a. Darne), John, Son
  Darne, Amelia, Wife
  Darne (Veale), John, Son
  Darne, Betsey, youngest sister
    of John and Thomas
  Gunnell, H. Jr., Wit.
  Watson, Thomas, Wit.
  Watson, William, Wit.
Hughes, Thomas, O:126, 1822
  Brookbank, Charles, Son-in-
    Law, dec'd.
  Hughes, Thomas, Son
  Hughes, Elisha, Son
  Hughes, Samuel, Son
  Hughes, —, Wife
  Taylor, Stacy, Dau.

Brown, William, Wit.
Stribling, Francis Jr., Wit.
Hinesling, Herman, O:142, 1822
Hinesling, Dorothy, Dau.
Hinesling, Mary, Dau.
Hinesling, Justis, Eldest Son
Hinesling, William, Son
Hinesling, Elizabeth, Wife
Ball, J., Wit.
Smith, George, Wit.
Sypherd, George, Wit.
Jenkins, John of Frederick Co., Md., O:143, 1822
Locker, Eleanor, Sister
Jenkins, Simon, Brother
Jenkins, William, Brother
Hooper, Mary, Sister
Hooper, Dorcas, Sister
McGill, Patrick Jr., Wit.
Luckett, Samuel, Wit.
Hook, John B., Wit.
Razor, Jacob, Admr. w.w.a.
Shover, Magdalena, O:145, 1822
Wenner, William Sr., Exor.
Karn, Adam, Exor.
Sanbower, Adam, Nephew, son of John
Sanbower, Christian, Nephew, son of John
Sanbower, Magdalena, Niece, dau. of John, w/o S. Rickart
Shover, Susanna, Niece, w/o George
Sager, Elizabeth, Niece, w/o Samuel
Sanbower, Catharine, Niece, dau. of John
Sanbower, Sarah, Niece, dau. of John
Sanbower, Susanna, Niece, dau. of John, w/o George Shover
Sanbower, Michael, Nephew, son of John
Sanbower, Elizabeth, Niece, dau. of John, w/o S. Sager
Sanbower, John, Brother
Sanbower, Henry, Nephew
Sanbower, Magdalena, Niece, dau. of Adam, w/o L. Roller, dec'd.
Sanbower, Adam, Nephew, son of Adam
Sanbower, John, Nephew, son of Adam
Sanbower, Adam, Brother
Shover, Charlotte, Gr-Niece, dau. of George & Elizabeth
Shover, George, Gr-Nephew, son of George & Elizabeth
Shover, George, husband of Elizabeth
Shover, Elizabeth, formerly Bauchman, Niece, dec'd.
Richart, Magdalena, Niece, w/o Simon
Roller, Magdalena, Niece, w/o Frederick,
Haeffner, formerly Bauchman, Catharine, Niece
Bauchman, Andrew, Brother
Bauchman, Catherine, Niece
Bauchman, Andrew, Nephew
Bauchman, Adam, Nephew
Bauchman, Elizabeth, Niece
Mann, John, Wit.
Potterfield, Daniel, Wit.
Boger, John H., Wit.
George, Elizabeth, O:146, 1809/22
Shover, John, Gr-Son
Shover, Simon's 6 children, Gr-children
Everhart, Jacob's 5 children, Gr-children
Richey, Samuel's 2 children, Gr-children
Verts, Jacob's 3 children, Gr-children
George, John, Son
Mills, William, Wit.
Shover, Adam, Wit.
Stoneburner, Frederick, Wit.
Hall, William, O:154, 1822
Hall, Mary, Wife
Hall, Deliah, Dau.
Hall, Mary, Dau.
Hall, William, Son

Hall, Sarah, Eldest Dau.
Hall, Jonathan, Eldest Son
Hall, Thomas, 2nd Son
Hall, Samuel, 3rd Son
Nixon, Joel, Wit.
Carr, Thomas, Wit.
Smith, David, Wit.
Bennett, Charles, O:172, 1822/23
Worsley, John, Exor.
Eaches, Ann, Dau.
Cassady, John H., Son-in-law, husband of Jane
Bennett, Jefferson, Son
Cassady, Jane, Dau.
McCowett, Elizabeth, Dau.
Wooddy, William Sr., O:225, 1821/23
Green, William Charles Mack G., Step-son, wife's son
Wooddy, Elizabeth, Wife
Wooddy, James, Son
Wooddy, David, Son
Wooddy, John, Son
Wooddy, Mary Jane, Dau.
Wooddy, Ruth Jones, Dau.
Hamerly, Sally, Dau.
Green, Chloe, Gr-mother of William
Wooddy, William, Son
Rose, Kitty, Dau.
Butler, James, negro boy
Blincoe, S., Wit.
Riley, Joshua, Wit.
Sowers, B. W., Wit.
Saunders, Henry, O:226, 1822/23
Saunders, Evrett, Son
Saunders, James, Son
Saunders, Cyrus, Son
Saunders, —, Wife
Saunders, Thomas, Son
Saunders, Presley, Son
Saunders, John, Son
Saunders, Crayton, Son
Saunders, Editha, Dau.
Saunders, Henry, Son
Saunders, Gunnell, Son
Saunders, Ramy, Son
Austin, Anna, Dau.
Austin, Ceselia, Gr-Dau., Anna's Dau.
Austin, Dorinda, Gr-Dau., Anna's Dau.
Austin, Henry, Gr-Son, Anna's son
Wilson, John T., Wit.
Rhodes, George, Wit.
Hall, Jonathan, Wit.
Rhodes, Tholemiah, O:238, 1821/23
Boley, Anna, Dau.
Rhodes, Samuel, Son
Allemong, Ruth, Dau.
Rhodes, Ruth, alias Allemong, Dau.
Jones, Letitia, Gr-Dau.
Cochran, Sarah, Dau.
Rhodes, Randolph, Son
Jones, Mary, Dau.
Cochran, James, Exor.
Rhodes, Mary, Gr-Dau., dau. of John
Rhodes, Tholemiah, Gr-Son, son of John
Rhodes, John, Son, dec'd.
Rhodes, Sarah, alias Cochran, Dau.
Rhodes, Anna alias Boley, Dau.
Rhodes, Eustius Howard, Son
Rhodes, Mary alias Jones, Dau.
Adams, William, Wit.
Wornell, John, Wit.
Fulton, Mahlon, Wit.
Triplett, Francis, O:258, 1821/23
Smith, Charlotte, Dau.
Peers, Mrs. Eleanor
Davis, Catharine, Gr-Dau.
Peers, Henry, son of Eleanor
Davis, Charlotte, Gr-Dau.
Triplett, Nathaniel, Son
Triplett, Daniel, Son
Triplett, Francis, Son
Triplett, William, Son
Triplett, John, Son
Triplett, Thomas, Son
Triplett, Nancy, Dau.
Binns, Charles, Wit.
Hamilton, E. G., Wit.
St. Clair, Alexander Robert, Wit.

Binns, John A., Wit.
Waterman, A. G., Wit.
Ball, Charles Burgess, O:263, u.d./1823
Ball, Fayette, Brother
Ball, —, Unborn child
Ball, Charles Burgess, Son
Ball, Isabella Graham, Dau.
Ball, Frances Washington, Dau.
Ball, Fayette Washington, Son
Ball, Ebenezer Burgess, Son
Ball, Lucy T., Wife
Wilson, Dr. John T., Friend
Mott, Thomas R., Exor.
Richards, George, Wit.
Gullatt, Charles, Wit.
Beatty, O. R., Wit.
Beans, Mathew, O:264, 1818/23
Beans, Rosanna, Gr-Dau.
Beans, Isaiah, Gr-Son
Beans, Mahlon, Gr-Son
Beans, Moses, Gr-Son
Beans, —, Wife
Beans, Uriah, Gr-Son
Beans, Minerva, Gr-Dau.
Beans, Jane, Gr-Dau.
Reece, David, Exor.
Roberts, Jonah, Gr-Son
Miller, Jeremiah, Exor.
Brown, William, Wit.
Brown, John, Wit.
Davis, Samuel, O:270, 1821/23/23
McConneley, Jane, Dau.
Garrett, Nancy, Dau.
Hoffman, Mary, Dau.
Bunnell, Elizabeth, Dau.
Dagg, Sarah, Dau.
Dagg, Samuel's child, Gt-Gr-Son
Davis, Samuel, Son
Dagg, John L., Gr-Son
Dagg, Samuel, Gr-Son, lately dec'd.
Davis, Joseph, Son
Davis, James, Son
Davis, William, Son
Davis, Sarah, Wife, dec'd. by 3/13/23
Davis, Harriet, Gr-Dau., dau of William

Powell, Burr, Wit.
Frey, Philip, Wit.
Helleard, James, Wit.
Bitzer, Harmon, Wit.
Boyd, Elizabeth, O:271, 1815/23/23
Davis, Samuel, child of James, she raised
Davis, Betsey (or Elizabeth) child of James, child she raised
Rogers, Hugh
Rogers, Hamilton, dec'd. in 1823
Rogers, Samuel, son of Hamilton
Harbert, Peggy, girl who lives with me
Waugh (alias Gibson), Lemuel
McVeigh, Jesse's 1st wife's children
Wilson, Jane, Sister, w/o Thomas
Boyd, Samuel, Husband, dec'd.
Bitzer, Poly, w/o John, child of Elizabeth Beaty, dec'd.
Beaty, Silas, child of Elizabeth Beaty, dec'd.
Bisco, Sally, w/o Thomas, child of Elizabeth Beaty, dec'd.
Beaty, Elizabeth, dec'd. by 1823
Davis, James, all his children
Powell, Burr, Wit.
Upp, John, Wit.
Gibson, A., Wit.
Smith, Hugh, Wit.
Sanders, Presly, O:273, 1823
Sanders, Cyrus G., Gr-Son
Sanders, John E., Gr-Son
Sanders, John, Exor.
Sanders, Emily, Gr-Dau.
Sanders, John W., Gr-Son
Sanders, Presly A., Gr-Son
Sanders, Thomas, Exor.
Sanders, Mary, Dau.
Sanders, —, Wife
Dware, James
Hoskins, Margaret, Gr-Dau.
Dware, Sally, Gr-Dau.
Sanders, Rachael A., Gr-Dau.

Joice, Thomas, Wit.
Saunders, Thomas R, Wit.
Hoskinson, William B., Wit.
Hough, Samuel, O:274, 1823
Hough, Samuel, Son
Hough, Jefferson, Son
Hough, John, Son
Hough, Robert R., Son
Hough, Edward, Son
Hough, Juliet, Dau.
Hough, Mary, Dau.
Hough, Ann, Dau.
Hough, Sarah, Dau.
Hough, Ann, Wife
Moore, Asa, Wit.
Phillips, Thomas, Wit.
Bond, Joseph, Wit.
White, Josiah, O:275, 1822/23
White, Rachel, Dau.
White, Josabed, Son
White, William, Son
White, Elizabeth, Dau.
White, Washington, Son
Love, Leah, Dau., w/o Thomas
Keith, Vincent Crawford, Gr-Son
Keith, Vincent's children, Gr-children
Keith, Vincent, Son-in-law, now in Ohio
Ellzey, L., Wit.
Dorrell, Thomas, Wit.
Hunt, John, Wit.
McArtor, Moses, Wit.
Janney, Israel, O:277, 1822/23
Janney, Samuel, Gr-Son, son of Abijah & Jane
Janney, Lott, Son, now in Ohio
Janney, Israel, Son
Janney, Jonathan, Son
Janney, Sarah Jane, Gr-Dau., dau. of David
Janney, Israel, Gr-Son, son of David
Janney, James, Gr-Son, son of David
Janney, David, Son, dec'd.
Janney, Phineas, Son
Janney, Tomzin, Gr-Dau., dau. of Abijah & Jane

Janney, Anna, Gr-Dau., dau. of Abijah & Jane
Janney, Richard, Gr-Son., son of Abijah & Jane
Janney, Asa, Gr-Son., son of Abijah & Jane
Janney, Jane, Dau., first w/o Abijah, dec'd-in-law
Janney, Hannah, Gr-mother of dau. Jane
Janney, Abijah, Son
Janney, Jane, Dau.
Janney, Daniel, Son
Janney, Phineas, Gr-Son, son of David
Janney, Pleasant, Dau.
Janney, Hannah, Gr.-Dau., dau. of Abijah & Jane
Taylor, Bernard, Wit.
Taylor, Jonathan Jr., Wit.
Taylor, Henry, Wit.
Taylor, Bernard Jr., Wit.
Frazer, Margaret, O:283, 1823
Taylor, John, Exor.
Taylor, Lucy A., dau. of John Taylor
Taylor, Margaret F., dau. of John Taylor
Riddle, Thomas F.
Frazer, Diana, Sister
Taylor, James W., son of John Taylor
Lewis, Charles, Wit.
French, Lewis, Wit.
Saffer, George, Wit.
Smith, Samuel, O:294, 1820/23
Holloway, Aaron, Son-in-law
Smith, Samuel, Son
Smith, Seth, Son
Smith, Jacob, Son
Smith, John, Son
Smith, Mary, Dau.
Smith, Kezia, Dau.
Smith, James, Son
Smith, Rachel, Dau.
Smith, Amos, Son
Reeder, Gourly, Wit.
Hatcher, Joseph, Wit.
Silcott, Jacob, Wit.

Waltman, Jacob Sr., O:307, 1823
  Deaver, Ann, Dau., dec'd.
  Deaver, Abraham, Gr-Son,
    child of Ann
  Deaver, Daniel, Gr-Son,
    child of Ann
  Deaver, Deborah, Gr-Dau.,
    child of Ann
  Deaver, Margreat, Gr-Dau.,
    child of Ann
  Deaver, Bazel, Son-in-law
  Ricard, Elizabeth
  Waltman, John, Son, dec'd.
  Chambers, William
  Wenner, Elizabeth, Dau.
  Wenner, John, Exor.,
    husband of Elizabeth
  Waltman, David, Gr-Son,
    son of John
  Waltman, Samuel, Gr-Son,
    son of John
  Waltman, Mariah, Gr-Dau., dau.
    of John
  Waltman, Jacob, Son
  Waltman, Elisebeth, Gr-Dau.,
    dau. of John
  Everhart, Sara, Gr-Dau., dau. of
    dau. Ann
  Everhart, Joseph, Gr-Son, son
    of dau. Ann
  Everhart, John, Gr-Son, son of
    dau. Ann
  Everhart, Jacob, Gr-Son, son of
    dau. Ann
  Moore, John, Wit.
  Smith, Jacob, Wit.
  Waters, Jacob, Wit.

Moore, Asa of Waterford, O:310, 1820/21/23
  Littler, Sarah Ann, Step-Dau.,
    wife's Dau.
  Phillips, Thomas, Exor.
  Taylor, Amy, Sister
  Deaver, Anne
  Bond, Joseph, Nephew
  Eaches, Ann
  Bond, Elizabeth, Sister
  Bond, James L., wife's Gr-Son
  Moore, Abner, Nephew
  Moore, James Jr., Nephew,
    son of James
  Moore, James, Brother
  Moore, Caleb, Nephew,
    son of Thomas
  Moore, Ann, Niece,
    dau. of Thomas
  Moore, Asa, Nephew,
    son of Thomas
  Moore, Mary, Niece,
    dau. of Thomas
  Moore, Thomas, Brother
  McCormick, Thomas,
    son of James
  McCormick, John, son of James
  Moore, —, Wife
  Morgan, Eliza
  Steer, Sarah, Niece
  Janney, Elizabeth, Niece
  McCormick, Mary
  Dorsey, Edward, Wit.
  Walker, Isaac, Wit.
  Stone, Daniel, Wit.
  Mendenhall, J., Wit.

Cowgill, Isaac, O:312, 1816/23
  Fry, Isaac, Son-in-law
  Silcott, Jacob, Son-in-law
  Cowgill, Sarah, Dau., dec'd.
  Cowgill, Thomas, Son
  Cowgill, Ruth, Dau.
  Cowgill, Mary, Wife
  —, Maria, Gr-Dau.
  —, Sarah's 2 Daus., Gr-Daus.
  Hibbs, Amos, Exor.
  Smith, Seth, Wit.
  Smith, Samuel Jr., Wit.

Ekart, Casper, O:313, 1823
  Cooper, Catharine, Sister
  Ekart, Ann, Wife
  Stevens, Henry
  Stevens, Eleanor, Dau.
  Anderson, Sarah, Dau.
  Gore, Truman, Wit.
  Beaty, John, Wit.
  Fry, Jacob, Wit.

Hunt, Major, O:314, 1823
  Reed, Hannah, w/o John
  Riley, Joshua, Exor.
  Hare, Jesse, son of William
  Hunt, Mary, Wife

Hunt, John, Brother
Hunt, John, Nephew,
  son of John
Hunt, Sandy, son of Joseph
Hare, James, son of William
Mercer, Joseph
Nixon, Joel, Exor.
McCabe, J. H., Wit.
Carr, Thomas, Wit.
McArtor, Jonathan, Wit.
McArtor, Moses, Wit.
Wine, Jacob, O:316, 1823
Wine, Catharine, Wife
Wine, George, Son,
  lives in Ohio
Wine, Daniel, Son
Hines, Catharine, Gr-Dau.
Hines, Hester, Dau.
Hines, Daniel, Gr-Son
Hines, Elizabeth, Gr-Dau.
Hines, Mary, Gr-Dau.
Hines, Linna, Gr-Dau.
Hines, William, Gr-Son
Huff, George, Son-in-law
Huff, Elizabeth, Dau.
Peacock, Sarah, Gr-Dau.
Gross, John, Gr-Son, Elizabeth
  Huff's son
Wine, John, Son
Boger, Catharine, Dau.
Boger, David, Son-in-law
Hough, William H., Wit.
Locker, Gerard, Wit.
Rawlings, Thomas, Wit.
Taylor, Mahlon, O:328, 1823
Taylor, Mary, Wife
Taylor, Joseph, Son
Taylor, Charlotte, Dau.
Taylor, Mahlon K., Son
Waters, Elizabeth, Dau.
Janny, Leatitia, Dau.
Faucet, Lydia, Dau.
Smith, Mary, Dau.
Taylor, Stacy, Dau.
Heaton, James, Wit.
Hurst, Jesse, Wit.
Jenkins, Samuel, O:342, 1818/24
Jenkins, Elijah, Son
Jenkins, Samuel, Gr-Son, son of
  Elijah

Blincoe, Sampson, Wit.
Perry, Benjamin W., Wit.
Powell, Albert O., Wit.
Beans, Matthew, O:343, 1824
Beans, Jane, Wife
Braden, Burr, Wit.
McDaniel, Archibald, Wit.
Brown, William Jr., Wit.
Souder, Margaret, O:344, 1823/24
Souder, Philip, Father, dec'd.
Souder, —, Mother
Souder, Michael, Brother
Cooper, Elizabeth Margaret,
  Niece, <18
Fry, Peter, Wit.
Fry, John, Wit.
Hamilton, John, Wit.
**Nichols, Rebeckah, O:362,
  1822/24**
Vernon, Rebeckah, Niece
Tavender, Miriam, Niece
Piggott, William, Exor.
Nickols, William, Exor.
Gregg, Phebe, Niece
Nickols, Mary, Niece
Nickols, Isaac, Husband, dec'd.
Gibson, John, Nephew
Gibson, Amos, Nephew
Gibson, Joseph, Nephew, son
  of Moses
Gibson, Lydia, Sister-in-law,
  Moses' wife
Gibson, Heber, Nephew, son of
  Moses
Gibson, Moses, Brother
Brooks, Hannah, Niece
Beans, Moses, O:366, 1824
Irey, Samuel, Exor.
Beans, Lattica, Wife
Beans, Mathew, Gr-father,
  dec'd.
Roberts, Sarah, Dau.
**Worthington, Joshua, O:372,
  1824**
Worthington, Elizabeth, Mother
Osburn, Joshua, Uncle
Osburn, Craven, Wit.
Osburn, Turner, Wit.
Hamilton, Norval, Wit.

Hamilton, John, Wit.
Osburn, Alfred, Wit.
Heslop, Isabella, O:406, 1819/21
Graham, George, Brother,
  dec'd.
Armistead, Robert, dec'd.,
  money due me from his
  estate
Armistead, Harriet M., Gr-Dau.
Armistead, George G., Gr-Son
Armistead, Frances A., Gr-Dau.
Armistead, Frances, Dau.
Armistead, Robert, Gr-Son
Armistead, Isabella G., Gr-Dau.
Taylor, John, negro
Taylor, Alfred, negro
Taylor, Robert, negro
  blacksmith
Tyler, Edmund, Wit.
Lacey, Elias, Wit.
Fishback, Ann E., O:408, 1820/24
Wherry, Elizabeth, Mother
Mines, John, Wit.
Wilson, John T., Wit.
Jenkins, Alse, O:409, 1824
Jenkins, Samuel, Husband,
  dec'd.
Henderson, Richard H., Son
Ewers, Levi G., Wit.
Mott, Thomas R., Wit.
**Beall, Thomas Brooke, of D.C.,
  O:416, 1808/12/16/20**
Turner, Frances
Peter, Mary
Peter, Miss Betsy
Peter, Mrs. Harriet
Wilson, Anna, Niece,
  dau. of Elizabeth Balch
Rose, Anna
Peter, Ann
Washington, Mrs. Elizabeth
Rose, Captain John, Exor.
Balch, Thomas, Nephew
Beall, Lucy, George's youngest
  Dau.
Balch, Stephen B., Exor.
Balch, Lewis P. W.
Balch, Elizabeth, Sister
Balch, Jane Whan, Niece,
  Elizabeth's Dau.
Balch, Eliza, Niece,
  Elizabeth's Dau.
Balch, Anna, Niece,
  Elizabeth's Dau.
Beall, Erasmus, Brother
Beall, Thomas, Nephew,
  son of Erasmus
Beall, George
Beall, Hez.
Hill, Avelina, Leithy's youngest
  Dau. in 1808
Hill, Leithy, father's former slave
Howes, Mary
Maffitt, Sally Miss, Friend
Magruder, George B., Wit.
Jones, Benjamin W., Wit.
Jones, Horatio, Wit.
Magruder, Peter W., Wit.
Harrison, Mrs.
Janney, Mary, O:429, 1823/24
Janney, Lydia, Dau.
Janney, Blackstone, Husband,
  dec'd.
Janney, Eli, Son
Hatcher, Samuel, Wit.
Janney, Daniel, Wit.
Piggott, Isaac, Wit.
Hatcher, Thomas, Wit.
Myers, Elijah, O:429, 1823/24
Paxson, Elijah, Gr-Son
Schooley, Sarah, Dau.
Schooley, Tacy, Dau.
Myers, —, Wife
Myers, Israel, Son
Myers, William, Son
Myers, Mary, Dau.
Myers, Mahlon, Son
Myers, Jonathan, Father, dec'd.
Moore, James, Wit.
Wood, Joseph, Wit.
Steer, Isaac E., Wit.
Moss, Thomas, O:440, 1824
Moss, —, Wife
Moss, John, Son
Moss, Carter, Son
Moss, Elizabeth, Dau.
Moss, Thomas, Son
Moss, Robert, Son
Moffett, Frances, Dau.

Moffett, Josiah, Son-in-Law,
  dec'd.
Moffett, David, Son-in-law,
  brother of Josiah
Moffett, Harriet, Gr-Dau., only
  dau. of David
Fouch, Susanna, Dau.
Tillett, Hannah, Dau.
Hammett, Sarah, Dau., dec'd.
Fouch, Thomas, Wit.
Fouch, Amos, Wit.
Jenners, Abiel, O:472, 1824
Jenners, —, five youngest
  children
Braden, John, Exor.
Jenners, Deborah, Wife
Jenners, —, three eldest
  children
Shepherd, Jonathan, O:473, 1824
Shepherd, —, Wife
Shepherd, William, Son
Shepherd, Edward, Brother
Evans, Eli, Wit.
Littleton, John, Wit.
Craven, Joseph, Wit.
Love, Rebeckah, O:474, 1824
Dillon, Abdon, Exor.
Nichols, Isach, Uncle, dec'd.
Nichols, Jonah, Brother
Love, Marah, Dau.
Love, Sarah, Dau.
Love, Nathan, Son
Love, Henry, Son
Love, William, Son, <21
Love, Lydia, Dau.
Carr, David, Wit.
Brown, William Jr., Wit.
Neptune, George, Wit.
Vernon, Daniel, O:483, 1824
Harber, Aaron, Nephew
Edwards, Sarah, Sister
Harber, Elizabeth, Sister
Smith, Hugh, Exor.
Vernon, Hester, Sister
Vernon, —, Wife
Vernon, Isaiah, Brother
Vernon, John, Brother
Grady, Edward B., Wit.
Gibson, David, Wit.
Gibson, Joshua, Wit.

Titus, Jane, O:495, 1823/24
Craig, Francis, Gr-Son
Craig, Jane, Gr-Dau.
Craig, Rebecca, Dau.
Carter, Joseph, Son-in-law
Craig, Nancy, Gr-Dau.
Pursel, John, Wit.
Emerson, Thomas, Wit.
Gibson, Amos, Wit.
Tribby, Mary, O:495, 1824
Tribby, Thomas, Husband,
  dec'd.
Blincoe, S., Wit.
Keene, John, Wit.
Moffett, Robert, Wit.
Scott, Stephen, O:496, 1822/24
Walker, Isaac, Exor.
Scott, —, Wife
Scott, Jacob, Son
Scott, Anna, Dau.
Scott, Isaac, Son
Scott, Elizabeth, Dau.
Scott, Hannah, Dau.
Scott, Joseph, Son
Scott, Rebecca, Dau.
Humphrey, Abner G., O:497, 1824
Johnston, James, Exor.
Humphrey, John G., Exor.
Humphrey, Abner, Son, <21
Humphrey, Polly, Wife
Humphrey, Thomas, Son, <21
Lodge, Joseph, Wit.
Richards, Baron, Wit.
Humphrey, Thomas G., Wit.
Carter, James, O:499, 1824
Carter, Jonathan, Brother
Vernon, Daniel, Exor.
Carter, —, three other Dau.'s
Carter, James, Son, dec'd.
Carter, Levi, Son
Carter, Ann, Dau.
Carter, Dellila, Dau.
Carter, Ann, Gr-Dau., dau. of
  James
Carter, Jonathan's children, Son
Kerrick, Thomas, Wit.
Brown, Thomas, Wit.
George, William, Wit.

Tribby, Thomas, O:501, 1820/24
McFarling, Elenor, Dau.
Love, James, Exor.
Reece, David, Exor.
Tribby, Thomas, Son
Tribby, James, Son
Tribby, John, Son
Tribby, Mary, Wife
Hughes, Elisha, Wit.
Brown, William, Wit.
Hughs, Thomas, Wit.
Hughs, Mathew, Wit.
Nichols, Jonah, Wit.
Moran, William Sr., P:9, 1823/24
Lyon, Jane, Gr-Dau., dau. of
  John Moran, w/o Alexander
Moran, John, Gr-Son,
  son of John
Moran, Catharine, Gr-Dau.,
  dau. of John
Moran, John M., Son, dec'd.
Moran, Sarah, Gr-Dau.,
  dau. of John
Moran, William, Gr-Son,
  son of John
Moran, Elizabeth, Gr-Dau.
Moran, Richard, Gr-Son,
  son of John
Moran, William, Son
Moran, Edward B., Son,
  in from Kentucky
Moran, Samuel, Son
Moran, Gustavus, Son
Cordell, William B. , Son-in-law,
  husband of Elizabeth
Cordell, Elizabeth B., Dau.
Stovin, Charles, Wit.
Stovin, John Lewis, Wit.
Thrift, William, Admr. w.w.a.
Roller, Conrad, P:21, 1821/25
Swank, Catharine, Dau.
Roller, Elizabeth, Wife
Crim, Conrad, Gr-Son
Roller, David, Son
Crim, Rosanna, Dau.
Roller, Jonathan, Son
Crim, Elias, Gr-Son
Roller, Frederick, Son
Crim, Adam, Gr-Son
Roller, Daniel, Son
Crim, Abraham, Son-in-law,
  husband of Rosanna
Roller, Conrad, Son
Roller, John, Son
Roller, Priscilla, Dau.
Roller, Elizabeth, Dau.
Shover, Simon, Wit.
McCabe, George, Wit.
Axline, Henry, Wit.
Slates, Frederick, Wit.
Veale, Thomas, P:29, 1825
Myers, Amelia, <21,
  dau. of Thomas
Myers, Mary, <21
  dau. of Thomas
Veale, John, Exor.
Myers, Elizabeth,
  infant's next friend
Bawlieson, John, Wit.
Muse, Mary, Wit.
Humphrey, Abner, P:57, 1824/25
McVeigh, Elizabeth, Dau.
Humphrey, Abner, Gr-Son,
  son of Abner G.
Currell, Permelia, Dau.
Beans, Hanna, Dau.
Humphrey, Thomas, Gr-Son,
  son of Abner G.
Settle, Elizabeth, Gr-Dau.
Humphrey, Abner G., Son,
  dec'd.
Settle, Isaac, Son-in-law
Hixson, Tace, Dau., dec'd.
Settle, Mary, Dau.
Humphrey, Thomas G., Son
Humphrey, John G., Son
Barton, Thomas, Wit.
Barton (Banks), James, Wit.
Grayson, John, Wit.
Grayson, George M., Wit.
Boggess, Ann, P:75, 1822/25
Boggess, Henley, Son
Boggess, Jane Eliza, Gr-Dau.
Boggess, Henley, Gr-Son
Boggess, Samuel, Gr-Son
Debell, Jeremiah, Wit.
Glascock, John, Wit.
Robinson, John L., Wit.

Thomas, Philip, P:76, 1824/25
Parsons, Lucy, housekeeper
Thomas, alias Parsons, Ubricka,
  Dau.
Parsons, Jefferson Conway,
  Son
Parsons, Ubricka, Dau.
Thomas, alias Parsons,
  Jefferson Conway, Son
James, Thomas, Exor.
Heaton, Jon, Exor.
Osburn, Craven, Wit.
Lovely, William E., Wit.
Rhodes, Samuel, P:132, 1823/25
Rhodes, Effa, Wife
—, Alcinda, Step-Dau.,
  dau. of Effa Rhodes
Rhodes, Randall, Brother
Rhodes, Nancy, Dau.
Rhodes, Elizabeth, Dau.
Rhodes, Samuel, Son
Rhodes, Alfred, Son
Rhodes, Tholemiah, Son, <21
Rhodes, Lydia, Dau.
Grady, E. B., Wit.
Russell, Charles, Wit.
Moore, Peter, Wit.
Mason, Mary, of Rasberry Plain, P:135, 1824/25
Williams, Wilson, Servant
Jackson, Fanny, slave
Diggs, Rachel, maid
Williams, John William, Servant
Mason, John Thomson, Son
Mason, Stevens T., Gr-Son,
  son of Armistead T.
Mason, William Temple T.,
  relation, Friend
Mason, Elizabeth B.,
  Dau.-in-law
Mason, Charlotte E., Dau.-in-law
Mason, Armistead Thomson,
  Son
McCarty, Emily, Dau.
Barry, Catharine A., Dau.
Moore, Ann, of Waterford, P:161, 1824/25
Bond, James L., Gr-Son
Harris, George, Son-in-law
Harris, Sarah Ann, Dau.

Walker, Isaac, Wit.
Hough, Amasa, Wit.
Schooley, Reuben, Wit.
Lamborn, Isaac, Wit.
Berkins, John, P:188, 1818/25
Berkins, Mary, Wife
Fredd, Joshua, Wit.
Janney, Stephen, Wit.
Spring, Andrew, P:190, 1825
Alt, Mary, Dau.
Spring, Jacob, Son
Fawley, Susannah, Dau.
Spring, Casper, Son
Fawley, Christiana, Dau.
Spring, Michael, Son
Fey (Fry), Elizabeth, Dau.
Spring, David, Son
Baker, Catherine, Dau.
Spring, John, Son
Spring, Andrew, Son
Spring, Joseph, Son
Akey, Simon, Wit.
Cordell, Samuel, Wit.
Hamilton, John, Wit.
Jones, Sarah, P:196, 1823/25
Smith, Elizabeth, Dau.
Jones, Richard, Son
Jones, John, Son
Jones, William, Son
Jones, Captain William,
  Husband, dec'd.
Jones, Philip, Son
Blincoe, Martha, Dau.
Jones, Thomas, Son
Rozel, Stephen, Wit.
Simpson, French, Wit.
Hughes, Isaac, Wit.
Cullison, Jeremiah, P:198, 1825
Solomon, Henrietta, Dau.
Rollison, Juliann, Gr-Dau.,
  dau. of John
Havener, Wady, Dau.
Beach, Priscilla, Dau.
Rollison, John, Son-in-law,
  husband of Elizabeth
Cheek, Sarah, Dau.
Rollison, Elizabeth, Dau., dec'd.
Cullison, Nancy, Dau.
Cheek, Barrach, Son-in-law,
  husband of Fanny

Cullison, William, Son
Cheek, Fanny, Dau., dec'd.
Cullison, Jeremiah, Son
Houser, Philip, Wit.
Hoskinson, Andrew T., Wit.
Hunter, John H., Wit.
Evans, Samuel, P:199, 1823/25
Evans, Evan, Son
Young, Israel
—, Hannah, Dau.
Evans, Jesse, Son
McArter, Johnathan, Wit.
Mateer, James, Wit.
Clendening, Samuel, Wit.
Burson, Joseph, P:203, 1819/25/25
Hutchison, Lydia, Dau.
Burson, Cyrus, Son
Wilson, Tamer, Dau.
Burson, Polly, Wife
Burson, Jesse, Son
Burson, Kitty, Dau.
Burson, John, Son
Green, Thomas, Wit.
Dorsey, William H., Wit.
Smith, Seth, Wit.
Whitacre, John, Wit.
Cooper, Frederick, P:296, 1825
Cooper, Jacob, Son
Rickard, Catharine, Dau., dec'd.
Cooper, Mary, Wife
Cooper, John, Son
Cooper, William, Son
Cooper, George, Son
Cordell, Alexander, Wit.
Compher, Peter, Wit.
Cooper, George, Wit.
Carpenter, William Sr., P:337, 1823/25
Thomas, Mary, Dau.
Keene, George, Exor.
Keene, Nancy, Dau.
Carpenter, James, Son
Carpenter, William Jr., Son
Carpenter, John, Son
Furr, Thompson, Wit.
Carpenter, William, Wit.
Gibson, Ann, P:337, 1825
Gibson, Lucinda, Niece
Gibson, Addison, Nephew

Gibson, James, Nephew
Gibson, Amos, Exor.
Gibson, Ruth, Niece
Nichols, Isaac, Exor.
Gibson, Delila, Niece
Gibson, Mary, Niece
Gibson, Elizabeth, Niece
Gibson, Nancy, Niece
Gibson, Almeda, Niece
Violett, Jemima, P:343, 1825
Violett, Edward, Husband, dec'd.
Violett, Sarah, Dau.
Murray, Samuel, Exor.
Galliher, Thomas H., Exor.
Violett,—, all my children
Lewis, Charles, Dau.
Guay (Guy), Mary, Dau.
Leith, Peggy, Dau.
Leigh, William G., Wit.
Leith, Theodorck, Wit.
Nichols, Samuel, P:350, 1825
Hatcher, Rebecca, Sister
Pancoast, John, Nephew
Pancoast, Lydia, Niece
Pancoast, Joshua, Nephew
Pancoast, Ruth, Sister, dec'd.
Piggott, William, Exor.
Dillon, Ann, Niece
Tate, Edith, Niece, w/o Levi
Hogue, William, Nephew
Nichols, Lydia, Sister
Nichols, Phebe, dau. of Jacob
Nichols, Charity, dau. of Jacob
Nichols, Isaac Jr., Nephew
Nichols, Samuel,
  son of Jacob & Margaret
Nichols, Samuel,
  son of William & Mary
Nichols, Samuel,
  son of Samuel & Mary
Nichols, Samuel,
  son of Swethe & Rebecca
Nichols, Isaac, Brother
Ellzey, Elizabeth, P:353, 1825
Armistead, Mary L.
Harrison, Maria P.
Russell, Margaret H.
Ellzey, Thomasin,
  Half Uncle, dec'd.

Index to Loudoun County Wills, 1757 - 1850   115

Harrison, Burr W., Nephew
McKinley, Elizabeth
Ellzey, Lewis, Brother
Harrison, Sarah C.
Ellzey, William, Brother
Harrison, Margaret L.
Ellzey, Sarah, Sister
Harrison, John M.
Ellzey, Mary, Sister
Harrison, Henry T., Nephew
Harrison, Thomas J.
Harrison, Catherine, Sister
Bayly, J., Wit.
Bayly, Richard P., Wit.
Ankers, John, Wit.
Tillett, Edward, Wit.
Dorsey, Dr. William H., P:356, 1825
Johnson, James, Friend
Smith, Seth, Wit.
Hall, Edward, Wit.
Wildman, John, P:359, 1824/25
Walters, Mary, Dau.
Wildman, James, Son
Wirnald, Rachel, Dau.
Wildman, Aaron, Son
Wildman, John, Son
Wildman, Enos, Son
Wildman, Jacob, Son
Wildman, Millary, Dau.
Wildman, Elenor, Dau.
Wildman, —, Wife
Wildman, Joseph, Son, dec'd.
Fouch, Thomas, Wit.
Hawling, Isaac W., Wit.
Donohoe, George, Wit.
Ingledue, Ann, P:360, 1823/25
Schooley, Reuben, Exor.
Richardson, Margaret, Sister
Ingledue, Blackstone, Brother
Schooley, Enoch, Wit.
Schooley, Eli L., Wit.
Boger, Elizabeth, P:379, 1825
Boger, Philip, Brother
Boger, Elizabeth, Mother
Winsell, George, Wit.
Hickman, Henry, Wit.
Boger, John, Wit.

Marlow, Edward, P:394, 1825
Marlow, —, my young children
Marlow, George, Son
Marlow, Henson, Son
Marlow, Thomas, Wit.
Shafer, Jacob, Wit.
Reitchie, Daniel, Wit.
Walsh, Elizabeth, Q:7, 1819/26
Rhodes, George, Exor.
Nixon, Mary, Gr-Dau.
Wildman, Elizabeth, Dau.
Wildman, Elizabeth, Gr-Dau.
Wildman, Nancy, Gr-Dau.
Wildman, Sarah, Gr-Dau.
Wildman, Juannah, Gr-Dau.
Wildman, Juliann, Gr-Dau.
Walsh, Thomas, Son
Walsh, George, Son
Maginnis, Edward, Wit.
Ervin, John, Wit.
Hogue, Joseph, Wit.
Gregg, William, Q:17, 1819/26
Wilkison, Elizabeth, Dau.
Hixson, Samuel, Son-in-law
Hixson, Ruth, Dau.
Steere, Rebekah, Dau.
Gregg, Aron, Son, dec'd.
Steere, Isaac, Son-in-law
Gregg, George, Son
Schooley, John, Exor.
Gregg, Rebekah, Wife
Gregg, Samuel, Son
Gregg, William, Gr-Son, son of Aron
Gregg, Sarah, Dau.
James, Elijah, Wit.
Minnix, Elijah, Wit.
Wilkison, William S., Wit.
Shaw, John, Q:20, 1825/26
Jacobs, William H., Son-in-law
Jacobs, Catharine, Dau.
Shaw, Rebecca, Wife
Shaw, Sidney, Son
Shaw, Mary, Dau.
Shaw, Susan Bailey, Youngest Dau., <21
Shaw, Eliza Ann, Dau.
Eskridge, Charles G., Wit.
Eskridge, Alfred A., Wit.

Nixon, James, Q:22, u.d./1826
  White, James, Gr-Son,
    son of Jane
  White, Thomas, Gr-Son,
    son of Jane
  White, William, Gr-Son,
    son of Jane
  Nixon, John, Brother
  Nixon, Mary, Gr-Dau.,
    dau. of William
  Nixon, Samuel, Gr-Son,
    son of William
  Nixon, William, Gr-Son,
    son of William
  Nixon, William, Son, dec'd.
  Lare, John
  Pusey, Mary, Dau.
  Pusey, Joshua, Exor.
  White, Jane, Dau., dec'd.
  Hanks, Ruth
  Jenners, Abiel, Wit.
  Jenners, William, Wit.
  Shumaker, Simon, Wit.

Settle, Susannah, Q:23, 1825/26
  McFarling, James, Exor.
  Cunningham, Huldah
  Settle, Daniel, Son
  Acres, Nancy, Dau.
  Settle, Newman, Son
  Lewis, Charles, Wit.
  Lee, Alexander, Wit.

Lewis, James, Q:44, 1811/26
  Lewis, Susannah H., Dau.
  Lewis, John H., Son
  Lewis, Jane F. L., Dau.
  Lewis, Nancy L., Dau.
  Lewis, Elizabeth C., Dau.
  Lewis, Catharine L., Dau.
  Lewis, James M., Son
  Lewis, Vincent L., Son
  Lewis, Willam B., Son
  Lewis, Martha J., Dau.
  Lewis, Charles, Exor.
  Berkley, John L., Exor.

Tavener, George, Q:64, 1823/26
  Hatcher, Sarah, Dau.
  Roach, Hannah, to live with my
    wife
  Roach, Lucinda, dau. of Hannah
    Roach
  Silcott, Barsheba, Dau.
  Batson, Tabitha, Dau.
  Tavener, Jonah, Son
  Tavener, Mary, Dau.
  Tavener, Betsy, Gr-Dau.,
    dau. of Mary
  Tavener, George, Son
  Tavener, George, Gr-Son,
    son of Eli
  Tavener, Hiram, Gr-Son,
    son of George
  Tavener, James, Son
  Tavener, Isaac, Son
  Tavener, Joseph, Son
  Tavener, Richard, Son
  Tavener, Eli, Son
  Tavener, Tabitha, Wife
  Wildman, Hannah, Dau.
  Sands, Jonah, Wit.
  Gregg, Joshua, Wit.
  Hamilton, C. B., Wit.
  Hamilton, Nancy, Wit.

Moore, James, Q:68, 1822/26
  Walker, Isaac, kinsman, Friend
  Talbott, Joseph, wife's dec'd.
    husband
  Janney, Elizabeth, Dau., dec'd.
  Janney, Alfred, Gr-Son
  Moore, Rebeckah, Wife
  Moore, Abner, Son
  Moore, James, Son
  Littleton, Hannah, w/o Joel
  Phillips, Thomas, kinsman,
    Friend
  Norwood, Mary Ann
  Steer, Sarah, Dau.
  Moore, Mary, Dau.-in-law,
    w/o Abner
  Williams, John, Wit.
  Smith, Seth, Wit.
  Mendenhall, J., Wit.
  Wilson, John C., Wit.

Powell, Cuthbert Jr., Q:79, 1826
  Powell, Cuthbert of Langollin,
    Exor.
  Powell, Charles, Friend
  Powell, Mary, Wife
  Powell, William A., Exor.
  Powell, —, Unborn child
  Powell, John, Brother

Powell, —, Mother
Powell, Alfred, Brother
Powell, Burr, Wit.
Powell, C. H., Wit.
Smith, F. W., Wit.
Warfield, David, Q:122, 1821/26
Warfield, Lott, Brother
Warfield, David, Nephew,
  son of Lott
Warfield, Alexander, Brother
Warfield, Dennis, Nephew,
  son of Alexander
Warfield, Charles, Brother
Wyatt, Rev. William E.
Johnson, Elizabeth, Sister,
  dec'd.
Johnson, Eliza Ann, Niece,
  dau. of Elizabeth
Johnson, Charles D. W.,
  Nephew, son of Elizabeth
Jones, Ann (or Nancy), Sister,
  dec'd.
Johnson, Thomas, Nephew,
  son of Elizabeth
Johnson, Caroline, Niece,
  dau. of Elizabeth
Johnson, Arthur L., Nephew,
  son of Elizabeth
Johnson, Evelina H., Niece,
  dau. of Elizabeth
Clagett, Misses Gr-children of
  Mrs. Susan Lee with whom I
  once lived
Bennett, Polly, Sister, dec'd.
Kendal, Mercy, Friend
Pearre, Sally, Sister
Birkhead, Hugh, Wit.
Cummins, Francis D., Wit.
Israel, Fielder, Wit.
Kitzmiller, Martin, Q:124, 1825/26
Kitzmiller, Archibald, Son, <21
Kitzmiller, Lydia, Dau.
Kitzmiller, William, Son, <21
Kitzmiller, Elizabeth, Wife
Mains, Archibald, Wit.
Carr, John, Wit.
Hunt, Eli, Wit.

Mott, Thomas R., Q:150, 1826
Mott, Mary C., Wife
Mott, Armistead, Son, <18
Mott, M. E., Dau., <18
Mott, Randolph, Son, <18
Ball, Charles, youngest son of
  C. B. Ball, dec'd.
Henderson, William,
  son of Richard H.
Hains, Stacy, Q:153, 1822/26
Hains, Thomas J., Son
Hains, Joseph, Son
Hains, John W., Son
Hains, Edward, Son
Hains, George W., Son
Hains, Hannah, Dau.
Hains, Manley R., Son
Kid, Sarah, Dau.
Ratcliffe, Cassy, Dau.
Cordell, Presley, Exor.
Langton, Margaret, Dau.
Morallee, Thomas, Wit.
Dailey, Aaron, Wit.
Morrison, Archibald, Q:155, 1826
Morrison, Archibald, son of
  John, Gr-Son
Morrison, Jane, Wife
Morrison, John, Son
Morrison, James' heirs, Son
Morrison, Rachel, Dau.
Morrison, Benjamin, Son
Morrison, Edward, Son
Morrison, Joseph, Son
Morrison, Elizabeth, Dau.
Morrison, Charity, Dau.
Morrison, Jane, Dau.
Morrison, Mary, Dau.
Morrison, Sary, Dau.
Burns, Philip, Wit.
Fry, John, Wit.
Baker, Philip, Wit.
German Script Name, Wit.
Chilton, Charles, Q:156, 1826
Chilton, Susan, Mother, dec'd.
Chilton, Charles, Uncle, dec'd.
Rust, Martha, Niece, dau. of
  Sally, <21
Rose, John, Exor.
Rust, Susan, Niece, dau. of
  Sally, <21

Rust, James William, Nephew,
 son of Sally, <21
Rust, Sally, w/o Manley T, Sister
Rust, John B., Nephew, son of
 Sally, <21
Taylor, Susan Ann, Sister,
 w/o Griffin
Rust, Thomas C., Nephew, son
 of Sally, <21
Richards, George, Wit.
Richards, Ann B., Wit.
Kincheloe, John, Q:159, 1826
Kincheloe, Brandt, Brother
Kincheloe, Hardwich, Brother
Kincheloe, William, Brother
Shepherd, Catherine G., dau. of
 Thomas
Waterman, A. G., Wit.
Luckett, Francis W., Wit.
Douglas, Margaret, Q:160, 1826
Tebbs, Margaret H. D., Niece
Douglas, Archibald N., Nephew
Peers, Ann, dau. of Mrs. Peers,
 Friend
Peers, Mrs., Friend
Douglas, Charles, Nephew
Binns, Elizabeth D., Wit.
Douglas, Lewis F., Wit.
Derry, Philip, Q:173, 1826
Derry, —, children
Derry, Barbary, Wife
White, B., Wit.
Conard, John, Wit.
Harding, Edward, Wit.
Filler, Jacob, Wit.
Gregg, Henry, Q:174, 1826
Purcell, Valentine V.
Gregg, Letty, Dau.
Gregg, Patty, Dau.
Hamilton, Charles B., Exor.
Taylor, Henry S. Trustee
Cockeril, Daniel, Exor.
Gregg, Jesse's children
Janney, Daniel, Wit.
Nichols, Isaac, Wit.
Gregg, Thomas, Q:175, 1826
Gregg, Stephen, Son
Gregg, Nathan, Brother
Osburn, Joshua, Wit.
Caldwell, S. B. T., Wit.

Heaton, Jonathan, Wit.
Reed, John, Wit.
**McDaniel, Martin Norris, Q:190,
 1816/26**
Dement, William, guardian of
 two eldest children
Bealle, David F., Exor.
McDaniel, —, Wife
McDaniel, Eleanor, Eldest Dau.
McDaniel,—, three youngest
 children
McDaniel, John William,
 Eldest Son
Macdaniel, George, Wit.
Macdaniel, John Jr., Wit.
Demont, Richard, Wit.
Frazier, Dian, Q:205, 1824/26
Cooper, Richard
Cooper, William Hiram
Cooper, Lucy Ann
Cooper, Nathaniel, Exor.
Lewis, Charles, Wit.
Timms, William S., Wit.
Duncan, Charles, Wit.
**Blincoe, Sampson, Q:206,
 1825/26**
Blincoe, —, two other children
Blincoe, Martha, Dau.
Blincoe, Sally E., Dau.
Blincoe, —, Unborn child
Blincoe, Martha S., Wife
Blincoe, Charles William, Son
Reeder, William, Q:207, 1826
Richards, William, Gr-Son's
 brother-in-law
Vickers, Anna, Dau.
Vickers, Abraham, Gr-Son
Hatcher, Sarah, Dau., dec'd.
Hatcher, Thomas, Gr-Son
Hatcher, William, Gr-Son
Humphrey, John, Gt-Gr-Son's
 brother-in-law
Hatcher, Hannah, Dau.
Reeder, Gourley, Son
Smith, Seth, Wit.
Gibson, Solomon, Wit.
Clico, Henry, Wit.
Whitmore, Polly, Q:209, 1826
Beaty, Catherine, Dau.,
 w/o John

Smith, William's heirs
  Whitmore, Michael, Brother
  Whitmore, Catherine
  Franks, Samuel
  Whitmore, George, Brother
  Beaty, Mary Elizabeth, Gr-Dau.
  Beaty, Susan, Gr-Dau.
  Beaty, John, Exor.
  Edwards, Charles W., Wit.
  Evans, Eli, Wit.
Cassady, John H., Q:210, 1823/26
  Hough, Samuel Jr., Exor.
  Cassady, Nancy or Ann
    MeGeath, second Wife
  Cassady, —, First Wife,
    sister of Nancy
  Cassady, William Henry, Son
  Cassady, Ann Catherine, Dau.
    child of Jane
  Cassady, Mary Elizabeth, Dau.,
    dau. of Jane
  Cassady, Jane, Wife
  McGeath, William, Father-in-
    law, father of Nancy
  Shawen, D., Wit.
  Paxon, Samuel, Wit.
  Paxon, John, Wit.
  Bennett, Jefferson, Wit.
Bronaugh, William, Q:212, 1819/26
  Brounaugh, Jane, Wife
  Brounaugh, Patrick H. William, Son
  Brounaugh, Ann C., Dau.
  Brounaugh, Jeremiah W., Son
  Brounaugh, George W., Son
  Brounaugh, William J., Son
  Brounaugh, John W. F., Son,
    dead by March 1824
  Brounaugh, Joseph W., Son
  Luckett, Francis W., Exor.
  Luckett, Sarah S., Dau.
  Magill, Mary D., Dau.
Love, Sarah, Q:264, 1824/27
  Pierpoint, Samuel, Exor.
  Love, Elizabeth, Sister
  Love, John P., Exor.
  Love, Thomas B., Wit.
  Pierpoint, Eli, Wit.

James, Anna, Q:284, 1822/27
  Nichols, William, Exor.,
    son of William
  Gore, Thomas, Exor.,
    son of Joshua
  James, Isaac, Son
  James, Thomas, Son
  James, James, Son
  Howel, Hannah, Dau.
  James, Elias, Son
  Heaton, Jonathan, Wit.
  Osburn, Morris, Wit.
  Howell, Elijah, Wit.
Marshall, William, Q:287, 1813/26
  Marshall, John, Brother
  Coleman, R., Wit.
  Harris, John A., Wit.
  Havener, Dominick, Wit.
Duncan, Susannah, Q:299, 1827
  Duncan, Susannah, Dau.
  Gardner, Nancy, Dau., dec'd.
  Duncan, Catherine, Dau.
  Power, Walter, Wit.
  Lee, Matthew P., Wit.
  Lee, Joshua, Wit.
Nichols, Nathan Jr., Q:300, 1827
  Nichols, Sarah, Wife
  Nichols, Nathan, Youngest Son
  Nichols, John, Eldest Son
  Nichols, George, Son
  Nichols, Albert, Son
  Nichols, Harriett, Dau.
  Nichols, Margaret, Dau.
  Nichols, Martha, Dau.
  Nichols, Ann, Dau.
  Nichols, Massey, Dau.
  Nichols, Sarah, Dau.
  Nichols, Mary Elizabeth, Dau.
  Coe, Albin, Son-in-law
  Osburn, Joshua, Exor.
  Thomas, Joseph, Wit.
  Thomas, Philip, Wit.
  Thomas, Joseph Jr., Wit.
  Nichols, Nathan, Wit.
Lewis, Joanna, Q:301, 1827
  Powell, Sarah, Dau.
  Green, John, Exor.
  Brent, Hugh, Son
  Wren, Patsy Newton, Gr-Dau.
  Brent, Willis, Son

Wren, Thomas, Son-in-law
Johnston, James, Friend
Dulaney, John P., Friend
Hall, Edward, Wit.
Smith, Henry, Wit.
Dunn, John, Q:303, 1827
Meade, Rev. William
Harrison, Burr William, Exor.
Beatty, Thomas B., Exor.
Dunn, Elizabeth, Wife
Beatty, Matilda C., w/o Thomas
Tutt, Eliza, Dau.
Powell, Burr, Wit.
Ball, Fayette, Wit.
Powell, William L., Wit.
Peers, Ann H., Wit.
Lodge, Willam, Q:332, 1825/27
Lodge, Christiana, Wife
Lodge, Laban, Son
Lodge, William, Son
Lodge, Abner, Son, lives in Ohio
Lodge, Joseph, Son
Lodge, Samuel, Son
Humphrey, Abner, Gr-Son,
  son of Mary
Humphrey, Thomas, Gr-Son,
  son of Mary
Humphrey, Mary, Dau.
Adams, William, Wit.
Janney, Stephen, Wit.
Janney, Aaron, Wit.
Janney, Jacob, Wit.
Thomas, Joseph, Wit.
Deale, William, Wit.
Hummer, William, Q:333, 1827
Hummer, Sarah, Dau.
Hummer, Richard, Brother
Hummer, Francis, Dau.
Hummer, William's heirs, Son
Hummer, Washington, Son
Hummer, Polly, Dau.
Hummer, Livi, Son
Hummer, Nancy, Dau.
Hummer, John, Son, dec'd.
Bridges, Benjamin, Exor.
Hummer, Eleanor, Dau.-in-law,
  w/o John
Minor, T. J., Wit.
Bell, William D., Wit.

Offutt, Hambleton, Wit.
Knight, William H., Wit.
Jenkins, William, Wit.
Bridges, John, Q:340, 1825/27
Ryan, Phillip
Bridges, Benjamin
Havner, Marcy
Cleveland, Johnston, Exor.
Havner, Sarah
Havner, Barbara
Havner, Mary
Havner, John
Havner, Martha
Havner, Joseph Redner
Darne, James, Wit.
Balenger, Henson, Wit.
Havener, Alexander, Wit.
Guider, Charles, Q:355, 1827
Guider, John, Son
Guider, Katy, Wife
Binns, John A., Exor.,
  son of Charles
Guider, Sarah Ann, Dau.
Morallee, Thomas, Wit.
Humphrey, Jane, Q:356, 1824/27
Gregg, Mary
Crossly, Ann and her children
Humphrey, John G., friend,
  Exor.
Walker, Martha & her children
Brown, Isacher's children
Brown, Craven
Snyder, Elizabeth & her children
Young, Abner H., Wit.
Humphrey, Abner G., Wit.
Humphrey, Thomas G., Wit.
Mains, Mary, Q:357, 1823/27
Vandevanter, Elizabeth, Dau.
Vandevanter, Mary, Gr-Dau.,
  dau. of Elizabeth
Vandevanter, Anne, Dau.,
  dec'd., has six children
Vandevanter, Elizabeth, Dau.,
  has seven children
Carr, Jane, Dau., has one child
Mains, William, Son, his 6
  children
Mains, Archibald, Son
—, my 20 Gr-children

Cordell, Presley, Wit.
Vandevanter, Gabriel, Wit.
Cline, John, Wit.
Garrett, Joseph, Q:358, 1827
  Garrett, Stephen, Son
  Garrett, John of Belmont Co.,
    Ohio
  Garrett, Mary, Dau.
  Garrett, Silas, Son
  Garrett, Rebecca, Dau.
  Garrett, Sarah, Dau.
  Garrett, Joseph, Son
  Garrett, Enoch, Son
  Hains, Joseph, Wit.
  Gilmore, William, Wit.
  Powell, Peyton, Wit.
  Wright, W. G., Wit.
Braden, Robert, R:20, 1827
  Braden, Noble S., Son
  Braden, Sarah, Dau., <21
  Braden, Elizabeth, Dau., <21
  Braden, Elizabeth, Wife
  Braden, Burr, Son
  Braden, William Fenton, Son
  Braden, Robert Jr., Son
  Braden, Hector W., Son
  Braden, James Adison, Son
  Dulaney, Mary E. , Dau.,
    w/o Zachariah
  Dulaney, Zachariah, Son-in-law
Rust, Peter, R:26, 1827/28
  Johnson, James, Exor.
  Froman, Hana, Dau.
  Rust, Peter, Son
  Dulaney, John, Exor.
  Hereford, Thomas, Exor.
  Hunt, Nancy, Dau.
  Rust, Margaret, Dau.,
    w/o Matthew of
    Frederick Co.
  Cramer, Thomas, Wit.
  Glass, Thomas, Wit.
  Jones, James, Wit.
James, David, R:93, 1818/28
  McKinney, Mary, Sister
  McKinney, Joseph, Nephew
  McKinney, George, Nephew
  James, Joseph, Brother
  James, Jane, Niece,
    dau. of Joseph
  James, Thomas, Nephew,
    son of Joseph
  Garrett, Joseph Sr., Exor.
  James, Joseph, Nephew,
    son of Joseph
  Skilman, Abraham, Wit.
  Lickey, William, Wit.
  Atwell, Jesse, Wit.
McNellage, James, R:95, 1827/28
  McNellage, Nancy, Wife
  Fadeley, Mary, Dau., w/o Jacob
  Harris, Isaac, Wit.
  Harris, James L., Wit.
  Martin, James L., Wit.
Carr, Thomas, R:159, 1828
  Carr, Archibald, Son
  Carr, —, minor children
  Carr, Joseph, Son
  Suffron, Mary Ann, Dau.
  Carr, —, Wife
  Nixon, Joel, Wit.
  Wade, Robert Jr., Wit.
  Sanders, Washington, Wit.
Saunders, Margaret, R:175, 1828
  Ruse, Polly, Dau.
  Saunders, Nicholas, Gr-Son,
    son of John
  Cooper, Nancy, Dau.
  Ruse, Sarah, Gr-Dau., dau. of
    Polly
  Saunders, —, Gr-Son, infant
    son of John
  Cooper, Hannah, Dau.
  Ruse, John, Gr-Son,
    son of Polly
  Sanders, George, Son
  Cooper, Betsy, Dau.
  Warner, Leonard, Brother
  Sanders, Peter, Son
  White, Thomas, Exor.
  Saunders, Hamilton, Gr-Son,
    son of George
  Saunders, John, Son
  Saunders, Westley, Gr-Son,
    son of John
  Saunders, Duanna, Gr-Dau.,
    dau. of George
  Morrison, Edward, Wit.
  Leslie, John, Wit.
  Hamilton, John Jr., Wit.

Brown, Samuel, R:180, 1827/28
Brown, Joseph, Brother
Brown, Betsy, Sister
Brown, Sarah's children, Sister
Brown, William, Brother
Taylor, Hannah, Sister
Brown, Sarah, Mother
Brown, Richard, Brother
Taylor, Yardley, Brother-in-law
Reece, David, Wit.
Brown, David, Wit.
Cooper, Alexander, R:180, 1828
Clifford, Elizabeth, Dau.,
   mother of Henry
Clifford, Henry, Gr-Son
Cooper, William, Son
Morallee, Thomas, Wit.
Manly, John S., Wit.
Shaw, John, Wit.
Mathias, John J., Wit.
Brown, John, R:181, 1823/26
Gregg, Hannah, Dau.
Potts, Lydia, Dau.
Nichols, Amer, Exor.
Gregg, Thomas, Son-in-law
Potts, Elizabeth, Dau.
Holmes, John, Exor.
Brown, John Harmon,
   Gr-Son, <21
Brown, Nathan, Son, dec'd.
Brown, William Holmes,
   Gr-Son, <21
Brown, Ann, Dau.-in-law
Brown, William, Brother
Kerrick, Stephen, Wit.
Pursel, John, Wit.
Hogue, Jesse, Wit.
Thornton, Charles, R:183, 1828
Belt, Alfred, Exor.
Knott, John Charles, Nephew,
   son of Sarah
Thornton, Mary, Dau., <16
Knott, Sarah, Sister
Thornton, Sarah, called Walters,
   Dau., <16
Knott, Julian, Nephew, son of
   Sarah
Walters, Sarah, Dau., <16
Jordan, John, Nephew

Jordan, Catharine, Niece
Dawson, Samuel, Wit.
Jackson, Benjamin, Wit.
Palmer, Elijah, Wit.
Hatcher, Noah, R:185, 1828
Nichols, Hannah, Oldest Dau.
Hatcher, John, Son, <21
Hatcher, Thomas Ellwood, Son
Hatcher, Elijah, Son
Hatcher, Rachel, Wife
Taylor, Stacy, Wit.
Taylor, Stacy Jr., Wit.
Taylor, Mahlon, Wit.
Gore, Solomon, R:205, 1826/28
Gore, Nancy, Dau.
Gore, Thomas, Son
Gore, Sarah, Dau.
Gore, William, Son
Gore, Joshua, Son
Gore, Jonathan, Son
Gore, John, Son
Gore, Rachel, Wife
Gore, Enos, Son
Gore, Joshua, Father, dec'd.
Janney, Daniel, Wit.
Hoge, William, Wit.
Hoge, Jesse, Wit.
Gore, Thomas, Wit.
Pursel, Samuel, R:206, 1826/28
Pursel, Samuel, Son
Pursel, Enos, Son
Pursel, Edwin, Son
Pursel, Jane, Dau.
Pursel, Mahlon, Son
Pursel, Margaret, Wife
Pursel, Hector, Son, <21
Pursel, Bernard, Son
Pursel, Hannah, Dau.
Pursel, Jonah, Son
Russel, Samuel, Wit.
Nichols, Isaac, Wit.
Taylor, Stacy Jr., Wit.
Gibson, Phebe, R:208, 1825/28
Brooke, Phebe, Gr-Dau.
Nichols, Phebe, Gr-Dau.
Nichols, Isaac, Son-in-law
Gregg, John, Son-in-law
Gibson, Phebe, Gr-Dau.
Gibson, John, Son

Pursel, John, Wit.
Janney, Daniel, Wit.
Gibson, Amos, Wit.
Fox, Mary, R:209, 1828
Shawen, William C.,
   Gr-Son, <21
Henry, America, Gr-Dau., <21
Fox, Delila, Niece
Braden, John, Brother
Fox, William, Nephew, <21,
   son of Cephus, dec'd.
Cordell, Presley, Wit.
Braden, Mary E., Wit.
Fouch, Thomas, R:238, 1827/28
Weldon, Nancy, Dau., of Prince
   William Co.
Fouch, —, Wife
Fouch, Amos, Son
Fouch, Thompson, Son
Fouch, Isaac, Son, late of Ky.
Fouch, Temple, Son, of
   Stafford Co.
Fouch, William, Son
Clagett, Henry, Wit.
Russell, Charley Ann Elizabeth
   Jane, Wit.
Middleton, William, R:245, 1828
Davis, Howell, Exor.
Harvey, Rebecca
Cockrill, John, Exor.
Rogers, Hugh Jr., Wit.
Rogers, Joseph, Wit.
Daniel, Eli, Wit.
Hoge, Jesse, R:250, 1828
Hoge, —, Wife
Hoge, William K., Son
Kenworthy, William
Gregg, Joshua Jr., Exor.
Gore, Joshua, Wit.
Hoge, William, Wit.
Janney, Daniel, Wit.
Hatcher, Rebecca, R:264, 1826/28
Nichols, Samuel, Brother, dec'd.
Hatcher, Thomas, Husband,
   dec'd.
Hatcher, William, dec'd.
   husband's brother
Hatcher, Gurley R., Gr-Son
Hatcher, Joseph, Son
Hatcher, Jonah, Gr-Son

Hatcher, Samuel, Son
Hatcher, Mahlon B., Gr-Son
Seaton, William, Gr-Son
Nichols, Isaac, Brother
Hoge, William, Nephew
Kerrick, Stephen, Wit.
Taylor, Yardley, Wit.
Hirst, Jonathan, Wit.
Dulin, John, R:265, 1827/28
Dulin, —, Mother, in Kentucky
Dulin, children
Dulin, Rebecca, Wife
Keene, Newton, Wit.
Havenner, John, Wit.
Havenner, Barbary, Wit.
Slater, Jacob, R:266, 1827/28
Carnes, Charlotte, Dau.
Souder, Mary, Dau.
Wean, Sarah, Dau.
Slater, Christena, Dau.
Slater, Samuel, Son
Slater, Catherine, Wife
Spring, Elizabeth, Dau.
Cordell, Susannah, Dau.
Slater, William, Wit.
Stuck, Ferdinando F., Wit.
Cordell, Samuel, Wit.
Ramey, Sanford, R:290, 1827/29
Cordell, Diana, Niece,
   w/o Alexander
Mason, Enoch, Exor.
Ramey, Jacob, Brother, dec'd.
Wilson, Presley, Exor.
Cordell, Alexander, Exor.
Ramey, Sanford I., Nephew
Ramey, Lydia, Wife
Edwards, Charles G., Wit.
Cordell, Presley, Wit.
Nichols, Isaac Sr., R:327, 1827/29
Hoge, William, Nephew
Hoge, James, Son-in-law
Hatcher, Thomas, Exor.
Hoge, Phebe, Gr-Dau.
Hoge, Joshua, Nephew
Hatcher, Catherine, Sister
Hoge, Rachel, Gr-Dau.
Hoge, Elizabeth, Gr-Dau.
Hoge, Isaac, Gr-Son, son of
   James & Rachel
Hatcher, Rebekah, Sister

Hoge, Jesse, Nephew
Hoge, Mary, Sister
Pancoast, John, Nephew
Pancoast, Lydia, Niece
Pancoast, Joshua, Nephew
Pancoast, Ruth, Sister, dec'd.
Nichols, William, Nephew,
  son of William
Gregg, Lydia, Niece
Tate, Edith, Niece, dau. of
  William Nichols
Nichols, Samuel, Nephew,
  son of William, dec'd.
Nichols, William, Brother
Dillon, Ann, Niece
Taylor, Henry S., Wit.
Taylor, Bernard Jr., Wit.
Janney, Jonas, Wit.
Taylor, Yardley, Wit.
Hatcher, Catherine, R:329, 1829
  Spencer, William, Son-in-law
  Hatcher, Isaac, Son
  Nichols, Jacob, Son-in-law
  Spencer, Sarah, Dau.
  Hatcher, James, Husband,
    dec'd.
  Nichols, Margery, Dau.
  Hatcher, James, Son
  Hatcher, Edith, Dau.
  Nichols, Swithin, Son-in-law
  Young, Elizabeth, Dau.
  Tavenner, Ann, Dau.
  Nichols, Rebecca, Dau.
  Young, David, Son-in-law
  Tavenner, Richard, Son-in-law,
    husband of Ann
  Tavenner, —, Ann's ten
    children, Gr-children
  Gregg, Abner, Son-in-law
  Gregg, Mary, Dau.
  Nichols, Samuel, Brother
  Smith, David, Wit.
  Gibson, William, Wit.
  Nichols, Thomas S., Wit.
Coleman, William, R:330, 1828/29
  Coleman, Edmond, Son
  Coleman, Julia, Dau.
  Coleman, Lydia, Wife
  Coleman, Thomas, Son
  Coleman, John J., Nephew

Vandevanter, Isaac, Wit.
Vandevanter, Gabriel, Wit.
Morgan, Eleanor, Wit.
Gunnell, George, Wit.
Wildman, Anna, R:373, 1828/29
  Williams, Lydia, Friend
  Roberts, Deborah, Niece
  Roberts, Joshua, Nephew
  Skiver, Delilah, Niece
  Steer, Isaac
  Downs, Ruth Ann, Gr-niece,
    dauther of Sintha
  Downs, Sintha, Niece
  Mendenhall, Hannah
  Janney, Sarah, dau. of Moses
  Irey, Jinilla, Niece
  Janney, Bulah, Friend
  Wildman, Abraham, Brother
  Roberts, Deborah, Sister
  Williams, John, Wit.
  Walker, Isaac, Wit.
  Janney, Moses, Exor.
Wirts, Jacob, R:375, 1828/29
  Grubb, Leah, Dau.
  Wirts, John, Son
  Wirts, Jacob, Son
  Wirts, Peter, Son
  Wirts, Mary, Dau.
  Wirts, Louinda, Dau.
  Wirts, William, Son
  Wirts, Henry, Son
  Conrad, Elizabeth, Dau.
  Grubb, Ebenezer Jr., Exor.
  Wirts, Susannah, Dau.
  Derry, Eliza, Dau., dec'd.
  Grubb, John, Wit.
  Sypherd, Matthew, Wit.
  Shover, Adam, Wit.
Matthew, Jonathan, R:376, 1815/29
  Matthew, Catherine, Wife
  Morris, Mahlon, Wit.
  Roberts, Robert, Wit.
  Beal, Thomas, Wit.
Potts, Susannah of Culpeper Co., R:376, 1827/29
  Potts, Enos
  Potts, Joshua
  Potts, Susannah, dau. of Jonas
  Potts, Isaiah

White, Maryann, Niece
Best, Elizabeth Ann,
 dau. of Enos
Best, Enos, Exor.
Favrow, George, Wit.
Favrow, William, Wit.
Eastham, Philip Jr., Wit.
Simpson, Hendley, Wit.
**Luckett, William, R:395,
1782/1783**
Luckett, Susanna, Dau.
Luckett, Thomas Hussey, Son
Luckett, Elizabeth, Dau.
Luckett, Ann, Dau.
Luckett, Leven, Son
Luckett, William, Son
Luckett, John, Son
Luckett, Virlinda, Dau.
Luckett, Eleanor, Dau.
Luckett, Charity, Wife
Harding, Garah, Wit.
Jacobs, John, Wit.
Hilton, Freeman, Wit.
**Luckett, Virlinda, R:399,
1782/1783**
Luckett, Kelly Collander, Niece,
 dau. of David, <16
Luckett, William Gesson,
 Nephew, son of David, <16
Luckett, Juliett, Niece,
 dau. of David, <16
Luckett, Luther, Nephew,
 son of David, <21
Luckett, William Francis,
 Nephew, son of Leven, <21
Luckett, John, Brother
Luckett, David, Exor.
Luckett, Samuel Noland,
 Nephew, son of John
Luckett, Susanna, Sister,
 w/o David
Luckett, Leven, Brother
Luckett, David Lawson,
 Nephew, son of David
Luckett, Francis William,
 Nephew, son of Leven, <21
Strington, Dorcas, Wit.
Beall, Thomas B., Wit.
Watkins, Leonard, Wit.

Mead, Margaret, R:401, 1829
Mead, —, six brothers and
 sisters
Taylor, Henry S., Exor.
White, Christeana, Sister
White, Margaret, Niece
Smith, David, Exor.
Popkins, Craven, Wit.
Bond, Asa M., Wit.
Bolon, Ferdinando, Wit.
McCarty, Dennis, R:402, 1824/29
McCarty, Richard Chichester,
 Son
McCarty, —, Wife
McCarty, Caroline G., Dau.
McCarty, George Washington,
 Brother
McCarty, Margaret, Dau.
McCarty, Dennis, Son
McCarty, Billington, Son
Taylor, R. I., Wit.
Mason, Thomas F., Wit.
Morrallee, Thomas, R:458, 1829
Purcell, Sarah, Wife's Niece
Morrallee, John, Brother
Morrallee, Michael, Brother
Morrallee, —, Wife
Binns, John A., Friend
Birkby, Thomas, Wit.
Smale, Simon, Wit.
Hixon, Mary, R:489, 1829
Miller, Rachel's children,
 Gr-child
Hixon, Catherine, Dau.
Hixon, Rheuben, Husband,
 dec'd.
Hixon, Noah, Son
Miller, Rachel, Dau.
Divine, Jacob, Wit.
Compher, Peter, Wit.
Shawen, George W., Wit.
Goodwin, Maria, S:67, 1829
Jackson, Rev. William, Exor.
Jackson, Mary Congreve,
 dau. of Thomas
Jackson, Rev. Thomas
Jackson, William Goodwin,
 son of Thomas
Goodwin, Thomas, Husband,
 dec'd.

Addison, Anthony, Wit.
Lee, Richard H., Wit.
Kalb, Susannah, S:94, 1829
Kalb, John, Husband, dec'd.
Ellzey, Mary, S:111, 1825/29
Pope, Mary L., formerly Armistead
Harrison, Sarah Elizabeth
Harrison, Maria P.
Harrison, Margaret L.
Harrison, Henry T.
Harrison, Thomas J.
Harrison, Kittey, Sister
Harrison, John T.
Harrison, Burr William, Nephew
Ellzey, William W.
Ellzey, Mary Cecelia
Ellzey, Rozannah M.
Ellzey, Frances
Ellzey, Alice Ann
Ellzey, Thomazin, dec'd. Half-Uncle
Ellzey, Lewis, Brother
Ellzey, William, Brother
Ellzey, Betsey, Sister
Ellzey, Ann Elizabeth
Russell, Margaret H.
Ellzey, Sally, Sister
Armistead, Elizabeth M.
Armistead, Mary L.
Bailey, J., Wit.
Bailey, Richard P., Wit.
Ankers, John, Wit.
Tillett, Edward, Wit.
Peyton, Mary D., Wit. [c]
Peyton, Ellen M. C., Wit. [c]
Harrison, James, Wit. [c]
Kalb, John, S:116, 1829
Everhart, Susannah, Dau.
Near, Matilda, Dau.
Kalb, Elijah, Son
Derry, Anna Barbara, Dau.
Kalb, Amanda, Dau.
Kalb, Susannah, Wife
Kalb, Samuel, Son
Kalb, Absalom, Son
Biggs, Mary, Dau.
Braden, Noble S., Wit.
Phillips, Thomas, Wit.
Grubb, Benjamin, Wit.

Gore, Joshua, S:129, 1830
Gore, William, Son
Gregg, Sarah, Dau.
Gore, Thomas, Son
Gore, Solomon, Son, dec'd.
Gore, Joseph, Son
Lovett, Ann, Dau.
Lovett, Jonathan, Son-in-Law, dec'd.
Hogue, William, Wit.
Janney, Daniel, Wit.
Hague, Thomas, Wit.
Taylor, Benjamin F., Wit.
Swart, Alexander, S:168, 1829/30
Swart, —, Unborn child
Swart, —, Wife
Grigsby, Lewis, Wit.
McNabb, William, Wit.
McPherson, William, Wit.
Adams, John R., Wit.
Kile, John, S:171, 1829/30
Anderson, Nancy, Dau.
Kile, George, Son
Bowman, Katty, Dau.
Kile, John, Son
Kile, Mary, Wife
Bowman, Elias L., Son-in-law
Burson, Elizabeth, Dau.
Brown, Christana, Dau.
Bowman, —, three Gr-children
Davis, Mary, Dau.
Luckett, Francis W., Wit.
Luckett, Ludwell, Wit.
Greenup, Christopher, S:195, 1817/18/30
Luckett, Susan, Dau.
Luckett, Craven P., Son-in-law
Greenup, Christopher, Son
Gamble, Nancy, Dau., w/o John G.
Gamble, John G., Exor.
Greenup, Wilson P., Son
Greenup, Charlotte V. C., Dau.
Greenup, Lucetta P., Dau.
Faw, Abraham, Partner
Hunter, William, Exor.
Pope, John, Exor.
Madison, John, Wit.
Slaughter, Gabriel, Wit.
Sneed, Achilles, Wit.

Shaffer, Michael, S:199, 1829/30
  Wince, Philip, Exor.
  Shaffer, Polly, Dau.
  Shaffer, Christiana, Dau.
  Shaffer, Elizabeth, Wife
  Shaffer, George, Son
  Shaffer, Lucinda, Dau.
  Shaffer, Henry, Son
  Shaffer, Elizabeth, Dau.
  Shaffer, Michael, Son
  Shaffer, Solomon, Son
  Wince, Catherine, Dau.
  Sockman, Sarah, Dau.
  Arnold, Michael, Wit.
  Pierpoint, Eli, Wit.
Lane, Epaminondas M., S:303, 1824/30
  Jett, Catharine Jane, Niece
  Jett, Peter friend, Exor.
  Lane, Catharine, Mother
  Lane, Dewit, Nephew
  Crane, Joseph, Nephew
  Crane, Emily, Niece
  Triplett, James L., Wit.
  Kile, George, Wit.
  Lacey, Elias, Wit.
Dodd, Jane, S:304, 1830
  Tribby, Elizabeth, Gr-Dau.
  Wilson, Lydia, Dau.
  Foreman, Sarah, Dau.
  Lacey, Ann, Dau.
  Dodd, Elizabeth, Dau.
  Dodd, Jesse, Gr-Son
  Dodd, Thomas, Son, dec'd.
  Dodd, John, Son
  Dodd, Samuel, Son
  Dodd, William, Son
  Hamilton, Charles B., Wit.
  Vandeventer, Isaac, Wit.
  Manning, Sally L., Wit.
Carter, Susanna, S:306, 1828/30
  Crozure, Eleanor, Sister
  Winder, Adah, Sister
  Galloway, Woodford, Nephew, sister's son
  Galloway, Sarah, Sister
  Penquite, Kesiah, Sister
  Bradfield, John, Brother
  Bradfield, Jonathan, Brother
  Bradfield, Edward, Brother
  Bradfield, William, Exor.
  Janney, Stephen, Exor.
  Lodge, Samuel, Wit.
  Janney, Jacob, Wit.
  Woodford, Elizabeth, Wit.
Perry, Benjamin W., S:331, 1830
  Perry, Samuel W., Brother
  Perry, Verlinda, Wife
  Boss, Samuel M., Wit.
  Burke, William B., Wit.
  Cordell, Martin, Wit.
Parsons, Solomon, S:335, 1830
  Parsons, Mary, Sister
  Dennis, black man
  Gover, Anthony P., Exor.
  Coffen, John
  Coffen, Mary F.
  Coffen, Mary, dec'd.
  Webber, Harriet Elford, Niece
  Wilson, Richard,
    late husband of Fanny B. B.
  Janney, John, Exor.
  Janney, Mary,
    dau. of Elisha & Mary
  Wilson, Fanny B. B.
  Maxwell, —, emancipated slave
  Marmaduke, Silas, Wit.
  Osburn, Mortimore, Wit.
  Janney, Aquila, Wit.
Violett, Elijah, S:352, 1819/30
  Violett, John, Son
  Violett, James, Son
  Violett, Phebe, Wife
  Violett, Jemima, Dau.
  Violett, Ashford, Son
  Violett, William, Son
  Violett, Mary, Dau.
  Rust, William, Wit.
  Brent, Willis, Wit.
  Glascock, Enoch, Wit.
Myers, Lambert, S:355, 1830
  Myers, Mary Ann, Dau., <21
  Myers, Abigail, Dau.
  Myers, Delilah, Dau.
  Myers, Jacob, Son
  Myers, Washington, Son
  Myers, Mary, Wife
  Myers, William, Son
  Myers, Lambert, Son
  Lee, George negro man

Schooley, William, Son-in-law
Braden, John, Wit.
Templer, William, Wit.
Hay, George, T:8, 1830
Ringold, Tench, Friend
Smith, Richard, Friend
Swann, Thomas, Friend
Ringold, Antoinette, Dau.
Hay, Eliza Kortwright, Wife
Hay, Charles, Son
Heifren, William, T:8, 1830
Wolikin, Judy, Sister
McCabe, John H., Exor.
Edwards, Samuel M., Wit.
Simpson, William, Wit.
Slates, Frederick, T:9, 1825/30
Holsman, Christine, Dau.
Slates, Adam, Son
Slates, Connard, Son
Slates, John Frederick, Son
Slates, —, Wife
Everheart, Jacob, Wit.
Everheart, John, Wit.
Roller, Daniel, Wit.
Birdsall, John, T:11, 1830
Birdsall, David, Son
Birdsall, Rebecca, Dau.
Brown, John, Exor.
Birdsall, infant, Dau.
Birdsall, Joel, Son
Birdsall, Benjamin, Son
Birdsall, John, Son
Birdsall, William, Son
Birdsall, Ann, Dau.
Birdsall, Mary, Wife
Carr, David, Wit.
Taylor, Joseph, Wit.
Goodin, John, Wit.
Harden, Elizabeth, of near Aldie, T:22, 1830
Harden, Henry, Son
Harden, William, Son
Eaton, Isaac, Wit.
Gulick, William, Wit.
Hatcher, John, T:41, 1829/30
Hatcher, Noah, Brother, dec'd.
Hatcher, Sarah, Wife
Chamblin, Mason, Exor.
Dillon, Ann, Sister
McVeigh, Eli, Wit.

Parmer, William C., Wit.
Chamblin, William, Wit.
Ewers, Thomas, T:42, 1830
Ewers, Mary, Wife
Ewers, Thomas, Nephew
Williams, Notley C., Wit.
Adam, William F., Wit.
Williams, James C., Wit.
Gore, Joseph, T:43, 1830
Whitacre, Caleb, Brother-in-law, husband of Phebe
Whitacre, Phebe, Sister
Whitacre, Alice, Sister
Sharp, Sarah, Niece, dau. of brother Thomas
Lovett, Daniel, husband of Rachel
Lovett, Christian, formerly Charuthers
Lovett, Rachel, formerly Charuthers
Lumm, Ruth
Lovett, Nancy, Niece, dau. of Joshua
Popkins, Craven, young man living with me
Charuthers, James, dec'd.
Osburn, Joshua, Exor.
Keath, Vincent, husband of Hannah
Keath, Nancy, formerly Charuthers
Keath, Joseph, son of Price & Nancy
Keath, Hannah, formerly Charuthers
Keath, Price, husband of Nancy
Kerrick, Phebe, formerly Charuthers
Kerrick, Thomas Phebe's husband
Kerrick, —, two eldest sons of Thomas & Phebe
Gore, Sarah, w/o nephew, William
Gore, Joseph, Nephew, son of Joshua
Gore, Thomas, Nephew, son of Joshua
Gore, Thomas, Brother

Gore, Joshua, Brother, dec'd.
Gore, William, Nephew
Gore, Solomon, Nephew, son of Joshua, dec'd.
Gore, Amos, Brother
Gregg, Sarah, Niece, dau. of brother Joshua
Charuthers, Thomas, dec'd.
Gore, Jonas, Brother
Webster, Anna, Niece, dau. of brother Thomas
Sharp, Jeptha, Sarah's 1st husband
Lovett, Edmund, husband of Christian
Hope, Massey, late Gore, Niece, dau. of Thomas Gore
Mead, Aquila, Wit.
Eaches, William S., Wit.

Heaton, Albert, T:92, 1826/31
Heaton, Jane Cecilia, Sister
Heaton, Lydia, Mother
Heaton, John Thomas William, Brother
Heaton, Townshend, Brother
Heaton, James Decatur, Youngest, Brother

Wilkenson, John, T:93, 1828/31
Smith, Seth, Exor.
Wilkenson, Anna, Dau.
Reeder, Gourley, Exor.
Wilkenson, Hannah, Dau.
Wilkenson, Mary, Dau.
Wilkenson, Joseph, Son, dec'd.
Wilkenson, Mary, Gr-Dau., dau. of Joseph
Wilkenson, John, Gr-Son, son of Joseph
Keen, George, Wit.
Walker, Craven, Wit.
Clark, Hamilton J., Wit.

Belts, Frederick, T:113, 1830/31
Wetsel, Mary, Dau.
Ruse, Susannah, Dau.
Axline, Elizabeth, Dau.
Belts, Marian, Wife
Naulton, Catharine, Dau.
White, Thomas, Exor.

Leslie, John, Wit.
Statler, John, Wit.
Ruse, John, Wit.

Heryford, John, T:128, 1783/94
Ansley, William, Son-in-law
Heryford, Thomas, Son
Ansley, Ann, Dau.
Heryford, Francis, Son
Heryford, Kitty, Dau.
Heryford, Elizabeth, Dau.
Heryford, Peggy, Wife
Heryford, John, Son
Heryford, Peggy, Dau.
Heryford, James, Son
Heryford, Robert, Son
Heryford, William, Son
Windsor, Thomas Sr., Wit.
Windsor, Thomas Jr., Wit.
Windsor, Richard, Wit.
Williamson, Jesse, Wit.
Triplett, Simon, Wit.
Triplett, Reuben, Wit.

Craven, Giles, T:130, 1823/31
Hunt, Mary, Dau.
Griggby, Sarah, Dau.
Whitacre, Lydia, Dau.
Craven, Lydia, Wife
Craven, Joel, Son
Craven, Hannah, Dau.
Cockrell, Hester, Dau.
Cockrell, Daniel, Exor.
Nichols, Thomas, Wit.
Bolon, William, Wit.
Nixon, James, Wit.
Daniel, Hiram, Wit.

Emery, Catharine, T:131, 1829/31
Arnold, Mary, Dau.
Shumaker, Catharine, Dau.
Emery, Elizabeth, Gr-Dau.
Wincel, George, Brother
Potterfield, Elizabeth, Dau.
Bumcrots, Christena
Grubb, John, Wit.
Filler, Henry, Wit.
Grubb, Benjamin, Wit.

Hough, Jane, T:215, 1831
Hough, Elizabeth, Dau.
Hough, William T., Son

Peacock, Nancy, Dau.
Steer, William, Exor.
Grubb, Harriet, Dau.
Woolford, Jane, Dau.
Jackson, Mary, Dau.
Hough, Rebecca, Dau.
Stone, Daniel, Wit.
Hough, Wm. H., Wit.
Wine, Daniel, Wit.
Gassaway, Thomas, T:216, 1830/31
Gassaway, Henrietta, Wife
Gassaway, Charles, Brother
Catlett, Polly, Sister
Darne, Elizabeth, Sister
Hillary, Thomas, Wit.
Williams, Zachariah, Wit.
Gassaway, John, Wit.
Aisqueth, Sally L., T:235, 1824/31
Aisquith, Charles, Son
Aisquith, Virginia, Dau.
Aisquith, William, Son
Aisquith, Edward, Son
Moore, Cato, Brother
Henderson, Richard H., Brother-in-law
Edwards, Samuel M., Wit.
Fry, Philip, T:282, 1824/31
Beltz, Susannah, Dau.
Fry, Daniel, Son
Fry, John, Son
Fry, Henry, Son
Fry, Michael, Son
Fry, Dorothy, Wife
Fry, Civilla, Dau.
Fry, Christina, Dau.
Kerner, Catharine, Dau.
Wealty, Elizabeth, Dau.
Grubb, John, Wit.
Grubb, Adam, Wit.
Grubb, James, Wit.
Tar, Aaron, Wit.
White, Washington, T:300, 1830/31
Updike, Barsina, Niece, dau. of Rachel
White, Elizabeth, Sister
White, Rachel, Sister
White, Albina, Niece, dau. of Rachel

Leslie, Samuel D., Wit.
Lodge, William, Wit.
Leslie, Benjamin, Wit.
James, Benjamin, T:307, 1830/31
Redmond, Andrew J., Gr-Son
Redmond, Nancy, Dau.
Redmond, Mary Ann, Gr-Dau.
James, Elizabeth, Dau., deaf & dumb
James, Mary, Dau., deaf & dumb
James, David, Son
James, Abigail, Dau.
James, Aaron, Son
James, Susan, Dau. deaf & dumb
Foley, Icy, Dau.
James, John, Wit.
James, Dean, Wit.
Baker, Elizabeth, T:333, 1828/31
Rust, Elizabeth
Rust, Peter C., husband of Elizabeth
Reid, Alfred, Exor.
Bailey, Sydnor, Son-in-law
Bailey, Susan Elizabeth, Gr-Dau.
Bailey, Nancy, Dau.
Rust, Alfred, Wit.
Miley, Benjamin, Wit.
Miley, John, Wit.
Fitzhugh, Ann, T:334, 1827/31
Battaile, Virginia C., Gr-Dau., child of Ann Maria
Battaile, Jane T., Gr-Dau., child of Ann Maria
Battaile, Lawrence, Son-in-law
Fitzhugh, John S., Gr-Son, son of William
Battaile, Ann Maria, Dau.
Fitzhugh, Sydnor B., Gr-Son, son of William
Harrison, Frances B., Gr-Dau., dau. of Elizabeth
Fitzhugh, Mary J., Gr-Dau., dau. of William
Harrison, Elizabeth T., Dau.
Fitzhugh, Cameron D., Gr-Son, son of William

Index to Loudoun County Wills, 1757 - 1850   131

Harrison, Ann, Gr-Son,
  dau. of Elizabeth
Fitzhugh, William C., Son
Harrison, Cecelia, Gr-Dau., dau.
  of Elizabeth
Harrison, Jane, Gr-Dau., dau. of
  Elizabeth
Harrison, Daniel P.,
  husband of Jane
Hopkins, Presly, Wit.
Harrison, H. T., Wit.
Armistead, John C., Wit.
Smith, T. W., Wit.
Drake, Thomas, T:347, 1831/32
Furgeson, Nancy, now living
  with me
Moore, Peyton, renter of mill
Humphrey, John G., Exor.
Offutt, Thornton F., Wit.
Johnson, Joseph, Wit.
Jenings, Edmund, T:354, 1829/32
Fairbanks, Charity, Niece
Rooles, Candy, Sister
Sappington, Jonathan, Nephew
Sappington, Mary, Sister, dec'd.
Sappington, Edmund, Nephew
Brooks, Elizabeth, Sister
Jenings, Seney, Wife
Waters, Plummer, Cousin
Rickard, George, Wit.
Unglesbee, Thomas, Wit.
Unglesbee, John, Wit.
Edwards, Charles Gray, Wit.
Murry, Elizabeth, T:356, 1831
Rose, Captain John, Exor.
Martin, Sally P., Dau.
Saunders, Thomas, Wit.
Clagett, Henry, Wit.
Watt, John G., Wit.
**Middleton, Studley, T:390,
  1822/23**
Rust, Peter's wife, Sister-in-law,
  dec'd. brothers relict
Luckett, Francis W., Exor.
Chinn, Samuel, Exor.
Middleton, —, children
Middleton, John, Brother, dec'd.
Middleton, Matilda, Dau.

Middleton, Ann, Wife
Powell, William L., Wit.
Titus, John, Wit.
Wynn, John, T:391, 1831/32
Wynn, Ulysses, Son
Craven, Mahlon, Exor.
Wynn, Susanna, Wife
Wynn, Mary Ann, Dau.
Sinclair, John, Wit.
Brown, Samuel, Wit.
Brown, Isaac M., Wit.
Russell, James, T:392, 1831/32
Niswanger, Christian, Exor.
Russell, Samuel
Neer, Hannah, Dau., dec'd.
Russell, —, children
Russell, —, Wife
Russell, Robert, Wit.
Marmion N., Wit.
Wager, Gerard B., Wit.
Bitzer, Harman, T:398, 1832
Hesser, Mary, Dau.
Bitzer, George, Son
Overfield, Anna, Dau.
Bitzer, John, Son
Bitzer, Harmon, Gr-Son,
  William's son
Bitzer, William, Son
Bitzer, Dorothy, Wife
Davis, William, Son-in-law
Davis, Catherine, Dau.
Skinner, Gabriel, Wit.
Reed, Joseph B., Wit.
Rogers, Asa, Wit.
Noland, Elizabeth, T:399, 1832
Cochran, Dr. Richard, brother's
  doctor
Noland, Peyton, Nephew,
  son of Samuel
Love, Jane, Sister
Noland, Louisa, Niece,
  dau. of Samuel
Noland, Samuel, Brother
Noland, Richard, Nephew,
  son of Lloyd
Noland, Burr, Nephew,
  son of Lloyd
Noland, Thomas, Nephew,
  son of Lloyd
Noland, Lloyd, Brother

Powell, H. B., Wit.
Iden, Samuel, Wit.
Cochran, Richard, Wit.
Moore, Margaret, U:20, 1830/32
  Aisquith, Sally L., Dau.
  Moore, Cato, Son
  Moore, Thomas, Son
  Henderson, Richard H., Wit.
  Henderson, Archibald Jr., Wit.
Filler, Henry, U:33, 1831/32
  Filler, Sarah, Wife
  Filler, —, my children
  Virts, Peter, Wit.
  Trittipo, William, Wit.
  Grubb, John, Wit.
Triplett, Enoch, U:34, 1823/32
  Triplett, Thomas, Eldest Son
  Triplett, Reuben, Son
  Triplett, Jesse, Son
  Triplett, James, Son
  Triplett, Elizabeth, Dau.
  Triplett, Mary, Wife
  Silcott, Jacob, Admr. w.w.a.
  Luckett, Francis W., Wit.
  Luckett, Sarah S., Wit.
Brown, David F., U:80, 1832
  Brown, Phebe, Sister
  Brown, Amanda, Sister
  Brown, Martha, Sister
  Brown, Eleanor, Sister
  Brown, Daniel, Father
  Sagars, George W., Exor.
  Brown, Rebecca, Sister
  Brown, Samuel, Brother
  Francis, John, Wit.
  Lumm, John, Wit.
  Monroe, William, Wit.
Campbell, Robert, U:123, 1829/32
  Curry, John, <21
  Campbell, Jane, Wife
  Curry, John Sr.
  McCarty, Henry
  Taylor, Henry S, Wit.
  Garrett, Enos, Wit.
  Vermilion, Jane, Wit.
  McArtor, Martha, Wit.
Beaty, Andrew, U:126, 1824/32
  Beaty, Mary, Wife
  Beaty, Robert, Son
  Beaty, James, Son
  Beaty, Keziah, Dau.
  Beaty, Betsy, Dau.
  Beaty, Mary, Gr-Dau.,
    dau. of James
  Osburn, Balaam, Exor.
  McCarty, Winifred, Dau.
  McCarty, Margaret, Dau.
  Turner, Mary, Dau.
  Sinclair, John, Wit.
  Shields, Alfred, Wit.
Smith, Mary, U:141, 1832
  Smith, Seth, Brother
  Galleher, Sarah, Dau.
  Galleher, Mary, Dau.
Mock, Jacob, U:148, 1831/32
  Taylor, Susannah, Dau.
  Hanks, Phebe, Dau.
  Mock, Elizabeth, Wife
  Mock, George, Oldest Son
  Mock, John Duval, Son, <21
  Mock, Mary Catherine,
    Dau., <18
  Roberts, Alice, Dau.
  Mock, —, three youngest sons
  Williams, John, Wit.
  Walker, Isaac, Wit.
  Conrad, D., Wit.
  Hough, S., Wit.
Fulton, Susan, U:222, 1832
  Madison, Rachiel, Dau.
  Obrien, Nancy, Gr-Dau.,
    dau. of Elizabeth Jacobs
  Cox, Rebecca, Dau.
  Jacobs, Elizabeth, Dau., dec'd.
  Fulton, William, Son
  Luckett, Matilda, Gr-Dau., dau.
    of Elizabeth Jacobs
  Fulton, Margaret, Dau.
  Fulton, James, Son
  Saunders, Thomas R., Wit.
  War, John, Wit.
  Dowdell, Thomas G., Wit.
Violet, Phebe, U:223, 1832
  Bishop, Jemima, Dau.
  Bishop, Aquilla, Son-in-law,
    Jemima's husband
  Violet, Ashford, Son
  Wright, Charles, Son-in-law
  Violet, John, Son
  Wright, Mary, Dau.

Index to Loudoun County Wills, 1757 - 1850   133

Violet, James, Son
Violet, William, maybe Son
Chilton, William, Wit.
Logan, Samuel, Wit.
Wright, John, Wit.
Darne, Thomas, U:234, 1831/32
Bell, Richard Thomas, Nephew
Bell, Elouiza
Darne, Addalaid
Lacy, Mariah
Turley, Alexander, Exor.
Darne, Alexander Hanson
  Contee, Nephew
Darne, Catherine, Wife
Lewis, Charles, Exor.
Turley, Charles William,
  Nephew
Lewis, James, Wife's dec'd.
  brother
Gregg, John, U:236, 1831/33
Gregg, George, Son, <21
Gregg, —, five sons
Gregg, Phebe, Wife
Nichols, Isaac, Exor.
Ewers, Levi G., Wit.
Nichols, Joshua, Wit.
Nichols, Joseph, Wit.
Hesser, Andrew, Wit.
Worsley, John, U:260, 1832/33
Worsley, Jane, 2nd Dau.
Worsley, Mary Ann, Eldest Dau.
Worsley, William, Son
Worsley, Frances,
  Youngest Dau.
Worsley, Eliza, 3rd Dau.
Worsley, Elizabeth, Wife
Clarke, Addison H., Wit.
Braden, John, Wit.
Mains, Archibald, Wit.
Fred, Joshua, U:298, 1833
Fred, Elizabeth, Dau.
Fred, Elizabeth, Wife
Fred, Mary Ann, Dau.
Fred, Joseph Hadley, Son
Fred, Sarah, Dau.
Smith, Seth, Wit.
Grayson, Richard,
  Commissioner

Humphrey, John G.,
  Commissioner
Humphrey, Thomas G.,
  Commissioner
Axline, John, U:299, 1826/33
Smith, Joseph, Gr-Son
May, William, Gr-Son
May, David, Gr-Son
May, Elizabeth, Dau., dec'd.
May, John, Gr-Son
Axline, Christina, Wife
Axline, Henry, Son
Axline, John, Son
Axline, Jacob, Son
Everhart, Charlotte, Dau.
Everhart, Catherine, Dau.,
  dec'd.
Everhart, Christina, Gr-Dau.,
  child of Catherine
Everhart, Elizabeth, Gr-Dau.,
  child of Catherine
Everhart, Israel, Gr-Son,
  child of Catherine
Everhart, Solomon, Gr-Son,
  child of Catherine
Everhart, Catherine, Gr-Dau.,
  child of Catherine
Everhart, Philip, Exor.
May, Leander, Gr-Dau.
Axline, David, Son
Grubb, D., Wit.
Bumcrats, John, Wit.
Arnold, Jacob, Wit.
Clowes, Joseph, U:300, 1833
Clowes, Nancy, Dau.
Clowes, Mary, Wife
Clowes, Elizabeth, Dau.
Clowes, Mary Jane, Dau.
Clowes, Thomas, Son
Janney, Daniel, Wit.
Canby, Joseph, Wit.
Vandeventer, Isaac Jr., Wit.
Whitacre, Alice, U:321, 1831/33
Craven, Albina, Dau.
Whitacre, Abner, Son
Whitacre, Thomas, Son
Whitacre, Thornton, Gr-Son,
  son of Thomas, <21
Whitacre, Tamer, Dau.
Whitacre, Ruth, Dau.

Whitacre, John, Son
Whitacre, Hannah, Dau.
Gore, Joseph, Brother
Gregg, Naomi, Dau.
Whitacre, Amos, Son
Rogers, Hamilton, Wit.
Nichols, Thomas, Wit.
Cost, Jacob, U:322, 1826/33
Cost, Mary Magdaline, Wife
Edwards, Charles G., Wit.
Hough, William H., Wit.
Gross, Henry, Wit.
Hawling, Mary, U:339, 1821/33
Hawling, John, Brother
Hawling, Elizabeth, Sister
Lewis, James M., Wit.
Surghnor, John, Wit.
Cridler, George, Wit.
Humphrey, Mary, U:349, 1823/29/33
McFarling, Rachel, Dau.
Lewis, Lewis
Jeams, Thomas, Son
McFarling, William
Jeams, Margaret
Moore, Samuel
Moore, Leary, Dau.
Jeams, Jesse
Ewers, Martha
Humphrey, Abner, Wit.
Humphrey, Thomas G., Wit.
Barton, Thomas, Wit.
Humphrey, Abner G., Wit.
Hesser, David, Wit. [c]
Tavenner, John, Wit. [c]
Garrott, Elisabeth, U:365, 1833
Russell, Catherine, Dau.
Russell, Robert Edgar, Gr-Son
Gulick, Ludwell, Wit.
Beatty, George, Wit.
Sanbower, Catherine, U:366, 1832/33
Sanbower, Ann, Mother
Sypherd, Sarah, Sister
Wenner, Jonathan, Wit.
Abraham, John, Wit.
Frazier, Mary, Wit.
Carr, John, U:371, 1833
Stewart, Henrey, Servant
Craven, Harriet, Servant

Craven, Giles, Servant
Craven, Violet, Servant
Craven, Caleb, Servant
Craven, Alfred, Servant
Craven, Charlet, Servant
Carr, David, Admr. w.w.a.
Vandeventer, Gabriel, Admr. w.w.a.
Berkley, John L., U:380, 1833
Berkley, Rufus, Son
Lee, Ann, Dau.
Lewis, Charles, Exor.
Lee, Matthew P., Exor.
Hancock, George, Wit.
Oden, Nathaniel S., Wit.
Tebbs, Foushee, Wit.
Jarvis, Washington, Wit.
Clayton, Israel, U:380, 1833
Clayton, Martha, Sister
Galloway, Nancy, Niece
Galloway, Madison
Lee, Catherine, Niece
Jackson, Benjamin, Wit.
Stephenson, James, Wit.
Hill, James, Wit.
Pagit, Timothy, V:4, 1829/33
Bond, Keziah, Dau.
Hutchison, Jamimah, Dau.
Pagit, James, Son
Pagit, Bayley, Son
Fagin, Jean, Dau.
Pagit, Mary, Dau.
Heath, Andrew, Wit.
James, Smith, Wit.
Hancock, George, Wit.
Summers, Jacob, Wit.
Poulson, Isabel, V:59, 1827/33
White, Robert & wife
Poulson, Susanna, Dau.
Poulson, Mary, Dau.
Reece, David, Exor.
Beans, Samuel, Exor.
Taylor, Stacy, Wit.
Hamon, Adam, Wit.
Schryock, Michael, V:64, 1824/33
Moffett, Elenor, Dau.
Moffett, Charles, Son-in-law, husband of Elenor
Fouch, Thomas, Exor.

Fox, Ezra, Son-in-law,
  husband of Polly
Fox, Margaret (alias Polly), Dau.
Schryock, George, Son
Schryock, Samuel, Son
Sanders, Thomas, Exor.
Schryock, Nancy, Dau.
Schryock, Susanna, Dau.
Harned, Rosanna, Dau., dec'd.
Schryock, Elizabeth, Dau.
Fouch, Thompson, Wit.
Fouch, Amos, Wit.
Wiley, Garitson, Wit.
Gregg, Nathan, V:65, 1831/33
Pursley, Jonah
Gregg, Nathan, Nephew,
  son of Thomas
Gregg, Susan, Sister
Gregg, Sarah, Niece,
  dau. of Thomas
Gregg, Thomas, Brother
Gregg, Samuel, Brother
Reese, David, Exor.
Roach, Asa, son of Sarah
Hollingsworth, Judith
Hollingsworth, Amanda,
  dau. of Judith
Roach, Sarah
Hamilton, Charles B., Exor.
Pursley, Maria Osborne
Tavenner, Richard, Wit.
Elgin, Gustavus, V:105, 1826/34
Elgin, Robert, Son-in-law,
  husband of Elizabeth
Elgin, Charles, Son
Elgin, William, Son,
  whereabouts unknown
Elgin, Elizabeth, Dau.
Elgin, Rebecah, Dau.
Elgin, Hamilton, Son
Elgin, Francis, Son
Elgin, Gustavus, Son
Elgin, Margaret, Dau.
Dulin, Nancy, Dau.
Shreve, Benjamin, Dau.
Elgin, Ignatius, Dau.
Elgin, Mathew, Dau.
Shumate, Murphey C.,
  Admr. w.w.a.

Echart, Adam, V:119, 1791
Echart, Casper, Son
Echart, Catherine, Wife
Cooper, Catherine, Dau.
Moul, George, Exor.
Harding, William H., Wit.
Hough, Samuel, Wit.
Tytus, Francis, Wit.
Compher, Catherine, V:142, 1833
Hines, Hugh's children
Adams, children, Sister
Winegardner, Levi, Exor.
Luckett, Samuel C., Dau.
Rogers, Thomas, Admr. w.w.a.
Compher, Peter, Brother
Compher, John's children,
  Brother
Compher, William, Brother
Compher, Jacob, Brother
Collins, Levi's children
Barry, Elisa Ann, V:143, 1833
Howard, Jacob, Brother
Corkran, Phebe, Dau.
Corkran, Eliza Ann, Dau.
Corkran, Rose Ann, Dau.
Timms, Jesse, Admr. w.w.a.
Tillett, Honor, V:176, 1834
Pool, Peggy, Dau.
Tillett, Nancy, Dau.
Tillett, Giles' children, Son
Tillett, Samuel A.'s children, Son
Jackson, Polly's children, Dau.
Clarke, Giles, Gr-Son,
  child of Effa
Saunders, Mahala's children,
  Dau.
Strauther, Sally's children, Dau.
Clarke, Lydia, Gr-Dau.,
  dau. of Effa
Clarke, Effa, Dau.
Clarke, James, Gr-Son,
  child of Effa
Clarke, Albert, Gr-Son,
  child of Effa
Edwards, Samuel M., Exor.
Saunders, Presley, Wit.
Edwards, Richard H., Wit.
Kitzmiller, Archibald M.,
  Admr. w.w.a.

Wherry, Elizabeth Ellzey, V:178, 1834
Wherry, Mary E., Dau.
Rogers, Hamilton, son of Hugh, Exor.
Roszel, Anna, Wit.
Powell, W. A., Wit.

Oatyer, Peter, V:204, 1829/33/34
Bridwell, James, Son-in-law, Sophia's husband
Bridwell, Sophia, Dau.
Moffett, Elizabeth, Dau.
Caylor, Catharine, Dau.
Oatyer, John, Son, dec'd.
Lafaber, Mary, Dau.
Caylor, Ann, Dau.
Caylor, Jacob, Son-in-law, husband of Catharine
Oatyer, Peter Jr., Gr-Son
Lafaber, William, Son-in-law
Oatyer, —, Wife
Wilson, John M., Exor.
Henderson, Richard H., Dau.
Edwards, Samuel M., Dau.
Hamilton, E. G., Wit.
Davis, Benjamin, Wit.

Lewis, Joseph of Clifton, V:209, 1830/34
Lufborough, Nathan, Exor.
Lewis, Charles, Uncle
Lewis, Dr. John H.
Lewis, Joseph, son of Dr. John H. Lewis
Lewis, Elizabeth, Wife
Nessmith, John, Wit.
Nessmith, Susan, Wit.
Shumate, Taliafarro, Wit.

Brown, Henry, V:212, 1834
Skillman, Abraham, Exor.
Brown, Henry, son of John
Brown, Hannah, dau. of John
Brown, Hamilton
Brown, Daniel
McKinley, Hannah
McKinley, Daniel
Brown, John
McKinley, Mary
Crosgrove, Sarah McKinley

Birdsall, Andrew, Wit.
Eaton, Isaac, Wit.
Birdsall, Thomas W. C., Wit.

Janney, Jonas, V:251, 1829/34
Janney, George, Son
Sands, Jonah, Son-in-law, husband of Sarah
Janney, Abel, Son
Sands, Sarah, Dau.
Janney, Elisha, Son
Hoge, Hannah, Dau.
Janney, Ruth, Dau.
Hoge, James, Son-in-Law, dec'd.
Janney, Jonas, Son
Taylor, Yardley, Wit.
Taylor, Bernard, Wit.
Janney, Daniel, Wit.
Taylor, Jonathan, Wit.

Skinner, Nathaniel, V:253, 1819/34
Skinner, William, Son
Skinner, Cornelius, Son
Skinner, John, Son
Skinner, Nathaniel, Son
Skinner, Martha, Wife
Skinner, James, Son
Skinner, Isaac, Son
Skinner, —, other children
Mercer, Charles Fenton, Wit.
Roach, Thomas C., Wit.
Noland, Thomas J., Wit.

Vandevanter, Isaac, V:269, 1834
Vandevanter, Gabriel, Nephew
Vandevanter, —, Wife
Braden, Flavious, Son, dec'd., of present wife
Vandevanter, Cornelius, Son
Vandevanter, William, Son, child of 1st wife
Sinclair, Leannah, Dau., child of 1st wife
Vandevanter, Mary Elizabeth, Dau.
Vandevanter, John, Son, child of 1st wife
Vandevanter, James H., Son
Vandevanter, Joseph, Son, child of 1st wife

Vandevanter, Fenton, Son,
  child of 1st wife
Vandevanter, Albert, Son
Chamblin, Dewannah, Dau.,
  child of 1st wife
Clarke, Addison H., Admr.
  w.w.a.
Janney, Eli, Wit.
Hamilton, C. B., Wit.
Schooley, William, V:313, 1834
Mitchel, Elizabeth, Dau.
Schooley, William, Son
Hughes, Ruth, Dau.
Schooley, Sarah, Dau.
Schooley, Richard, Son
Schooley, Henry, Son
Schooley, Reubin, Son
Schooley, James, Son
Clarke, Addison H., Wit.
Schooley, Mahlon, Wit.
Schooley, John Jr., Wit.
Rathie, John Baptiste, V:322, 1832/34
Rathie, —, children
Rathie, Elizabeth, Wife
Newton, John, Wit.
Mills, James, Wit.
Garner, James, Wit.
Wright, Charles, V:341, 1834
Wright, Mary, Wife
Baker, Richard, Wit.
Wright, Alfred, Wit.
Brooks, Ebenezer, Wit.
Kalb, Susanna, V:342, 1833/34
Beeler, Amanda, Dau.
Biggs, Mary, Dau.
Everhart, Susanna, Dau.
Kalb, Elijah, Son
Neer, Matilda, Dau.
Derry, Anna, Dau.
Kalb, Samuel, Son
Kalb, Absalom, Son
Grubb, John, Wit.
Saunders, George, Wit.
Hamilton, John, Wit.
Brown, Isaac Sr., V:344, 1834
Tavenner, Jonathan, Exor.
Barton, Hannah
Baldwin, Ruth, Dau.
Burson, Patsey, Dau.

Brown, Mariah, Isaac's wife,
  Dau.-in-law
Brown, Isaac, Son
Brown, David E., Son
Brown, John, Son
Brown, James, Son
Bennett, Susan W., Dau.
Brown, Sarah, Wife
Machlan, Mary, Dau.
Plaster, Henry Jr., Exor.
Tavenner, Sarah, Dau.
Wood, Lydia, Dau.
Clowes, Edith P., Dau.
Walker, Thornton, Wit.
Trahern, Thomas, Wit.
Plaster, Michael, Wit.
Peers, Eleanor, V:346, 1832/34
Wilson, Elizabeth, Friend
Jordan, Nancy, Sister
Powell, William A., Exor.
Adie, Rev. George
Lee, Anna, Niece
Diggs, John, Servant
Lee, Richard H., husband of
  Anna
Henderson, Orra M., Wit.
Henderson, Richard H., Wit.
Davis, Harriot, Wit.
Rogers, Thomas, Admr. w.w.a.
Beveridge, John, V:374, 1821/28
Ellzey, Col. William, Exor.
Fouch, Thomas, Exor.
Smith, Sarah, Dau., of 1st wife
Beveridge, Andrew, Son,
  son of Mary
Beveridge, Susanah, Dau.,
  dau. of Mary
Beveridge, Noble, Son,
  child of 1st wife
Beveridge, John, Son,
  child of 1st wife
Beveridge, William, Son,
  child of 1st wife
Beveridge, Thomas, Son,
  child of 1st wife
Beveridge, Mary, Wife
Kelly, Edward, Wit.
Skinner, Nathan, Wit.

Dowling, Edward, W:1, 1834/35
  Potts, Ezekiel, Exor.
  Dowling, Rachel, Sister
  Dowling, —, Mother
  Dowling, Mary, Wife
  Dowling, Henry M., Exor.
  Brown, John, Wit.
  Smith, John, Wit.
  Evans, Jesse, Wit.
Abel, George, W:37, 1831/35
  Abel, Catherine, Wife
  Abel, George, Son
  Abel, —, other 10 children
  McIlhaney, James, Wit.
  Osburn, Joshua, Wit.
  White, John, Wit.
  Grubb, E., Wit.
Peugh, Samuel, W:39, 1835
  Peugh, Elisha M., Son
  Peugh, Mary Ellen, Gr-Dau.,
    dau. of Jonah
  Peugh, Rebecca Jane, Gr-Dau.,
    dau. of Elisha
  Peugh, Leonidus, Gr-Son.,
    son of Jonah
  Peugh, Jonah, Son-in-law
  Peugh, Abel Marks, Gr-Son,
    son of Elisha
  Peugh, Margaret Elizabeth,
    Gr-Dau., dau. of Elisha
  Peugh, Samuel Braden, Gr-Son,
    son of Jonah
  Peugh, Mary, Wife
  Ewers, Jonathan, Exor.
  Peugh, Susana, Dau.,
    w/o Jonah
  Peugh, Mary, Dau.-in-law,
    w/o Elisha M.
  Jackson, Benjamin, Wit.
  Jackson, Ebenezer, Wit.
  Wright, William, Wit.
Best, James, W:40, 1828/35
  Tippett, Elizabeth, Gr-Dau.,
    dau. of Martha Dodd
  Osburn, Joshua, Exor.
  Hallins, Fanny, Gr-Dau.,
    dau. of Martha Dodd
  Sinclair, Jane, Dau.
  Dodd, James, Gr-Son,
    child of Martha
  Best, Joseph, Son
  Dodd, Sarah, Gr-Dau.,
    child of Martha
  Best, Enos, Son
  Dodd, Thomas, Gr-Son,
    child of Martha
  Best, William, Son
  Dodd, Martha, Dau., dec'd.
  Best, John, Son
  Best, Thomas, Son
  Best, James, Son
  Pursell, Samuel Jr., Wit.
  Pursel [sic], Enos, Wit.
  Hollingsworth, John, Wit.
McArter, Jonathan, W:51, 1834/35
  McArter, Moses, Son
  McArter, James, Son
  McArter, Rebecca, Dau.
  McArter, Mahlon, Son
  McArter, William, Son
  McArter, Rebecca, Gr-Dau.,
    dau. of Mahlon
  McArter, Thomas, Gr-Son,
    son of Mahlon
  McArter, Mary, Gr-Dau.,
    dau. of Mahlon
  McArter, Rachel, Gr-Dau.,
    dau. of Mahlon
  McArter, Jonathan, Son
  Saxton, Elizabeth
  Reiley, Elizabeth, Dau.
  White, Thomas, Exor.
Harrison, William Butler, W:54, 1835
  Wilson, Julia A., Dau.
  Harrison, Russell B., Son
  Harrison, Burr W., Exor.
  Mason, William T. T., Exor.
  Boss, S. M., Wit.
  Saunders, Evritt, Wit.
Grubb, Ebenezer Sr., W:56, 1832/35
  Smith, Sarah, Dau.
  Vickers, Rosanah, Dau.
  Grubb, Jacob, Step-son
  Grubb, John, Son
  Grubb, Mary, Wife
  Grubb, William, Son
  Grubb, Nancy, Dau.
  Grubb, Ebenezer, Son

Grubb, Curtis, Son
Grubb, Benjamin, Son
Coe, Catherine, Dau.
Conard, Rachel, Dau.
Cunard, Mary, Dau.
Lee, Theodrick, Wit.
Cockerill, S. W., Wit.
Vincel, John, W:90, 1830/35
Vincel, Philip, Son
Vincel, George, Son
Vincel, Mary Magdeleana, Wife
Vincel, Solomon, Son
George, John, Wit.
Bottenfield, Samuel, Wit.
Bottenfield, Adam, Wit.
Grayson, Benjamin, W:145, 1824/32/35
Grayson, Nancy, Wife
Grayson, Richard O., Son
Grayson, George M., Son
Grayson, Elizabeth O., Dau.
Grayson, Robert, Son
Grayson, William, Son
Grayson, Mary D., Dau.
Wirtz, William Jr., Wit.
Wolforde, George W., Wit.
Smallwood, John, Wit.
Selden, Wilson Cary, W:151, 1831/35
Selden, Wilson Cary, Son
Selden, Mary B., Wife
Selden, —, my younger children
Cutler, G. C., Wit.
Alexander, Charles H., Wit.
Alexander, Wm. Fontaine, Wit.
Shaffer, Elizabeth, W:152, 1835
Shaffer, Elizabeth, Dau.
Shaffer, Solomon, Son
Taylor, Joseph A., Wit.
Pierpoint, Eli, Wit.
Love, Eli A., Wit.
Marks, Thomas, W:153, 1832/35
Marks, Keziah, Wife
Croley, Clementine, Dau.
Crook, Charles, of Henderson Co., Ky., Wit.
Crews, Williamson, of Henderson Co., Ky., Wit.

Shoemaker, George Sr., W:157, 1829/35
Shoemaker, Mary, Wife
Shoemaker, George, Son
Shoemaker, Jacob, Son
Shoemaker, —, six more children
Potterfield, Daniel, Wit.
Boland, Daniel, Wit.
Shoemaker, Simon Sr., Wit.
Hamilton, Charles B., W:241, 1835
Reese, David, Exor.
Hamilton, James, Brother
Hamilton, Nancy, Wife
Hamilton, John, Brother
Hamilton, —, my children
Janney, Daniel, Wit.
Purcell, V. V., Wit.
Garrott, Erasmus, W:242, 1832/35
Garrott, Sarah, Wife
Johnson, Joseph A., Wit.
West, Joseph, Wit.
Hilleary, Tilghman, Wit.
Frye, Christopher, W:244, 1835
Frye, Margaret, Wife
Edwards, Samuel M., Wit.
Hammat, Edward, Wit.
Wooddy, James, Wit.
Fadley, Jacob, Wit.
Ellzey, William, W:258, 1830/35
Ellzey, —, Wife
Ellzey, William W., Eldest son
Ellzey, Thomas L., Son
Ellzey, Mary, Sister, dec'd.
Ellzey, Eliza, Sister, dec'd.
Gray, Frances W., Dau.
Gray, William H., Son-in-law
Ellzey, —, other dau.'s
—, wife's adopted Dau.
Chichester, George Mason, W:275, 1835/36
Bowie, Robert Gilmer, Exor.
Mason, William T. T., Exor.
Chichester, Sarah, Dau.
Cichester, —, Wife
Chichester, —, children
Harrison, Burr W., Wit.
Powell, W. A., Wit.

Neer, James, W:316, 1835/36
  Neer, Susana, Wife
  Neer, Elizabeth, Dau.
  Neer, John, Son
  Neer, George, Son
  Neer, Josiah, Son
  Neer, Mahaly, Dau.
  Shriver, Jacob, Exor.
  Neer, James, Son
  Waters, Jacob, Wit.
  Nyswanger, Christian, Wit.
  Nisewanner, John, Wit.
  Jacobs, Adam, Wit.
Drish, Ellenor, W:353, 1834/36
  Drish, Wilson J., Son
  Summers, Jacob, Wit.
  Elmore, Charles, Wit.
  Gulick, George, Wit.
  Gore, Tilghman, Admr. w.w.a.
Grubb, James, W:355, 1835/36
  Grubb, Adam, Brother
  Grubb, John Sr., Cousin
  Grubb, Elizabeth, Mother
  Grubb, Mary, Sister
  Grubb, William D., Brother
  Housholder, Gideon, Wit.
  Cogsil, Harvey, Wit.
  Janney, Amos, Wit.
Souder, Susana, X:13, 1829/36
  Souder, John, Son
  Souder, Mary, Dau.
  —, Margaret, Gr-Dau., dau. of Susanna, <18
  Souder, Elizabeth, Dau.
  Souder, Anthony, Son
  Souder, Peter, Son
  Souder, Rachel, Dau.
  Souder, Michael, Son
  Hickman, Henry, Wit.
  Miles, Benjamin, Wit.
  Wirtz, Peter, Wit.
Wornel, James, X:25, 1835/36
  Wornel, Charlotte, Wife
  Wornel, Elizabeth, Dau.
  Wornel, Agnes, Dau.
  Anderson, Nancy, Dau.
  Wornel, John, Son
  Barton, Sally, Dau.
  Sinclair, John, Wit.
  Eidson, Joseph F., Wit.
  Powell, Peyton, Wit.
  Lynn, James F., Wit.
Orem, Henry, X:51, 1834/36
  Claspy, Mary, Dau.
  Wise, Joseph, Step-son
  Orem, Lucinda Jane, Dau., <21
  Burson, Anne, Dau.
  Orem, Henry, Son
  Shoemaker, Pamelia, Dau.
  Orem, Sarah Elvira, Dau.
  Orem, Massie
  Orem, Armsistead, Son
  Orem, Enos, Son
  Orem, Jane, Wife
  Beans, Isaiah B., Exor.
  Noland, George W., Wit.
  Stone, William, Wit.
  Glascock, Thomas P., Wit.
Burson, Mary, X:53, 1835/36
  Torreyson, Lidia, Dau.
  Hutchison, Mary, Gr-Dau.
  Burson, Hester, Dau.
  Burson, Jesse, Son
  Burson, John, Son
  Burson, Cyrus, Son
  Burson, Jehu, Son
  Burson, Joseph, Husband, dec'd.
  Leith, Theodrick, Wit.
  Jackson, Benjamin, Wit.
Acres, Walter, X:55, 1835/36
  Bell, Susanna
  Bell, Nancy wife's child, Step-Dau.
  Saffer, William, Exor.
  Saffer, Susanna, wife's child, Step-Dau.
  Cunningham, Hulda, wife's child, Step-Dau.
  Tharp, Polly
  Cunningham, Wilmoth, wife's child, Step-Dau.
  Cunningham, Robert, Son-in-law [sic; probably step-son]
  Acres, Nancy, Wife
  Lewis, John, Wit.
  Hoff, Joshua, Wit.
  Hoff, Silas, Wit.

Index to Loudoun County Wills, 1757 - 1850   141

Filler, Benjamin, X:56, 1836
Filler, Mary, Wife
Marlow, Thomas J., Wit.
Shaffer, Jacob, Wit.
Cullison, William, X:57, 1836
Cullison, Nancy, Wife
Havner, Joseph, Nephew
Wilson, John M., Dau.
Muse, Thomas H., Wit.
Havner, James, Wit.
Reese, Elizabeth, Wit.
Coleman, Edmund W., X:58, 1836
Coleman, Caroline, Wife
Tebbs, Julia E., Sister
Coleman,—, two children, <21
Morgan, Jane C., Sister
Saunders, R. G., Wit.
Ramey, Sanford J., Wit.
Tebbs, A. S., Wit.
Gregg, Susan, X:60, 1836
Gregg, Elizabeth, Niece,
  dau. of Samuel
Gregg, Nathan, Nephew,
  son of Thomas
Gregg, Mary Jane, Niece,
  dau. of Samuel
Gregg, Samuel, Nephew,
  son of Thomas
Gregg, Thomas, Nephew,
  son of Thomas
Gregg, Nancy, Niece,
  dau. of Thomas
Gregg, Susan, Niece,
  dau. of Samuel
Gregg, Sally, Niece,
  dau. of Thomas
Gregg, Samuel, Brother, dec'd.
Gregg, Smith, Nephew,
  son of Thomas
Gregg, Henry, Nephew,
  son of Thomas
Gregg, Sarah Ann, Niece,
  dau. of Samuel
Gregg, Thomas, Brother, dec'd.
Gregg, Susan, Niece,
  dau. of Thomas
Gregg, Stephen, Nephew,
  son of Thomas
Vail, Nancy, Niece, w/o Nathan

Gregg, Harmon, Nephew,
  son of Thomas,
McIlhany, James, Wit.
Pierpoint, Samuel, Wit.
Morrison, Jane, X:61, 1830/36
Morrison, Joseph, Son
Lasley, Rachel, Dau.
Marchant, Mary, Dau.
Whiteman, Sarah, Dau.
Grubb, Hetty, Dau.
Morrison, James, Son
Chapeleare, Levy
Morrison, Benjamin, Son
Morrison, Jane, Gr-Dau.,
  dau. of John
Morrison, Elizabeth, Dau.
Morrison, Jane, Dau.
Morrison, John, Son
Morrison, Edward, Son
Harper, Samuel, Wit.
Frye, John, Wit.
Fanney, Amos, Wit.
Elgin, Walter, X:139, 1836
Rogers, Walter Thomas, infant,
  Gr-Son, son of Nancy
Rogers, Nancy, Dau., dec'd.
Fulton, Mary, Dau.
Elgin, William, Son
Elgin, Ignatius, Son
Elgin, Samuel, Son
Elgin, Walter, Son
Elgin, Sally, Dau.
Elgin, Rebecca, Dau.
Elgin, John, Son
Elgin, Diadama, Dau.
Elgin, Mordicai, Son
Fulton, William, Son-in-law
Jackson, Asa, Wit.
Littleton, John, Wit.
Shreve, B. Jr., Wit.
Taylor, Stacy, X:147, 1835/36
Beans, Leatitia, Dau.
Smith, Sarah, Dau.
Taylor, Benjamin F., Son
Hughes, Fanny, Dau.
Taylor, Stacy, Son
Taylor, Samuel B., Son
Taylor, Mahlon K., Son
Taylor, Ruth, Wife
Taylor, Timothy, Youngest Son

Purcell, Samuel J., Wit.
Hatcher, Thomas E., Wit.
Osburn, Mary, X:167, 1836
Pursel, Volney, Gr-Son, son of Jonah & Maria, < 21
Pursel, Harrison, Gr-Son, son of Jonah & Maria, < 21
Pursel, Maria, Dau.
Pursel, Jonah, Son-in-law
Osburn, Balaam, Wit.
Mains, Archibald, X:179, 1832/36/36
Sugars, Joseph
Chamblin, Archibald, Gr-nephew
Carr, Washington Mains, Nephew, <21,
Chamblin, Dewanna, Niece, w/o Mason
Carr, John, Brother-in-law, dec'd., father of Washington Mains Carr
Mains, Archibald, Nephew, son of William,
Vandevanter, Elizabeth, Sister
Vandevanter, Mary, Niece
Vandevanter, Ann, Sister, dec'd.
Vandevanter, Ann Eliza, Niece
Carr, Jane, Sister, dec'd.
Mains, William, Brother
Vandevanter, Gabriel, Nephew
Sinclair, Leanna, Niece
Mains, John, Brother, dec'd.
Downs, John, Wit.
Harrison, Burr W., Wit.
Edwards, Samuel M., Wit.
Robertson, John, X:183, 1836
Robertson, Tamar, Dau.
Robertson, Seth, Son
Robertson, William, Son
Robertson, Elizabeth, Wife
Robertson, Sarah, Dau.
Robertson, Elizabeth, Dau.
Robertson, Mary, Dau.
Robertson, Helah, Dau.
Jackson, S. A., Wit.
James, Elijah, Wit.
Trahern, Sarah, X:209, 1835/37
Trahern, Thomas, Friend
Trahern, Samuel
Trahern, Israel
Trahern, Isaac's heirs
Trahern, James' heirs
Walker, Thornton, Wit.
McGeath, James, Wit.
Ogdon, Robert, X:210, 1832/37
Stevens, Sally, Dau.
Stevens, Hannabel, Gr-Son
Stevens, Ann Eliza, Gr-Dau.
Stevens, Thomas, Gr-Son
Stevens, Rosamond, Gr-Dau.
Stevens, Robert, Gr-Son
Stevens, John, Gr-Son
Ogdon, Robert, Son
Ogdon, Hezekiah, Son
Ogdon, William, Son
Ogdon, Nancy, Dau.
Ogdon, Benjamin, Son
Ogdon, Andrew, Son
McIlhany, James, Wit.
Beans, Samuel, Wit.
Beans, Paxson, Wit.
Kline, Jno. Nicholas, X:212, 1834/37
Ashby, Delilah, Dau.
Bridenbaugh, Maria L., Dau.
Kline, John, Son
Kline, Elizabeth, Dau.
Kline, David, Son
Kline, Nicholas, Son
Wright, Jotham, Wit.
Jarvis, Washington, Wit.
Hutchison, Reuben, X:213, 1837
Smith, Alexander M., Gr-Son
Hutchison, Joseph, Son, child of 1st marriage
Smith, Mary Ann, Gr-Dau.
Hutchison, Leah, Wife
Smith, Maria, Gr-Dau.
Hutchison, Cynthiana, Gr-Dau., dau. of Alexander
Shumate, Maria, Gr-Dau.
Hutchison, Susanna, Dau., child of 2nd marriage
Hutchison, Mary Jane, Dau., child of 2nd marriage
Hutchison, Henry B., Son, child of 2nd marriage
Hutchison, Robert P., Son, child of 2nd marriage

Hutchison, James, Son,
  child of 1st marriage
Hutchison, Alexander, Son,
  child of 1st marriage
Hutchison, John, Wit.
Hutchison, Beverly, Wit.
Binns, Charles, X:240, 1835/37
Tebbs, Hannah Sim, Dau.
McCabe, Margaret Hannah
  Douglas, Dau.
Binns, Anne Alexander, Dau.
Binns, Elizabeth Douglas, Dau.
Binns, Charles William Douglas,
  Son
Binns, John Alexander, Son
Binns, Hannah, Wife
Henderson, Richard H., Exor.
Rogers, Thomas, Exor.
Timms, Jesse, X:240, 1837
Timms, Betsey, Dau.
Timms, Jane, Dau.
Timms, John, Exor.
Timms, Henry, Son
Taylor, William, Exor.
Webster, Mary Jane, Gr-Dau.
Luck, Jordan, Wit.
Mount, Thomas A., Wit.
Elgin, Gustavus Sr., Wit.
Potterfield, Adam, X:260, 1837
Potterfield,—, all my children
Potterfield, Mary, Wife
Potterfield, Samuel, Brother
Potterfield, Elizabeth
Vincel, Solomon, Wit.
Bumcrots, John, Wit.
Cooper, George Jr., Wit.
Butler, Moses (F.N.), X:278, 1837
Butler, Hannah, Wife
Butler, Melvina, Dau.
Drish, William D., Exor.
Lambaugh, Thomas, Wit.
Rogers, Thomas, Wit.
Stoutseberger, John, X:278, 1836/37
Stoutseberger, Margarett, Wife
Stoutseberger, Samuel, Son
Stoutseberger, Jacob, Son
Crumbaker, Solomon,
  Son-in-law
Hamilton, C. B., Wit.

Yakey, Simon, Wit.
McCutcher, Samuel, Wit.
Presgraves, Richard, X:291, 1837
Presgraves, Ann, Dau.
Presgraves, John Thomas, Son
Presgraves, Nancy, Wife
Presgraves, Milly, Dau.
Presgraves, Lydia, Dau.
Hutchison, Lucinda, Dau.
Hutchison, Melvin, Son-in-law
Presgraves, Richard H., Exor.
Presgraves, William W., Exor.
Lewis, Charles, Wit.
Ellmore, Edward, Wit.
Ellmore, Edward Sr., Wit.
Kenworthy, William, X:356, 1824/37
Kenworthy, Isaac, Brother,
  dec'd., of Washington
  County, Pa.
Hancock, Mary, Sister
Kenworthy, Rebecca, Wife
Hopkins, Gerard T., Friend
McPherson, Isaac, Friend
Blackburn, Amy, Sister
Hewes, John, Friend
Williams, Rebecca, Cousin,
  dau. of Abner
Blackburn, William, Nephew
Hoge, William K., son of Jesse,
  son of wife's brother
Williams, Abner, Cousin
Hancock, William, Nephew
Ellicott, E., Wit.
Kenworthy, Rebecca, X:358, 1829/37
Fisher, Lydia, mother of
  Rebecca
Everitte, Rebecca Kenworthy
Hancock, Mary, mother of Mary
Fisher, John, father of Rebecca
Everitte, Eli, father of Rebecca
Hogue, William, Brother
Fisher, Rebecca,
  Husband's Niece
Williams, John, Exor.
Everitte, Ann,
  mother of Rebecca
Hancock, Joel, father of Mary

Hancock, Mary, Husband's
  Niece
Gregg, Joshua, Wit.
Hoge, Thomas, Wit.
Hoge, James, Wit.
Abel, Catharine, X:360, 1837
Hatcher, Jonah, Exor.
Abel, George, Son
Abel, Ann Catharine, Gr-Dau.
Wigginton, Presley, Wit.
Shriver, Jacob, Wit.
Conard, Joseph, Wit.
Coleman, Thomas W., X:360, 1829/37
Coleman, —, two sisters and
  one brother
Coleman, Fanny, Wife
Kelly, Joseph, Wlt.
Coleman, Thomas, Wit.
Rumsey, Marianne, Wit.
Lovett, Daniel, X:368, 1837
Taylor, Christian C., Dau.
Marshall, Ruel
Lovett, Thomas Alfred, Son
Lovett, Joseph Tazewell,
  Youngest Son
Lovett, Edmund Landon
  Osburn, Son
Lovett, Daniel Clinton, Son
Lovett, James Peyton, Son
Gore, Enos, Wit.
Fulton, David, Wit.
Davis, Howel, X:370, 1836/37
Tavenner, Benjamin, son of
  Mary, Gr-Son, <21
Tavenner, William, Gr-Son, son
  of Mary, <21
Tavenner, Richard, Gr-Son, son
  of Mary, <21
Tavenner, Elizabeth, Gr-Dau.,
  dau. of Mary, <21
Tavenner, Catharine, Gr-Dau.,
  dau. of Mary, <21
Tavenner, Sarah Ann, Gr-Dau.,
  dau. of Mary, <21
White, Eden, Son-in-law
  husband of Hannah
Davis, Lucinda, Dau.
Davis, Joseph, Son

Davis, Benjamin, Son
Davis, Amanda, Dau., <21
Warner, Acinda, Gr-Dau.
Davis, Sarah, Wife
Hicks, Charles, Gr-Son, <21
Tavenner, Mary, Dau., dec'd.
White, Hannah, Dau.
Gore, Sarah, Dau.
Everitt, Nancey, Dau.
Gore, Sarah's four children,
  <21
Eaton, Isaac, Wit.
Nixon, Joel, Wit.
Newman, Jesse, Y:1, 1837
Newman, Nathan, Brother
Pain (Payne), Nancy
Marlow, George, Wit.
Spinks, John, Wit.
White, Benjamin, Y:1, 1827/37
White, Richard, Son
White, Edon, Son
White, Mary, Wife
White, Louisa, 4th Dau.
White, Rebecca's children,
  2nd Dau.
White, Elizabeth, 3rd Dau.
White, Nancy, Eldest Dau.
Nixon, Joel, Wit.
Tavenner, Eli, Wit.
Hamilton, C. B., Wit.
Heath, Lydia, Y:3, 1837
Church, Louisa, Niece
James, Susanna, Niece
Heath, John, Nephew,
  son of Isaac
Buck, Reuhama, Sister
James, Sarah, Sister
Hawley, Catharine's children,
  Sister
Heath, Richard, Nephew,
  son of Isaac
Heath, Andrew, Brother
Heath, Charles, Nephew,
  son of Isaac
Heath, Isaac, Brother
Heath, Gustavus, Nephew,
  son of Isaac
Hutchison, John, Exor.
Hutchison, Beverly, Trustee
Hancock, G., Wit.

James, Dean, Wit.
Hawley, Jeremiah, Wit.
Taylor, Mary, Y:44, 1836/37
Taylor, Joseph, Son
Taylor, Mahlon K., Son
Taylor, Timothy Jr., Wit.
Heaton, Townsend, Wit.
Heaton, John T. M., Wit.
Rogers, Thomas, Y:107, 1837/38
Rogers, Edwin, Son
Elgin, Francis, Son-in-law
Rogers, Walter Thomas, Gr-Son
Elgin, Lucy Alice, Gr-Dau.
Rogers, Elizabeth, Wife
Elgin, Mary Elizabeth, Gr-Dau.
Elgin, Thomas Gustavus, Gr-Son
Elgin, Mary Jane, Dau.
Latham, John, Wit.
Dowdell, Sampson G., Wit.
Ewell, Jesse Jr., Wit.
Updike, Rufus, Y:129, 1837/38
Updike, Sally, Dau.
Carter, Jane, Dau.
Updike, Nancy, Dau.
Updike, John, Son
Updike, Samuel, Son
Updike, Edon, Son
Updike, Phebe, Dau.
Updike, Peggy, Dau.
Updike, Amos, Son
Taylor, Charles, Wit.
Osburne, Phineas, Wit.
Hampton, James, Wit.
Sanbower, Ann, Y:130, 1837/38
Rickard, Mary, w/o Simon
Sypherd, Sarah, Dau.
Sanbower, Adam
Sanbower, Michael
Sanbower, Julian
Sagar, Elizabeth, w/o Samuel
Shover, Susan, w/o George
Wenner, Jonathan, Wit.
Thrashere, John, Wit.
Russell, William, Wit.
Harden, Thomas Sr., Y:142, 1837/38
Harden, Mary, Wife
Nalls, Carr Bailey, Wit.
Chappell, James, Wit.

Love, Jane, Y:142, 1837/38
Berkeley, Frances, Niece
Cochran, Catherine, Niece
Noland, Ellen, Niece, dau. of Lloyd, <21
Noland, Lloyd, Brother
Noland, Burr P., Nephew
Noland, Catherine, Sister
Noland, Thomas, Nephew
Noland, Jane Elizabeth, Niece, <21
Noland, Richard, Nephew
Noland, Louisa, Niece, <21
Cochran, Richard, Wit.
Smith, James W., Wit.
Hale, H. D., Wit.
Powell, Humphrey B., Exor.
Lacey, Naomi, Y:145, 1825/38
Beard, Benjamin, Nephew
Beard, Jonathan, Nephew
Beard, Orpah, Sister
Beard, Ellen, Niece
Lacey, Huldah, Sister
Lacey, Ruth, Sister
Hutchison, Alexander, Wit.
Beatty, William T. C., Wit.
Lacey, Mesheck, Wit.
Palmer, Samuel, Y:208, 1832/38
Palmer, Edith, Dau.
Palmer, Israel, Son
Palmer, Samuel, Son
Palmer, Benjamin, Son
Palmer, Elizabeth, Dau.
Palmer, Rachel, Dau., [married, but name not shown]
Palmer, Priscilla, Dau.
Chamblin, Charles, Exor.
Chamblin, James H., Wit.
Chamblin, Rush, Wit.
Rogers, Elmina, Wit.
Chamblin, Dewanner, Wit.
Taylor, Timothy, Y:218, 1834/38
Taylor, Timothy, Son
Taylor, Leatitia, Dau., married, but name not shown
Taylor, William, Son
Taylor, Benjamin, Son
Hill, Olivia, Gr-Dau.
Taylor, Charles, Son
Roane, Mary, Dau.

Bartlett, Johnston, Gr-Son
Bartlett, Minor, Gr-Son, <21
James, Ellwood B., Wit.
Osburn, Phineas, Wit.
Nichols, Thomas, Wit.
Nickols, Nathan, Y:220, 1824/38
Nickols, Jane, Wife
Nickols, —, Son
Bradfield, Ann, Dau.
Nickols, Abraham, Exor.
Bradfield, John, Exor.
Alder, Jane, Dau.
Alder, George H., Exor.
Nichols, Thomas, Wit.
Nichols, Joel, Wit.
Tracey, Everit, Wit.
Chew, John Sr., Y:221, 1834/37/38
Osburn, Mary, Dau.
McKnight, Margaret (Jacobs), Gr-Dau.
Gustine, Mary, Gr-Dau.
Gustine, Elinor, Dau.
Jacobs, Augustus, Gr-Son, son of Elizabeth
Chew, Margaret, Wife
Jacobs, Elizabeth, Dau., dec'd.
Chew, Henry, Gr-Son, son of Henry, <21
Jacobs, Lemuel, Gr-Son, son of Elizabeth
Chew, Lemuel, Gr-Son, son of William
Jacobs, Almira, Gr-Dau., dau. of Elizabeth
Chew, Mary, Gr-Dau., child of William
Jacobs, Caroline, Gr-Dau., dau. of Elizabeth
Chew, Mary B. , Dau.-in-law, mother of Caroline & James Edward
Jacobs, Ferdinand, Gr-Son, son of Elizabeth
Tailor, Elizabeth (Jacobs), Gr-Dau.
Jacobs, Emily, Gr-Dau., dau. of Elizabeth
Chew, Roger, Son
Jacobs, Cornelius, Gr-Son, son of Elizabeth
Carrington, Margaret, Dau.
Chew, Henry, Son
Chew, William, Son
Chew, James Edward, Gr-Son, <21
Chew, Caroline, Gr-Dau.
Chew, John, Son
Chew, Nancy, Dau.
Jacobs, Prestley, Son-in-law
Osburn, Balaam, Exor.
Osburn, Joshua, Exor.
Young, John B., Wit.
McCullough, W. H., Wit.
Grady, Edward B., Wit. [c]
Wornal, John, Wit. [c]
Campbell, John, Y:254, 1838
Sullivan, Eliza
Sullivan, John, son of Eliza
Summers, William, Wit.
Grubb, William Jr., Wit.
Hough, Bernard, Wit
Janney, James C., Wit.
Copeland, Andrew, Wit.
Aldridge, Joseph W., Y:254, 1838
Aldridge, John, Brother
Aldridge, Andrew, Brother
Lickey, John W., Wit.
Aldridge, Harriet, Wit.
Simpson, John, Wit.
Campbell, John, Y:254, 1838
Campbell, John, Son
Campbell, Robert, Son
Campbell, Asa, Son
Campbell, James, Son
Cockerill, Delilah, widow of Lee
Hunter, Nancy, Y:256, 1838
Rollison, Fanny, Niece, daugther of John
Havener, Julyan, Niece, w/o Silas
Havener, Silas, Nephew
Havener, Ann Elizabeth, Gr-niece, dau. of Silas
Dawson, Charles, Wit.
Wilson, John M., Wit.
Dawson, S., Wit

Lacey, Huldah, Y:257, 1825/38
Lacey, Ruth, Sister
Lacey, Naomi, Sister
Beard, Ellen, Niece
Beard, Orpah, Sister
Beard, Benjamin, Nephew
Beard, Sandy, Nephew
Beard, Jonathan, Nephew
Hutchison, Alexander, Wit.
Beatty, William T. C., Wit.
Lacey, Mesheck, Wit.
Hutchison, J., Wit.
Copeland, James, Y:258, 1836/38
Copeland, Pleasant, Dau.
Copeland, Sarah, Dau.
Clapper, Zillah, Dau.
Copeland, Elizabeth, Dau.
Copeland, Jane, Dau.
Copeland, Craven A., Son
Copeland, Sarah, Wife
Copeland, Nancy, Dau.
Evans, Hannah, Dau.
Evans, Evan, Exor.
Vanvacter, Solomon, Wit.
Pierpoint, Eli, Wit.
Love, Eli A., Wit.
Williams, Hannah, Y:258, 1835/38
Williams, Sydnor, Son
Hamilton, C. B. Jr., Wit.
Schooley, J. P., Wit.
Luckett, Samuel C., Wit.
Marks, Sarah, Y:272, 1836/38
Marks, Elisha, Husband, dec'd.
Marks, Anna, Dau.
Richards, Barton, Wit.
Fred, Joseph, Wit.
Smith, Seth, Wit.
Williams, Martha, Y:273, 1837/38
Conner, Martha, Gr-Dau.
Alliston, Wilfred, Wit.
Conner, John, Wit.
Powell, William L., Wit.
Rogers, Hamilton Jr., Y:310, 1838
Rogers, Samuel, Brother
Rogers, Thomas, Brother
Rogers, —, Mother
Hughes, Martha, Wit.
Rogers, Dinah, Wit.
Holmes, Elizabeth, Wit.

Beavers, Samuel, Y:334, 1838
Beavers, Washington, Son
Palmer, Harriet, Dau.
Garrett, Eliza, Dau.
Beavers, Thomas, Son
Beavers, Julian Ann, Dau.
Beavers, Sarah M., Wife
Beavers, John A., Son
Leith, Theodrick, Wit.
Taylor, Jane, Wit.
Beavers, John, Wit.
Walker, Benjamin, Wit.
White, Elizabeth, Y:336, 1831/38
White, Washington
White, Rachel
Updike, Barsina,
  dau. of Rachel White
White, Albina, dau. of Rachel
Leslie, Samuel D., Wit.
Leslie, Benjamin, Wit.
Lodge, William, Wit.
Wright, Jotham, Y:355, 1838/39
Jarvis, Louisa, Dau.
Wright, John A., Son
Wright, Mary E., Dau.
Wright, Mary Ann, Wife
Edwards, Samuel M., Wit.
Peck, Asa, Wit.
Maulsby, Benjamin, Wit.
Newton, Joseph T., Y:361, 1838/39
Newton, Augustus, Brother
Harper, Dr. William
Newton, Mary A., Gr-Dau.
Newton, Frances F., Gr-Dau.
Newton, Nelly S. , Dau.-in-law,
  son's widow
McIntyre, Lucy
Wise, George P., Exor.
McIntyre, R., Exor.
Newton, William, Wit.
Owens, James T., Wit.
Cranwell, John S., Wit.
Ewers, Jonathan, Y:392, 1839
Whitacre, Hannah, Dau.
Ewers, Phebe, Wife
Ewers, William, Son
Ewers, Jonathan, Gr-Son
Ewers, Franklin, Gr-Son
Ewers, Mary, Dau., <21

Jackson, Benjamin, Wit.
Garrett, Silas, Wit.
Nichols, Joseph, Wit.
Noble, George, Y:422, 1836/39
Noble, Patsy, Dau.
Noble, Catharine, Dau.
Noble, Sarah Elizabeth, Dau.
Noble, Dorothy, Dau.
Noble, Franklin, Son
Noble, John, Son
Noble, Elisa, Dau.
McDanniel, Ann, Gr-Dau., <21
Noble, Nancy, Wife
McDanniel, Mason, Gr-Son, <21
Noble, William, Son
Noble, Thomas, Son
Noble, Warren (Peter), Son
McDanniel, Mary, Dau., dec'd.
Tillett, Samuel, Y:424, 1838/39
Tillett, John Love, Son
Tillett, Eleanor, Wife
Tillett, Jane, Dau., w/o Samuel
Tillett, —, all my children
Rogers, Hamilton, Exor.
Moore, John, Wit.
Elgin, Ignatius, Wit.
Skinner, Samuel, Z:22, 1839
Rousseau, Frances, Sister
Skinner, Nathan Sr., Friend
Ewell, Jesse Jr., Wit.
Skinner, Nathaniel, Wit.
Brown, Edwin C., Z:46, 1839
Mitchell, Henry, Servant
Brown, George M, Son
Brown, Edwin C., Son
Bailey, Harriet A., Dau.
Bailey, Stephen G., Son-in-law
Brown, Elizabeth, Wife, dec'd.
Stowers, Mrs., Son's aunt
Weeks, James, Wit.
Smith, James W., Wit.
Simpson, R. T., Wit.
Gibson, A. M., Wit.
Rogers, Asa, Exor.
Wilson, James B., Z:48, 1838/39
Lanham, Amelia, Gr-Dau.
Wilson, Juliet, Dau. [married name not shown]
Wilson, Nelson B., Son
Lanham, Bethania, Gr-Dau.

Wilson, —, Wife
Oden, Nathaniel S., Wit.
Oden, James S., Wit.
DeButts, Samuel Welby, Z:58, 1839
DeButts, —, Mother
DeButts, —, Wife
DeButts, John P., Son
DeButts, —, Unborn child
Dulaney, John P., Exor.
Hereford, Margaret, Wit.
Edwards, Charles G., Wit.
Bennett, James H., Wit.
Griffith, Israel T., Z:89, 1838/39
Lowe, Amelia Ann
Osburn, Richard, Admr. w.w.a.
Osburn, Joshua, Admr. w.w.a.
Roszel, Anna, Z:96, 1832/39
Roszel, Phebe
Mines, Martha
Ball, Ebenezer B.
Ball, Lucy T., Wit.
Potter, Elizabeth, Wit.
Roszel, Stephen G., Admr. w.w.a.
Powell, Burr, Z:98, 1829/39
Conrad, Elizabeth W., Dau.
Harrison, Sarah H., Dau.
Powell, William L., Son
Noland, Richard, Gr-Son, son of Ann
Powell, Cuthbert, Brother
Noland, Burr, Gr-Son, son of Ann
Powell, Humprhrey B., Son
Noland, Thomas, Gr-Son, son of Ann
Powell, George Cuthbert, Son
Noland, Catherine, Gr-Dau., dau. of Ann
Powell, Catherine, Wife
Noland, Ann W., Dau., dec'd.
Powell, Francis W., Son
Heaton, Lydia, Z:102, 1830/39
Heaton, James Decatur, Son
Heaton, Jane Cecila, Dau.
Heaton, Townsend, Son
Heaton, Albert, Son
Heaton, John Thomas William, Son

Heaton, Dr. James, Husband,
  dec'd.
Taylor, Timothy, Wit.
Osburn, Joel, Wit.
Whaley, William, Z:125, 1839/40
Whaley, —, Wife
Keene, Newton, Exor.
Francis, John, Wit.
Jenkins, Thomas, Wit.
Parker, Hannah, Z:126, 1829/40
Fry, Mary, Niece
Ellzey, Rosannah, Niece, dec'd.
Ellzey, Rosannah's three
  Dau.'s, Gr-nieces
Dunn, Elizabeth
Stribling, Cecelia, Niece, dec'd.
Stribling, —, Cecelia's children
White, Thomas, Nephew
White, James, Nephew, dec'd.
Jones, Polly's Dau., Gr-niece
McIlhany, Taliaferro M.
White, Nancy, Niece
Janney, Rachel, Niece
McIlhany, James, Nephew
White, —, children of James
Jones, Polly, Niece, dec'd.
Kilgour, Louisa, Niece, dec'd.
McIlhany, Mortimer, Nephew
White, Benniah, Nephew
McIlhany, John, Gr-nephew,
  son of Mortimer, <21
White, Robert, Nephew
Clendening, Samuel, Wit.
Marmaduke, John A., Wit.
Marmaduke, Silas, Wit.
**Wren, Sarah, a free woman of
  color, Z:127, 1835/40**
Jennings, William, Gr-Son
Jennings, John, Gr-Son
Jennings, Sally, Gr-Dau.
Jennings, Laura, Gr-Dau.
Hamilton, James L., Wit.
Harris, James S., Wit.
Martin, James L., Wit.
Swann, Thomas, Z:144, 1839/40
Swann, William, Son
Mercer, Jane, Gr-Dau.,
  dau. of Mary
Mercer, Mary S., Dau.
Swann, Robert P., Son

Swann, Thomas Jr., Son
Swann, Wilson C., Son
Mercer, M., Wit.
Clagett, Henry, Wit.
Magill, Henry D., Wit.
Mercer, Thomas L., Wit.
Brown, John, Z:146, 1840
Schooley, Elizabeth, Dau.
Steer, Mary Esther, Dau.-in-law,
  son John's widow, now
  remarried
Frame, Anna, Dau.
Steer, Jonah,
  husband of Mary Esther
Frame, James
Brown, William, Son
Myers, Hannah, Dau.
Brown, John, Son, dec'd.
Brown, David, Son
Brown, Sarah, Dau.
Birdsall, Mary, Dau.
Janney, Daniel, Wit.
Heaton, Townsend, Wit.
Birdsall, John B., Wit.
Williams, John, Z:148, 1837/40
Williams, William, Son
Williams, Rachel, Dau.
Williams, —, Wife
Williams, Abner, Brother
Steer, William E., Exor.
Jolliffe, William, Wit.
Walker, Isaac, Wit.
Janney, Moses, Wit.
Schelfield, William, Wit.
Steer, Joseph, Wit.
Coale, Lewis, Wit.
Russell, Samuel, Z:153, 1839/40
Russell, Ann, Mother
Russell, James, Father, dec'd.
Derry, Peter, Wit.
Fouke, Isaac, Wit.
Nyswanger, Christian, Wit.
Greenlease, James, Z:179, 1840
Vandevanter, Mary, Dau.
Vandevanter, Joseph,
  Son-in-law
Greenlease, Catharine, Dau.
Greenlease, James, Son
Greenlease, Polly, Sister
Greenlease, Charles, Son

Greenlease, Eliza, Dau.
Greenlease, William, Son
Greenlease, Hamilton, Son
Greenlease, Catharine, Wife
Clarke, Addison H., Wit.
Brown, Joseph, Wit.
Rice, William H, Wit.
Curry, John, Wit.
Sanders, Ann, Z:180, 1839/40
Gregg, George,
    Sarah Ann's father
Gregg, Sarah Ann, Niece
Vandevanter, Mary Ann L.,
    Step-Dau.
Sanders, Britton, Husband
Smith, Martha L., Niece
Gregg, Elisha, Sarah Ann's
    Gr-father
Gray, John, Wit.
Gray, Asher W., Wit.
Smith, Daniel G., Wit.
Sinclair, James, Wit.
Fairhurst, George, Z:181, 1835/40
Bolon, Joseph, John's child
Bolon, William, John's child
Bolon, Ezra
Bolon, John, dec'd.
Bolon, Rebecca
Bolon, Enoch, John's child
Fairhurst, David, brother
    John's Gr-child
Wilson, Mary
Bolon, Silas, John's child
Zimmerman, Eliza, Sister
Ellis, Ezar
Fairhurst, John, Brother
Hoge, Rachel, Niece,
    child of Rachel
Oram, Hiram
Fairhurst, John, brother
    John's Gr-child
Hoge, Rachel, Gr-Niece, dec'd.,
    dau. of sister Phebe
Mead, Lavina
Hoge, Isaac, Gr-nephew,
    child of Rachel
Hoge, Elizabeth, Gr-niece,
    child of Rachel
Hoge, Phebe, Gr-niece,
    child of Rachel

Taylor, Bernard, Exor.
Taylor, Yardley, Exor.
Hirst, Jonathan, Wit.
Gibson, Joseph, Wit.
Hirst, Eli P., Wit.
Alford, Charles, Z:182, 1840
Gildea, Rev. John B., Catholic
    clergyman
Coghlan, Edward, Exor.
Donohoe, Patrick, Wit.
McDaniel, Archibald, Wit.
Feagins, William D., Wit.
Heatherby, Thomas, Z:238, 1810/40
Heaton, Dr. James, Brother-in-
    law, wife's brother
Heatherby, Mary, Wife
Heaton, Lydia, Wit.
Osburn, Patience, Wit.
Chamblin, Charles, Z:262, 1840
Rogers, Thomas, Son-in-law
Atwell, Harriett, Dau.
Atwell, William, Son-in-law
Chamblin, Mason, Son
Chamblin, Ruth, Wife
Chamblin, Rush, Son
Chamblin, Jared, Son
Chamblin, James H., Son
Chamblin, Burr, Son
Janney, John, Wit.
Luckett, F. W., Wit.
Brown, Isachar, Z:273, 1840
Brown, Urey Jane, Gr-Dau.,
    Samuel's Dau., <21
Gregg, Thomas, Son-in-law
Gregg, Mary, Dau.
McMullen, Edith
Brown, James children,
    Gr-children
Brown, Joel, Son
Brown, Hannah, Wife, dec'd.
Brown, Craven, Son
Brown, Giles, Son
Brown, Samuel, Son
Brown, William, Son
Brown, Thomas, Son
Brown, Margaret, present Wife
Chamblin, Mason, Exor.
Smith, David, Wit.

Griffith, Philip, Wit.
Pursel, Enos, Wit.
Ish, Jacob, Z:274, 1839/40
Prosser, Margaret, Dau.
Ish, Lucinda, Dau.
Carnes, Naomi, Dau.
Ish, Mary, Dau.
Humphrey, Thomas, Son-in-law
Humphrey, Phebe, Dau.
Simpson, Elizabeth, Dau.
Ish, William King, Son
Ish, Robert Alexander, Son
Ish, Susannah, Wife
Ish, John, Son
Ish, George Henry, Son
James, Dean, Wit.
Adam, William F., Wit.
Skinner, Nathaniel, Wit.
Adams, Francis, Wit.
Kemp, Henry, of Maryland, Z:277, 1833/40
Hoffman, Henry W., Son-in-law
Buckey, David, Son-in-Law, dec'd.
Hoffman, Margaret, Dau.
Buckey, Elizabeth, Dau.
Kemp, William, Son
Kemp, Daniel, Son
Kemp, Lewis, Son
Kemp, Henry, Son
Richardson, Davis, Exor.
Bayly, John, Wit.
Harding, John L., Wit.
Steiner, William, Wit.
Booth, John, Z:279, 1839/40
Booth, Nancy, Dau.
Booth, John, Son
Booth, James, Eldest Son
Booth, Lydia, Dau.
Wiard, Michael, Exor.
Wenner, Jonathan, Wit.
George, John, Wit.
George, John Jr., Wit.
Harris, Isaac, Z:302, 1840
Brisco, Eliza H., Dau.
Brisco, Caroline E., Gr-Dau.
Brisco, Richard L. L., Gr-Son
Majors, Hannah A. J., Gr-Dau.
Weedon, Sarah J., Gr-Dau.
Harris, Samuel M., Son

Harris, —, Wife
Harris, Isaac, Son
Harris, James S., Son
Harris, William P., Son
Sanders, Thomas, Exor.
Saunders, Thomas R., Wit.
Saunders, Gunnell, Wit.
Hall, Elizabeth, Z:311, 1840
Hall, William, Exor.
Hall, —, all my children
Skillman, Alcinda, Sister
Nixon, Joel, Wit.
Skillman, William French, Wit.
Coe, John W., Z:311, 1840
—, Charles, negro man
Rogers, Thomas, Wit.
Cullen, John, Wit.
Hixon, D., Wit.
Turner, George, Admr. w.w.a.
Beveridge, John, Z:328, 1831/40
Beveridge, Kesiah, Wife
Rogers, Asa, Wit.
Swart, William R., Wit.
McFarland, Alfred, Wit.
Hereford, Thomas A., Z:342, 1840/41
Champ, Sarah, negro
Champ, Eliza, negro
Champ, Nancy, negro
Champ, Joseph, negro
Smith, Lucy, negro
Champ, Betsey, negro
Hereford, Thomas Short's children, Son, dec'd.
Hoe, Alfred, Slave
Hereford, Margaret S., Gr-Dau.
Hereford, Theoderick M., Son
Hereford, Alice Thornton, Wife
Champ, Peggy, negro
Fred, Thomas, Exor.
Megeath, James, Wit.
Palmer, William C., Wit.
Hereford, John B., Wit.
Fortney, Susan, Z:353, 1840/41
Birkby, Charles, son of Thomas, about 14 years
Birkby, Thomas, neighbor
Birkby, Joseph, Exor.
Torrison, William, Wit.

Watson, Lemuel, Wit.
Illegible, George, Wit.
Henderson, Richard Henry, Z:372, 1839/41
Henderson, Mary Garnett, Dau.
Henderson, Orra Moore, Wife
Henderson, Fenton Mercer, Son
Henderson, Sarah Moore, Dau.
Henderson, Robert, Son
Henderson, Annie, Dau.
Henderson, Janet, Dau.
Henderson, William Henry, Son
Henderson, Thomas, Son
Henderson, Margaret, Dau.
Fouch, Mary McD., Z:389, 1839/41
Russell, Elizabeth, Sister
Russell, Charley Ann Elizabeth Jane, Niece
Harrison, Burr W., Wit.
Fouch, Eden, Wit.
Baker, Samuel, Z:397, 1837/41
Baker, George, Son
Baker, Philip, Son
Baker, Elizabeth, Dau.
Baker, John, Son
Axline, Christina, Dau.
Baker, Adam, Son
Grubb, John, Wit.
Wunder, H. S., Wit.
Frye, Daniel, Wit.
Phillips, Thomas, Z:407, 1841
Williams, Willis L., Son-in-law
Phillips, Rachel, Wife
Phillips, Thomas Jr., Son
Miller, Amy Ann, Dau.
Miller, William H, Son-in-law
Williams, Sarah M., Dau.
Braden, Noble S., Exor.
Bond, T. M., Wit.
Bond, Asa M., Wit.
Gover, Jesse, Wit.
Fulton, Robert, Z:414, 1836/41
Fulton, Richard Evans, son of Elisha W., nephew of 2nd wife, Gr-Son
Fulton, Robert Massie, Son
Fulton, Mary, 2nd wife, dec'd.
Fulton, Jane E., Dau.-in-law
Fulton, Elisha Wynkoop, Son

Fulton, Mary Elizabeth, Gr-Dau., dau. of Elisha W., niece of 2nd wife
Fulton, David Powell, Son
Fulton, John, Son
Fulton, William, Son
Richards, George, Wit.
Janney, John, Wit.
Elgin, Gustavus Jr., Wit.
Elgin, John, Wit.
Brewer, Edward, Z:426, 1841
Brewer, Ann, Dau.
Brewer, John, Son
Brewer, Martha, Wife
Brewer, —, rest of my children
Belt, Alfred, Wit.
Magill, Henry D., Wit.
Rawlings, William, Wit.
Beatty, Mary, 2A:1, 1840/41
McIlroy, Elizabeth, Dau.
Beatty, Joseph W., Gr-Son
Beatty, William, Son
Beatty, Patsey, Dau.-in-law, Joseph William's mother
Beatty, Thomas, Son
Rhodes, George, Exor.
Nixon, Joel, Wit.
Nixon, Asbury, Wit.
Gover, Samuel, Wit.
Gover, John, Wit.
Smith, Clement, 2A:6, 1823/41
Cox, Clement, Exor.
Smith, Walter, Brother
Ringgold, Walter S., Exor.
Smith, John A., Exor.
Smith, Richard, Brother
Stull, John J., Wit.
Suter, Alexander, Wit.
Waugh, A. P., Wit.
Cox, John, Wit.
Lacey, Sarah, 2A:34, 1838/41
Conner, Lucinda, Gr-Dau.
Paxson, Jane, Gr-Dau.
Paxson, Eliza, Gr-Dau.
Paxson, Thompson Mason Chichester, Gr-Son
Heath, Diademia, Dau.
Schooley, Mahlon, Exor.
Steer, Isaac E., Exor.

Vermillion, Garrison, Wit.
Braden, Noble S., Wit.
Everhart, Susannah, 2A:58, 1841
Everhart, Elijah Danner, Son
Everhart, George Marlow, Son
Everhart, Matilda Irrebella, Dau.
Everhart, Nathaniel William, Son
Everhart, William Nathaniel, Son
Ropp, Nicholas, Wit.
Ropp, Samuel, Wit.
Smith, John, Wit.
Conard, John, 2A:59, 1841
Edwards, Elizabeth, Dau.
Potts, Ann, Dau.
Conard, Mary, Youngest Dau.
Conard, Joseph, Son
Conard, Abner, Youngest Son
Conard, Jonathan, Son
Conard, John, Son
Conard, David, Eldest Son
Conard, Barbara, Wife
Filler, Sarah Eldest Dau.
Derry, Peter, Wit.
Lay, George, Wit.
Clendening, William, Wit.
Hixon, Fleming, 2A:60, 1839/41
Hixon, Betty, Dau.
Dulaney, Elizabeth Ann
Anderson, A. S., dec'd.
Anderson, Eleanor
Anderson, Ellen, Niece
Braden, H. W., Exor.
Braden, Noble S., Exor.
Edmonds, R. L., Wit.
Sprote, L. W., Wit.
Illegible name, Wit.
Richards, Samuel, 2A:93, 1838/41
Richards, Elizabeth, Wife
Richards, Lydia, Gr-Dau.
Richards, Barton, Son
Richards, Thomas, Son
Lang, Elizabeth A., Dau.
Newlon, Hannah, Dau.
Newlon, Richard Manly, Gr-Son
Walker, Thornton, Wit.
Weadon, John, Wit.

Hodgson, William Ludwell, 2A:94, 1840/41
Irwin, Frances, dau. of James
Irwin, James
Irwin, Elizabeth, dau. of James
Lee, Alfred, son of Charles
Wilson, Thomas Irwin
Wilson, Hannah, mother of Thomas
Hoffman, Peter E.
Hann, Matthias, 2A:102, 1840/41
Hann, Elizabeth, Dau.
Hann, James Fenton, Youngest Son, <21
Hann, Mary, Wife
Hann, David Franklin, Oldest Son
Fred, Thomas, Wit.
Smith, Seth, Wit.
Gulick, Martha, 2A:103, 1839/41
Weeks, Clarissa, Niece
Lovett, Lucinda, Niece
Dowdell, James H., Nephew
Dowdell, Sampson G., Nephew
Dowdell, Theodore C., Nephew
Creel, Lucretia, Niece
Gulick, George, Wit.
Gulick, Sanford, Wit.
King, William, Wit.
Rogers, Elizabeth, Wit.
Rogers, Hamilton, Wit.
Gulick, Francis, Wit.
McCormick, Mary, 2A:112, 1842
Knox, Janet P.
Knox, Thomas P. father of Janet
Lawrence, John E. C., Gr-Son
Annin, Helen C., Dau.
Lawrence, Emily, Dau., dec'd.
Gray, John, Exor.
Seeders, William, Wit.
Seeders, Sarah S., Wit.
McDonaugh, James Jr., Wit.
McKenna, Anne Cecelia, 2A:131, 1840/42
McKenna, James L., Husband
Love, Cecelia Matilda, Niece
Lee, Richard Henry, Brother
Lee, Cassius F., Cousin
Lee, Flora, Mother, dec'd.

Adie, George, Wit.
Lee, Emily L., Wit.
Grayson, Richard O., 2A:132, 1841/42
Grayson, Benjamin, Father, dec'd.
Grayson, —, six children
Grayson, George M., Brother
Lufborough, James H., Exor.
Carter, Elizabeth O., Wit.
Carter, George, Wit.
Mason, Westwood T., 2A:133, n.d./1842
Mason, —, Wife
Mason, William T. T.
Macrae, Amelia A., Wit.
Wallace, Elizabeth C., Wit.
Filler, Jacob, 2A:134, 1841/42
Crim, Matilda, Dau.
Arnold, Emeline, Dau.
Filler, Jonathan Heaton, Son
Filler, Jacob Abner, Son
Filler, Elizabeth, Dau.
Filler, Solomon, Son
Filler, Sarah, Wife
Filler, Sarah Ann, Dau.
Filler, John Milton, Son
Filler, Joseph Henry, Son
Smith, John, Wit.
Hawes, Daniel J., Wit.
Porter, Jesse, Wit.
Lowe, Amelia A., 2A:134, 1841/42
Cridler, Rachel, Sister
Hough, Mary, Sister
Smallwood, Jane, Mother
Cridler, Andrew, Brother-in-law, Rachel's husband
Hough, Samuel, Brother-in-law, Mary's husband
Lowe, Edward, Husband
Pusey, Joshua, Exor.
Braden, Noble S., Wit.
Walker, Nathan, Wit.
Heaton, Townsend, 2A:135, 1841/42
Heaton, John T. W.
Heaton, James Decatur
Heaton, Jane Cecila
Heaton, Albert, Brother

Rose, Robert, 2A:154, 1839/42
Casey, Susana, dec'd.
Rose, Christopher, Brother, dec'd.
Rose, John Casey, Adopted Son
Garrett, Stephen, Exor.
Gulick, William, Exor.
Sinclair, John, Wit.
Beatty, William, Wit.
Adams, William F., Wit.
Smith, William, 2A:155, 1841/42
Taylor, Yardley, Nephew
Hoge, Sarah Ann, Gr-Dau., dau. of Lydia Janney
Hoge, William K., husband of Sarah Ann
Zimmerman, Elizabeth
Smith, William, Gr-Son, son of Jonas
Smith, William, Gr-Son, son of John
Shepherd, Ann, Dau.
Smith, Jonas, Son
Smith, John, Son
Shepherd, Thomas, Son-in-law
Janney, Lydia, Dau., w/o Elisha
Janney, Jonas, Son-in-law
Janney, Ruth Hanah, Gr-Dau., dau. of Elisha & Lydia
Janney, Pleasant, Dau., w/o Jonas
Janney, Eliza Pleasant, Gr-Dau., dau. of Elisha & Lydia
Janney, William, Gr-Son, son of Jonas
Janney, Elisha, Son-in-law
Taylor, Mahlon K., Wit.
Nichols, Thomas, Wit.
Shoemaker, Naylor, Wit.
Taylor, Jonathan, Wit.
Wilson, Julia A., 2A:158, 1842
Wilson, —, my children
Harrison, Burr W., Exor.
Gray, William H., Exor.
Powell, Lucy P., Wit.
Magill, Henry D., Wit.
Davis, Harriet, Wit.
Ellzey, Alice A., Wit.

Index to Loudoun County Wills, 1757 - 1850 155

Roszel, Stephen G., 2A:184, 1839/42
Roszel, Stephen Samuel, Son
Roszel, Stephen George, son of Dr. Stephen Wesley Roszel, dec'd., <21
Roszel, Mary, Wife
Roszel, George Washington, Son
Roszel, Stephen Calvert, Son
Roszel, Phebe, Sister
Roszel, Nancy, Sister
Roszel, Stephen McKendree, Son
Roszel, Stephen Daniel Bosley, son of Dr. Stephen Wesley Roszel, dec'd., <21
Woodard, Octavia, Dau.
Conner, Sarah Ann Amelia, Dau.
Mount, Stephen G. Roszel
Mount, Mary Ann, Dau.
Merryman, Mary
Roszel, Stephen G., Gr-Son, son of Stephen Calvert
Donohoe, Sarah, Sister
Roszel, Stephen Asbury, Son

Squires, Thomas, 2A:185, 1842
Squires, John, Son
Squires, Henson W., Son
Squires, Nancy, Dau.
Littleton, Fielding, Exor.
McCarty, Dennis, Wit.
Short, John P. H., Wit.

Hatcher, Edith, 2A:207, 1841/42
Spencer, William, Brother-in-law, husband of Sarah, dec'd.
Spencer, Sarah, Sister
Nichols, Jonah, Nephew, son of Margery
Nichols, Margery, Sister, dec'd.
Nichols, James, Nephew, son of Margery
Nichols, Samuel, Nephew, son of Margery
Nichols, Joshua, Nephew, son of Margery
Nichols, Ann, Niece, dau. of Margery
Nichols, Elizabeth S., Niece, dau. of Margery
Nichols, William N., Nephew, son of Margery
Nichols, Phebe L., Niece, dau. of Margery
Nichols, Swithen, Brother-in-law, husband of Rebecca
Nichols, Jacob, Brother-in-law
Nichols, John E., Nephew, son of Margery
Nichols, Rebecca, Sister
Mead, Manly, husband of Mary A.
Mead, Mary A., Niece, dau. of Margery Nichols
Tavenner, Jonathan, Nephew, son of Ann
Tavenner, James, Nephew, son of Ann
Cohagan, Mary, Niece, dau. of Ann Tavenner
Tavenner, Richard, Nephew, son of Ann
Torrison, Lewis, husband of Catharine
Tavenner, Samuel, Nephew, son of Ann
Tavenner, George, Nephew, son of Ann
Cohagan, Aquila, husband of Mary
Tavenner, Ann, Sister, dec'd.
Torrison, Catharine, Niece, dau. of Ann Tavenner
Tavenner, Jonah, Nephew, son of Ann
Tavenner, William, Nephew, son of Ann
James, Elijah, husband of Sarah
James, Sarah, Niece, dau. of Ann Tavenner
Young, Elizabeth, Sister
Young, David, Brother-in-law
Hatcher, Isaac, Brother
Hatcher, Isaac, Nephew, son of Isaac
Hatcher, James, Brother
Gibson, William, Wit.

Silcott, Mortimer, Wit.
Hamilton, Mary, Wit.
Davis, Harriett B., Wit.
Nichols, Isaac, Wit.
Dagg, Susan G., 2A:217, 1841/42
McCullough, Mary Jane
McCullough, Clarissa P., Sister
McCullough, John Robert
McCullough, Susan Dagg
Grady, Ury
Powell, John L., Exor.
Chew, James E., Wit.
Luke, Catharine, Wit.
Howell, Mahala, Wit.
Fredd, Thomas, Wit.
Hoge, William, 2A:218, 1842
Hoge, Thomas, Son
Hoge, James, Son
Hoge, Jonathan, Son
Hoge, Mary, Wife
Taylor, Benjamin F., Wit.
Hoge, John G., Wit.
Gore, Thomas, Wit.
Janney, Daniel, Wit.
Hoffman, John, 2A:228, 1835/42
Birckhead, Mary Eliza, Niece
Latimer, James, Brother-in-law, of Philadelphia
Latimer, Sophia, Sister
Hoffman, Harriet Emily, Niece, dau. of Jeremiah
Hoffman, David, Brother
Hoffman, Jeremiah, Brother
Hoffman, Samuel, Brother
Hoffman, Peter, Brother
Hoffman, Jacob's heirs, Brother
Hoffman, Eliza, Sister
Dunglison, Robley, Wit.
Carroll, C. R., Wit.
Poor, J. H., Wit.
Bales, Hannah, 2A:231, 1842
Milbourn, Emily Iden
Bronaugh, P. H. W., Wit.
Milbourn, Sarah Ann, Wit.
Milbourn, Gideon W., Wit.
Carr, David, Admr. w.w.a.
Carter, William, 2A:231, 1841/42
Carter, Margaret, Wife
Bowles, James, Wit.

Bowles, Samuel, Wit.
Gregg, George, Wit.
Elgin, Ignatius, 2A:259, 1831/42
Elgin, Robert, Nephew
Edwards, Samuel M., Wit.
Hamilton, Erasmus G., Wit.
Watt, John G., 2A:259, 1842
Watt, Duanna, Wife
Phelps, Rev. Elisha P., husband of Mary Winifred
Phelps, Mary Winifred, wife's Niece
Edwards, Samuel M., Wit.
Binns, Elizabeth D., Wit.
Richards, George, Wit.
Holmes, William, 2A:264, 1841/42
Brown, Ann, Dau.
Hoge, William, Gr-Son, son of Samuel Sr.
Hoge, Samuel, Gr-Son, son of Samuel Sr.
Holmes, Elisha, Son
Hoge, James, Son-in-law
Holmes, John, Son
Hoge, Phila, Dau.
Hoge, Washington, Gr-Son, son of Samuel Sr.
Holmes, William, Son
Holmes, Warner, Son
Vansickle, Mahala, Dau.
Vansickle, William, Gr-Son, son of Sarah
Cockerell, Keziah, Dau.
Janney, Sophia, Dau.
Vansickle, Emanuel, Gr-Son, son of Sarah
Craven, Abigail, Dau.
White, Mary, Dau.
Hughes, John H., Wit.
Brown, John H., Wit.
Taylor, Benjamin F., Wit.
Silcott, Jesse, 2A:266, 1842
Silcott, —, ten children, all living, two unmarried Daus.
Silcott, Mesheck, Son
McIlhany, James, Exor.
Hatcher, Thomas E., Wit.
Roal, Joshua, Wit.
Jackson, Ephraim, Wit.
Hough, William N., Wit.

White, Nancy, 2A:274, 1842
McVeigh, Mary E., Dau.
White, Robert, Son
Davisson, Theodore, Son
Davisson, Frederick A., Son
Milton, Richard & wife
White, Agnes B., Dau.
White, James B.
Milton, Ann Cecilia, Dau.
Milton, Alexander
McIlhany, James, Wit.
Kilgore, James M., Wit.
Kilgore, J. Mortimer, Wit.
Hatcher, Thomas, 2A:277, 1842
Hatcher, Jonah, Brother
Hatcher, Nancy L., Wife
Beatty, Mary Jane
Beatty, Eliza,
  mother of Mary Jane
Rogers, Thomas, Wit.
Bolon, William, Wit.
Gover, Jesse, 2A:278, 1835/42
Gover, Miriam, Wife
Gover, —, my children
Griffith, I. T., Wit.
Bond, Asa M., Wit.
Janney, Moses, Wit.
Roach, James Sr., 2A:284, 1840/43
Roach, Phinehas, Son
Roach, Mahlon, Son
Roach, James, Son
Leslie, Samuel, Wit.
Smith, Abraham, Wit.
Torryson, Lewis, Wit.
Leslie, Joseph, Wit.
Phillips, Rachel, 2A:285, 1842/43
Morgan, Eliza
Phillips, Thomas, Husband, dec'd.
Phillips, Thomas, Son
Gover, Miriam
Miller, Amy Ann, Dau.
Miller, Edgar, Gr-Son
Miller, Mordecai, Gr-Son
Miller, William
Williams, Thomas, Gr-Son
Williams, Sarah, Dau.
Steer, William B., Wit.
Steer, Samuel L., Wit.
Gover, Jesse, Wit.
Hughes, Thomas, 2A:307, 1843
Hughes, Martha, Wife
Hughes, —, all my children
Holmes, Elijah, Exor.
Taylor, Benjamin F., Exor.
Janney, Daniel, Wit.
Janney, Elisha, Wit.
Clowes, Mary, 2A:320, 1843
Simms, John, son of Charity, slave
Clowes, Thomas, Son
Simms, Charles,
  son of Charity, slave
Clowes, Mary Jane, Dau.
Simms, Charity, slave
Simms, James, a.k.a. Bob,
  son of Charity, slave
Clowes, Joseph, Husband, dec'd.
Clowes, —, all my children
Janney, Eli, Wit.
Taylor, Benjamin F., Wit.
Vandevanter, A. M., Wit.
Lewis, Charles, 2A:328, 1841/43
Stoven, Charles James
Lewis, Vincent L., Nephew, son of James
Lewis, John H., Nephew, son of James, dec'd.
Lewis, Fisher Ames, Exor.
Lewis, Catharine, daugther of John
Lester, Elizabeth B., Niece, dau. of James Lewis
Lewis, William Berkley, Nephew, son of James
Lewis, James, Brother, dec'd.
Lewis, Martha J., Niece, dau. of James
Lewis, Nancy L., Niece, dau. of James, dec'd.
Lewis, Jonathan, son of John
Lewis, Susan H., Niece, dau. of James
Beard, Lewis
Jenings, Nancy, daugther of James
Jenings, Sarah, of Kentucky

Hancock, Jane T. L., Niece,
  dau. of James Lewis
Darne, Catharine L., Niece,
  dau. of James Lewis
Jenings, James, dec'd.
Mankin, Lewis F., Wit.
Hancock, G., Wit.
Lee, Matthew P., Wit.
Selden, Wilson Cary, 2A:329, 1842/43
  Selden, Eliza Armistead, Wife
  Selden, John, Half-Brother
  Selden, Eleanor Love, Dau.
  Alexander, Dr. William F., Brother-in-law
  Rogers, Thomas, Exor.
  Harrison, Henry T., Exor.
  Knox, Thomas P., Wit.
  Bowie, Robert G., Wit.
  Cross, W., Wit.
Barrett, Robert, 2A:337, 1843
  Brown, James, Nephew
  Barrett, James, Nephew
  Harper, Thurza
  Rogers, Thomas, Exor.
  Vandevanter, Armstead, Exor.
  Marlow, George, Wit.
  Peacock, William, Wit.
Vermillion, Benjamin, 2A:337, 1843
  Vermillion, Maria, Wife
  Veal, E. C., Wit.
  Wilson, John M., Wit.
  Edwards, Samuel M., Wit.
Hereford, Alice T., 2A:338, 1843
  Eggborn, George, Brother-in-law, husband of Harriet
  Eggborn, Susan Emily, Niece
  Ratluff, Lucinda H., Sister
  Fitzhugh, Thomas, Father, dec'd.
  Northan, Elizabeth C., Sister, now in Kentucky
  Eggborn, Harriet H., Sister
  Eggborn, George, Exor.
  Barton, Benjamin C., Wit.
  Walker, Mary Eleanor A., Wit.
  Gill, John L., Wit.
  Osburn, Balaam, Wit.

Russell, David, 2A:361, 1843
  Russell, James, Father, dec'd.
  Russell, Esther Ann, Wife
  Littlejohn, Ruth A., Sister, dec'd.
  Russell, John L.
  Allstadt, John H.
  Russell, Emily, Sister, dec'd.
  Russell, Catherine, Sister, dec'd.
  Russell, James Horatio, Son
  Grubb, Ebenezer, Wit.
  Clendening, William Jr., Wit.
  Fowke, Isaac, Wit.
Cooper, Phillip, 2A:362, 1843
  Cooper, John, Son
  Cooper, —, Wife
  Cooper, George, Son
  Baker, Sally, Dau.
  Baker, Adam, Son-in-law
  Cooper, Elias, Son
  White, Thomas, Wit.
  Orrison, Ananias, Wit.
  Peacock, Elijah Jr., Wit.
Canby, Joseph, 2A:384, 1843
  Gilpin, Letitia, Sister
  Wilson, Mary, Niece
  Canby, Mary, Wife
  Janney, Jonas, Exor.
  Gore, Joseph, Wit.
  Hughes, Wm. H., Wit.
Demory, Peter, 2A:385, 1843
  Dowling, Daniel, Gr-Son
  Harding, Edward, Son-in-law
  Harding, Elizabeth, Dau.
  Coe, Mary, Gr-Dau.
  Coe, Cynthia Ann, Gr-Dau.
  Dowling, Rachel, Gr-Dau.
  Demory, Mary, Wife
  Demory, Mahlon, Son
  Demory, Enos, Son
  Demory, William, Son
  Demory, Louisa, Dau.
  Wigginton, Presley, Wit.
  Grubb, John, Wit.
  Grubb, William Jr., Wit.
Walker, Ruth, 2A:388, 1842/43
  Walker, Garrett, Husband
  Smith, John, Gr-father
  Megeath, Joseph P., Wit.

Lynn, Michael, Wit.
Milhollen, Henry, Wit.
Wood, Joseph, 2A:389, 1843
Janney, Mary J., Dau.
Wood, Joseph, Son
Wood, Lidia, Wife
Shawen, David, Exor.
Janney, Asa, Son-in-law
Steer, Isaac, Wit.
Beach, Lial T., Wit.
Frye, Margaret, 2A:402, 1837/43
Edwards, Samuel M.
Wilson, Milly, colored woman
Wilson, Norvil, Methodist minister
Waters, Benjamin, Exor.
Stenchecun, Rebecka, Husband's Niece
Frye, Rev. Christopher, Husband, dec'd.
Martin, Sarah P., w/o James
Moss, Thomas, Clerk of Fairfax
Martin, Mary Frye, dau. of James, Husband's Gr-niece
Martin, Elizabeth Murry, dau. of James Husband's Gr-niece
Minor, Daniel
Martin, Joseph F., husband's relation
Martin, Margaret Frye, dau. of James, Husband's Gr-niece
Martin, Angelina, Husband's Niece
Martin, James L., Husband's Nephew
Mitchell, George, colored man
Martin, Sarah Loueza, dau. of James, Husband's Gr-niece
Moss, Alfred, son of Thomas
Hughes, George, coloured boy
Tippet, Charles B., Methodist minister
Minor, Robert Moss, son of Daniel
Andrews, Margaret Frye, Nancy's Dau.
Andrews, Nancy
Andrews, Rev. Wells, Nancy's husband
Waters, Dorothy, w/o Benjamin

Binns, Anne Alexander, Wit.
McIlhany, M., Wit.
Smoot, George H., Wit.
Campbell, William, Wit.
Cassady, Jane H., 2A:405, 1843
Cassady, Ann Catharine, Dau.
Cassady, Mary Elizabeth, Dau.
Cassady, Charles Thomas, Son
Janney, Eli, Friend
Reece, David, Friend
Vandevanter, Gabriel, Friend
Rogers, Thomas, Wit.
Vandevanter, A. M., Wit.
Bogar, Elizabeth, 2A:417, 1838/44
Arnold, Rebecca, Gr-Dau.
Arnold, Adam, Gr-Son
Arnold, Elizabeth, Gr-Dau.
Vincel, Mary, Dau.
Vincel, John, Son-in-law, husband of Mary
Bogar, Philip, Son
Bogar, Jacob, Son
Bogar, Michael, Son
Bogar, Samuel, Son
Bogar, John, Son
Shumaker, Jacob, Wit.
Bogar, John, Wit.
Miles, Benjamin, Wit.
Binns, Hannah, 2A:418, 1833/44
Binns, Charles, Husband
Binns, Ann A., Dau.
Binns, Elizabeth D., Dau.
Edwards, Thomas W., Wit.
Edwards, Samuel M., Wit.
Offutt, O., Wit.
Rose, John, 2A:419, 1836/44
Binns, Mary M., Dau.
Richards, Anna B., Dau.
Richards, George, Son-in-law
Rose, Anna, Wife
Wilson, Charlotte F., Dau.
Edwards, Samuel M., Friend
Clagett, Dr. Thomas H., Friend
Goings, Nelly, slave
Davis, Rev. John, Methodist minister
Goings, Laura, dau. of Nelly, slave
Rust, Sally
Chilton, Charles William

Eskridge, Charles G., Wit.
Campbell, Samuel, Wit.
Edwards, John S., Wit.
Edwards, Richard H., Wit.
Janney, John, Wit.
Rogers, Thomas, Wit.
Luckett, Leven, 2B:1, 1842/43
  Gunn, James
  Holland, John
  Luckett, Thomas H. husband of Matilda, Son-in-law
  Luckett, Henry Fenton, Son
  Luckett, Alfred, Son
  Luckett, Matilda D., Dau.
  Luckett, David's heirs
  Luckett, Horace, Son
  Luckett, Ludwell, Son
  Luckett, —, Wife
  Luckett, Leven, Son
  Luckett, Robert T., Son
  Luckett, William F., Son
  Luckett, Francis W., Son
  Luckett, William, Father, dec'd.
  Offutt, Elizabeth
  Offutt, Thomas' heirs
Luckett, Lettice, 2B:5, 1842/44
  Luckett, Leven, Son
  Luckett, Ludwell, Son
  Luckett, Alfred, Son
  Luckett, Robert T., Son
  Luckett, Matilda D., Dau.
  Luckett, Horace, Son
  Luckett, William, Father, dec'd.
  Powell, G. Cuthbert, Wit.
  Littleton, Fielding, Wit.
Gideon, Peter, 2B:6, 1835/43
  Morris, Mahlon, Son-in-law
  Blue, Sarah, Dau.
  Blackburn, James
  Gideon, George, Son
  Gideon, William, Son
  Gore, Mark, Son-in-law
  Gore, Elizabeth, Dau.
  Gideon, Henry, Son
  Gideon, Catherine, Wife
  Evans, Mary, Dau.
  McIlhany, James, Wit.
  Clendening, William, Wit.
  Follin, Edward, Wit.

McGavack, William, 2B:7, 1844
  McGavack, Patrick, Brother
  McGavack, James, Brother, dec'd.
  Graham, Tamar, Sister, dec'd.
  Ramey, Sanford I., Exor.
  Davisson, Theodore N., Wit.
  Russell, William, Wit.
Nixon, John, 2B:24, 1845
  Myers, William
Wright, Nancy, 2B:39, 1844
  Moss, John, Son-in-law
  Brooks, David, negro man
  Wright, Joseph H., Son
  Wright, William, Son
  Wright, Patterson's heirs
  Braden, Noble S., Wit.
  Wright, Samuel, Wit.
  Hunt, Mary, Wit.
Elgin, Robert, 2B:40, 1844
  Elgin, Robert, Son
  Elgin, —, all my children
  Elgin, Gustavus Fayette, Son
  Shumate, M. C., Wit.
  Elgin, Francis, Wit.
  Fulton, William, Wit.
Gilbert, Joseph, 2B:40, 1843/44
  Gilbert, Joseph, Gr-Son
  Gilbert, Melvina, Gr-Dau.
  Gilbert, Sinai, Dau.
  Oden, James S., Exor.
  Bradshaw, Walter N., Wit.
  Oden, Nathaniel S., Wit.
Sanders, George, 2B:53, 1844
  Sanders, Hamilton, Son
  Sanders, Elizabeth, Wife
  Sanders, Duanna, Dau.
  White, Thomas, Exor.
  Orrison, Ananias, Wit.
  Crusen, Jacob, Wit.
  Donahoe, Patrick, Wit.
Gochnauer, Jacob, 2B:54, 1844
  Lovett, Jonathan
  Norton, Nathaniel
  Gochnauer, William, Son
  Peyton, Betsy, free woman of color
  Kile, George
  Gochnauer, Elizabeth, Wife
  Luckett, Ludwell, Exor.

Weadon, John, Wit.
Murray, E. C., Wit.
Davis, John L., Wit.
Gray, John, 2B:56, 1843/44
Janney, John, Friend
Waterman, Augustus, of
  Rockingham, to be guardian
  of son Albert
Gray, W. H., Friend
Douglas, Charles, Friend
Gray, Rebecca, Dau.
Gray, Isabella, Dau.
Gray, Henrietta, Dau.
Gray, Robert, Son
Gray, Asher, Son
Gray, Sally, Dau.
Gray, Albert, Son
Beaty, Betsy G., 2B:103, 1843/44
Beaty, Kiziah, Sister
Simpson, Elizabeth
Simpson, Emily, Niece
Simpson, John, Exor.
Smarr, Susan
McCarty, Peggy, Sister
McCarty, Margaret Elizabeth
Turner, Mary Jane, Niece
Turner, Eusebia, Niece
McCarty, Billington
Luckett, Robert T., Wit.
Luckett, Horace, Wit.
Ish, William K., Wit.
Canby, Mary, 2B:104, 1844
Brooks, Philips of Ohio
Gilpin, Letitia, Sister-in-law
Thatcher, Mary, Cousin
Taylor, Benjamin F., Exor.
Hughes, Elias, Brother, dec'd.
Hughes, Martha, Sister-in-law
Hughes, Thomas, Brother,
  dec'd.
Hughes, Elias, Nephew
Gore, Thomas, Wit.
Gore, Joseph, Wit.
Humphrey, Sarah, 2B:105, 1844
Humphrey, Thomas M.
Humphrey, Thomas L., Son
Humphrey, Willliam, Gr-Son
Osburn, Addison, Wit.
Palmer, W. C., Wit.

Grubb, William Sr., 2B:107, 1832/44
Copeland, Mary, Dau.
Campbell, James, Son-in-law
Campbell, Rebecca, Dau.
Grubb, Mary, Wife
Grubb, Nancy, Dau.
Grubb, Rachel, Dau.
Grubb, James, Son
Grubb, John, Son
Sackman, Elizabeth, Dau.,
  dec'd.
Gregg, Sarah, Dau.
Sackman, John Martin,
  Gr-Son, <21
Chamblin, Nelson, Wit.
Grubb, Richard, Wit.
Grubb, Edward, Wit.
Grubb, Benjamin, Wit.
Beaty, Silas, 2B:109, 1842/44
Beaty, —, six children of
  present wife
Beaty, —, Wife
Beaty, John, Son
Rogers, Asa, Exor.
Powell, H. B., Wit.
Rogers, William H., Wit.
Ashby, F. W., Wit.
Gibson, S. M., Wit.
Steer, Isaac, 2B:121, 1837/44
Russell, Joshua, Son-in-law
Hough, Ann, Dau.
McPherson, Mary, Dau.
Steer, Elizabeth, Wife
Hough, Mary, Gr-Dau.,
  dau. of Ann
Hough, Isaac, Gr-Son,
  son of Ann
McPherson, Samuel, Son-in-law
Steer, Rachel, Dau.
Wood, Lydia, Dau.
Steer, J. H., Gr-Son, son of
  Joseph
Wood, William S., Gr-Son
Steer, Jonah, Son
Steer, William B., Son
Steer, Joseph, Son

Wright, Patterson, 2B:125, 1825/44
Dulaney, William, Son-in-law
Dulaney, Rachel, Dau.
Wright, William, Son
McKim, Patty, Dau., dec'd.
Wright, Joseph, Son
Myers, Anne, Dau.
Wright, Nancy, Wife
McGarvick, Polly, Dau.
Wright, Aron, Son
Myers, Mahlon, Son-in-law
Wright, Effy, Dau.
Edwards, Charles G., Wit.
Hough, William H., Wit.
McGarvick, Israel, Wit.
Moffett, Robert, Admr. w.w.a.
Paterson, John, 2B:149, 1844
Patterson, James, Brother
Kent, William
Brown, Dr. Isaac, my physican
Furr, William, Exor.
Humphrey, Thomas L., Wit.
Wiley, William, Wit.
Newlon, Charles A., Admr.
Lynn, Joseph R., 2B:151, 1843/44
Davis, Verlinda N., Dau.
Cole, Rebecca, Dau.
Taylor, Joshua
Lynn, Sarah Gertrude, Dau of this union
Lynn, Seymor
Lynn, Pammelia, Wife
Lynn, Luther L., Son
Lynn, Maria V., Dau.
Lynn, John T., Son
Lynn, William M., Son
Rogers, William trustee for Dau.
Currell, John's J.'s children, wife's children
Hixson, Harriet R., Dau.
Fairfax, Captain Henry
Hutchison, Beverly, Wit.
Cochran, William B., Wit.
Axline, David, 2A:152, 18 30/44
Axline, Christena, Dau.
Axline, Daniel, Son
Axline, Elizabeth, Dau.
Axline, Louisa, Dau.
Axline, Catharine, Dau.
Axline, Emanuel, Son
Axline, —, Wife
Axline, David, Son
Householder, Gideon, Wit.
Householder, Adam, Wit.
Arnold, Jacob, Wit.
Bumcrots, John, Wit.
Iden, Samuel, 2B:172, 1844/45
Iden, Eli, Son
O'Neal, Thomas, Son-in-law
Taylor, Mahlon K., son of Mahlon, Exor.
Iden, Sarah, Wife
Craven, Hannah, Dau.
Craven, Mahlon, Son-in-law
Iden, Randel, Son
Iden, Thomas, Son
Heaton, James D., Wit.
Purcel, James H., Wit.
Taylor, Bernard Jr., Wit.
Brown, Sarah, 2B:173, 1836/45
Wood, Joseph, Son-in-law
Bennett, Susan W., Dau.
Brown, Isaac, Husband, dec'd.
Gillespey, Susan W., formerly Bennett, Dau.
Leith, Theo., Wit.
Hereford, William T., Wit.
Hutchison, Henry H., Wit.
McLin (Maclin), Mary, Wit.
Beveridge, Noble, 2B:174, 1843/45
Auchincloss, Hugh, John's father
Auchincloss, John, Friend
Hamilton, Henry H., employee
Noland, Lloyd, husband of Elizabeth
Smith, Marion Noble, Gr-Niece, dau. of Benjamin
Smith, Benjamin, Nephew
Gibson, Dr. William, husband of Sarah
Gibson, Sarah Noble, Niece
Noland, Lloyd, Gr-nephew, son of Lloyd
Powell, Virginia, dau. of William
Noland, Richard W. N., Gr-nephew, son of Lloyd

Powell, Gertrude,
   dau. of Humphrey B.
Noland, Elizabeth Winn, Niece
Powell, Humphrey B., Exor.
Noland, Burr P., Gr-nephew,
   son of Lloyd
Powell, Dr. William L.
Janney, John, Exor.
Powell, George Cuthbert, Wit.
Powell, F. W., Wit.
Smith, James W., Wit.

Wright, Joseph, 2B:278, 1844/45
Wright, Edward S., Son, <21
Wright, Sarah Ann, Dau., <21
Wright, Julius J., Son, son of
   Mary Jane
Wright, Lewis B., Son,
   son of Mary Jane
Wright, Catharine, Wife
Wright, Mary Jane, 1st Wife,
   dec'd.
Wright, Elizabeth A., Dau.,
   dau. of Mary Jane
Wright, John E., Son,
   son of Mary Jane
Wright, Nancy, Mother, dec'd.
Steer, Jonah, Wit.
Bond, Edward, Wit.
Russell, William, Exor.

Megeath, Gabriel, 2B:320, 1843/45
Haines, Mary Ann, Dau.
Megeath, James, Son, dec'd.
Megeath, Samuel, Son
Megeath, Martha, Wife
Megeath, Alfred, Son
Megeath, Joseph P., Son
Hoge, Thomas, Wit.
Nichols, William, Wit.

Furr, Enoch, 2B:327, 1831/45
Furr, William Gilmore, Son
Littleton, Hannah, Dau.
Littleton, John K., Son-in-law
Furr, Jeremiah, Son
Furr, Betsy, Dau.
Urton, Besheba, Dau.
Urton, Norman, Son-in-law
Berkley, Tacey, Dau.
Furr, Edwin, Son
Furr, Sarah, Wife

Humphrey, Joseph, Exor.
Lloyd, Joseph A., Wit.
Poston, Leonard R., Wit.
Nalls, Carr Bailey, Wit.
Littleton, Fielding, Wit.

Clayton, Martha, 2B:340, 1845
Moore, Susan
Huffman, Phebe, Sister
Galloway, Madison
Galloway, Nancy
Clayton, William, Father, dec'd.
Clayton, William, Brother
Luke, Catharine, Niece
Luke, John Whalen
Luke, John W., Nephew
Moore, Mason
Osburn, Jonah, Wit.
Grady, Edward B., Wit.
Palmer, Elizabeth A., Wit.

Nichols, Charity, 2B:341, 1840/45
Nichols, Phebe, Sister, dec'd.
Young, Rebecca
Young, William, Exor.
Megeath, Joseph P., Wit.
Janney, Daniel, Wit.
Nichols, Swithen, Wit.

Matthews, Catherine, 2B:379, 1845
Shield, Catherine, Gr-Dau.
Matthews, Mary Catherine,
   Gt-Gr-Dau.
Matthews, Jonathan, Husband,
   dec'd.
Matthews, John, Gt-Gr-Son
Matthews, Simon, Gr-Son,
   dec'd.
Matthews, Sarah Ann Eliza,
   Gt-Gr-Dau.
Matthews, Jonathan, Gt-Gr-Son
Matthews, Jesse, Gt-Gr-Son
Matthews, Jonathan, Gr-Son,
   dec'd.
Matthews, William, Gt-Gr-Son
Matthews, Rodney, Gt-Gr-Son
Matthews, Sarah Elizabeth,
   Gt-Gr-Dau.
Thompson, Jonah, husband of
   Sarah
Thompson, Sarah, Gr-Dau.

Byrns, John, husband of
 Elizabeth
Shield, Alfred, husband of
 Catherine
Byrns, Elizabeth, Gr-Dau.
Hough, William, Wit.
Harding, Edward, Wit.
Conard, Jonathan, Wit.
Clendening, William, Wit.
Hancock, George, 2B:411, 1843/45
Hancock, Ebin T., Son
Hancock, Edmoney, Dau.
Hancock, Fenton M., Son
Hancock, —, Wife
Jett, Peter, Wit.
Alexander, Robert, Wit.
Millan, George W., Wit.
Wilson, William T., Wit.
Wilson, John S., Wit.
Hutchison, Thomas, Wit.
Lacey, Elias, 2C:10, 1845
Lacey, Alexander Israel, Son
Lacey, Mary Jane, Dau.
Lacey, Mesheck Henry, Son
Lacey, Benjamin R., Son
Moore, John, Wit.
Davis, Alexander, Wit.
Stover, Edwin A., Wit.
James, Dean, 2C:11, 1845
James, Sally, Wife
James, David B., Son
Greenlease, Mary, 2C:18, 1845
Greenlease, George F.
Greenlease, William S., Nephew
Greenlease, Lydia E., Gr-niece, dau. of William
Wine, Ann E.'s children
Coleman, John I., Wit.
Mankin, Lewis F., Wit.
Veale, John, Wit.
Nixon, John, 2C:24, 1845
Nixon, John, Nephew, son of George
Nixon, Jonah, Half-Brother, dec'd.
Nixon, George, Half-Brother, dec'd.

Carruthers, Sarah, Gr-niece, Gr-Dau. of half-sister
Carruthers, William, Gr-nephew, Gr-Son of half-sister
Day, Emily, wife's niece
Day, Dr., husband of Emily
Nixon, Jonah, Nephew, son of Jonah
Walters, James, Brother-in-law
Brown, Sarah, widow of William
Kerrick, Anne, housekeeper
Barre, Mahala, Niece, dau. of half-sister
Brown, William, dec'd.
Janney, Eli, Exor.
Nichols, Thomas, Exor.
Taylor, Benjamin F., Exor.
Nixon, Joel, Wit.
Myers, Elijah P., Wit.
Laycock, James, Wit.
Taylor, Henry S., Wit.
Householder, Gideon, 2C:27, 1845
Householder, Adam, Son
Householder, Julia Ann, Wife
Darr, Samuel, former occupant of house
Hamilton, Caroline, Dau.
Householder, —, all my children
Hamilton, James William, Exor.
Karne, Adam, Exor.
Karn, Michael, Wit.
Grubb, John, Wit.
Francis, Thomas, 2C:30, 1845
Francis, Thomas, Exor.
Francis, Leannah, Wife
Carter, Sarah Jane
Gulick, Elisha
Nichols, William, Wit.
Hoge, Thomas, Wit.
Megeath, Samuel, Wit.
Catlett, Charles I., 2C:31, 1844/45
Catlett, Ann F., Wife
Catlett, Fairfax, Son, dec'd.
Catlett, Erskine, Son
Minor, Louisa Fairfax, Dau.
Minor, John West, Son-in-law
Catlett, Esther Ann, Dau.-in-law, widow of Fairfax
Knox, Thomas P., Wit.

Eskridge, Charles G., Wit.
Rust, P. C., Wit.
King, Tacey, 2C:35, 1835/45
  Daniel, Tacey, Dau.
  Daniel, Joseph H., Son
  Hixson, David, Exor.
  Hixson, Benjamin, Wit.
  Gibson, Levi, Wit.
  Hixson, John H., Wit.
  Rogers, William, Admr. w.w.a.
Dailey, Jesse, 2C:40, 1845
  Surghnor, Sally, Dau.
  Crissey, Mary, Gr-Dau.,
    dau. of Betsy Surghnor
  Dailey, Hugh, Son, dec'd.
  Surghnor, Betsy, Dau., dec'd.
  Surghnor, John Jr., Gr-Son,
    son of Betsy
  Tygert, Anne, Dau.
  Dailey, Mary, Wife
  Cooper, Eleanor, Dau.
  Ball, Charles B., Exor.
  Birkby, Thomas, Wit.
  Nixon, Joel L., Wit.
  Johnson, Peter W., Wit.
Clagett, Henry, 2C:43, 1845
  Clagett, Thomas H., Brother
  Birkby, Rev. Thomas
  Birkby, Charles, son of Rev.
    Thomas Birkby
  Cross, William, Wit.
  Bowie, Robert G., Wit.
Edwards, Rebeckah, 2C:49, 1839/45
  McNealy, Sarah Moran, Niece
  Lyon, Jane, w/o Alexander
  Moran, John, Nephew
  Moran, Elizabeth, Niece
  Lyon, Catharine,
    dau. of Alexander
  Lyon, Alexander
  Lewis, Jonathan, Nephew
  Lewis, Catharine, Niece
  Lyon, Rebeckah,
    dau. of Alexander
  Fouch, Amos, Wit.
  Lewis, Charles, Wit.
  Darne, Catharine, Wit.

Bolen, Elizabeth, 2C:58, 1839/45
  Bolen, Edward, Husband, dec'd.
  Bolen, Emily, Dau. [married
    name not shown]
  Coombs, Jane, Dau.
  Bolen, William, Son
  Carter, Landon, Wit.
  Carter, William, Wit.
  Smith, Seth, Wit.
  Gregg, George, Wit.
Bitzer, Conrad, 2C:59, 1844/45
  Wolf, Ann C., Gr-Dau.
  Dowell, Elisha, Son-in-law
  Kincheloe, Hardwick,
    husband of Mary
  Dowell, John A., Gr-Son, dec'd.
  Kincheloe, Mary A., Gr-Dau.
  Dowell, Anna, Dau.
  Dowell, Conrad R., Gr-Son
  Dowell, William F., Gr-Son
  Brown, David, Wit.
  Reece, David, Wit.
  Roberts, Stephen, Wit.
Bruce, Eliza S., 2C:64, 1845/46
  Gibson, Eliza B., Niece
  Gibson, Judith Ann, Niece
  Bruce, Judith, Sister
  Gibson, Mayland, Brother-in-law
  Bruce, John, Brother
  Carter, John A., Wit.
  Gibson, Joshua, Wit.
Dawson, Samuel, 2C:70, 1845/46
  Dawson, Sarah Ann, Wife
  Gassaway, Henrietta, Sister
  Dawson, Charles G., Son
  Dawson, Mason, Son
  Dawson, Elizabeth H., Dau.
  Dawson, Mellinda H., Dau.
  Dawson, Nicholas, Son
  Dawson, Eugenia T., Dau.
  Dawson, Elizabeth, Mother
  Dawson, Roger T., Son
  Dawson, Arthur, Son
Walraven, Josiah, 2C:94, 1827/46
  Walraven, Lydia, Wife
  Osburn, Joshua, Exor.
  Cochran, James, Wit.
  Chamblin, Charles, Wit.

Chittenden, Ann Eliza C., 2C:104, 1843/46
  Chittenden, William B., Husband
  Turner, Rev. Jesse H.
  Gerberding, C. O., Wit.
  Fry, Joshua J., Wit.
  Lawson, Thomas, Wit.

Lyons, Peter, 2C:105, 1837/46
  Roane, W. H., Friend
  Pryor, William
  Crump, George P., Friend
  Roane, S. A., dau. of W. H., friend's Dau.
  Chamberlayne, Dr. L. W., Friend
  Lyons, —, Sister

Love, James D., 2C:108, 1846
  Love, Susan Ann, Wife
  Love, Fenton, Brother
  Love, Mary R., Sister
  Jones, John Jr., Exor.
  Turner, Samuel, Wit.
  Heaton, James D., Wit.
  Edwards, Charles G., Wit.

Osburn, Craven, 2C:108, 1846
  Worthington, Cassandra, Niece
  Worthington, Elizabeth, Sister
  Worthington, Lucy, Niece
  Worthington, Joseph, Nephew
  Worthington, Sarah, Niece
  Osburn, Sarah, Niece, dau. of Herod
  Osburn, Hector, Brother
  Osburn, Thomas William, Nephew, son of Herod
  Osburn, Herod, Brother
  Fox, Amanda O., Niece
  Young, Emily, Niece, dec'd.
  Shutt, Caroline F., Niece
  Osburn, Norval, Brother
  Fox, Joseph B.
  Worthington, Nancy, Niece
  Worthington, Harriet, Niece

Steer, Beulah W., 2C:109, 1845/46
  Steer, Joseph, Husband

Compher, John, 2C:133, 1846
  Fawley, Elizabeth, Dau.
  Compher, Elizabeth, Wife
  Kern, Margaret, Dau., dec'd.
  Spring, Lydia Ann, Dau.
  Compher, Samuel, Son
  Bartlett, Sarah, Dau.
  Stoneburner, Catharine, Dau.
  Compher, William, Son
  Compher, Jonas, Son
  Compher, Mary, Dau.
  Compher, Joseph, Son
  Compher, John, Son
  Hamilton, C. B., Wit.
  Slater, William, Wit.
  Edwards, R. H., Wit.

Potts, Edward, 2C:156, 1845/46
  Gardner, Sally, Niece, dec'd., 1st w/o Francis Gardner of Jefferson Co.
  Osburn, Betsy, Sister
  Potts, —, Wife
  Janney, James C., Exor.
  Potts, John, Nephew, dec'd.

Stuck, Peter, 2C:157, 1846
  Everhart, Jacob, Gr-Son
  Hon, Margaret, Gr-Dau.
  Wenner, Sarah, Dau.
  Everhart, Elizabeth Lane, Gr-Dau.
  Hon, George, Gr-Son
  Slater, William
  Stuck, Mary, Dau.
  Short, Susan, Gr-Dau.
  Stuck, Ferdinando F., Son
  Short, George, Gr-Son
  Short, Cornelia, Gr-Dau.
  Stuck, Nancy, Dau.
  Schooley, Jonas P., Exor.
  Stuck, Lydia M.
  Stuck, Elizabeth, Wife
  Price, Samuel H., Wit.
  Thrasher, Luther A., Wit.
  Waltman, Emanuel, Wit.

Hirst, Jesse, 2C:176, 1841/46
  Hirst, Heston Gr-—, Father
  Hirst, Rebecca, Dau.
  Hirst, Jonathan, Son
  Hirst, Heston, Son
  Hirst, Mary, Wife
  Hirst, Eli, Son
  Taylor, Yardley, Wit.
  Young, Thomas J., Wit.
  McMullen, George, Wit.

Index to Loudoun County Wills, 1757 - 1850 167

Carter, George of Oatlands, 2C:187, 1841/46
Carter, Benjamin Grayson, Son
Carter, George, Son
Carter, Elizabeth O., Wife
Carter, John Tasker, Brother
Grayson, Benjamin Sr., Father-in-law
Lufborough, James H., Wit.
Grayson, Richard O., Wit.
Lack, William, Wit.

Saunders, Susannah C., 2C:189, 1844/46
Bentley, Charles, emancipated
White, Mary E., Gr-Dau.
White, Josiah T., Gr-Son
White, George, Gr-Son
Saunders, Thomas R., Son
Saunders, Catharine A. R., Dau.
Saunders, Aaron R., Son
Saunders, Curtis R., Son
Saunders, Alcinda, Gr-Dau., dec'd.
Saunders, Susan R., Dau.
Saunders, Rosabel C., Gr-Dau.
Saunders, Delia, Gr-Dau.
Saunders, Anna Lee, Gr-Dau.
Saunders, R. G., Wit.
Saunders, Evritt, Wit.
Magill, Henry D., Wit.

Vandevanter, Mary, 2C:191, 1838/46
Nettle, William, Exor.
Vandevanter, James H., Son
Pidgeon, Milly, Half-sister
Vandevander, Cornelius, Son
Vandevanter, Isaac, Exor.
Paul, Sarah, Half-sister
Tebbs, Algernon S., Wit.
Morgan, Jane C., Wit.

Ramey, Lydia, 2C:217, 1844/46
Braden, John, Exor.
Ramey, Jacob, Brother-in-law, dec'd.
Ramey, Jane, Niece, dau. of Jacob
Ramey, Nancy (or Ann), Niece, dau. of Jacob
Ramey, Sanford, Husband, dec'd.
Ramey, Elizabeth, Niece, dau. of Jacob
Gregg, Nathan, Wit.
Orrison, Jonah, Wit.
Hough, Eliz., Wit.
Leslie, John, Admr. w.w.a.

Hockings, Joseph, 2C:219, 1843/46
Hockings, Joseph, alias Joseph Kent, orphan boy raised
Kent, alias Hockings, Joseph's children
Hockings, Samuel, Brother
Hockings, Bridget, Mother
Kelley, Rebekah, Sister
Hockings, John, Half-brother
Kelley, Rebekah's children
Hockings, John, Nephew, son of Samuel
Sinclair, John, Wit.
Elgin, John, Wit.
Thrift, William, Wit.
Simpson, John, Admr. w.w.a.

Plaster, Mary, 2C:228, 1846
Plaster, —, my children
Hamilton, Sarah, Mother
Plaster, Michael, Brother-in-law
Plaster, George, Husband, dec'd.
Roby, Andrew, Wit.
Plaster, David H., Wit.

Saunders, Elizabeth, 2C:228, 1845/46
Saunders, Benjamin, Son
Saunders, Washington, Son
Saunders, Philip, Son
Saunders, James, Son
Saunders, Elizabeth, Dau.
Taylor, Benjamin F., Wit.
White, Richard, Wit.
White, Adin, Wit.

Hay, Elizabeth K., 2C:239, 1837/46
Rogers, Harriet Murray, Gr-Dau.
Rogers, Hortensia Monroe, Gr-Dau.
Rogers, Mary Custis, Gr-Dau.
Gouverneur, Maria Hester, Sister
Adams, John Quincy, Exor.

Smith, Richard M., Exor.
Stanard, Robert, Wit.
Stanard, Robert C., Wit.
Lyons, James, Wit.
Brown, Sarah S., 2C:245, 1846
  Birdsol, Mary, Sister
  Frame, Anna, Sister
  Brown, Eliza, Sister-in-law
  Birdsol, Ann, Niece
  Birdsol, Rebecca, Niece
  Birdsol, Mary Ellen, Niece
  Brown, Esther Ann, Niece
  Schooley, Eliza Ann, Niece
  Frame, David James, Nephew
  Schooley, Elizabeth, Sister, dec'd.
  Schooley, Charles, Nephew
  Schooley, Jonathan, Nephew
  Brown, David, Exor.
  Vandevanter, Washington, Wit.
  Taylor, Mahlon K., Wit.
  Walker, Isaac, Wit.
Piggott, William, 2C:247, 1846
  Piggott, Mary, Wife
  Piggott, Jesse, Son
  Piggott, Mary, Dau.
  Brown, Sarah, Dau.
  Brown, William, Son-in-law, husband of Sarah
  Brown, Elizabeth, Dau.
  Brown, Richard, Son-in-law, husband of Elizabeth
  Tavener, Phebe, Dau.
  Tavener, Lott, Son-in-law, husband of Phebe
  Piggott, Isaac, Son
  Piggott, Burr, Son
  Piggott, Jesse, Son
  Piggott, Mary, Dau.
  Taylor, Yardley, Wit.
  Janney, Jacob, Wit.
  Taylor, Jonathan, Wit.
  Taylor, Richard Henry, Wit.
Richards, William of Richland County, Ohio, 2C:248, 1844/46
  Alexander, James
  Richards, Jesse, Son
  Richards, Isaac, Son
  Richards, Alfred, Son
  Richards, Leven, Son
  Richards, Thomas, Son
  Clark, Emily, Dau.
  Newlon, Rachel, Dau.
  Gory, Betsy, Dau.
  Newlon, Polly, Dau.
  Kent, Elsinda, Dau.
  Kent, George, Son-in-law
  Hand, William, Son-in-law, Elsinda's former husband
  Hand, —, 3 Daus. of William & Elsinda, Gr-Daus.
  Gory, Abel
  Newlon, Nimrod, Exor.
  Jackson, B., Wit.
  Scott, George, Wit.
  Andrews, Samuel, Wit.
Mercer, Margaret, 2C:252, 1843/46
  Mercer, Thomas S., Nephew
  Mercer, Richard S., Nephew
  Mercer, John, Brother
  Mercer, Jane B., Niece
  Mercer, William R., Nephew
  Mercer, James M., Nephew
  Mercer, George D., Nephew
  Mercer, Wilson C., Nephew
  Mercer, Sophia E., Niece
  Mercer, Mary M., Niece
  Mercer, Mary S., Sister-in-law, w/o John
  Randall, A., Wit.
  Randall, H. K., Wit.
  Hagner, R. H., Wit.
  Hagner, Frances R., Wit.
Lodge, William, 2C:265, 1846
  Humphrey, Thomas L., Nephew
  Humphrey, Abner G., Nephew
  Lodge, Samuel, Brother
  Lodge, Abner, Brother
  Lodge, Joseph, Brother
  Hill, Mary, Sister
  Hall, David, Wit.
  Bleakly, William, Wit.
  Gallaway, Madison, Wit.
Powell, Sarah, 2C:266, 1842/46
  Powell, Catherin, Dau.
  Powell, William, Gr-Son
  Heskit, Henny, Dau.
  Hooper, Ann, Dau.

Riticor, Elijah, Wit.
Ish, Robert A., Wit.
Paxson, William, 2C:266
Paxson, —, Wife
Paxson, Griffith, Son
Paxson, George W., Gr-Son,
  son of Griffith
Purcel, Rachel, Dau.
Paxson, Jacob, Son
Paxson, Jane, Gr-Dau.,
  dau. of Jacob
Paxson, David, Gr-Son,
  son of Jacob
Paxson, Samuel, Son
Bond, Asa M., Wit.
Rickard, George, Wit.
Verts, William, Wit.
Yakey, Simon, 2C:267, 1846/47
Yakey, John, Son
Yakey, Martin, Son, dec'd.
Yakey, Martin's widow and
  children
Frazier, Samuel H., Wit.
Spring, Casper, Wit.
Crumboyer, Samuel W., Wit.
Fred, Joseph Sr., 2C:268, 1846/47
Fred, Joshua, Brother, dec'd.
Fred, Joseph Hadley, Nephew,
  son of Joshua
Richards, Barton, Friend
Galleher, William, Friend
Humphrey, Thomas G, Friend
Moreland, Sarah, Dau.
Moreland, Samuel, Son-in-law
Luntz, Jane, Dau.
Luntz, Lorenzo, Son-in-law
Bloxham, Clarissa, Dau.
Bloxham, Ephram, Son-in-law
Smith, Seth, Wit.
Fry, Michael, 2C:281, 1847
Fry, Mary, Wife
Fry, Enos, Son
Fry, Joseph Henry, Son
Arnold, Catharine, Dau.
Arnold, Simon, Son-in-law
Fry, Susana, Dau.
Fry, Rebecca, Dau.
Fry, Elizabeth, Dau.
Fry, Anna, Dau.
Fry, Emily Jane, Dau.

Smith, Job, Exor.
Baker, Adam, Wit.
Householder, Adam, Wit.
Householder, Gideon, Wit.
Love, Susannah, 2C:293, 1846/47
Love, Mary R., Dau.
Nichols, Phanny, Dau.-in-law
Love, James D., Son
Love, Fenton M., Son
Nichols, Thomas, Son
Nichols, Jonah, Son
Love, Rebecca, dec'd's
  children, Gr-children
Brown, David, Wit.
Reece, David, Wit.
Shepherd, Jacob R., 2C:294, 1846/47
Shepherd, Nancy, Wife
Patten, Mary Ann, Dau.
Thomas, Hariet Hannah, Dau.
Dean, Sarah Brobst, Dau.
Shepherd, Jane Eliza, Dau.
Shepherd, Francis Coke, Son
Shepherd, Melville Roberts, Son
Day, John, Exor.
Megeath, Samuel, Wit.
Mount, John E., Wit.
Welsh, James, Wit.
Mason, Charlotte E., 2C:296, 1844/47
Mason, Armistead T.,
  Husband, dec'd.
Mason, Stevens T., Son
Rust, George Jr.
Luckett, F. W., Wit.
Sinclair, James, Wit.
Jones, John Jr., 2C:297, 1846/47
Craven, Sarah, Sister
Simpson, Mary, Gr-mother,
  dec'd.
Jones, Martha, Sister
Jones, Mary, Sister
Jones, John, Father
Simpson, John, Exor.
Simpson, French, Wit.
Wynkoop, William B., Wit.
Ish, Susan, 2C:317, 1846/47
Simpson, Eliza, Gr-Dau.
Prosser, Mary, Dau.
Ish, George H., Son

Ish, Robert A., Son
Ewell, Jesse, Wit.
Riticor, Elijah, Wit.
Stoutsenberger, Samuel, 2C:327, 1846/47
Stoutsenberger, Albert C., Son
Stoutsenberger, Elvina, Dau.
Stoutsenberger, Mary C., Wife
Stoutsenberger, Jacob, Exor.
Hepburn, Margaret, 2C:328, 1836/47
Hepburn, Martha, Dau.
Osburn, Joshua, Wit.
Osburn, Herod, Wit.
Osburn, Norval, Wit.
Russell, Sarah E., 2C:343, 1846/47
Russell, Thaddeus, Son
Russel [sic], John, Husband
McCarty, George N.
Russell, Emily, Dau.
Russell, Jane, Dau.
Russell, Sally, Dau.
Russell, William, Son
Russell, Anthony, Son
Russell, Nancy, Dau.
Russell, Elizabeth, Dau.
McCarty, Stephen N., Exor.
McCarty, George W., Wit.
McCarty, Richard C., Wit.
McCarty, George B., Wit.
Cockran, William B., Wit.
Morrallee, Sarah, 2C:344, 1845/47
Pettitt, Nancy, Niece
Purcell, George, Brother
Purcell, Elizabeth, Niece
Purcell, Thomas, Nephew
Purcell, Jane, Niece
Purcell, Mary, Niece
Purcell, Eleanor, Niece
Smale, Simon, Wit.
Smale, John, Wit.
Newton, William, Wit.
Willett, Sarah, 2C:344, 1844/47
Tavenner, Elizabeth Ann, Niece
Tavenner, Louisa Ann, Niece
Tavenner, Nancy, Sister
Reece, David, Exor.
Sands, Jonah, Wit.
Reese, Solomon, Wit.

Tavenner, Charles H., Admr. w.w.a.
Buckner, Ariss, 2C:326, 1828/47
Buckner, Lucy, Wife
Furr, Sarah, 2C:355, 1846/47
Furr, Enoch, Husband, dec'd.
Furr, William Gilmore, Son
Furr, Desdemona, Gr-Dau., dau. of Jeremiah C.
Furr, Jeremiah C., Son
Thomas, Elizabeth, Dau.
Grady, Dr. Frank, Friend
Smith, Seth, Wit.
Fred, Joseph H., Wit.
Marshall, Benjamin, 2C:377, 1847
Perry, Mildred, Dau.
Longbeam, Benjamin
Lanham, William A., Wit.
Oden, Nathaniel S., Wit.
Smith, John S., Wit.
Gibson, Levi, 2C:378, 1847
Gibson, Juliet Ann, Dau.
Gibson, Selden M., Son
Rogers, Hamilton, Wit.
Rogers, William H. Jr., Wit.
Barrett, John, of Frederick Co., Maryland, 2C:380, 1846/47
Barrett, George Washington, Son
Barrett, William, Son
Barrett, Alisabeth, Dau.
Barrett, Mandy, Dau.
Lynch, William, Exor.
Remsburg, Sebastian, Exor.
McGaughen, Philip, Wit.
Padgett, Alfred, Wit.
Walter, John, Wit.
Hamilton, James, 2D:15, 1842/47
Hamilton, Cassandra, Wife
Hamilton, James L., Son
Smith, D. G., Wit.
Hamilton, Erasmus T., Wit.
Rogers, Thomas, Wit.
Peirce, Susannah, 2D:33, 1847
Grubb, William D., Friend
Grubb, Elizabeth, Friend, mother of William D.
Grubb, Catherine, Friend, w/o William D.
Fry, Daniel, Exor.

Index to Loudoun County Wills, 1757 - 1850　　　　　171

Householder, Adam, Exor.
Bronaugh, J. W., Wit.
Arnold, Simon, Wit.
Arnold, Joseph, Wit.
Fitzhugh, William C., 2D:54, 1845/47
Fitzhugh, Syndor B., Son
Fitzhugh, Dugal Cameron, Son
Fitzhugh, Matilda, Wife
Fitzhugh, John Spencer, Son
Fitzhugh, —, all my children
Dixon, H. T., Wit.
Baker, William, Wit.
Ashby, Robert S., Wit.
Henry, Edward H., Wit.
Braden, John, 2D:56, 1846/47
Braden, Mary, Wife
Braden, Rodney C., Son
Vandevanter, Cecelia E., Dau.
Braden, Oscar S., Son
Braden, Noble S., Wit.
Gregg, Stephen, Wit.
Carter, Ferdinando A. F., of Shelby County, Missouri, 2D:58, 1841/48
Carter, Pammelia Jane, Wife
Carter, Ann Elizabeth, Dau., only child
Carter, Joseph, Brother
Collins, Joseph, youth living with me
Louthan, Henry, Exor.
Foley, B. W., Wit.
Buford, Alexander, Wit.
Taylor, James W., Admr. w.w.a.
Tavenner, Mariam, 2D:81, 1848
Gregg, Phebe, Sister
Nichols, Mary, Sister
Nichols, Joshua
Nichols, Jonah
Nichols, Jonah, child of Jonah
Nichols, Mariam, child of Jonah
[Gibson], George, Brother
Nichols, Isaac Sr., Wit.
Gregg, John, Wit.
Gregg, William, Admr. w.w.a.

Jacobs, John Price, of Tazewell County, Illinois, 2D:91, 1845/48
Jacobs, Lamuel, Son, dec'd.
Jacobs, Hyland, Son, dec'd.
Jacobs, William, Son
Jacobs, Roswell P., Son
Jacobs, Ryland P., Son
Wrenn, Elizabeth, Dau.
Triplet, Mary, Dau.
Williams, Isaac, Exor.
Burton, R. W., Wit.
Holland, J. B., Wit.
Burnham, Ira, Wit.
Hawling, John, 2D:109, 1832/48
Fouch, Nancy, Sister
Hawling, Mary, Sister
Hawling, Elizabeth, Sister
Birdsal, Rachel, 2D:110, 1846/48
Birdsal, Andrew M., Son
Birdsal, John, Son, dec'd.
Birdsal, Mary, Dau.-in-law, widow of John
Birdsal, John, Gr-Son, son of John
Birdsal, Benjamin, Son
Birdsal, Elizabeth, Dau.
Birdsal, Hannah, Dau.
Sands, Ruth, Dau.
Sands, Thomas, Son-in-law
Goodin, Anna, Dau.
Janney, S. M., Wit.
Janney, Jacob, Wit.
Hirst, Jonathan, Wit.
Denham, Oliver, 2D:110, 1843/48
Denham, Amos, Nephew
Denham, Amos, Brother
Powell, H. B., Exor.
Bartlett, Burgess D., Wit.
Moran, John M., Wit.
Gassaway, Charles, 2D:111, 1848
Gassaway, Catharine B., Wife
Gassaway, Eliza
Edwards, Deborah
Luckett, Francis W., Exor.
Tebbs, A. Sidney, Wit.
Sinclair, James, Wit.

Swart, John, 2D:112, 1848
  Swart, Elizabeth, Sister
  Swart, Maria, Sister
  Lee, Matthew P., Wit.
  Taylor, George B., Wit.
  Riticor, John, Wit.

Dorsey, Edward, 2D:113, 1846/48
  Dorsey, Presly K., Son
  Dorsey, Alfred, Son
  Dorsey, Allen M., Son, dec'd.
  Dorsey, Hamilton M., Son
  Dorsey, Edward H., Gr-Son
  Dorsey, Charles W., Gr-Son
  Dorsey, Jonathan E., Gr-Son
  Dorsey, Emery W., Gr-Son
  Hough, John, Wit.
  Hough, Samuel, Wit.
  Schooley, Presley N., Wit.

Vansickler, Philip, 2D:114, 1843/48
  Vansickler, Hester, Wife
  Vansickler, John, Son
  Vansickler, Philip, Son
  Holmes, Lydia, Dau.
  Holmes, John, Son-in-law
  Hamton, James, Son-in-law
  Hamton, —, Wit.
  Simpson, Samuel, Wit.
  Jones, John Jr., Wit.

Baldwin, James E., 2D:132, 1846/48
  Baldwin, Mahlon, Father, dec'd.
  Baldwin, Ruth, Mother
  Tavenner, Sarah Jane, Wit.
  Tavenner, Jonah, Admr. w.w.a.

Dishman, Samuel, 2D:132, 1847/48
  Dishman, Marcus, Son
  Ward, Emily, Dau.
  Ward, Elisabeth, Gr-Dau.
  Skilman, Martha, Gr-Dau., dau. of Maria
  Sinclair, Milly, Dau.
  Dishman, James T., Son
  Sinclair, John
  Skilman, Maria, Dau.
  Skilman, Abraham, Son-in-law
  Skilman, Marcus, Gr-Son, son of Maria
  Skilman, James, Gr-Son, son of Maria
  McVeigh, Jesse, Wit.
  Rogers, Richard L., Wit.
  Rogers, Asa, Wit.
  Littleton, Eli, Wit.

Simpson, Susannah, 2D:143, 1842/48
  Zimmerman, Samuel, Brother
  Zimmerman, Elizabeth, Sister
  Backhouse, George, Wit.
  Thompson, John H., Wit.
  Thompson, James, Wit.

Taylor, Bernard, 2D:143, 1847/48
  Taylor, Sarah, Wife
  Taylor, Yardley, Son
  Taylor, Jonathan, Son
  Taylor, Henry Smith, Son
  Taylor, Bernard, Son
  Taylor, Nancy, Dau.
  Bond, Sarah Alice, Dau.
  Janney, Maria Wilson, Dau.

Nichols, Isaac, 2D:163, 1844/48
  Wilson, Elizabeth, Dau.
  Wilson, William, Son-in-law
  Nichols, Thomas, Son
  Nichols, Joshua, Son
  Nichols, Joseph, Son
  Perdue, Miriam, Dau.
  Hatcher, Lydia, Dau.
  Hatcher, Mary, Gr-Dau., child of Lydia
  Hatcher, Isaac, Gr-Son, child of Lydia
  Hatcher, Phebe, Gr-Dau., child of Lydia
  Hatcher, Miriam, Gr-Dau., child of Lydia
  Hatcher, Louisa, Gr-Dau., child of Lydia
  Hatcher, Sarah, Gr-Dau., child of Lydia
  Nichols, William, Son
  Logan, Sarah, Dau.
  Mead, Phebe, Dau.
  Brown, Thomas, Wit.
  Gregg, John, Wit.
  Gregg, William, Wit.
  Ewers, Jonathan, Wit.

Index to Loudoun County Wills, 1757 - 1850

Gore, Elizabeth, 2D:164, 1839/48
Roper, James W., Son
Roper, Wager, Gr-Son,
  child of James W.
Roper, Ellen Cecelia, Gr-Dau.,
  child of James W.
Wilkinson, Eleanor, Friend
Nettle, William, Exor.
Worsley, William, Wit.
Conrad, A. M. H., Wit.
Costs, Jonathan, Wit.

Skinner, Nathaniel, 2D:167, 1848
Oden, Nathaniel S., Nephew
Oden, Mary, Sister
Skinner, John, Brother
Foley, Martha, Sister
Wayland, Sarah, Sister
Norris, Harriet, Niece
Brooks, Frances C., Niece
Skinner, James, Brother, dec'd.
Skinner, Isaac, Brother
Rogers, Nathaniel, Nephew
Ewell, Jesse, Wit.
Hutchison, Beverly, Wit.
Adams, Francis T., Wit.

Miller, George, 2D:171, 1848
Miller, John, Son
Miller, Armistead, Son
Miller, Mahlon, Son
Miller, —, Wife
Miller, —, all my children
Dorrell, George
Porter, Jesse, Wit.
Turner, Samuel, Wit.

Craig, Rebecca, 2D:174, 1844/48
Craig, William, Son
Craig, James, Son
Craig, Samuel, Son
Eaton, Malinda, Dau.
Hatcher, Jane, Dau.
Gulick, Ann, Dau.
Brown, Thomas, Wit.
Brown, Phebe, Wit.
Nichols, Mary, Wit.

Gibson, Esther, 2D:186, 1828/48
Logan, Alice, Dau.
Gibson, William, Son
Hickes, Rachel, Dau.
Gibson, Joseph, Son
Bowles, Isaac G., Gr-Son

Bowles, Samuel, Gr-Son
Bowles, William, Gr-Son
Bowles, David, Gr-Son
Bowles, Emmily, Gr-Dau.
Bowles, Allcinda, Gr-Dau.
Hogue, Rachel, Gr-Dau.
Bowles, James, Son-in-law
Gibson, Moses, Son
Armistead, John B., Wit.
Nesmith, John, Wit.
Logan, Samuel, Wit.
Carter, Landon, Wit.
Logan, Alfred, Wit.

Thomas, Daniel, 2D:186, 1848
Thomas, John, Brother, dec'd.
Thomas, Mary Ann, Wife
Thomas, Maria, Dau.
Thomas, Nancy, Dau.
Thomas, Ellen, Dau.
Thomas, Mary, Dau.
Thomas, Nathaniel, Son
Scanland, Sophronia, Dau.
Dorsey, Eliza (Virginia E.), Dau.
Thomas, Maziah, Son
Mintur, Duany, Dau.
Wertenbaker, Sarah, Dau.
Dorsey, Martha, Dau.
Dorsey, Paul E. , Son-in-law,
  husband of Virginia E.
Hutchison, Lemuel, Wit.
Stephenson, W. A., Wit.
Frazier, Thomas, Wit.
Harrison, John M., Wit.
Lauck, Isaac G., Wit.

Wade, John, 2D:189, 1848
Wade, Hannah, Wife
Barrett, Caroline M. E., Dau.
Barrett, John F., Son-in-Law,
  dec'd.
Barrett, John Wade, Gr-Son
Barrett, Francis, Gr-Son
Barrett, Campbell Boyd, Gr-Son
Barrett, Harriet Ann, Gr-Dau.
Green, Euphemia, Wit.
Clarke, A. H., Wit.

Cullison, Nancy, 2D:215, 1847/48
Muse, Mary, Sister
Saunders, Elizabeth, Sister
Saunders, —, 2 Daus. of
  Elizabeth, Nieces

Muse, —, 2 sons of Mary,
  Nephews
Miller, Julian Ann, Servant
Miller, Margaret Ellen, Servant
Wilson, John M., Exor.
Coleman, John J., Wit.
Dorrell, George W., Wit.
Murray, Elizabeth, Wit.
Muse, John, Wit.
Waltman, Jacob, 2D:216, 1846/48
Waltman, Mary, Wife
Waltman, Mortimer, Son
Waltman, Mary Catherine, Dau.
Waltman, Caroline, Dau.
James, Sarah Ann, Dau.
Waltman, Armistead, Son
Waltman, Milton B., Son
Beevers, John
James, Richard, Exor.
Hamilton, C. B., Wit.
Luckett, Samuel C., Wit.
Lovett, David, 2D:259, 1841/49
Lowe, Susannah, Housekeeper,
  dec'd.
Lowe, Amanda,
  child of Susannah
Lowe, Tazewell,
  child of Susannah
Lowe, Landon,
  child of Susannah
Lowe, Mortimer, child of
  Susannah
Heaton, Townshend, Exor.
Osburn, Craven, Exor.
Adams, Richard, Wit.
Janney, Jonas, Wit.
Pursel, Bernard, Wit.
Pursel, Samuel Jr., Wit.
Chamblin, Mason, Wit. [c]
Osburn, Abner, Wit. [c]
Lovett, Tazewell, Son [c]
Lovett, Amanda, Dau. [c]
**Darrell, Margaret, 2D:260,
  1847/49**
Dorrell, Thomas, Son
Wright, Charlotte, Dau.
Wright, Nancy Johnson,
  Gr-Dau., dau of Charlotte
Ramey, Sanford I., Exor.
Schooley, Ephraim, Wit.

Steer, James M., Wit.
Schooley, John Jr., Wit.
Lacey, Ruth, 2D:279, 1825/49
Lacey, Naomi, Sister
Lacey, Huldah, Sister
Beard, Jonathan, Nephew,
  son of Orpha
Beard, Orpha, Sister
Hutchison, Alexander, Wit.
Beatty, William T., Wit.
Lacey, Meshack, Wit.
Hutchison, J., Wit.
Powell, Cuthbert, 2D:285, 1848/49
Powell, Cuthbert H., Son
Powell, John S., Son
Powell, Charles L., Son
Powell, —, Wife
Powell, —, all my children
Gray, William H., Exor.
**Elgin, Charles W. of Mobile,
  Alabama, 2D:287, 1836/49**
Elgin, John, Brother
Elgin, Armistead, Brother
Elgin, Francis, Brother
Elgin, Isabella, Sister
Jones, William Jefferson, Exor.
Childers, N., Wit.
Leach, Fielding, Wit.
Iglehart, Thomas H., Wit.
Tavenner, Joseph, 2D:294, 1849
Tavenner, Ann, Wife
Tavenner, John, Son
Tavenner, Mahlon, Son
McDaniel, Sarah, Dau.
McDaniel, John, Gr-Son,
  child of Sarah
McDaniel, Nancy, Gr-Dau.,
  child of Sarah
McDaniel, Elizabeth, Gr-Dau.,
  child of Sarah
McCarty, Elizabeth, Dau.
Tavenner, Levi, Son
Tavenner, Hannah, Dau.
Tavenner, Susan, Dau.
Nichols, Catharine, Dau.
Thompson, Ann, Dau.
Tavenner, Mary, Dau.
Nichols, Jonah, Exor.
Taylor, Henry S., Exor.
Tavenner, William, Wit.

Hamilton, E. J., Wit.
Taylor, Lewis, Wit.
Downs, James, 2D:295, 1849
Downs, —, Mother
Gray, Robert W., Exor.
Mott, Armistead R., Wit.
Rathie, Benjamin D., Wit.
Osburn, Joshua, 2D:296, 1847/49
Osburn, Hector, Brother
Osburn, Norval, Brother
Osburn, Herod, Brother
Osburn, Sally, Niece,
  dau. of Herod
Osburn, Thompson, husband of
  Sally
Osburn, William T., Nephew,
  son of Herod
Worthington, Joseph, Nephew
Hamilton, Nancy Worthington,
  Niece
Craven, Cassandra
  Worthington, Niece
Thomas, Sally Worthington,
  Niece
Thomas, Joseph,
  husband of Sally
Allen, Lucy Worthington, Niece
Allen, Edgar, husband of Lucy
Young, Emily Worthington's
  Dau., Gr-niece
Ebersole, Harriet Worthington,
  Niece
Fox, Amanda O. Leslie, Niece
Fox, Joseph B.
Shutt, Caroline F., Niece
Shutt, Jacob,
  husband of Caroline
Osburn, Landon, Brother, dec'd.
Worthington, Elizabeth, Sister
Hamilton, Landon, Gr-nephew,
  son of Hannah
Hamilton, Hannah Worthington,
  Niece, dec'd.
Worthington, Joshua, Nephew,
  dec'd.
McIlhany, James, Wit.
Janney, James C., Wit.
Kilgour, James M., Wit.

Powell, George Cuthbert, 2D:317
Powell, Marietta Fauntleroy,
  Wife
Powell, Humphrey B., Brother
Pursel, Margaret, 2D:327, 1842/49
Pursel, Mahlon, Son
Pursel, Enos, Son
Pursel, Samuel, Son
Pursel, Jonah, Son
Pursel, Bernard, Son
Pursel, Edwin, Son
Pursel, Hector, Son
Pursel, Hannah, Dau.
Urton, Jane, Dau.
Vanvacter, Solomon, Wit.
Nichlols sic, Thomas J., Wit.
Palmer, William C., 2D:327, 1849
Palmer, —, Wife
Palmer, —, my children
Chamblin, William, Exor.
Weadon, John, Exor.
Fred, Frenk L., Wit.
Fred, Burr P., Wit.
Osburn, Addison, Wit.
Ball, Mary, 2D:328, 1849
Beach, Charlotte, Dau.
Gover, Henry T., Exor.
Braden, Noble S., Wit.
Russell, George W., Wit.
Carter, Jonathan, 2D:345, 1849
Carter, Elizabeth, Wife
Carter, Francis M., Son
Carter, Benjamin Franklin, Son
Carter, John R., Son
Carter, George W., Son
Wright, Ellen, Gr-Dau.
Wright, Elizabeth, Gr-Dau.
Carter, Richard R., Son
Carter, Hannah E., Dau.-in-law,
  w/o Richard R.
Latham, Sarah
Rust, James
Carter, James, Gr-Son,
  son of Hannah
Carter, Franklin, Gr-Son,
  son of Hannah
Wright, Robert L., Son-in-law
Wright, Sarah Catharine, Dau.,
  dec'd.
George, Phebe, Sister

Simpson, John, Wit.
Simpson, James R., Wit.
Hoge, Thomas, Wit.
Craig, William T. J., Wit.
McIntyre, Mary, 2D:356, 1848/49
McIntyre, Ellen, Dau.
McIntyre, Lucy, Dau.
Glascock, Catharine, Dau.
Moore, Laura F., Dau.
Boss, Samuel M., Wit.
Tebbs, A. Sidney, Wit.
Blincoe, Martha, 2D:357, 1847/49
Blincoe, Virginia, Dau.
Blincoe, Charles, Son
Ward, Mary, Dau.
Ward, William N., Son-in-law
Blincoe, —, my 6 children
Magill, Henry D., Wit.
Edwards, Mary L., Wit.
Seaton, Hiram, 2D:382, 1849
Seaton, Nancy, Wife
Seaton, James, Son
Seaton, John, Son
Seaton, Robert, Son
Seaton, Hiram, Son
Seaton, Townshend, Son
Seaton, William, Son
Carter, John A., Wit.
Dawson, G. H., Wit.
Benton, William, Wit.
Harrison, John M, Wit.
Handley, David, 2D:383, 1849
Handley, —, Wife
Handley, Betsy, Dau.
Handley, Harriet, Dau.
Powell, John L., Trustee
Taylor, Timothy, Trustee
Fred, Thomas, Exor.
Stringfellow, Benjamin, Wit.
Taylor, Charles, Wit.
Everhart, Philip, 2D:384, 1849
George, Isaiah, Gr-Son,
  son of dau. Delilah
Wirts, John, Gr-Son,
  son of dau. Delilah
Everhart, Henry Wunder,
  Gr-Son, son of Daniel
Everhart, Daniel, Son, dec'd.
Copeland, Delilah, Dau.
Everhart, Solomon, Son
Wincel, Philip, Son-in-law
Everhart, —, all my children
Neer, Jesse, Wit.
Neer, Samuel A., Wit.
Grubb, John, Wit.
Davis, William, 2D:391, 1850
Davis, Sarah D., Dau.
Gochnauer, Harriet A., Dau.
Davis, Margaret A., Dau.
Gochnauer, Joseph, Son-in-law
Davis, Thomas S., Exor.
Bitzer, George L., Wit.
Bitzer, James H., Wit.
Tavenner, Jonah, Wit.
Lafever, William, 2E:1, 1847/50
Havener, Rachel, Dau.
Havener, Bassil, Son-in-law
Arundell, Honnor, Dau.
Arundell, Joseph, Son-in-law
Lafever, William, Son
Lafever, Henry, Son
Lafever, Peter, Son
Lafever, Samuel, Son
Lafever, John, Son
Fouch, Amos Sr., Wit.
Fouch, Ellen, Wit.
Power, Robert, Wit.
Cost, Peter, 2E:2, 1848/50
Cost, —, Wife
Cost, John, Brother
Cost, Jacob, Brother, dec'd.
Gross, Elizabeth, Sister
Yeakey, Barbara, Sister, dec'd.
Cost, Jonathan dec'd.
Cost, Jacob F., Admr. w.w.a.
Fulton, William, Wit.
Magill, Henry D., Wit.
Hardy, Hugh M., Wit.
Smith, David, 2E:21, 1832/50
Newport, Rachel, Only Dau.,
  now in Belmont County, Ohio
Newport, Jonah C., Son-in-law,
  now in Belmont County, Ohio
Taylor, Yardley, Exor.
Taylor, Benjamin F., Exor.
Taylor, Jonathan, Wit.
Hirst, Jonathan, Wit.
Janney, Elisha, Wit.

Index to Loudoun County Wills, 1757 - 1850

Cross, James, 2E:50, 1845/50
Cross, Nancy, Wife
Bullard, Lucy, Dau.
Bullard, R. D., Son-in-law
Cochran, Fanny, Dau.
Cross, Lewis, Son
Elgin, Elizabeth, Dau.
Cochran, Elizabeth Ann,
  Gr-Dau.
Cross, William, Son
Cross, James, Son
Littleton, John, Wit.
Ball, Henry A., Wit.
Cross, Nancy, Wit.
Dodd, John, 2E:51, 1850
Dodd, Thomas, Brother, dec'd.
Dodd, Jane, Mother, dec'd.
Divine, Betsy, Sister
Divine, Jacob, Brother-in-law
Dodd, Mary, Niece,
  dau. of Betsy
Dodd, Lucinda, Niece,
  dau. of Betsy
Vandevanter, Isaac, Exor.
Paxson, Samuel, Wit.
Vandevanter, Gabriel, Wit.
Gregg, Nathan, Wit.
Vandevanter, A. M.,
  Admr. w.w.a.
Wenner, Sarah, 2E:95, 1849/50
Stuck, Peter, Father, dec'd.
Wenner, Jonathan, Husband,
  dec'd.
Washington, Sarah J., Dau.
Wenner, Lydia J.,
  Youngest Dau.
Souder, John, Exor.
Price, S. H., Wit.
Edwards, Charles G., Wit.
Edwards, Richard H., Wit.
Zimmerman, Eliza, 2E:96, 1850
Zimmerman, Henry,
  Husband, dec'd.
Gibson, Nancy, lives with me
Gibson, Miner, son of Nancy
Gibson, Samuel, son of Nancy
Hirst, Jonathan, Exor.
Gibson, Joseph, Exor.
Smith, Seth, Wit.
Janney, Jacob, Wit.

Fred, Mary Ann, 2E:96, 1850
Triplett, Sarah Ann, Sister
Triplett, Uriel, Brother-in-law
Triplett, Gordan, Nephew,
  child of Sarah Ann
Triplett, —, Nephew
Triplett, Mary E., Niece
Fred, Eliza Ann, Sister
Fred, Joseph H., Brother
Littleton, Richard C., Exor.
Chamblin, A. G., Wit.
Chamblin, John L., Wit.
Skinner, John, 2E:201, 1850
Oden, Nathaniel S., Nephew
Ewell, Jesse, Wit.
Adams, Francis T., Wit.
Elgin, Gus. Sr., Wit.
Arnold, Noah, 2E:201, 1850
Arnold, Emeline, Wife
Arnold, Jacob, Father
Grubb, John, Wit.
Arnold, Simon, Wit.
Cooper, Michael, Wit.
Stuck, Elizabeth, 2E:201, 1845/50
Short, Cornelia, Gr-Dau.
Stuck, Lydia M., Gr-Dau.
Hough, Philip, Brother
Stuck, Jane, Gr-Dau.,
  dau. of F. F.
Stuck, Ferdinando F., Son
Stuck, Mary, Dau.
Stuck, Nancy, Dau.
Price, Samuel H., Exor.
Janney, John, Wit.
Wright, C. F., Wit.
Stoneburner, J. C., Wit.
Filler, Lydia M. Gr-Dau.,
  late Stuck, [c]
Huff, Philip, Dau. [c]
Osburn, John, 2E:203, 1832/50
Osburn, Anna, Wife
Osburn, Bushrod, Son
Osburn, Tarlton, Son
Alder, George H, Wit.
Osburn, Richard Jr., Wit.
Lorentz, Julia A., 2E:204, 1850
Lorentz, Jacob A., Husband
Lorentz, Laura, Dau.
Hodgson, Sydney L., Brother
Hodgson, Caroline O., Sister

Osburn, Abner, Wit.
Wheeler, Mary S., Wit.
Bradfield, George W., Wit.
Nyswanger, Christian, 2E:223, 1850
Nyswanger, Henry, Father, dec'd.
Nyswanger, Catharine, Mother
Nyswanger, Mary, Wife
Nyswanger, James Henry, Son
Nyswanger, Samuel Andrew, Son
Nyswanger, Christian Thomas, Son
Nyswanger, John William, Son
Nyswanger, Jacob R., Son
Nyswanger, Harriet Jane, Dau.
Nyswanger, Emily Virginia, Dau.
Waters, Susannah, Dau.
Jackson, Monica, Slave
Smith, Jobe, Exor.
Fowk, Isaac, Wit.
Derry, Christian, Wit.
Nyswanger, John, Wit.
Clendening, William, Admr. w.w.a.

Rhodes, Euphamia, 2E:225, 1850
Rhodes, Samuel, Son
Rhodes, Alfred, Son
Rhodes, Tholemiah, Son
Turnipseed, Alcinda, Dau.
Willett, Elizabeth, Dau.
Hibbs, Nancy, Dau.
Rhodes, Lydia, Dau.
Willett, George
James, Robert, Exor.
Allen, Edmund, Wit.
Arnett, William, Wit.
Arnet sic, Moses, Wit.
Fawley, John, 2E:226, 1848/50
Fawley, Edith, Wife
Fawley, Sarah Elizabeth, Dau.
Goodhart, Mary, Dau.
Stock, Christena, Dau.
Frey, Margaret, Dau.
Fawley, Edith, Dau.
Fawley, Henry, Son
Fawley, Jeremiah, Son
Fawley, Charles, Son
Frey, Joseph, Son-in-law
Luckett, Samuel C., Wit.
Titus, Tunis, Wit.
Schooley, Jonas P., Wit.
Baker, George, Wit.

SUPERIOR COURT RECORDS

Mercer, John F., A:31, 1810/12
Mercer, Charles F., Brother
Tutt, Ann Mason
Wildman, Joseph, A:34, 1817
Wildman, Martin, Son
Wildman, Joseph, Son
Wildman, John, Son
Wildman, —, Wife
Shreve, Benjamin, Wit.
Elgin, Gustavus, Wit.
Elgin, Gustavus Jr., Wit.
McMackin, Alexander, A:35, 1815/17
Duncan, Catharine, Dau.
Lingham, Mary, Dau.
Cordell, Martha, Dau.
Tablor, Ann, Dau.
Henderson, Mary, Gr-Dau., dau. of Elizabeth
Henderson, Elizabeth, Dau., dec'd.
Henderson, Alexander, Gr-Son, son of Elizabeth
Henderson, Lawson, Gr-Son, son of Elizabeth
McMackin, William, Son
Skinner, Sarah, Dau.
Cordell, Martin, Son-in-law
Henderson, John, Exor.
Newton, John, Wit.
Jacobs, Thomas, Wit.
Murrey, Samuel, Wit.
Mason, Armistead T., A:45, 1818/19
Mason, Mary, Mother
Mason, Charlotte Eliza, Wife
Mason, —, Son
Mason, John T. Jr., Brother
Barry, William T., Brother-in-law
Barry, Catherine, Sister
Mason, Emily, Sister
Mason, Stephen T., Brother
Mason, William Temple T., Exor.
Mason, Thomson, Exor.

Van Buskirk (Buskirk), Abraham, A:49, 1815/19
Van Buskirk, Ann, Wife
Osburne, Ann, Dau.
Beavers, Margaret, Dau.
Waltman, Sary, Dau.
Jinkins, Elizabeth, Dau.
Buskirk, John Seanor, Gr-Son
Buskirk, John, Son
Nichols, Nathan, Exor.
Beavers, John, Exor.
Hatcher, John, Wit.
Chamblin, Mary, Wit.
Griffith, Rebecca, A:59, 1822
Price, Sarah, Sister
Clapham, Samuel, Brother
Mason, Elizabeth Clapham, Niece
Price, Matilda Rebecca, Niece
Chichester, Sarah Elizabeth, Gr-Dau.
Mason, Thompson F., Exor.
Potter, Elizabeth, Wit.
Hamilton, Dewanner, Wit.
Potter, Mary F., Wit.
Taylor, William, A:76, 1822
Rodgers, Elizabeth, Sister
Taylor, —, my 3 sisters
Taylor, David, Nephew
Taylor, Robert I., Exor.
Clagett, Henry, Wit.
Smarr, William, Wit.
Shover, Simon, A:77, 1821
Shover, Mary, Dau.
Shover, Sophia
Saurbaugh, Elizabeth
Marlowe, John S., Wit.
Alder, Latimore, Wit.
Swart, James, A:147, 1833
Swart, Elizabeth, Wife
Daniel, Elizabeth, Dau., child of 1st marriage
Skillman, Lucinda, Dau., child of 1st marriage, Dau.
Walker, Mary Ann, Dau., child of 1st marriage, Dau.

Swart, Barnet, Son,
  child of 1st marriage
Swart, James, Son, dec'd.,
  of 1st marriage
Simpson, Matilda, Dau., dec'd.,
  of 1st marriage
Swart, Amelia Jane, Dau.,
  of 2nd marriage
Swart, Samuel, Son,
  of 2nd marriage
Swart, Charles Fenton, Son,
  of 2nd marriage
Swart, Fayette Washington,
  Son, of 2nd marriage
Swart, James William, Son,
  of 2nd marriage
Swart, Burr, Son,
  of 2nd marriage
Henderson, Richard H., Exor.
Hamilton, Erasmus G., Wit.
Edwards, Samuel M., Wit.
Pancoast, John, A:154, 1834
  Pancoast, John, Son
  Pancoast, Joshua, Son
  Pancoast, Lydia, Dau.
  Dillon, Anna, Dau.
  Hatcher, James, Wit.
  Ewers, Barton, Wit.
  Ewers, Thomas, Wit.
Cleveland, Johnston, A:156, 1834
  Newman, Frances, Niece
  Cockerill, Ann, Niece
  Coleman, Sarah, Niece
  Coleman, John J, Nephew
  Coleman, James R., Nephew
  Newman, Robert M., Exor.
  Mershon, William, Wit.
  Mershon, James, Wit.
  Powell, John, Wit.
  Cleveland, George, Brother
Lee, Ludwell, A:180, 1836
  Lee, Ellen, Dau.
  Lee, Emily, Dau.
  Lee, Dr., Son
  Lee, Bowles, Son
  McKenna, J. L., Wit.
  Lee, Ed. J., Wit.
  Selden, Wilson C., Admr. w.w.a.

**Gabby, William of Maryland,
  A:216, 1833/41**
  Peebles, Emily, Wife's niece
  Gabby, Emily, Niece,
    dau. of Joseph
  Gabby, Joseph, Brother
  Gabby, Emily, Wife, dec'd.
  Lawrence, John Curtis E.
  Annin, Helen C.
  Fullerton, William G.,
    son of Humphrey
  Gabby, James, Brother
  Gabby, Archibald, Brother
  Burns, Jennet, Sister
  Cooper, Jane, Sister
  McCormick, Mary, Gr-mother of
    J. C. E. Lawrence
  Fletcher, Charles A., Dau.
  Strite, Abraham, Dau.
  Wolfinger, Jacob, Dau.
Waters, Catharine, A:220, 1835/45
  Waters, Barbara, Dau.
  Waters, Jacob, Son
  Waters, —, my eight children
  Virts, Edw., Wit.
  Boland, Daniel, Wit.
  Smith, George, Wit.
  Waters, Levi, Admr. w.w.a.
**Singleton, Mary Ann, A:229,
  1831/43**
  Tompson, French, Nephew
  Tompson, Benjamin, Brother
  Tompson, Daniel, Brother
  Singleton, Washington G.
  Murry, Josiah, Exor.
  Hicks, K. G., Wit.
  Settle, Thomas G., Wit.
Adams, Margaret, A:230, 1843
  Hereford, Margaret, Niece
  Hereford, Mary, Niece
  Hereford, John, Brother
  Hereford, M. A. B., Niece
  Hereford, John Burr, Nephew
  Hereford, Margaret, tombstone
    to be erected
  Adams, John, tombstone to be
    erected
  Adams, Margaret, tombstone to
    be erected [apparently her
    own]

Hereford, Ann C., tombstone to
  be erected
Wharton, Catherine, tombstone
  to be erected
Rogers, William A., Wit.
Rawlings, William, Wit.
Carr, William B., Wit.
**Mason, Stevens T., A:269,
  1844/48**
Mason, —, Mother
Mason, Westwood T.
**Hamilton, Erasmus G., A:270,
  1845/49**
Hamilton, Matthew G., Brother
Hamilton, James
Hamilton, Cassandra,
  w/o James
Fox, Erasmus H.,
  son of George K.
Hamilton, James, son of
  Samuel G., dec'd.
**Cochran, Stephen, A:278,
  1849/50**
Kees, Polly, Sister
Stenson, Stephen, Nephew
Stenson, Prudence, Sister
Rector, Peggy, Sister
Cochran, Jane, Sister
Burson, Anna, Sister
Gregg, Anameraca,
  dau. of Gibson
Cochran, John, Brother
Cochran, James, Brother
Megeath, Joseph P., Exor.
Gregg, Gibson, Wit.
Elwell, A. G., Wit.
Vansickler, Emanuel, Wit

DEEDS PARTLY PROVED
PART 3

(These did not qualify to be recorded for some reason; some not fully proved, some rejected, etc.--not part of the official record.)

Willson, Alexander,
   DPP 10034, 1791
   Willson, William, Gr-Son
   Willson, James, Gr-Son
   Willson, Alexander, Gr-Son
   Willson, Elizabeth, Gr-Dau.
   Hixon, Eleanor
   Faris, James, Brother
   Gadis, George, Exor.
   Closon, John Sr., Wit.
   Shaw, Amos, Wit.
   Devison, Adam, Wit.

Whelan, James, DPP 10038, 1804
   Whelan, Timothy,
     Brother, dec'd.
   Whelan, Catharine, Sister
   Whelan, Margaret, Sister
   Whelan, Judith, Sister
   Whelan, Winnifred, Sister
   Figh, Terrence
   Hamilton, James, Exor.
   Huff, Phili, Wit.
   Mull, David, Wit.

Wildman, Elenor,
   DPP 10039, 1826
   Wildman, John,
     Husband, dec'd.
   Beard, Lewis, renunciation, Wit.
   Hamilton, C. B., renunciation, Wit.

Goodin, David, DPP 10040, 1825
   Goodin, Ann, Wife
   Goodin, John, Son
   Goodin, David, Son, <21
   Goodin, Maria, Dau.
   Goodin, Sarah, Dau.
   Goodin, Rachel, Dau.
   Goodin, Martha, Dau.
   Goodin, Elizabeth, Dau.
   Goodin, Kitty, Dau.
   Sands, Jonah, Exor.
   Buffington, William, Wit.
   Kerrick, Stephen, Wit.

Edwards, Joseph,
   DPP 10043, 1822
   Edwards, Lydia, Wife
   Edwards, James, Son
   Edwards, Heneritta, Dau.
   Edwards, Jonathan, Son
   Edwards, John Thomas, Son
   Lewis, Charles, Exor.

Stoneburner, Adam,
   DPP 10045, 1825
   Stoneburner, —, Wife
   Stoneburner, —, 3 children
   Morris, John, Exor.
   Curtis, John W., Wit.
   Mann, John, Wit.
   Ridenbaugh, Mahala, Wit.

Howell, William, DPP 10048, 1816
   Howell, Jesse, Son
   Howell, Abner, Son
   Howell, Abel, Son
   West, Margaret, Dau.
   Nichols, Nathan Sr., Exor.
   Cunard, Edward Jr., Wit.
   Farnsworth, Jonathan, Wit.
   Bishop, John, Wit.

Smith, Elizabeth,
   DPP 10049, 1824
   Smith, Margaret, Dau.
   Smith, Elenor, Dau.
   Wilson, Dr. John T., Exor.
   Edwards, Samuel M., Wit.
   Binns, C., Wit.

Suddarth, William,
   DPP 10050, 1784
   Suddarth, Lawrence, Son
   Suddarth, Mary Ann, Dau.
   Suddarth, Owen, Gr-Son,
     son of William
   Suddarth, William, Gr-Son,
     son of William
   Gillmore, Ann, Dau.
   Peyton, Ann, Niece, dau. of
     John & Margaret Smith
   Suddarth, William, Son, dec'd.
   Gillmore, Robert
   Lane, Hardage, Exor.
   Bush, Abraham, Exor.
   Summers, George, Wit.

Smith, Temple, Wit.
Doyal, Sarah, Wit.
Thatcher, Joshua,
DPP 10053, 1793
Thatcher, Silvester, Son
Head, George, Wit.
Wade, Jesse, DPP 10053, 1809
Wade, James, Son
Wade, Mary, Wife
Fleming, Robert, Exor.
Harris, John A., Wit.
Jefferson, John, Wit.
Blincoe, Mark, Wit.
Summers, Henry, Wit.
Martin, John, DPP 10054, 1805
Clored, alias Matthews,
   Christiana, Friend
Craven, Abner, Friend
Wunder, Thomas, Wit.
Hanby, John, DPP 10055, 1798
Hanby, Mary, Wife
Harding, Elihu, Nephew
Harding, Job, Nephew
Harding, William H., Nephew
Harding, Mary, Sister
Bennett, Charles, Wit.
Binns, John, Wit.
Hatcher, John, DPP 10057, 1801
Hatcher, Sarah, Wife
Hatcher, Noah, Son
Hatcher, Joshua, Son
Hatcher, William, Son
Hatcher, John, Son
Dillon, Ann, Dau.
Tavenner, George Sr., Exor.
Roberts, Joseph, Wit.
Kerrick, Stephen, Wit.
Hollingsworth, Levi, Wit.
Craney, Patrick of Culpeper Co.,
DPP 10058, 1798
Craney, William, Brother
Craney, Edward, Brother
Binns, Charles, Exor.
Murrey, Samuel, Exor.
Wilson, Robert, Wit.
Addams, Thomas Sr., Wit.
Heaton, Benjamin, Wit.

Pugh, Samuel, of Richmond Co.,
DPP 10059, 1771
Pugh, David, Son
Pugh, Samuel, Son
Pugh, Sarah, Dau.
Pugh, Mary, Dau.
Pugh, David, Brother
Hon, George, Exor.
Hon, John, Exor.
Boyed, Hannah, Wit.
Roberson, James, Wit.
Pike, Jonathan,
DPP 10060, 1788
Thomas, Mary, dau. of William
Talbut, Henry
Sears, William B.
Thomas, Moses, Wit.
Smith, Edward, Wit.
Talbut, Hugh, Wit.
Brian, Martha,
DPP 10061, no date
Brian, Jane, Dau.
Brian, Mary, Dau.
Brian, Daniel, Son
Hess, John, Son
Bronaugh, Rebecca,
DPP 10064, 1827
Bronaugh, Sarah, Dau.
Skinner, Rebecca, Dau.
Bronaugh, James C.,
   Son, dec'd.
Bronaugh, Martin, Son-in-law
Skinner, Usher, Son-in-law
Grayson, John W., Wit.
Payne, Elizabeth, Wit.
Skinner, Jacob, DPP 10066, 1820
Skinner, Sucky, Wife
Phillips, Thomas, Wit.
Janney, David, Wit.
Tomkins, Marcy,
DPP 10067, 1800
Rowen, Sarai, Dau.
Tomkins, Betsey,
   Youngest Dau.
Tomkins, Polly, Dau.
Tomkins, Nancy, Dau.
Tomkins, Benjamin, Son

Tomkins, Asahel, Son
Tomkins, Jonah, Son
Rowan, George, Son-in-law
Littlejohn, John, Wit.
Littlejohn, Monica, Wit.
Ferguson, Mary, DPP 10069, 1822
　Layten, Charlotte, Sister
　Lawson, Randal, negro boy
　Hungerford, William Barton,
　　Brother
　Fiffe, Elenor, Sister
　Oneal, Margaret, Sister
　Fiffe, Ann, Niece
　Ferguson, Amos, Husband
　Gibson, Abner, Exor.
　Sinclair, John, Exor.
　Burson, Stephen T., Wit.
　Kent, Thomas, Wit.
　Ferguson, Emily, Wit.
Rhodes, John, DPP 10072, 1805
　Rhodes, Nancy, Wife
　Rhodes, Mary, Dau.
　Rhodes, Tholemiah, Son
　Russell, Robert, Father-in-law
　Inness, Alexander, Wit.
　Inness, William, Wit.
Bissott, Dublin, DPP 10073, 1805
　Bissott, Nancy, Wife
　Bissott, Rachel, Youngest Dau.
　Bissott, Jerry, Son
　Bissott, Dauphany, Dau.
　Bissott, Minty, Dau.
　Bissott, Amy (Anny), Dau.
　Bissott, Zilpah, Dau.
　Moore, James, Exor.
　Phillips, Thomas, Exor.
　Moore, Asa, Wit.
　Braden, John, Wit.
Gill, James, DPP 10074, 1767
　Gill, Elizabeth, Mother
　Gill, George, Brother
　Lane, James, Wit.
　Miller, John, Wit.
West, Mary, DPP 10075, 177:
　Ellzey, Elizabeth, dau. of
　　William, Cousin [probably
　　incorrect and should be
　　Niece]
　Ellzey, William, Brother
　Hancock, Elizabeth, Sister

Hogue, Morgan, DPP 10076, 1793
　Hogue, Ann, Wife
　Hogue, Elizabeth, Mother
　Emrey, George, Wit.
　Murrey, Samuel, Wit.
Rice, James, DPP 10077, 1810
　Rice, Berthamy, Wife
　Rice, William, Son, of 1st wife
　Rice, Leonard, Son, of 1st wife
　Rice, John, Son, of 1st wife
　Rice, Susannah, Dau.,
　　of 1st wife
　Rice, Jane, Dau., of 1st wife
　Rice, Jesse, Son
　Rice, Isaac, Son
　Rice, James, Son
　Rice, Sampson, Son
　Rice, Rebeckah, Dau.
　Braden, Robert, Exor.
　Bennett, Charles Jr., Exor.
　Vandevanter, Isaac, Wit.
　Vandevanter, Joseph, Wit.
　Vandevanter, John, Wit.
　Lacey, David, Wit.
McNathan, James,
**　DPP 10078, 1805**
　McNathan, Tabitha, Wife
　Fox, George
　Jefferson, James
　Kilgore, George, Exor.
　Jefferson, John, Exor.
　Minor, Thomas E., Wit.
Fulkerson, Benjamin,
**　DPP 10079, 1795**
　Fulkerson, Allice, Wife
　Fulkerson, Philip, Son, <21
　Fulkerson, Josia, Son
　Fulkerson, Sarah, Dau., < age
　Fulkerson, Benjamin, Son, <21
　Fulkerson, William, Son, <21
　Fulkerson, Anna, Dau., < age
　Carr, Joseph, Exor.
　Bonham, Benjamin, Wit.
　Baldwin, Joseph, Wit.
Stephens, Anne,
**　DPP 10081, 1772**
　Stephens, Lewis, Son
　Pretsill, John, Gr-Son
　Pretsill, Isaac, Gr-Son
　Pretsill, Fredrick, Gr-Son

Index to Loudoun County Wills, 1757 - 1850

Pretsill, Charity, Dau.
Pretsill, Isaac, Son-in-law
Johnson, Rachel, mulatto
Goff, James, Wit.
Murshite, Martha, Wit.
Smith, Winneford,
  DPP 10082, 1815
Smith, Charles, Son
Simpson, Nancy, Dau.
Coe, John W., Wit.
Coe, Edward M., Wit.
Coe, Robert, Wit.
Kelly, James M., DPP 10084, 1794
Kelly, Edward, Brother
Kelly, Margret, Sister
Kelly, Mary, Sister
Kelly, Monica, Sister
Harrison, M. Jr., Wit.
Jenkins, Reuben, Wit.
King, Osborn, DPP 10088, 1797
Coleman, James
Binns, John, Exor.
Smith, Pusey, Wit.
Varnes, John, Wit.
Strup, M., Wit.
King, Osburn, DPP 10091, 1797
Hulls, Levan
King, John, son of John, dec'd.
King, Reuben,
  son of John, dec'd.
King, Osborn,
  son of John, dec'd.
King, Smith, son of John, dec'd.
Binns, John, Exor.
Boggess, Henley, Wit.
Roach, Edmund, Wit.
Strup, M., Wit.
Watter, John, Wit.
Battson, Hanah, DPP 10094, 1826
Swart, Wm.'s children
Rogers, Phebe, Sister
Swart, James, Brother
Swart, William, Nephew
Smith, Hugh, Exor.
Denham, O., Wit.

Overfield, Benjamin,
  DPP 10096, 1813
Overfield, Mary, Wife
Lewis, Nancy, Eldest Dau.
Lewis, Sarah, Youngest Dau.
Overfield, Martin, Eldest Son
Overfield, Samuel, 2nd Son
Overfield, Peter, Son
Overfield, John, Son
Butcher, John H., Wit.
Malin, Elisha, Wit.
Malin, Elizabeth, Wit.
Ansel, Leonard Sr.,
  DPP 10124, 1804
Ansel, Peator, Son
Ansel, Michael, Son
Ansel, Leonard, Son
Ansel, Melcher, Son
Ansel, Martin, Son
Ansel, Beckey, Dau.
Ansel, Catarine, Dau.
Ansel, Dorety, Dau.
Ansel, Susanna, Dau.
Stouseberger, John, Exor.
Francis, Enoch, Wit.
Steere, Isaac, Wit.
Snider, William, DPP 10126, 1799
Snider, Jacob, Son
Snider, William, Son
Snider, Henry, Son
Snider, Peter, Son
Snider, Catherine, Wife
Shry, Elizabeth, Dau.
Vere, John, Wit.
Etcher, John, Wit.
Dawson, William, Wit.
Everhart, Christian Sr.,
  DPP 86429, 1802
Everhart, Maria Sybilla, Wife
Everhart, Christian, Son
Everhart, William, Son
Fishel, John, Gr-Son
Lamm, Ann Mary, Dau., dec'd.
Lamm, Mary, Gr-Dau.
Everhart, Lorence, Son
Everhart, Jacob, Son

Everhart, Casper, Son
Everhart, Philip, Son
Everhart, Michael, Son
Sipher, Susanna, Dau.
Derry, Barbara, Dau.
Bagley, Christina, Dau.
Snoke, Elizabeth, Dau.
Smith, Frederick, Wit.
George, John Sr., Wit.
George, John Jr., Wit.

Index to Loudoun County Wills, 1757 - 1850   187

INDEX

—A—

Abbett
  Joseph, 12
  Richard, 12
Abel
  Ann, 144
  Catherine, 138
  George, 138, 144
Abit
  Jobe, 34
Able
  Catharine, 55
Abraham
  John, 134
Acres
  Nancy, 116, 140
  Walter, 140
Adam
  John, 62
  Matthew, 64
  Robert, 21
  Susanah, 73
  William, 128, 151
Adams
  Abraham, 97
  Ann, 36
  Elizabeth, 1, 54
  Esther, 97
  Francis, 36, 151, 173, 177
  Gabriel, 1
  James, 22, 31
  John, 126, 167, 180
  Kerid, 97
  Margaret, 180
  Mary, 100
  Philip, 1
  Richard, 174
  Samuel, 82, 89
  Sarai, 18
  Thomas, 18
  Wesley, 54
  William, 1, 97, 105, 120, 154
Addams
  Thomas, 183
Addison
  Anthony, 126
Adie
  George, 137, 154
Adomas
  Rachel, 47
Aisqueth
  Sally, 130
Aisquith
  Charles, 130
  Edward, 130
  Sally, 132
  Virginia, 130
  William, 130
Akey
  Simon, 113
Aldamus
  William, 24
Alder
  George, 54, 146, 177
  Jane, 146
  Latimore, 179
Aldridge
  Andrew, 146
  Harriet, 146
  John, 146
  Joseph, 146
Alexander
  Charles, 139
  David, 96
  Elizabeth, 54
  James, 168
  John, 31
  Mary, 76
  Richard, 31
  Robert, 164
  Susanna, 76
  William, 139, 158
Alford
  Charles, 150
Allder
  George, 93
  James, 54
Allemong
  Ruth, 105
Allen
  Ann, 19
  David, 48
  Edgar, 175
  Edmund, 178
  Elizabeth, 19, 49
  Else, 19
  James, 48
  Joseph, 19, 48
  Lucy, 175
  William, 18, 19, 48
Allison
  Bryan, 31
Alliston
  Wilfred, 147
Allstadt
  John, 158
Alt
  Mary, 113
Ambler
  Lewis, 86
Amour
  Laurence, 75
Anderson
  A. S., 153
  Ann, 28
  Eleanor, 153
  Ellen, 153
  Nancy, 126, 140
  Rebecca, 19
  Robert, 91
  Sarah, 64, 108
Andrews
  John, 5, 7
  Margaret, 159
  Nancy, 159
  Samuel, 168
  Wells, 159
Ankers
  John, 115, 126
Annin
  Helen, 153, 180
Ansel
  Beckey, 185
  Catarine, 185
  Dorety, 185
  Leonard, 185
  Martin, 185
  Melcher, 185

Ansel
  Michael, 185
  Peator, 185
  Susanna, 185
Ansell
  Leonard, 48
Ansley
  Ann, 48, 129
  William, 48, 129
Arden
  Aaron, 63, 87
Armat
  Thomas, 16
Armistead
  Elizabeth, 126
  Frances, 110
  George, 110
  Harriet, 110
  Isabella, 110
  John, 131, 173
  Mary, 58, 114, 126
  Robert, 58, 110
Armstrong
  Susanna, 94
Arnet
  Alexander, 7
  Moses, 178
  Ruth, 7
  Samuel, 7
  Thomas, 3
Arnett
  Samuel, 72
  Thomas, 72
  William, 178
Arnold
  Adam, 159
  Catharine, 169
  Elizabeth, 159
  Emeline, 154, 177
  Jacob, 81, 90, 133, 162, 177
  Joseph, 171
  Mary, 90, 129
  Michael, 127
  Noah, 177
  Rebecca, 159
  Simon, 169, 171, 177
Arundell

  Honnor, 176
  Joseph, 176
Asbury
  Joseph, 39, 43
  Rebecca, 39
Ashby
  Delilah, 142
  F. W., 161
  Robert, 171
Ashford
  Anna, 59
  Dilla, 59
  Elizabeth, 59
  Jane, 59
  John, 59
  Michael, 59
  Rebeckah, 59
  Sarah, 49
  William, 59
Ashton
  Joseph, 48
Askin
  John, 100
Atchley (Askley)
  Joshua, 15
Ater
  Abraham, 45
  George, 45
  Isaac, 45
Athey
  Hezekiah, 68
Atterbury
  William, 2
Atwell
  Harriett, 150
  Jesse, 85, 121
  Peggy, 85
  Thompson, 85
  William, 85, 150
Auchincloss
  Hugh, 162
  John, 162
Austin
  Anna, 105
  Ceselia, 105
  Henry, 105
Awbery
  Mary, 6
Awbrey

  Francis, 30
  Henry, 30
  Jemima, 29, 30
  John, 29
  Philip, 30
  Rhoda, 29
  Richard, 26, 30
  Samuel, 26, 29
  Thomas, 29
  Towny, 30
  William, 26, 30
Axline
  Adam, 28
  Catharine, 162
  Christena, 162
  Christina, 133, 152
  Daniel, 162
  David, 90, 133, 162
  Elizabeth, 129, 162
  Emanuel, 162
  Henry, 112, 133
  Jacob, 133
  John, 133
  Louisa, 162

—B—

Backhouse
  George, 172
Baer
  George, 46
Bagley
  Christina, 186
  John, 30
Bagus
  Mary, 5
Bailey
  Harriet, 148
  J., 126
  Nancy, 130
  Richard, 126
  Stephen, 148
  Susan, 130
  Sydner, 84
  Sydnor, 130
Baily
  Sydnor, 90

Baker
  Adam, 152, 158, 169
  Barbary, 28
  Bitty, 13
  Catherine, 113
  Cathiren, 28
  Christian, 28
  Daniel, 28
  David, 28
  Dorothy, 52
  Elizabeth, 13, 130, 152
  George, 152, 178
  Hannah, 28
  Isaac, 13
  Jacob, 28
  John, 152
  Joseph, 13
  Joshua, 22
  Mary, 13, 22, 27, 28
  Nathan, 13
  Philip, 28, 117, 152
  Rachel, 13, 22
  Richard, 137
  Sally, 158
  Samuel, 28, 70, 152
  Sarah, 22
  Ule, 28
  William, 5, 7, 13, 22, 28, 171
Balch
  Anna, 110
  Eliza, 110
  Elizabeth, 110
  Jane, 110
  L. P. W., 101
  Lewis, 110
  Stephen, 110
  Thomas, 110
Baldwin
  James, 172
  Joseph, 184
  Mahlon, 40, 172
  Ruth, 137, 172
Balenger
  Henson, 120
Bales
  Hannah, 156

Ball
  B., 117
  Burgess, 52
  Charles, 52, 100, 106, 117, 165
  Ebenezer, 106, 148
  Fayette, 52, 106, 120
  Frances, 52, 106
  George, 52
  George Washington, 75
  Henry, 100, 177
  Isaac, 74
  Isabella, 106
  J., 104
  Lucy, 106, 148
  Martha Dandrige, 52
  Mary, 175
  Mildred, 52
  Stephen, 46
  William, 53
Ballenger
  Casandria, 86
  William, 12
Baltzer
  Conrad, 72
Banks, 112
Barb
  Mary, 19
Barker
  John, 16
Barkley
  Barbary, 27
  Thomas, 63
Barkly
  Benjamin, 27
Barnett
  Margaret, 47
  Mary, 100
Barre
  Mahala, 164
Barrett
  Alisabeth, 170
  Campbell, 173
  Caroline, 173
  Francis, 173
  George, 170
  Harriet Ann, 173
  James, 158

  John, 170, 173
  Mandy, 170
  Robert, 158
  William, 170
Barrington
  Barbara, 98
  Elizabeth, 98
Barrot
  Thomas Mattox, 7
Barrow
  Elizabeth, 50
  John, 50
  Margaret, 50
  Thomas, 50
  William, 50
Barry
  Catharine, 113
  Catherine, 179
  Elisa Ann, 135
  William, 179
Bartel
  Eva, 11
Bartlett
  Alley, 60
  Burgess, 171
  Daniel, 35, 60
  Gardner, 60
  James, 27, 68
  John, 60
  Johnston, 146
  Mary, 28, 60
  Minor, 146
  Samuel, 28, 60
  Sarah, 166
  Stacey, 60
  Thomas, 60
  William, 60
Barton
  Benjamin, 158
  Hannah, 137
  James, 112
  Joseph, 87
  Rachel, 87
  Sally, 140
  Thomas, 78, 79, 112, 134
Batson
  Betsey, 91
  Elizabeth, 91

Batson
  Hannah, 91
  James, 48, 91
  John, 48, 91
  Polly, 91
  Susanna, 91
  Tabitha, 116
  William, 91
Battaile
  Ann, 130
  Jane, 130
  Lawrence, 130
  Virginia, 130
Battson
  Elizabeth, 79
  Hanah, 185
  Hannah, 79
  James, 18, 78, 79
  John, 18, 79
  Margery, 18
  Mehaley, 79
  Nancy, 79
  Polly, 79
  Thomas, 79
  William, 79
Baty
  Jean, 2
Bauchman
  Adam, 104
  Andrew, 104
  Catherine, 104
  Elizabeth, 104
Baugh
  Jacob, 61
Bawlieson
  John, 112
Bayles
  John, 10, 17
Bayley
  Elizabeth, 33
  John, 63
  Joseph, 33
  Mountjoy, 33
  Pierce, 33, 34, 43
  Robert, 33
  Samuel, 33
  William, 33
Baylis
  John, 17

Bayly
  Albert, 51
  George, 51
  Hesekiah, 19
  J., 115
  Jane, 19
  John, 51, 151
  Leah, 51
  Mary, 50
  Mountjoy, 51
  Pierce, 50
  Polly, 51
  Richard, 115
  Robert, 51
  Samuel, 51
  Susannah, 50
  William, 51
Bazell
  Ezekiel, 43
Beach
  Charlotte, 175
  Elizabeth, 30
  Joel, 30
  Lial, 159
  Priscilla, 113
Beal
  Hannah, 66
  Joseph, 43, 66
  Thomas, 66, 77, 124
Beale
  Charles, 88
  David, 54
Beales
  Amos, 95
Beall
  David, 82
  Elizabeth, 55
  Erasmus, 110
  George, 110
  Hez., 110
  Lucy, 110
  Thomas, 110, 125
Bealle
  David, 118
Beans
  Aaron, 56
  Absalam, 95
  Amos, 54
  Hanna, 112

  Isaiah, 95, 106, 140
  Jacob, 54
  James, 54
  Jane, 106, 109
  John, 95
  Lattica, 109
  Leatitia, 141
  Levi, 95
  Mahlon, 106
  Mathew, 106, 109
  Matthew, 54, 56, 109
  Minerva, 106
  Moses, 106, 109
  Paxson, 142
  Rachael, 95
  Rebecca, 54, 95
  Rosanna, 106
  Samuel, 95, 134, 142
  Timothy, 54, 95
  Uriah, 106
  William, 14, 54, 95
Beard
  Benjamin, 145, 147
  Ellen, 145, 147
  Jonathan, 145, 147, 174
  Joseph, 66, 96
  Lewis, 157, 182
  Orpah, 51, 145, 147
  Orpha, 174
  Sandy, 147
  Stephen, 96
Beatey
  David, 74
  Elizabeth, 74
  John, 74
  Robert, 74
  William, 74
Beatty
  Anna, 92
  Eleanor, 92
  Eliza, 157
  Elizabeth, 96
  George, 134
  Jane, 92
  John, 63, 92
  Joseph, 152
  Mary, 152, 157
  Matilda, 120

Beatty
 O. R., 106
 Patsey, 152
 Silas, 96
 Thomas, 92, 120, 152
 William, 145, 147, 152, 154, 174
Beaty
 Andrew, 8, 132
 Betsy, 132, 161
 Catherine, 118
 Elizabeth, 66, 106
 George, 66
 James, 132
 John, 108, 118, 119, 161
 Keziah, 132
 Kiziah, 161
 Mary, 119, 132
 Robert, 132
 Silas, 106, 161
 Susan, 119
 William, 8, 42, 66
Beaver
 Bazil, 82
Beavers
 James, 8
 John, 8, 147, 179
 Joseph, 8
 Julian, 147
 Margaret, 179
 Martha, 8
 Mary, 13
 Polly, 43
 Robert, 8
 Samuel, 8, 147
 Sarah, 147
 Thomas, 8, 147
 Washington, 147
 William, 8
Beazer
 John, 76
Beck
 Martha, 55
Beckenbaugh
 Jacob, 92
Becraft
 Peter, 42

Bedom
 Hannah, 103
Beeler
 Amanda, 137
Beeson
 Phebe, 3
Beevers
 John, 174
Bell
 Elizabeth, 5, 92
 Elouiza, 133
 George, 98
 Nancy, 140
 Richard Thomas, 133
 Susanna, 140
 William, 5, 120
Belt
 Alfred, 122, 152
Belts
 Frederick, 129
 Marian, 129
Beltz
 Catharine, 62
 Susannah, 130
Benedum
 Peter, 94
Benham
 John, 22
 Robert, 22
Bennet
 Phebe, 29
Bennett
 Ann, 47
 Charles, 45, 57, 65, 72, 73, 84, 100, 105, 183, 184
 Duhanna, 47
 Elizabeth, 84
 James, 148
 Jefferson, 105, 119
 Joseph, 47
 Judith, 102
 Mary, 44
 Patty, 47
 Polly, 47, 117
 Sally, 47
 Samuel, 47
 Susan, 137, 162

Bentley
 Charles, 167
Benton
 William, 176
Berkeley
 Frances, 145
Berkins
 John, 113
 Mary, 113
Berkley
 Ann (Nancy), 30
 Benjamin, 30
 Burgess, 30
 Catharine, 30
 Elizabeth, 11
 Fanna Rogers, 30
 George, 30, 68, 92
 John, 11, 30, 40, 68, 92, 116, 134
 Moses, 30
 Reuben, 11, 23, 30
 Rufus, 134
 Scarlett, 11, 49
 Susanna, 30
 Tacey, 163
 William, 30
Bernard
 William, 25
Berry
 Fielding, 98
Besicks
 Priscilla, 101
Best
 Elizabeth, 125
 Enos, 125, 138
 James, 8, 138
 John, 8, 138
 Joseph, 138
 Martha, 8
 Thomas, 8, 138
 William, 138
Betts
 Andrew, 47
Bever
 Rebecca, 45
Beveridge
 Andrew, 137
 John, 55, 57, 137, 151

Beveridge
  Kesiah, 151
  Lucy, 91
  Mary, 137
  Noble, 58, 82, 91,
    96, 137, 162
  Susanah, 137
  Thomas, 60, 137
  William, 91, 137
Biggs
  Mary, 126, 137
Binns
  Ann, 159
  Anne, 54, 143, 159
  Betsey, 81
  C., 44, 60, 82, 182
  Charles, 24, 30, 39,
    54, 58, 71, 81, 89,
    105, 120, 143,
    159, 183
  Dewanner, 81
  Elizabeth, 81, 118,
    143, 156, 159
  Hannah, 143, 159
  John, 24, 48, 54, 58,
    81, 106, 120, 125,
    143, 183, 185
  Luisa, 81
  Mary, 81, 159
  Nancy, 81
  Sarah, 97
  Simon, 39, 54, 58,
    81, 93
  Thomas, 54, 96
  Thomas Nelson, 81
  William, 54, 97
Birckhead
  Mary, 156
Bird
  Derrick, 53
Birdsal
  Andrew, 171
  Benjamin, 171
  Elizabeth, 171
  Hannah, 171
  John, 171
  Mary, 171
  Rachel, 171

Birdsall
  Andrew, 136
  Ann, 128
  Benjamin, 128
  David, 128
  Hannah, 97
  infant, 128
  Joel, 128
  John, 128, 149
  Mary, 128, 149
  Rebecca, 128
  Thomas, 136
  William, 128
Birdsol
  Ann, 168
  Mary, 168
  Rebecca, 168
Birkby
  Charles, 151, 165
  Joseph, 151
  Thomas, 90, 125,
    151, 165
Birkhead
  Hugh, 117
Bisco
  Sally, 106
Biscoe
  Sarah, 96
Bishop
  Anne, 97
  Aquilla, 132
  Cathrun, 51
  Daniel, 38
  Jemima, 132
  John, 24, 182
  Mary, 24
Bisicks
  Hindley, 101
  James, 102
  Jesse, 101
Bissott
  Amy, 184
  Dauphany, 184
  Dublin, 184
  Jerry, 184
  Minty, 184
  Nancy, 184
  Rachel, 184
  Zilpah, 184

Bitzer
  Conrad, 165
  Doratha, 40
  Dorothy, 131
  George, 131, 176
  Harman, 131
  Harmon, 106, 131
  James, 176
  John, 106, 131
  Polly, 96
  Poly, 106
  William, 131
Blackburn
  Amy, 143
  J., 32, 77
  James, 160
  Richard, 32
  William, 143
Bland
  Robert, 17
Blare
  Charles, 59
  James, 59
  Jean, 59
  John, 59
Bleakly
  William, 168
Blincoe
  Charles, 118, 176
  Elizabeth, 75
  Mark, 183
  Martha, 113, 118,
    176
  S., 105, 111
  Sally, 118
  Sampson, 54, 86, 88,
    90, 109, 118
  Virginia, 176
Blincoe:, 98
Blinston
  William, 40
Blinstone
  Thomas, 39
  William, 39
Bloxham
  Clarissa, 169
  Ephram, 169
Blue
  Sarah, 160

Index to Loudoun County Wills, 1757 - 1850

Blunt
  Susan, 82
Bockins
  Godfrey, 68
Bodine
  Cornelius, 21
  Elizabeth, 21, 46
  Idah, 21
  Isaac, 8, 21
  Jacob, 8, 21
  John, 21, 32
  Mary, 21
  Sarah, 21
Bogar
  Elizabeth, 159
  Jacob, 159
  John, 159
  Michael, 102, 159
  Philip, 159
  Samuel, 159
Boger
  Catharine, 109
  David, 109
  Elizabeth, 115
  John, 104, 115
  Philip, 115
Boggess
  Ann, 84, 112
  Henley, 54, 84, 90, 112, 185
  Henly, 91
  Jane, 112
  Jemima, 32
  Samuel, 50, 54, 64, 84, 112
  Susannah, 83
  Vincent, 54
Boland
  Daniel, 139, 180
Bolen
  Edward, 165
  Elizabeth, 165
  Emily, 165
  William, 165
Boley
  Anna, 105
Bolin. *See* Bowlin
Bolon
  Elizabeth, 54

Enoch, 150
Ezra, 150
Ferdinando, 125
John, 150
Joseph, 150
Rebecca, 150
Silas, 150
William, 129, 150, 157
Bonam
  Sarah, 54
Bond
  Asa, 125, 152, 157, 169
  Edward, 163
  Elizabeth, 108
  James, 108, 113
  Joseph, 65, 68, 84, 107, 108
  Keziah, 134
  Nancy, 88
  Sarah Alice, 172
  T. M., 152
Bonham
  Benjamin, 184
Bonhem
  Jonathan, 54
Bonsall
  Jane, 70
Boone
  Hannah, 33
Booram
  John, 28
Booth
  James, 1, 151
  John, 1, 151
  Lydia, 151
  Nancy, 151
  Robert, 1
Borbridge
  J. R., 44
Boss
  Mary, 96
  Peter, 96
  S. M., 138
  Samuel, 96, 127, 176
Boswell
  Ann, 69
  William, 97

Bottenfield
  Adam, 139
  Samuel, 139
Botterfield
  Adam, 24
Bottonfield
  Elisabeth, 69
Botts
  Aaron, 4
  Ann, 5
  Archibald, 35
  Joshua, 46
  Judah, 46
  Margaret, 35
  Moses, 46
  Sarah, 35
  Seth, 4
  Sibacah, 4
Boulton
  David, 7, 17
  Margaret, 7
Bover
  R. H., 96
Bower
  Barnett, 24
Bowie
  Robert, 158, 165
  Robert Gilmer, 139
Bowles
  Allcinda, 173
  David, 173
  Emmily, 173
  Isaac, 173
  James, 156, 173
  Samuel, 156, 173
  William, 173
Bowlin
  Jane, 63
Bowman
  Elias, 126
  George, 46
  Katty, 126
Boyce
  Rachel, 49
Boyd
  Betty, 20
  Elizabeth, 54, 106
  James, 20
  Jane, 20

Boyd
  John, 20
  Nancy, 20
  Samuel, 54, 106
  Thomas, 20
  William, 20, 22
Boyde
  Elizabeth, 79
Boydstone
  Benjamin, 20
  Mary, 20
Boyed
  Hannah, 183
Boyer
  George, 24
Brabham
  Thomas, 73
Braden
  Burr, 109, 121
  Elizabeth, 42, 84, 121
  Flavious, 93, 136
  H. W., 153
  Hector, 121
  James Adison, 121
  John, 72, 73, 74, 93, 111, 123, 128, 133, 167, 171, 184
  Joseph, 35, 38, 41, 49, 52, 65, 72, 73, 74, 85, 93
  Mary, 85, 93, 123, 171
  Noble, 93, 121, 126, 152, 153, 154, 160, 171, 175
  Oscar, 171
  R., 102
  Robert, 38, 41, 42, 44, 57, 72, 73, 76, 78, 81, 85, 86, 93, 101, 121, 184
  Rodney, 171
  Sarah, 73, 93, 121
  William, 121
Bradfield
  Ann, 146
  Benjamin, 67, 88, 94
  Edward, 127

  George, 178
  Hannah, 29
  James, 88
  John, 127, 146
  Jonathan, 79, 127
  Nancy, 76
  William, 127
Bradock
  Deborah, 80
Bradshaw
  Walter, 160
Branner
  Phillip, 23
Braves
  Joseph, 96
Brent
  Caty, 27
  Charles, 43, 44, 47
  George, 27
  Hannah, 22
  Hugh, 27, 119
  Joannah, 27
  Martain, 27
  Sarah, 27
  Thomas, 27
  Willis, 27, 119, 127
Brewer
  Ann, 152
  Edward, 152
  Elizabeth, 3
  Henry, 38
  John, 38, 152
  Martha, 152
  Nancy, 53
Brian
  Daniel, 183
  Jane, 183
  Martha, 183
  Mary, 183
Brickell
  Elizabeth, 16
  Wright, 16
Bridenbaugh
  Maria, 142
Bridges
  Benjamin, 120
  John, 120
Bridwell
  James, 136

  Sophia, 136
Brisco
  Caroline, 151
  Eliza, 151
  Richard, 151
Briscoe
  Matilda, 92
Broden
  Robert, 97
Bronaugh
  J. W., 171
  James, 50, 183
  Jeremiah, 50
  John, 50
  Martin, 183
  P. H. W., 156
  Rebecca, 50, 183
  Rosa, 50
  Sally, 50
  Sarah, 183
  William, 50, 53, 66, 70, 73, 82, 119
Brookbank
  Charles, 103
Brooke
  Benjamin, 88
  Deborah, 14
  Elizabeth, 14
  Hannah, 5, 14
  Phebe, 122
Brooks
  Aaron, 47
  Alice, 47
  David, 160
  Ebenezer, 137
  Elizabeth, 131
  Frances, 173
  Hannah, 109
  Philips, 161
Brooner. *See* Bruner
Brounaugh
  Ann, 119
  George, 119
  Jane, 119
  Jeremiah, 119
  John, 119
  Joseph, 119
  Patrick, 119
  William, 119

Index to Loudoun County Wills, 1757 - 1850

Brown
Aaron, 40
Abraham, 44
Alexander, 98
Amanda, 132
Andrew, 20
Ann, 40, 122, 156
Benjamin, 1, 45
Betsey, 12
Betsy, 81, 122
Brown Jon., 70
Catharine, 27, 76
Christana, 126
Coleman, 30, 39
Craven, 120, 150
Daniel, 132, 136
David, 122, 132, 137, 149, 165, 168, 169
Edwin, 148
Eleanor, 132
Eliza, 168
Elizabeth, 40, 80, 148, 168
Esther, 53, 168
George, 27, 40, 54, 59, 62, 67, 70, 76, 148
Giles, 150
Hamilton, 136
Hannah, 27, 53, 54, 76, 80, 81, 93, 136, 150
Harmon, 76
Henry, 13, 53, 92, 136
Hyram, 76
Isaac, 26, 27, 30, 44, 76, 131, 137, 162
Isachar, 150
Isacher, 120
Jacob, 40, 77
James, 46, 77, 80, 99, 137, 150, 158
Jehue, 40
Joel, 150
John, 15, 27, 31, 40, 44, 53, 67, 76, 77, 78, 85, 103, 106, 122, 128, 136, 137, 138, 149, 156
Joseph, 5, 9, 39, 81, 122, 150
Judith, 89
Leah, 40
Margaret, 76, 80, 103, 150
Mariah, 137
Martha, 30, 132
Mary, 12, 30
Mason, 80
Mercer, 12
Molly, 5
Moses, 40, 67
Nathan, 85, 122
Nimrod, 76
Phebe, 63, 132, 173
Rachel, 40
Rebecca, 132
Reed, 39
Richard, 24, 40, 81, 122, 168
Sally, 76
Samuel, 81, 99, 122, 131, 132, 150
Sarah, 13, 40, 76, 81, 89, 98, 122, 137, 149, 162, 164, 168
Susanna, 76
Tamar, 40
Thomas, 27, 29, 39, 40, 111, 150, 172, 173
Urey, 150
Uriah, 80
Vincent, 80
William, 12, 14, 20, 23, 24, 27, 40, 43, 45, 53, 57, 62, 80, 81, 93, 104, 106, 109, 111, 112, 122, 149, 150, 164, 168
Winifred, 45

Browne
Elizabeth, 23
Mary, 24

Browner
William, 46

Bruce
Eliza, 165
John, 165
Judith, 165

Bruner
Margaret, 85

Buchannan
Ann, 37

Buck
Reuhama, 144

Buckey
David, 151
Elizabeth, 151

Buckley
Elijah, 32
James, 6
John, 32
Joshua, 32, 43
Samuel, 32
William, 32

Buckner
Ariss, 56, 71, 170
Lucy, 170
Thornton, 68

Buffington
James, 20
William, 182

Buford
Alexander, 171

Bullard
Lucy, 177
R. D., 177

Bumcrats
John, 133

Bumcrots
Christena, 129
Christianna, 90
John, 90, 143, 162

Bunnell
Elizabeth, 106

Burgoine
Ann, 102
Joseph, 102

Burgoyne
  Joseph, 65, 100
Burk
  John, 10
  Rhoda, 10
Burke
  William, 127
Burnham
  Ira, 171
Burnhouse
  Christian, 55
  Rosina, 55
Burns
  Jennet, 180
  John, 12
  Philip, 117
  William, 71
Burrel
  Jonathan, 62
Burson
  Aaron, 89, 98
  Ann, 6
  Anna, 181
  Anne, 89, 140
  Benjamin, 1, 6, 29, 35
  Cyrus, 114, 140
  Elizabeth, 126
  Esther, 35
  George, 29, 35
  Hannah, 35
  Hester, 140
  Isaiah, 89
  James, 29, 35, 44, 89
  Jehu, 140
  Jesse, 99, 114, 140
  John, 44, 89, 114, 140
  Jonathan, 29, 35, 44, 89
  Joseph, 5, 6, 15, 29, 53, 66, 89, 114, 140
  Kitty, 114
  Laban, 89
  Lydia, 89
  Mary, 140
  Moses, 89
  Patsey, 137
  Polly, 114
  Rebecca, 89
  Rebeckah, 28
  Ruth, 89
  Sarah, 1, 29, 35, 89
  Silas, 35
  Stephen, 184
  Susannah, 89
  Thomas, 35
Burton
  Elizabth, 37
  R. W., 171
Bush
  Abraham, 182
  Mary, 43
Buskirk
  John, 179
Bussell
  Sally, 65
Butcher
  Elizabeth, 17
  Hannah, 76
  Jane, 17
  John, 17, 55, 60, 185
  Samuel, 17, 60
  Susan, 55
  Susannah, 17, 60
Butler
  Hannah, 143
  James, 105
  Linney, 36
  Mary, 98
  Matilda, 102
  Melvina, 143
  Moses, 143
Byland
  David, 14
  Elizabeth, 15
  Jesse, 14
  Martha, 14
  Rachel, 14
  Samuel, 15
Byrne
  Bennadic, 23
Byrns
  Elizabeth, 164
  John, 164

—C—

Cadwallader
  Jane, 49
Cain
  Mary, 89
Caldwell
  Jean, 38
  Joseph, 38, 97
  Moses, 38
  S. B. T., 118
Calihan
  Catharine, 58
Calvert
  George, 55
Cambell
  Andrew, 43
  James, 43
  John, 43
  Robert, 43
  William, 43
Cameron
  Mary, 80
Campbell
  Aens., 1, 4, 29
  Andrew, 44
  Asa, 146
  Elizabeth, 76, 84
  James, 65, 146, 161
  Jane, 44, 60, 72, 78, 132
  John, 40, 76, 81, 146
  Marion, 21
  Mary, 101
  Matthew, 21
  Rebecca, 161
  Robert, 132, 146
  Samuel, 160
  William, 159
Canby
  Benjamin, 46
  Benjamin Hough, 45
  John, 89, 90
  Joseph, 133, 158
  Mary, 158, 161
  Samuel, 41
Cannaday
  James, 8

Index to Loudoun County Wills, 1757 - 1850 197

Canton
  Elizabeth, 27
  Mark, 27
  Sarah, 27
Carder
  Mary, 31
Carlile
  David, 8, 26, 65
Carnahan
  George, 89
Carnes
  Charlotte, 123
  Naomi, 151
Carney
  John, 94
Carpenter
  James, 114
  John, 114
  William, 114
Carr
  Archibald, 121
  Daniel, 41
  David, 111, 128, 134, 156
  Eliza Ann, 78
  Elizabeth, 44, 60, 72, 78
  James, 44, 60, 72, 78
  Jane, 78, 120, 142
  John, 41, 44, 60, 78, 91, 117, 134, 142
  Joseph, 41, 44, 49, 51, 53, 60, 72, 78, 84, 121, 184
  Margaret, 44, 60
  Mary, 44, 60, 72, 78, 91
  Peter, 41, 77, 78
  Presley, 55
  Sally, 41
  Samuel, 44, 60, 72, 78, 102
  Thomas, 41, 44, 60, 72, 78, 105, 109, 121
  Washington, 142
  William, 41, 56, 78, 181

Carrington
  Margaret, 146
  Timothy, 34
  Winney, 25, 34
Carrol
  Cynthia, 14
  Demse, 14
  Mary, 14
  Rachel, 14
  Rebekah, 14
  Sandford, 14
  Sarah, 14
  William, 14
Carroll
  C. R., 156
  Demse, 33
  Frances, 9
  Sanford, 9
  William, 9
Carruthers
  Ann, 69
  Christian, 69
  Hannah, 69
  James, 69
  Phebe, 69
  Rachel, 69
  Sarah, 164
  Thomas, 69
  William, 164
Carter
  Ann, 52, 111, 171
  Asa, 79
  Benjamin, 167, 175
  Cassius, 101
  Charles S., 101
  Dellila, 111
  Dempey, 79
  Edith, 76
  Edon, 79
  Edward, 52, 82, 101
  Efraim, 92
  Elam, 52
  Elihu, 52
  Elizabeth, 52, 154, 167, 175
  Ephriam, 52
  Fanny, 52, 92
  Ferdinando, 171
  Francis, 175

  Franklin, 175
  G., 86
  George, 68, 154, 167, 175
  Hannah, 45, 49, 52, 58, 79, 175
  Henry, 79
  James, 45, 52, 79, 92, 111, 175
  Jane, 145
  Janet, 20
  John, 21, 52, 79, 92, 101, 165, 167, 175, 176
  Jonathan, 91, 111, 175
  Joseph, 111, 171
  Landon, 165, 173
  Levi, 111
  Mahlon, 79
  Margaret, 42, 156
  Mary, 101
  Mima, 85
  Molly, 52
  Morris, 21, 52, 92
  Pammelia, 171
  Peter, 7, 52
  Richard, 65, 91, 175
  Sarah, 164
  Susanna, 127
  William, 41, 48, 156, 165
Cartnail
  John, 94
  Susan, 94
Caruthis
  James, 52
Casady
  John, 97
Casey
  Leven, 72
  Susana, 154
Casidy
  John, 74
  Thomas, 74
Cassady
  Ann, 119, 159
  Charles, 159
  Jane, 105, 119, 159

Cassady
  John, 105, 119
  Mary, 119, 159
  Nancy, 119
  William Henry, 119
Castle
  Rebekah, 68
Castleberry
  Sarah, 11
Castleman
  Massey, 30
Catlett
  Ann, 164
  Charles, 164
  Erskine, 164
  Esther, 164
  Fairfax, 164
  Polly, 130
Cavan
  James, 83
  Patrick, 21, 27
Cavans
  Patrick, 20
Cavens
  Edward, 77
  Joseph, 64
  William, 6, 64
Cavin
  William, 19, 38
Cavins
  John, 15, 37, 82
  Joseph, 38
  Robert, 37
  William, 13, 37
Caylor
  Ann, 136
  Catharine, 136
  Jacob, 136
Chalfant
  Robert, 22
Chamberlayne
  L. W., 166
Chamberlin
  John, 12
Chambers
  Ann, 1
  Viallator, 1
  William, 1, 108

Chamblain
  John, 93
Chamblin
  A. G., 177
  Ann, 35
  Archibald, 142
  Burr, 150
  Charles, 35, 145, 150, 165
  Dewanna, 137, 142
  Dewannah, 137
  Dewanner, 145
  Eleanor, 35
  James, 145, 150
  Jane, 35
  Jared, 150
  John, 35, 59, 88, 177
  Mary, 88, 179
  Mason, 128, 142, 150, 174
  Nelson, 161
  Rush, 145, 150
  Ruth, 150
  Sarah, 35
  William, 35, 128, 175
Champ
  Betsey, 151
  Eliza, 151
  Joseph, 151
  Nancy, 151
  Peggy, 151
  Sarah, 151
Champe
  Ann, 3
  John, 3
  Susy, 3
  Thomas, 3
Chandlee
  Deborah, 78
  George, 78
  Hannah, 78
  Mahlon, 78
Chaney
  Mary, 7
Chapeleare
  Levy, 141
Chapman
  Thomas, 45

Chappell
  James, 145
Charuthers
  Christian, 128
  James, 128
  Rachel, 128
  Thomas, 129
Cheek
  Barrach, 113
  Fanny, 114
  Sarah, 113
Chew
  Caroline, 146
  Henry, 146
  James, 146, 156
  John, 50, 146
  Joseph, 24
  Lemuel, 146
  Margaret, 146
  Mary, 146
  Nancy, 146
  Roger, 146
  William, 146
Chichester
  Anne, 95
  Daniel, 82
  George, 82, 95, 139
  Richard, 95
  Sarah, 139, 179
Childers
  N., 174
Chilton
  Ann, 10, 11
  Catherine, 26
  Charles, 90, 117, 159
  Elisabeth, 3
  George, 10
  James, 11
  John, 11, 26
  Mark, 11
  Martha, 11
  Mary, 10, 26
  Nancy, 11
  Sally, 90
  Sarah, 11, 26, 37, 74
  Steerman, 3, 26
  Sturman, 11
  Susan, 117
  Susanna, 90

Chilton
  Susannah, 90
  Thomas, 10, 11, 26, 57, 90
  William, 26, 74, 133
Chinn
  Charles, 7
  Christopher, 7, 9
  Elijah, 7, 9
  Elizabeth, 7, 9, 91
  Hugh, 51
  John, 7
  Judy, 51
  Rawleigh, 7, 9, 91
  Richard, 51
  Robert, 51
  Samuel, 91, 131
  Thomas, 8, 51, 87, 91
Chittenden
  Ann, 166
  William, 166
Church
  Louisa, 144
Cimmings
  Ann, 94
Clack
  Spencer, 8
Clage
  Joseph, 4
Clagett
  Henry, 123, 131, 149, 165, 179
  Misses, 117
  Thomas, 159, 165
Claggett
  Charles, 35
  Mary, 35
  Monica, 35
  Thomas, 35
Clandenning
  Samuel, 77
Clandinen
  Saml., 9
Clanke
  Eve, 35
Clapham
  Elizabeth, 75
  J., 10, 29, 58

  Joseph, 57
  Josias, 10, 13, 26, 30, 35, 36, 48, 57
  Rebeckah, 57
  Samuel, 36, 57, 73, 75, 77, 89, 90, 179
Clapman
  Josias, 61, 62
Clapper
  Zillah, 147
Clark
  Charles, 9, 11
  Emily, 168
  Hamilton, 129
  Mary, 11
  Susanna, 9
  Thomas, 23
Clarke
  A. H., 173
  Addison, 133, 137, 150
  Albert, 135
  Effa, 135
  Giles, 135
  James, 135
  Lydia, 135
  Richard, 78
Claspy
  Mary, 140
Claypole
  James, 24
  Joseph, 24
  Sabilla, 51
Claypoole
  James, 40, 66
Clayton
  Amos, 93
  Israel, 93, 134
  Martha, 93, 134, 163
  Nancy, 93
  Sally, 93
  William, 93, 163
Clendenen
  Ruth, 81
Clendening
  Samuel, 99, 114, 149
  William, 153, 158, 160, 164, 178

Clendinan
  Samuel, 12
Clerk
  Ann, 34
Cleveland
  Alexander, 36
  Darkes, 31
  Frances, 36, 39
  George, 36, 39, 180
  Hannah, 36
  James, 36, 39
  Johnson, 39, 88
  Johnston, 36, 71, 75, 88, 120, 180
  Marey, 31
  William, 31
Clews
  Joseph, 24
  Thomas, 24
Clico
  Henry, 118
Clifford
  Elizabeth, 122
  Henry, 122
  Obediah, 71
Climor
  Christian, 41, 44
Cline
  John, 121
  Margaret, 72
  William, 72
Clip
  John, 72
  Mary, 72
Clise
  John, 12
Clored
  Christiana, 183
Closon
  John, 182
Clowes
  Edith, 137
  Elizabeth, 37, 133
  Hannah, 37
  Joseph, 37, 69, 133, 157
  Mary, 37, 133, 157
  Nancy, 37, 133
  Phebe, 37

Clowes
  Ruth, 37
  Thomas, 37, 69, 133,
    157
Coale
  Lewis, 149
Cochran
  Andrew, 58
  Catherine, 145
  Elizabeth, 177
  Fanny, 177
  James, 58, 76, 103,
    105, 165, 181
  Jane, 181
  John, 181
  Nathan, 18
  Richard, 58, 79, 91,
    131, 132, 145
  Sarah, 105
  Stephen, 181
  William, 58, 162
Cochrane
  Richard, 57, 98
Cocke
  Catesby, 41
  Lucy, 41
  Washington, 41
  William, 24, 27, 41
Cockerell
  Jeremiah, 30
  Keziah, 156
  Thomas, 9
  William, 38
Cockeril
  Daniel, 118
  Joseph, 90
Cockerill
  Ann, 26, 180
  Benjamin, 17, 25,
    31, 55
  Christopher, 26
  Delilah, 146
  Jeremiah, 17, 39
  John, 17, 26
  Lee, 146
  S. W., 139
  Sandford, 17
  Thomas, 17, 61

Cockran
  William, 170
Cockrell
  Daniel, 129
  Francis, 60
  Hester, 129
  Joseph, 60
  Susannah, 10
  Thebea, 60
Cockrill
  John, 123
Coe
  Albin, 119
  Catherine, 86, 139
  Cynthia, 158
  David, 86
  Edward, 83, 86, 185
  Elizabeth, 66
  John, 86, 151, 185
  Mary, 158
  Menan, 83, 86
  Robert, 86, 185
  William, 86
Coffen
  John, 127
  Mary, 127
Cogel
  Amey, 59
  Joseph, 59
Coghlan
  Edward, 150
Cogsil
  Harvey, 140
Cogswell
  Joseph, 11
Cohagan
  Aquila, 155
  Mary, 155
Coldwell
  Moses, 65
Cole
  Mary, 4, 12
  Rebecca, 162
  William, 12, 100
Coleman
  Ann, 88
  Caroline, 141
  Edmond, 124
  Edmund, 141

Elenor, 3
Fanny, 144
Frances, 39, 88
Hannah, 39, 88
J. W., 97
James, 3, 10, 88,
  180, 185
John, 88, 124, 164,
  174, 180
Johnson James, 88
Julia, 124
Lydia, 97, 124
Richard, 3, 102
Sarah, 55, 88, 180
Thomas, 55, 97, 124,
  144
William, 97, 124
Coleman:, 119
Collett
  William, 38
Collings
  Joseph, 12
Collins
  Joseph, 171
  Levi, 135
Comber
  Peggy, 73
Combs
  Andrew, 13
  Israel, 13, 85
  John, 13, 77
  Joseph, 13
  Mahlon, 13, 50
  Mary, 13
  Rebecca, 13
  Samuel, 13, 14, 35
  Stephen, 27
  Tacy, 76
Compher
  Catherine, 135
  Elizabeth, 166
  Jacob, 135
  John, 58, 135, 166
  Jonas, 166
  Joseph, 166
  Mary, 166
  Peter, 88, 114, 125,
    135
  Samuel, 166

Compher
  William, 135, 166
Compton
  Craven, 33
  Cynthia, 33
  Jack, 33
  Mildred, 33
Conard
  Abner, 153
  Barbara, 153
  David, 102, 153
  John, 70, 118, 153
  Jonathan, 153, 164
  Joseph, 144, 153
  Mary, 153
  Rachel, 139
Conn
  Coxon, 11
  Hamilton, 97
  Henrietta, 97
  Hugh, 11
  Josias, 11
  Leanna, 97
  Mary, 11
  Ruth, 11
Connally
  Ann, 31
  John, 31
  Mary, 31
  Sanford, 31
  William, 31
Connard
  Anthony, 94
  John, 24
  Jonathan, 22, 24
Conner
  John, 147
  Lucinda, 152
  Margaret, 6
  Martha, 147
  Richard, 44
  Sarah, 155
Connoly
  Cornelius, 37
  Margaret, 37
Conrad
  A. M. H., 173
  Ann, 57
  Anthony, 57
  D., 132
  Edward, 43
  Elizabeth, 57, 124, 148
  Gulielme, 43
  John, 43, 57
  Jonathan, 43, 57
  Joseph, 57
  Nathan, 57
  Samuel, 57
  Sarah, 57
Conrads
  James, 6
Cook
  Samuel, 99
Cooke
  Catharine, 88
  Edward, 88
  H. S., 88
  John, 88
  Stephen, 88
  William, 60, 92
Cookus
  Lydia, 62
Coombs
  Jane, 165
Cooms
  David, 101
Coonce
  Adam, 72
  Henry, 72
  Mary, 71
  Nicholas, 71
Coop
  George, 66
Cooper
  Agnes, 25
  Alexander, 16, 71, 122
  Apollos, 8
  Benjamin, 22
  Betsy, 121
  Catharine, 88, 108
  Cathariny, 23
  Catherine, 135
  Daniel, 87
  Eleanor, 165
  Elias, 158
  Elizabeth, 109
  Frederick, 23, 88, 114
  George, 88, 90, 114, 143, 158
  Hannah, 121
  Jacob, 88, 114
  Jane, 180
  John, 87, 88, 114, 158
  Lucy, 118
  Mary, 114
  Michael, 87, 177
  Nancy, 121
  Nathaniel, 118
  Peter, 87
  Philip, 88
  Phillip, 158
  Richard, 118
  Sarah, 11, 54
  William, 114, 118, 122
Copeland
  Andrew, 66, 146
  Bennet, 66
  Craven, 147
  David, 66
  Delilah, 176
  Elizabeth, 147
  James, 66, 147
  Jane, 147
  John, 99
  Jonathan, 66
  Mary, 161
  Nancy, 66, 147
  Pleasant, 147
  Sally, 66
  Sarah, 147
Cordall
  Jacob, 38
Cordell
  Alexander, 114, 123
  Diana, 123
  Elizabeth, 112
  Martha, 179
  Martin, 127, 179
  Presley, 83, 101, 117, 121, 123
  Presly, 94
  Samuel, 113, 123

Cordell
  Susannah, 123
  William, 112
Corder
  Judith, 31
Corkran
  Eliza, 135
  Phebe, 135
  Rose, 135
Corneluson
  Conrod, 18
  Cornelus, 18
  Garrett, 18
  John, 18
  Mary, 18
  Peter, 18
Cost
  Barbara, 75
  Beator (Peter), 75
  Beckey, 75
  Catarine, 75
  Elisabeth, 75
  Francis, 75
  George, 75
  Jacob, 43, 75, 134, 176
  John, 75, 176
  Jonathan, 176
  Mary, 134
  Peter, 176
Costalow
  Jane, 66
Costs
  Jonathan, 173
Cotton
  Frances, 33
  John, 31
  Mary, 31
  William, 10, 31, 33, 56
Coutsman
  Catharine, 58
  Jacob, 6, 58
Coutzman
  Catherine, 19
  Clarissa, 20
  Hannah, 19
  Jacob, 19, 20
  Louisa, 19

Covan
  Patrick, 32
Cowgill
  Dorothy, 41
  Hannah, 41
  Isaac, 41, 108
  James, 41, 48
  Joseph, 41
  Mary, 108
  Ralph, 41, 48
  Ruth, 108
  Sarah, 41, 108
  Tamer, 41
  Thomas, 108
Cowill
  Isaac, 79
Cox
  Clement, 152
  Jane, 9
  John, 152
  Joseph, 31
  Rebecca, 132
Crafe
  Philip, 24
Crague
  Margaret, 3
Craig
  Francis, 111
  Isaac, 77
  James, 77, 173
  Jane, 111
  John, 6
  Nancy, 111
  Rebecca, 77, 111, 173
  Robert, 77
  Samuel, 77, 173
  William, 77, 173, 176
Craige
  James, 27
Cramer
  Thomas, 121
Crane
  Emily, 127
  Joseph, 127
Craney
  Edward, 183
  Patrick, 183

  William, 183
Cranwell
  John, 78, 147
Cravan
  Giles, 54
  James, 54
  John, 54
Craven
  Abigail, 156
  Abner, 61, 183
  Albina, 133
  Alfred, 134
  Caleb, 134
  Cassandra, 175
  Charlet, 134
  Giles, 51, 129, 134
  Hannah, 129, 162
  Harriet, 134
  James, 28, 52
  Joel, 129
  Joseph, 111
  Lydia, 129
  Mahlon, 131, 162
  Sarah, 169
  Violet, 134
Creager
  Elizabth, 45
Crecelius
  Rudolph, 9, 11, 23
Creel
  Lucretia, 153
Crews
  Williamson, 139
Crider
  Peggy, 97
Cridler
  Andrew, 154
  George, 134
  Rachel, 154
Crim
  Abraham, 112
  Adam, 112
  Conrad, 112
  Elias, 112
  Matilda, 154
  Rosanna, 112
Crissey
  Mary, 165

Index to Loudoun County Wills, 1757 - 1850

Croley
  Clementine, 139
Crook
  Charles, 139
Crooks
  James, 46, 55, 68
  Mary, 55
Crosgrove
  Sarah, 136
Cross
  James, 177
  John, 49
  Joseph, 49
  Lewis, 177
  Nancy, 177
  Robert, 49
  W., 158
  William, 49, 165, 177
Crossly
  Ann, 120
Crowe
  Hiland, 96
  Martha, 103
Crozure
  Eleanor, 127
Crumbacker
  Elizabeth, 43
  Eve, 43
  Jacob, 43
  John, 43
Crumbaker
  Solomon, 143
Crumboyer
  Samuel, 169
Crump
  George, 166
Crumrine
  Catherine, 58
  Michael, 58
  Philip, 58
Crupper
  Ann, 80
  Benjamin, 80
  Elisha, 80
  John, 80
  Kitty, 80
  Leven, 80
  Richard, 18, 24, 80
  Serepta, 80
  Thomas, 80
  William, 80
Crusen
  Jacob, 160
Cuddy
  Michael, 60
Cullen
  John, 151
Cullison
  Jeremiah, 38, 113, 114
  Nancy, 103, 113, 141, 173
  William, 114, 141
Culverhouse
  Franky, 91
  James, 91
Cummings
  John, 87
  Rebecka, 65
  Robert, 98
Cummins
  Francis, 117
Cunard
  Edward, 67, 76, 78, 182
  Mary, 139
Cunnard
  Adah, 88
  Calvin, 88
  Edward, 76, 88
  Esther, 29
  Jonathan, 13
  Luther, 88
Cunningham
  Ann, 56
  Hulda, 140
  Huldah, 116
  Rachel, 42
  Robert, 140
  Wilmoth, 140
Currell
  James, 33
  John, 162
  Permelia, 112
Currlane
  Robert, 83
Curry
  John, 132, 150
Curtis
  Helen, 21
  James, 77
  John, 25, 182
  Levi, 81
  Mary, 21, 77
  Nancy, 98
  Samuel, 86
  Thomas, 86
Cutler
  G. C., 139

—D—

Dagg
  John, 93, 106
  Samuel, 106
  Sarah, 106
  Susan, 156
Dailey
  Aaron, 117
  Hugh, 165
  Jesse, 165
  Mary, 165
Daily
  Aaron, 40
  John, 94
Daniel
  Benjamin, 49
  Eli, 123
  Elizabeth, 179
  Esther, 49
  Hiram, 129
  James, 49
  Joseph, 49, 57, 69, 86, 165
  Joshua, 38, 57
  Samuel, 49
  Tacey, 165
  William, 49, 88
Danniel
  Jane, 23, 64
  Josh., 37
  Joshua, 15, 23, 68
  Tracy, 103

Danniell
  Elizabeth, 74
  Jane, 74
  Joshua, 74
  Nancy, 74
  Stephen, 74
Darne. *See* Veale
  Addalaid, 133
  Alexander, 133
  Amelia, 103
  Betsey, 103
  Catharine, 158, 165
  Catherine, 133
  Elizabeth, 130
  James, 120
  John, 103
  Thomas, 103, 133
  William, 97
Darnes
  Amelia, 103
Darr
  Conrod, 16
  Leonard, 103
  Samuel, 164
Darrell
  Margaret, 174
  Sarah, 30
Daub
  Henry, 11
David
  Elijah, 24
  Isaac, 16
  James, 24
  Jenkin, 5, 16
  Joan, 24
  John, 16
  Margaret, 16
  Mary, 16
Davis
  Abel, 57
  Abraham, 47, 94
  Abram, 38
  Agnes, 48
  Alexander, 164
  Amanda, 144
  Amos, 15
  Ann, 57, 83, 91
  Benjamin, 57, 136, 144

Betsey, 106
Betty, 45
Catharine, 79, 105
Catherine, 131
Charlotte, 105
Daniel, 94
David, 43, 48
Elizabeth, 1, 57, 94, 99
Ellis, 47
Enoch, 8
Evan, 10, 14, 36
Hannah, 47, 57
Harriet, 106, 154, 156
Harriot, 137
Howel, 144
Howell, 57, 83, 123
Jacob, 94
James, 94, 106
Jason, 94
Jinkin, 36
Joannah, 48
John, 1, 5, 8, 17, 18, 30, 36, 37, 40, 58, 94, 99, 103, 159, 161
Jonathan, 1, 45
Joseph, 94, 106, 144
Lucinda, 144
Margaret, 1, 36, 176
Mary, 8, 17, 36, 86, 87, 99, 126
Morris, 73
Nathan, 5, 8, 58
Polly, 94
Rachel, 1, 32, 57, 77
Reason, 29
Rebecca, 103
Samuel, 94, 106
Sarah, 1, 57, 94, 106, 144, 176
Solomon, 69, 94
Thomas, 1, 36, 86, 94, 96, 103, 176
Verlinda, 162
William, 94, 106, 131, 176

Davisson
  Frederick, 65, 157
  Lemuel, 65
  Margaret, 65
  Nancy, 65
  Nathaniel, 65
  Theodore, 65, 157, 160
Dawson
  Ann, 58
  Arthur, 165
  Charles, 58, 146, 165
  Elizabeth, 165
  Eugenia, 165
  G. H., 176
  John, 64
  Mason, 165
  Mathias, 18, 58
  Matilda, 88
  Mellinda, 165
  Nicholas, 165
  Roger, 165
  S., 146
  Samuel, 75, 122, 165
  Sarah, 165
  William, 185
Day
  Dr., 164
  Emily, 164
  John, 169
Daymeed. *See* Daymud
Daymud
  Jacob, 34, 63
DBell
  George, 75
  Mary, 32
  William, 32
Deagon
  Henry, 94
Deale
  William, 120
Dean
  Sarah Brobst, 169
Deaver
  Abraham, 108
  Ann, 108
  Anne, 108
  Bazel, 108
  Daniel, 108

Index to Loudoun County Wills, 1757 - 1850　　　　205

Deaver
  Deborah, 108
  Margreat, 108
Debell
  Dorcus, 49
  Jeremiah, 112
  John, 7, 49, 56
  William, 7, 49, 55
DeButts
  John, 148
  Samuel, 148
DeGras
  Joseph, 57
Dehaven
  Abraham, 4, 9
  Ann, 9
  Elizabeth, 9
  Hannah, 9
  Isaac, 9
  Jacob, 9
  Jesse, 9
  Rebecca, 9, 15
  Sarah, 9
  William, 9
Delaplane
  Catharine, 87
Deliforce
  Catharine, 88
Dement
  Benoni, 1
  William, 118
Demery
  Elizabeth, 66
  John, 66
  Margaret, 66
  Peter, 66, 70
Demit
  Jane, 70
  Sinclear, 70
Demont
  Richard, 118
Demory
  Enos, 158
  John, 72
  Louisa, 158
  Mahlon, 158
  Mary, 158
  Peter, 158
  William, 158

Denham
  Amos, 171
  O., 185
  Oliver, 91, 171
Dennis
  James, 79
  Lettes, 79
  Margaret, 78
  Matilda, 79
  Thomas, 78, 79
  William, 79
Dent
  Mary, 9
  Rhoda, 9
  William, 9
Derflinger
  Catherine, 61
  Daniel, 61
  Eve, 61
  Frederick, 61
  Henry, 61
  Mary, 61
  Thomas, 61
Derry
  Andrew, 81
  Anna, 126, 137
  Baltzer, 70
  Barbara, 70, 186
  Barbary, 118
  Catherine, 47
  Christian, 178
  Eliza, 124
  Jacob, 70, 81, 91
  Peter, 81, 149, 153
  Philip, 70, 118
Dever
  Abraham, 100
  Ann, 100
  Daniel, 100
  Deley, 100
  Margarate, 100
Devison
  Adam, 182
Dickey
  James, 17
Diggs
  John, 137
  Rachel, 113

Dillard
  Anne, 35
  John, 35
Dillon
  Abdon, 61, 111
  Ann, 114, 124, 128,
    183
  Anna, 180
  Betsey, 63
  Daniel, 56
  James, 12, 20, 21,
    26, 31, 39, 51, 61
  Mary, 49, 61
  Moses, 61
  Samuel, 65
  William, 4, 5, 12, 29
Dishman
  James, 172
  Marcus, 172
  Samuel, 41, 172
Divers
  Catherine, 52
  John, 52
  Margaret, 52
  Mary, 52
Divine
  Betsy, 177
  Bonham, 74
  Jacob, 125, 177
Dixon
  H. T., 171
  Hannah, 31
Dnisor
  John, 51
Dodd
  Elizabeth, 127
  James, 138
  Jane, 127, 177
  Jesse, 127
  John, 6, 35, 70, 127,
    177
  Lucinda, 177
  Martha, 138
  Mary, 177
  Samuel, 127
  Sarah, 138
  Thomas, 127, 138,
    177
  William, 81, 127

Donahoe
  Patrick, 160
Donaldson
  —, 17
  Ann, 22
  Betsey, 69
  Daniel, 22
  James, 4, 69
  Mary, 69
  Sally, 22
  Stephen, 22, 69
  Susannah, 69
  William, 47
Done
  Mary, 54
Donohoe
  George, 115
  Patrick, 150
  Samuel, 102
  Sarah, 155
Donohow
  Margrate, 1
Doring
  Polly, 102
Dorrell
  George, 173, 174
  John, 40
  Thomas, 40, 107, 174
Dorris
  Martha, 15
Dorsett
  Samuel, 46
Dorsey
  Alfred, 172
  Allen, 172
  Charles, 172
  Edward, 77, 78, 85, 86, 102, 108, 172
  Eliza, 173
  Emery, 172
  Hamilton, 172
  Jonathan, 172
  Martha, 173
  Mary, 85
  Patty, 77
  Paul, 173
  Presly, 172
  Virginia, 173
  William, 114, 115
Dorsthimer
  Charles, 75
Doubleday
  Sally, 88
Doud
  John, 97
Doudle
  Trecey, 87
Dougherty
  James, 25
Douglas
  Archibald, 118
  Catherine, 82
  Charles, 118, 161
  Evelyn, 94
  Hugh, 75, 82, 89
  Lewis, 118
  Margaret, 118
  Patrick, 82, 92, 94
Douglass
  Archibald, 89
  Charles, 89
  Elizabeth, 23
  Hannah, 23
  Hugh, 23
  Lewis, 89
  Louisa, 89
  Margaret, 89
  Mary, 45
  Nancy, 23
  Patrick, 23
  Peggy, 23
  Sarah, 23
  William, 23
Dow
  Alexander, 59
  Anna, 59
  Janet, 59
  Peter, 59
Dowdell
  James, 153
  Sampson, 145, 153
  Theodore, 153
  Thomas, 132
Dowell
  Anna, 165
  Conrad, 165
  Elisha, 165
  John, 165
  Mary, 102
  William, 165
Dowling
  Daniel, 158
  Edward, 138
  Henry, 138
  Mary, 138
  Rachel, 138, 158
Downman
  Rawleigh, 7
  William, 7
Downs
  Henry, 79
  James, 175
  John, 99, 142
  Nancy, 79
  Ruth, 124
  Sintha, 124
  Walter, 79
  William, 79
Doyal
  Sarah, 183
Drake
  Anna, 51
  Jacob, 76
  James, 76
  Thomas, 76, 131
  Uriee, 76
Drane
  John, 19
Drean
  John, 24
Drish
  Ellenor, 140
  Susanna, 80
  William, 143
  Wilson, 140
Drum
  George, 21
Dudley
  John, 32
Dulaney
  Elizabeth, 153
  John, 120, 121, 148
  Mary, 121
  Rachel, 162
  William, 162
  Zachariah, 93, 121

Dulany
  Morris, 60
Dulin
  children, 123
  Edward, 78, 84
  John, 78, 123
  Mary, 32, 78, 84
  Nancy, 135
  Rebecca, 123
  Rebecka, 84
  William, 32, 57, 74, 78
Dunbar
  William, 27
Duncan
  Catharine, 179
  Catherine, 119
  Charles, 118
  Joshua, 6
  Susannah, 119
Dunglison
  Robley, 156
Dunkin
  Anna, 70
  Benjamin, 68
  Catharine, 68
  Charles, 42, 68
  Coleman, 68
  George, 68
  Henry, 68
  John, 98
  Mason, 68
  Nancy, 68
  Samuel, 98
  Susanna, 68
  William, 68
Dunn, 54
  Elizabeth, 120, 149
  John, 120
Dunnington
  George, 6
Durham
  Catherine, 54, 60
  Caty, 81
  Lee, 54, 60
  Nancy, 60, 81
Dutton
  James, 40, 63

Duty
  Simpson, 90
Dware
  James, 106
  Sally, 106
Dyel
  Elizabeth, 4
  James, 4
  Leonard, 4
  Littes, 4
  Rebecca, 4
  Sarah, 4
  Stasey, 4
  Tibithe, 4
  William, 4
Dyer
  Ann, 4
  Hannah, 28
  James, 4
  John, 28

—E—

Eacha
  Martain, 23
Eaches
  Ann, 105, 108
  Joseph, 93
  William, 129
Eastham
  Philip, 125
Eaton
  Isaac, 128, 136, 144
  Malinda, 173
  Mary, 11
Ebersole
  Harriet, 175
Eblen
  Jane, 38
Eblin
  Elisia, 35
  Hannah, 35
  Isaac, 35, 45
  Jannet, 35
  John, 35, 45, 49
  Mary, 35, 45
  Peter, 35
  Rachel, 35
  Samuel, 35, 45

Sarah, 35
Echart
  Adam, 135
  Casper, 135
  Catherine, 135
Ecton
  Drucilla, 25
  Francis, 25
  Theodore, 25
Edelen
  Robert, 54
Edmonds
  R. L., 153
Edwards
  Amos, 26
  Catherine, 10
  Charles, 97, 99, 102, 119, 123, 131, 134, 148, 162, 166, 177
  Deborah, 171
  Edward, 42, 74
  Elizabeth, 153
  Elvira, 97
  Gilbert, 101
  Heneritta, 182
  James, 182
  John, 10, 160, 182
  Jonathan, 73, 74, 182
  Joseph, 74, 182
  Lydia, 182
  Mary, 176
  R. H., 166
  Rebecca, 73
  Rebeckah, 165
  Richard, 135, 160, 177
  Samuel, 82, 94, 128, 130, 135, 136, 139, 142, 147, 156, 158, 159, 180, 182
  Sarah, 73, 74, 111
  Thomas, 99, 159
Eggborn
  George, 158
  Harriet, 158
  Susan Emily, 158

Eidson
  Joseph, 140
Ekart
  Ann, 95, 108
  Caspar, 95
  Casper, 108
Elgin
  Armistead, 174
  Charles, 74, 135, 174
  Diadama, 141
  Elizabeth, 22, 135, 177
  Francis, 22, 54, 135, 145, 160, 174
  Frederick, 54
  George, 22, 41
  Gus., 177
  Gustavus, 22, 41, 135, 143, 152, 160, 179
  Hamilton, 135
  Ignatius, 22, 135, 141, 148, 156
  Isabella, 174
  Jessey, 22
  John, 141, 152, 167, 174
  Lucy, 145
  Margaret, 22, 135
  Mary, 145
  Mathew, 135
  Mordicai, 141
  Nancy, 22
  Rebecah, 135
  Rebecca, 141
  Rebeccah, 22
  Robert, 135, 156, 160
  Sally, 141
  Samuel, 141
  Sarah, 54
  Thomas, 145
  Walter, 22, 141
  William, 22, 41, 54, 135, 141
Eliot
  M—, 11
Ellgin
  Francis, 58
  Frederick, 55
  Gustavus, 58
  William, 55
Ellicott
  E., 143
Elliot
  George, 74
  John, 15
  Mary, 74
  Thomasin, 15
Elliott
  Catharine, 10
  David, 73
  Elizabeth, 78
  Henson, 88
  James, 40
  Peter, 55
  Samuel, 73
Ellis
  Elias, 4, 9, 14
  Ellis, 47
  Ezar, 150
  Jassa, 4
  Marget, 4
  Mary, 4
  Nancy, 4
  Robert, 4
  Ruth, 4, 63
  Samuel, 4
Ellis (or Eales)
  Jane, 25
Elliss
  Thomas, 82
Ellmore
  Edward, 143
Ellzey
  Alice, 76, 126, 154
  Ann, 126
  Betsey, 126
  Eliza, 139
  Elizabeth, 67, 76, 114
  Fanny, 56
  Frances, 126
  John, 26
  L., 107
  Lewis, 26, 43, 69, 115, 126
  Lucy, 43
Lydia, 26
Margaret, 43
Mary, 67, 76, 115, 126, 139
Prudence, 26
Rosannah, 149
Rozannah, 126
Sally, 76, 126
Sarah, 43, 115
Thomas, 139
Thomasin, 114
Thomazin, 126
William, 18, 43, 51, 56, 67, 76, 115, 126, 137, 139, 184
Ellzey:, 99
Elmore
  Charles, 140
Elwell
  A. G., 181
Emary
  Catharine, 90
  Elizabeth, 90
  Jacob, 90
Emerson
  Thomas, 111
Emery
  Catharine, 129
  Elizabeth, 129
Emmit
  William, 101
Emrey
  George, 24, 184
  Jacob, 37
  Stephen, 23
Emry
  Adam, 81
  Elizabeth, 81
  Mary, 81
English
  David, 58
  King, 42
  Susanna, 30
Ervin
  James, 103
  John, 115
  Peggy, 42
Eskeridge
  William, 60

Eskridge
  Alfred, 115
  Ann, 18
  Charles, 18, 30, 39,
    115, 160, 165
  William, 42
Etcher
  John, 185
Ethel
  Winefred, 4
Ethel (or Ethell)
  John, 4
Ethell
  John, 5
  Winniford, 5
Evans
  Alexander, 19
  Ann, 57
  Anney, 32
  Asahel, 98
  Barten, 72
  Catharine, 57, 93
  Catherine, 8
  Charity, 32
  David, 5, 12
  Deborah, 98
  Eleazer, 98
  Eli, 111, 119
  Elisabeth, 10, 19
  Elizabeth, 5, 61, 98
  Evan, 114, 147
  George, 44
  Griffith, 3, 5
  Hannah, 114, 147
  Henry, 57
  Isaac, 61
  Isabella, 103
  James, 103
  Jesse, 114, 138
  John, 5, 8, 12, 36,
    57, 58, 98, 103
  Joshua, 5, 10, 12
  Margaret, 103
  Martha, 12, 57
  Mary, 5, 8, 10, 26,
    32, 58, 67, 103,
    160
  Nancy, 98
  Rachel, 98
  Rebekah, 103
  Richard, 5
  Robert, 67, 103
  Samuel, 32, 114
  Sarah, 8, 44, 98
  Susanna, 98
  William, 5, 8, 10, 12,
    14, 32, 57, 58, 93
  Zachariah, 19
Everhard
  Charlotte, 9
  Elizabeth, 9
  Jacob, 9
Everhart
  Ann, 108
  Casper, 186
  Catherine, 133
  Charlotte, 133
  Christian, 185
  Christina, 133
  Daniel, 176
  Elijah, 153
  Elizabeth, 133, 166
  George, 153
  Henry Wunder, 176
  Israel, 133
  Jacob, 100, 104, 108,
    166, 185
  John, 100, 108
  Joseph, 101, 108
  Lorence, 185
  Maria Sybilla, 185
  Matilda, 153
  Michael, 186
  Nathaniel, 153
  Philip, 133, 176, 186
  Sara, 108
  Sarah, 101
  Solomon, 133, 176
  Susanna, 137
  Susannah, 126, 153
  William, 153, 185
Everheart
  Jacob, 128
  John, 128
Everitt
  Nancey, 144
Everitte
  Ann, 143
Eli, 143
Rebecca, 143
Evernham
  Sarah, 27
Ewell
  Jesse, 145, 148, 170,
    173, 177
Ewers
  Amy, 50
  Barton, 56, 60, 180
  Eden, 82
  Franklin, 147
  Gregg, 82
  Hannah, 56, 63, 82
  Helen, 56
  Jonathan, 56, 63,
    138, 147, 172
  Levi, 110, 133
  Martha, 82, 134
  Mary, 63, 128, 147
  Phebe, 147
  Rachel, 60
  Thomas, 56, 63, 128,
    180
  William, 49, 147

—F—

Fadeley
  Jacob, 83, 102, 121
  Mary, 121
Fadley
  Jacob, 139
Fagin
  Jean, 134
Fairbanks
  Charity, 131
Fairfax
  Henry, 162
Fairhurst. *See*
  Farrhouse
  David, 150
  Eliza, 63
  George, 36, 63, 93,
    150
  Jeremiah, 63
  John, 37, 63, 150
Fanner
  Mealy, 94

Fanney
  Amos, 141
Faris
  James, 182
Farnsworth
  Henry, 17
  John, 64
  Jonathan, 182
Farr
  Nicholas, 92
Farrhouse
  George, 73
Farro
  Ann, 102
Farrow
  Elizabeth, 24
  J., 24
  Joseph, 24
  Mary, 24
  Sarah, 24
  Thomas, 24
  Thornton, 24
Faucet
  Lydia, 109
Favrow
  George, 125
  William, 125
Faw
  Abraham, 126
Fawley
  Barbara, 52
  Charles, 178
  Christiana, 113
  Edith, 178
  Elizabeth, 166
  Henry, 178
  Jacob, 52, 75
  Jeremiah, 178
  John, 99, 178
  Sarah, 178
  Susannah, 113
Feagan
  Daniel, 27
Feagins
  William, 150
Fearst
  Christien, 49
  Cunrod, 49
  Hannah, 49

Feirst
  Christian, 13
  John, 13
  Peter, 13
Fenton
  Michael, 96
Ferguson
  Abner, 21
  Amos, 184
  Ann, 21
  Elijah, 21
  Emily, 184
  Francis, 21
  James, 54
  Jane, 21
  Mary, 184
  Ruth, 21
  Samuel, 21
  Sarah, 21
  Urias, 88
Fey
  Elizabeth, 113
Fichter
  John, 90
Field
  Elizabeth, 96
  George, 96
  Jamima, 39
  Jemima, 19
  John, 3, 5, 15, 19, 96
  Luke, 99
  Margaret, 99
  Thomas, 15, 19, 96
  William, 15, 19, 46, 55, 96
Fielder
  Hizziah, 33
Fields
  Elizabeth, 23
Fierce
  Elizabeth, 67
Fierst
  Ann, 12
  Christian, 12
  Elizabeth, 12
  John, 12
  Peter, 12
  Sarah, 12

Fiffe
  Ann, 184
  Elenor, 184
Figh
  Terrence, 60, 182
Filler
  Benjamin, 141
  Elizabeth, 154
  Henry, 129, 132
  Jacob, 118, 154
  John, 154
  Jonathan, 154
  Joseph, 154
  Lydia, 177
  Mary, 141
  Sarah, 132, 153, 154
  Solomon, 154
Fine
  Catharine, 48
  Peter, 48
Finety
  Jemimah, 84
Firth
  George, 84, 99
Fishback
  Ann, 110
Fishel
  John, 185
Fisher
  Catherine, 102
  John, 143
  Lydia, 143
  Rebecca, 143
Fitch
  James, 88
Fitchcharles
  Philipina, 47
Fitzgerald
  James, 15
Fitzhugh
  Ann, 130
  Cameron, 130
  Dugal, 171
  John, 130, 171
  Mary, 130
  Matilda, 171
  Sydnor, 130
  Syndor, 171
  Thomas, 158

Fitzhugh
  William, 131, 171
Fitzsimons
  Mary, 41
Fleming
  Robert, 183
Fletcher
  Charles, 180
  Nancy, 28
  Sarah, 28
  William, 28
Flicklinger
  John, 32
Flitter
  Sarah, 78
Floyd
  Sarah, 25, 34
Fohley
  John, 94
Foley
  B. W., 171
  Icy, 130
  Martha, 173
Follin
  Edward, 160
Forbes
  Samuel, 62
Foreman
  Peter, 25, 37
  Sarah, 127
Forg
  Francis, 8
Forgh
  Adam, 9
Forguson
  Abigail, 21
Fort
  Andrew, 58
  Polly, 58
Fortney
  George, 94
  Henry, 94
  John, 94
  Susan, 94, 151
Foster
  Edward, 103
  Isabel, 2
Fouch
  Abraham, 20

  Alice, 7
  Amos, 111, 123,
    135, 165, 176
  Ann, 47
  Daniel, 41
  Eden, 152
  Ellen, 176
  George, 40
  Hugh, 20
  Isaac, 29, 33, 36, 40,
    41, 123
  Jack, 20
  Jacob, 7, 20
  Jonathan, 20, 36, 41
  Mary, 20, 41, 152
  Nancy, 171
  Susanna, 111
  Susannah, 6
  Temple, 123
  Thomas, 33, 36, 41,
    52, 58, 111, 115,
    123, 134, 137
  Thompson, 86, 123,
    135
  William, 41, 123
Fouke
  Isaac, 149
Foutch
  Mary, 1
Foutt
  Elizabeth, 24
  Eve, 24
  Frederick, 24
  George, 24
  Hannah, 24
  Philip, 24
Fowk
  Isaac, 178
Fowke
  Isaac, 158
  Mary, 50
  William, 60
Fox
  Alfred, 72
  Amanda, 166, 175
  Amos, 31
  Ann, 15
  Anna, 98
  Bartleson, 41

  Betsey, 95
  Bushrod, 72
  Catheren, 45
  Cemelio, 93
  Cephus, 72, 123
  Delila, 123
  Elisha, 59
  Elizabeth, 14, 42, 72,
    73, 93, 95, 98
  Erasmus, 181
  Ezra, 135
  Frances, 95
  Francis, 72
  Gabriel, 15, 19, 61
  George, 98, 181, 184
  Grace Minton, 85
  James, 14, 23
  Joseph, 166, 175
  Malinda, 85
  Margaret, 135
  Mary, 45, 72, 73, 93,
    95, 123
  William, 10, 14, 15,
    19, 44, 45, 52, 72,
    74, 123
Foye. *See* Frye
Frame
  Anna, 149, 168
  David James, 168
  James, 149
Francis
  Enoch, 68, 185
  John, 132, 149
  Leannah, 164
  Thomas, 164
Frank
  Samuel, 84
Franks
  Samuel, 119
Frazer
  Catharine, 100
  Diana, 107
  Dinah, 100
  James, 19, 100
  Margaret, 100, 107
  Nancy, 100
Frazier
  Dian, 118
  Mary, 134

Frazier
 Samuel, 169
 Thomas, 173
Fred
 Burr, 175
 Eliza, 177
 Elizabeth, 133
 Frenk, 175
 Joseph, 59, 133, 147, 169, 170, 177
 Joshua, 59, 133, 169
 Mary, 133, 177
 Rebeckah, 59
 Sarah, 133
 Thomas, 59, 151, 153, 176
Fredd
 Joshua, 113
 Thomas, 156
Freeman
 Hezekiah, 35
 Mary, 35
French
 Ann, 98
 George, 59
 James, 11, 21, 98
 Lewis, 98, 107
 Margaret, 98
 Mason, 84, 98
 Reuben, 98
Frey
 Henry Joseph, 72, 81
 Joseph, 178
 Margaret, 178
 Philip, 91, 106
Frier
 Daniel, 10
 Hannah, 10
 James, 8, 10
 Pheby, 10
 Robert, 10, 22
Frits
 George, 72
Froman
 Hana, 121
Fry. See Fey
 Anna, 169
 Christina, 130
 Civilla, 130

Daniel, 130, 170
Dorothy, 130
Elizabeth, 169
Emily, 169
Enos, 169
Henry, 70, 130
Henry Joseph, 70
Isaac, 108
Jacob, 108
John, 87, 109, 117, 130
Joseph, 169
Joshua J., 166
Mary, 149, 169
Michael, 130, 169
Peter, 109
Philip, 130
Rebecca, 169
Susana, 169
Frye
 Christopher, 139, 159
 Daniel, 152
 Elizabeth, 58
 John, 58, 141
 Lewis, 58
 Margaret, 139, 159
 Philip, 87
 Terence, 58
Fryer
 Robert, 10
Fryor
 Robert, 12
Fulkerson
 Allice, 184
 Anna, 184
 Benjamin, 184
 Josia, 184
 Philip, 184
 Sarah, 184
 William, 184
Fullerton
 Humphrey, 180
 William, 180
Fulton
 David, 48, 144, 152
 Elisha, 152
 James, 48, 132
 Jane, 152

John, 65, 152
Leanah, 48
Mahlon, 105
Margaret, 132
Mary, 141, 152
Milly, 48
Richard, 152
Robert, 16, 48, 152
Sarah, 44
Susan, 132
Thomas, 94
William, 132, 141, 152, 160, 176
Furgeson
 Nancy, 131
Furman
 Elizabeth, 49
Furr
 Betsy, 163
 Desdemona, 170
 Edwin, 163
 Enoch, 163, 170
 Jeremiah, 163, 170
 Minor, 78
 Sarah, 163, 170
 Thompson, 114
 William, 162, 163, 170

—G—

Gabby
 Archibald, 180
 Emily, 180
 James, 180
 Joseph, 180
 William, 180
Gadis
 George, 182
Gallaher
 Feabey, 80
Gallaway
 Madison, 168
Galleher
 David, 42
 Mary, 132
 Sarah, 132
 William, 42, 169

Galliher
  Thomas, 114
Galloway
  Amos, 93
  Israel, 93
  Madison, 134, 163
  Nancy, 134, 163
  Polly, 93
  Sarah, 127
  Woodford, 127
Gamble
  John, 126
  Nancy, 126
Gante
  Daniel, 64
Gardner
  Arthur, 90
  Elender, 3
  Essers, 31
  Francis, 166
  Jeremiah, 64
  Joseph, 29, 72
  Mary, 10, 12
  Nancy, 119
  Sally, 166
Garner
  James, 137
  Mahlon, 93
Garret
  Archabald, 76
  Barton, 76
  Elizabeth, 76
Garrett
  Eliza, 147
  Enoch, 121
  Enos, 132
  John, 121
  Joseph, 121
  Mary, 121
  Nancy, 106
  Rebecca, 121
  Sarah, 82, 121
  Silas, 121, 148
  Stephen, 121, 154
Garrott
  Elisabeth, 134
  Erasmus, 139
  Sarah, 139

Gassaway
  Catharine, 171
  Charles, 130, 171
  Eliza, 171
  Henrietta, 130, 165
  John, 130
  Thomas, 130
Geen
  Narcissa, 85
Geesling
  Ann, 19
George
  Elizabeth, 70, 104
  Isaiah, 176
  Jesse, 83
  John, 70, 99, 104, 139, 151, 186
  Phebe, 175
  Thomas, 4, 6, 48
  William, 45, 48, 111
Gerberding
  C. O., 166
Gerrard
  Susannah, 56
Gess
  John, 3
Gheen. See Geen
  James, 57
Ghoram
  Margaret, 31
Gibbs
  Anne, 12
  James, 31, 84
  James Lewin, 23
  William, 12
Gibson
  A., 106, 148
  Abner, 98, 184
  Addison, 114
  Almeda, 114
  Amos, 78, 109, 111, 114, 123
  Ann, 114
  Aron, 34
  David, 80, 111
  Delila, 114
  Dinah, 34
  Ealse, 34
  Eliza, 165

  Elizabeth, 114
  Esther, 173
  George, 49, 171
  Heber, 109
  Isaac, 34
  James, 34, 114
  Jesse, 34
  John, 34, 78, 109, 122
  Jonathan, 34, 85
  Joseph, 34, 109, 150, 173, 177
  Joshua, 111, 165
  Judith, 165
  Juliet, 170
  Lemuel, 106
  Levi, 165, 170
  Lucinda, 114
  Lydia, 109
  Mary, 20, 92, 114
  Mayland, 165
  Miner, 177
  Miriam, 34
  Moses, 34, 109, 173
  Nancy, 114, 177
  Phebe, 122
  Rachel, 34, 59
  Ruth, 34, 114
  S. M., 161
  Samuel, 177
  Sarah, 162
  Selden, 170
  Solomon, 118
  Susannah, 34
  Thomas, 18, 34
  William, 124, 155, 162, 173
Gideon
  Catherine, 160
  George, 160
  Henry, 160
  Peter, 160
  William, 160
Gilbert
  Joseph, 24, 160
  Melvina, 160
  Sinai, 160
Gildea
  John, 150

Giles
  Sally, 71, 83
Gill
  Ann, 97
  Cornalas, 53
  Daniel, 97
  Elizabeth, 184
  George, 184
  James, 184
  John, 98, 158
  Levi, 97
  Uriah, 97
Gillespey
  Susan, 162
Gillmeyer
  Catharine, 101
  Elizabeth, 101
  Francis, 101
  George, 101
  Jacob, 101
  John, 101
  Joseph, 101
  Sarah, 101
  Taresa, 101
Gillmore
  Ann, 182
  Robert, 182
Gilmore
  William, 121
Gilpin
  Letitia, 158, 161
Gist
  Constant, 17
  Elizabeth, 42
  Henson, 17
  John, 17
  Mary, 17
  Nathaniel, 17, 45
  Sarah, 17
  Thomas, 17
  William, 17, 45
Glascock
  Catharine, 176
  Enoch, 84, 127
  John, 112
  Thomas, 140
Glasgow
  Catharine, 93
  Henry, 94

Glass
  Thomas, 121
Glasscock
  Daniel, 76
  Uree, 76
Gleasor
  Jacob, 52
Gochnauer
  Elizabeth, 160
  Harriet, 176
  Jacob, 160
  Joseph, 176
  William, 160
Goff
  James, 185
Goings
  Laura, 159
  Nelly, 159
Gold
  Ann, 43
  Joseph, 43
Goodhart
  Mary, 178
Goodin
  Amos, 8, 53
  Ann, 171, 182
  Anna, 171
  David, 8, 26, 53, 95, 182
  Elizabeth, 182
  Jean, 53
  John, 8, 53, 128, 182
  Kesiah, 8
  Kitty, 182
  Maria, 182
  Martha, 8, 53, 182
  Mary, 53
  Rachel, 182
  Rebekah, 8, 53
  Samuel, 8, 26, 53
  Sarah, 8, 53, 182
Gooding
  Anna, 30
Goodwin
  Maria, 125
  Thomas, 125
  William, 75
Gordon
  Mary, 34

Gore
  Amos, 129
  Ann, 29
  Anne, 33
  Betsey, 26
  Elizabeth, 33, 160, 173
  Enos, 122, 144
  Hannah, 33
  John, 60, 122
  Jonas, 129
  Jonathan, 26, 122
  Joseph, 35, 37, 38, 77, 126, 128, 134, 158, 161
  Joshua, 24, 26, 33, 52, 54, 69, 74, 77, 119, 122, 123, 126, 129
  Mark, 33, 160
  Nancy, 122
  Rachel, 122
  Sarah, 24, 33, 74, 122, 128, 144
  Solomon, 122, 126, 129
  Thomas, 26, 29, 33, 69, 75, 119, 122, 126, 128, 156, 161
  Tilghman, 140
  Truman, 108
  William, 77, 122, 126, 129
Gorham
  Ann, 11
  Harving, 11
  Lamken, 11
  Priscilla, 83
  Sanford, 11
  Thomas, 14
  William, 11
Gorr. *See* Gore
Gory
  Abel, 168
  Betsy, 168
Goteley
  Elizabeth, 3

Gourley
  Absalom, 95
  Grace, 95
  Hannah, 95
  Johnathan, 95
  Joseph, 95
  Susannah, 95
  Thomas, 95
  William, 95
Gouverneur
  Maria, 167
Gover
  Abinah, 86
  Albina, 100
  Ann, 86
  Anna, 100
  Anthony, 86, 100, 127
  Elizabeth, 78
  Hannah, 86, 100
  Henry, 175
  Jesse, 86, 100, 152, 157
  John, 152
  Mary, 78
  Miriam, 157
  Rachel, 86, 100
  Robert, 86, 100
  Samuel, 78, 86, 100, 152
  Sarah, 86
Grady
  E. B., 113
  Edward, 61, 93, 97, 98, 111, 146, 163
  Frank, 170
  James, 17, 46
  Susannah, 61
  Ury, 156
Graham
  George, 110
  John, 23, 26, 38
  Tamar, 160
Grant
  Esther, 69
  Mary, 53, 69
  William, 68

Gray
  Albert, 161
  Asher, 150, 161
  Daniel, 76
  Frances, 139
  Henrietta, 161
  Isabella, 161
  John, 150, 153, 161
  Rebecca, 161
  Robert, 161, 175
  Sally, 161
  Samuel, 57
  W. H., 161
  William, 139, 154, 174
Grayson
  Benjamin, 63, 76, 87, 139, 154, 167
  Elizabeth, 139
  George, 112, 139, 154
  John, 112, 183
  Mary, 139
  Nancy, 50, 87, 139
  Richard, 133, 139, 154, 167
  Robert, 64, 139
  Spence, 18
  William, 64, 139
Green
  Chloe, 105
  Cloe, 84
  Elizabeth, 85
  Euphemia, 173
  Fielding, 44
  Frances, 44
  George, 44
  Gerrard, 44
  James, 44
  John, 20, 44, 119
  Margaret, 67
  Nancy, 92
  Richard, 18
  Ruth, 2
  Thomas, 44, 114
  William, 44, 84, 105
Greenlease
  Catharine, 149, 150
  Charles, 149

Eliza, 150
George, 164
Hamilton, 150
James, 149
Lydia, 164
Mary, 164
Polly, 149
William, 150, 164
Greenlees
  James, 51
Greenup
  Charlotte, 126
  Christopher, 21, 22, 24, 126
  Lucetta, 126
  Wilson, 126
Greenwood
  Caleb, 9
Gregg
  Aaron, 59, 90
  Abner, 62, 99, 124
  Amos, 31, 59
  Amy, 31
  Anameraca, 181
  Aron, 115
  Betsey, 62
  Caleb, 62
  Dinah, 37
  Easther, 59
  Elisha, 39, 95, 150
  Elizabeth, 39, 141
  Esther, 65, 99
  five sons, 133
  George, 9, 31, 39, 90, 95, 115, 133, 150, 156, 165
  Gibson, 181
  Hannah, 39, 53, 78, 82, 122
  Harmon, 141
  Henry, 118, 141
  Isaac, 37, 41
  Israel, 50, 59
  Jacob, 49, 50
  Jesse, 118
  John, 27, 31, 37, 39, 43, 59, 62, 72, 82, 99, 122, 133, 171, 172

Gregg
  Joseph, 29, 37, 56, 65
  Joshua, 62, 99, 116, 123, 144
  Josiah, 37, 41
  Letty, 118
  Levi, 31, 37, 41
  Lydia, 74, 85, 124
  Mahlon, 62, 76
  Margaret, 77, 90
  Martha, 95
  Mary, 31, 37, 39, 65, 120, 124, 141, 150
  Nancy, 59, 141
  Naomi, 134
  Nathan, 43, 118, 135, 141, 167, 177
  Patty, 118
  Persillah, 59
  Phebe, 109, 133, 171
  Rebeckah, 29, 31, 50, 59
  Rebekah, 115
  Richard, 31, 59
  Ruth, 39, 65
  Sally, 141
  Samuel, 12, 31, 37, 43, 50, 59, 66, 115, 135, 141
  Sarah, 39, 41, 95, 115, 126, 129, 135, 141, 150, 161
  Smith, 141
  Stephen, 28, 41, 43, 62, 82, 118, 141, 171
  Susan, 135, 141
  Susanna, 20, 43, 62
  Susannah, 43
  Thomas, 37, 39, 41, 43, 50, 59, 62, 75, 82, 87, 118, 122, 135, 141, 150
  William, 39, 41, 59, 90, 115, 171, 172
Gregory
  Ann, 73
  Evelina, 73
  James, 73
  Louiza, 73
Griffith
  Ann, 15
  Charles, 4
  David, 13
  I. T., 157
  Israel, 69, 75, 148
  John, 24
  Mary, 10
  Nancy, 68, 69, 75
  Philip, 151
  Rebecca, 24, 179
  Richard, 48, 53, 69, 84
  Sarah, 10, 69, 75
  Thomas, 98
Grigg
  Martha, 26
Griggby
  Sarah, 129
Griggs
  George, 6
Grigsby
  James, 46
  Lewis, 82, 126
Grimes
  Edward, 4
  Nicholas, 4
  Philip, 4
  Samuel, 92
  William, 4
Gross
  Elizabeth, 176
  Henry, 75, 134
  John, 109
Grove
  Elizabeth, 3
  William, 3
Groves
  William, 7
Grubb
  Adam, 101, 130, 140
  Benjamin, 126, 129, 139, 161
  Catherine, 170
  Curtis, 139
  D., 133
  E., 138
  Ebenezer, 79, 124, 138, 158
  Edward, 161
  Elizabeth, 140, 170
  Harriet, 130
  Hester, 79
  Hetty, 141
  Jacob, 138
  James, 130, 140, 161
  John, 90, 101, 124, 129, 130, 132, 137, 138, 140, 152, 158, 161, 164, 176, 177
  Leah, 124
  Mary, 138, 140, 161
  Nancy, 138, 161
  Rachel, 161
  Richard, 161
  William, 59, 138, 140, 146, 158, 161, 170
Grymes
  Anna, 47
  Edward, 47
  Jain, 47
  John, 47, 53
  Nicholas, 47
  Sandford, 47
  Silvester, 47
  William, 47
Guay
  Mary, 114
Guider
  Charles, 120
  John, 120
  Katy, 120
  Sarah Ann, 120
Gulick
  Aaron, 69
  Ann, 173
  Elisha, 164
  Elizabeth, 69
  Fardinan, 69
  Ferdinando, 96
  Francis, 69, 96, 153
  George, 96, 140, 153
  John, 69
  Leannah, 96

Index to Loudoun County Wills, 1757 - 1850   217

Gulick
  Leanor, 69
  Ludwell, 134
  Martha, 153
  Moses, 34, 69, 86, 96
  Sanford, 153
  William, 128, 154
Gullatt
  Charles, 106
Gunn
  James, 55, 160
  Jane, 55
  John, 25, 55
Gunnell
  Elizabeth, 22
  George, 124
  H., 103
  Henry, 44, 92
  John, 19, 44
  William, 25
Gunnell:, 98
Gustine
  Elinor, 146
  Mary, 146
Guy. *See* Guay
Kesanders, 64
Kesiar, 64
Mary, 55, 64
Nancy, 55
Rhoda, 64
Sampson, 64
Samuel, 50, 64
Tase, 64

—H—

Haddocks
  John, 17
Hadducks
  Barbara, 49
Haden
  Barsheba, 27
  John, 27
Haeffner
  Catharine, 104
Hagarman
  Adrian, 48

Hagner
  Frances, 168
  R. H., 168
Hague
  Ann, 5, 20, 23
  Francis, 5, 20, 39
  Hannah, 20
  Hiram, 50
  Isaac, 5, 12, 20, 31, 39
  John, 5
  Jonah, 5
  Mary, 20
  Rebeckah, 20
  Samuel, 5, 20
  Sarah, 20
  Thomas, 20, 39, 126
Haines
  Mary, 163
  Simeon, 37
  Stacey, 38
Hains
  Daniel, 99
  Edward, 117
  George, 117
  Hannah, 117
  Hephzidah, 49
  John, 117
  Joseph, 117, 121
  Manley, 117
  Mary, 49, 99
  Sarah, 49
  Simeon, 24, 49
  Stacy, 49, 117
  Thomas, 49, 117
Halbert
  Ailsey, 43
  James, 43
  Katey, 43
  Lyddia, 43
  Michael, 43
  Rosanna, 32
  Rosey, 43
  Sally, 43
  Thomas, 43
  William, 43
Hale
  Elizabeth, 90
  George, 70

H. D., 145
  Peggy, 50
  William, 70, 90
Hall
  Amy, 18
  Ann Remey, 17
  Bety, 7
  David, 168
  Deliah, 104
  Edward, 115, 120
  Elizabeth, 151
  James, 3
  Jane, 25
  John, 2, 7
  Jonathan, 105
  Josiah, 87
  M., 94
  Mary, 18, 44, 72, 78, 104
  Samuel, 105
  Sarah, 105
  Thomas, 105
  William, 44, 52, 59, 104, 151
Hallar
  Peter, 23
Halley
  Barton, 96
  Catharine, 96
Halling
  Jemima, 29
  John, 29
  William, 29
Hallins
  Fanny, 138
Haman
  George, 9
Hamby
  John, 3
Hamerly
  Sally, 105
Hamilton
  Ann, 16, 20, 84, 100
  Betsey, 68
  C. B., 116, 137, 143, 144, 147, 166, 174, 182
  Caroline, 164
  Cassandra, 170, 181

Hamilton
  Charles, 84, 118,
    127, 135, 139
  Dewanner, 179
  E., 20
  E. G., 105, 136
  E. J., 175
  Elizabeth, 20, 84
  Erasmus, 156, 170,
    180, 181
  Hannah, 175
  Henry, 162
  James, 13, 16, 55,
    60, 62, 65, 102,
    139, 149, 164,
    170, 181, 182
  Jane, 13, 16, 84
  John, 13, 38, 57, 65,
    77, 79, 89, 99,
    109, 110, 113,
    121, 137, 139
  Landon, 175
  Mary, 13, 156
  Matthew, 181
  Nancy, 116, 139, 175
  Norval, 109
  Robert, 7, 16, 20, 64
  Sarah, 167
Hammat
  Edward, 82, 139
  George, 30, 82
  Giles, 82
  James, 82
  John, 82
  Polly, 82
  Samuel, 82
  Sarah, 82
  William, 82
Hammatt
  George, 16
Hammerly
  John, 82
Hammett
  Sarah, 47, 111
Hammon
  Ephraim, 11
Hammond
  Mildred, 52
  Thomas, 52

Hamon
  Adam, 134
Hampton
  Elizabeth, 3
  James, 145
  Jeremiah, 96
  Mary, 42
Hamrick
  James, 5
Hamton
  Elizabeth, 38
  James, 172
Hanby
  John, 4, 183
  Mary, 183
Hancock
  Alethea, 11
  Ebin, 164
  Edmoney, 164
  Elizabeth, 67, 184
  Fenton, 164
  G., 144, 158
  George, 134, 164
  Jane, 158
  Joel, 143
  Mary, 143, 144
  William, 143
Hancocke
  Mary, 19
  William, 1, 19
Hand
  William, 168
Handley
  Betsy, 176
  David, 176
  Harriet, 176
Hanes
  Rachel, 86
Hanks
  Elizabeth, 11
  John, 15
  Phebe, 132
  Ruth, 116
Hann
  David, 153
  Elizabeth, 153
  James, 153
  John, 93
  Mary, 153

  Matthias, 153
  Nancy, 93
Hanna
  John, 58
Hannah. *See* Hanne
Hanne
  John, 58
  Thomas, 58
Hanson
  Arryaner, 40
  Gustavus, 40
  Sarah, 40
Harber
  Aaron, 111
  Elizabeth, 111
Harbert
  Peggy, 106
Harbourt
  Peggy, 68
Harden
  Elihu, 39
  Elizabeth, 128
  Henry, 128
  Mary, 145
  Thomas, 10, 145
  William, 128
Harding
  Ann, 44, 54
  Betsey, 81
  Caty, 81
  Edward, 118, 158,
    164
  Elihu, 44, 183
  Elizabeth, 64, 158
  Frances, 64
  Garah, 125
  Henry, 64
  J., 70
  Job, 183
  John, 151
  Joseph, 64
  Lewis, 64
  Mary, 183
  Nancy, 81
  Pressley, 64
  Susannah, 81
  William, 39, 54, 64,
    135, 183

Index to Loudoun County Wills, 1757 - 1850

Hardy
  Hugh, 176
  Joshua, 42
Hare
  James, 109
  Jesse, 108
Harl
  Elizabeth, 44
  John, 11
  Leven, 25
Harlan
  Mary, 64
Harman
  Peter, 37
Harmon
  Susanna, 56
Harned
  Rosanna, 135
Harper
  John, 55
  Nicholas, 58
  Samuel, 141
  Thomas, 55
  Thurza, 158
  Walter, 60
  William, 12, 147
Harris
  Acey, 23
  Amos, 62
  Ann, 3
  Asa, 52
  Catherine, 32
  Daniel, 28
  David, 3
  Elizabeth, 14, 32, 96
  George, 113
  Henry, 16
  Isaac, 55, 63, 87, 102, 121, 151
  James, 121, 149, 151
  John, 13, 20, 67, 85, 96, 119, 183
  Joseph, 3
  Mary, 9, 23
  Peggy, 51
  Samuel, 3, 9, 23, 102, 151
  Sarah, 32, 113
  Thomas, 23

Harrison
  Alexander, 21, 76, 80
  Ann, 131
  Burr, 9, 115, 120, 126, 138, 139, 142, 152, 154
  Catherine, 43, 115
  Cecelia, 131
  Daniel, 131
  Eliza, 21
  Elizabeth, 130
  Frances, 130
  George, 50
  H. T., 131
  Henry, 115, 126, 158
  James, 126
  Jane, 131
  John, 20, 115, 126, 173, 176
  Kittey, 126
  M., 49, 185
  Margaret, 115, 126
  Maria, 114, 126
  Matthew, 43, 51
  Mrs., 110
  Peyton, 9
  Russell, 138
  Sarah, 115, 126, 148
  Thomas, 115, 126
  William, 138
Harriss
  Ann, 13
  Jacob, 13
Hart
  Thomas, 80
  William, 97
Hartman
  Catherine, 23
  Mathias, 23
Harven
  Ann, 86
Harvey
  Rebecca, 123
Harvy
  Elizabeth, 81
Hase
  Frederick, 92

Hatcher
  Catharine, 92
  Catherine, 56, 85, 123, 124
  Edith, 56, 85, 92, 124, 155
  Elijah, 122
  George, 20, 92
  Gurley, 123
  Hannah, 87, 118
  Isaac, 56, 85, 124, 155, 172
  James, 20, 40, 85, 92, 124, 155, 180
  Jane, 72, 173
  John, 20, 31, 92, 122, 128, 179, 183
  Jonah, 123, 144, 157
  Joseph, 85, 91, 97, 107, 123
  Joshua, 40, 183
  Louisa, 172
  Lydia, 172
  Mahlon, 97, 123
  Margery, 85
  Mary, 92, 172
  Miriam, 172
  Nancy, 157
  Noah, 122, 128, 183
  Phebe, 172
  Rachel, 122
  Rebecca, 85, 96, 114, 123
  Rebeckah, 91
  Rebekah, 56, 123
  Samuel, 85, 91, 92, 96, 110, 123
  Sarah, 116, 118, 128, 172, 183
  Thomas, 20, 85, 91, 92, 96, 110, 118, 122, 123, 142, 156, 157
  William, 20, 92, 97, 118, 123, 183
Hatfield
  Thomas, 4
Hatten
  Rosanna, 63

Hauge
  Isaac, 11
Haugue
  Francis, 16
Havener
  Alexander, 120
  Ann, 146
  Bassil, 176
  Dominick, 119
  Julyan, 146
  Rachel, 176
  Silas, 146
  Wady, 113
Havenner
  Barbary, 123
  John, 123
Havner
  Barbara, 120
  James, 141
  John, 120
  Joseph, 120, 141
  Marcy, 120
  Martha, 120
  Mary, 120
  Sarah, 120
Hawes
  Daniel, 154
Hawley
  Abram, 40
  Absolom, 58
  Barton, 86
  Catharine, 144
  Jeremiah, 145
  John, 40, 86
  Mary, 86
Hawling. *See* Halling
  Elizabeth, 134, 171
  Isaac, 115
  John, 3, 4, 29, 134, 171
  Mary, 134, 171
Hay
  Charles, 128
  Eliza Kortwright, 128
  Elizabeth, 167
  George, 128
Haynie
  Bridgar, 2

Hays
  Nancy, 33
  William, 33
Head
  George, 183
  John, 49, 50
  Mary, 86, 100
Headen
  Richd., 3
  Samuel, 30
Headman
  Mary, 58
Headon
  Jennie, 30
Heald
  Rachel, 102
Heath
  Andrew, 96, 103, 134, 144
  Charles, 144
  Diademia, 152
  Gustavus, 144
  Isaac, 49, 57, 96, 144
  John, 144
  Lydia, 96, 144
  Richard, 144
Heatherby
  Mary, 150
  Thomas, 150
Heaton
  Albert, 129, 148, 154
  Benjamin, 183
  Dr. James, 70
  James, 39, 55, 69, 94, 99, 109, 129, 148, 149, 150, 154, 162, 166
  Jane, 129, 148, 154
  John, 129, 145, 148, 154
  Jon, 113
  Jonathan, 70, 88, 99, 103, 118, 119
  Lydia, 55, 129, 148, 150
  Townsend, 145, 148, 149, 154
  Townshend, 129, 174

Heifren
  William, 128
Helleard
  James, 106
Helm
  Charles, 68
  Elizabeth, 63
  John, 68
  Mary, 68
  Meredith, 68
  Sarah, 68, 71
Henderson
  Alexander, 179
  Amy, 8, 98
  Annie, 152
  Archibald, 132
  Elizabeth, 179
  Fenton, 152
  Henry, 98
  Jane, 98
  Janet, 152
  John, 98, 179
  Lawson, 179
  Margaret, 152
  Mary, 152, 179
  Molly, 98
  Orra, 137, 152
  Richard, 75, 82, 110, 117, 130, 132, 136, 137, 143, 152, 180
  Robert, 152
  Samuel, 32, 97, 98
  Sarah, 152
  Thomas, 152
  William, 64, 98, 117, 152
Henings
  Hannah, 16
Henning
  Ignatious, 83
  Persiller, 83
  Thomas, 83
Henry
  America, 123
  Edward, 171
  James, 64
  John, 28
  Matilda, 57

Hepburn
  Margaret, 170
  Martha, 170
Herdy
  Leannah, 38
Hereford
  Alice, 151, 158
  Ann, 181
  Francis, 73
  John, 180
  M. A. B., 180
  Margaret, 148, 151, 180
  Mary, 180
  Theoderick, 151
  Thomas, 121, 151
  William, 162
Herring
  John, 16
Hervey
  Ann, 97
Heryford
  Elizabeth, 129
  Francis, 129
  James, 129
  John, 129
  Kitty, 129
  Peggy, 129
  Robert, 129
  Thomas, 129
  William, 129
Heskett
  Mary, 95
  William, 64
Heskit
  Henny, 168
Heslop
  Isabella, 110
Hess
  John, 183
Hesser
  Andrew, 67, 99, 133
  Betty, 67
  Cornelia, 99
  David, 99, 134
  Emiline, 99
  Hannah, 99
  John, 99
  Lucinda, 99

  Mary, 99, 131
  Nancy, 99
  Sarah, 99
Heth
  Andrew, 21
  Haner, 21
Hetherley
  Thomas, 61
Hetherly
  Thomas, 20
Hewatson
  Benjamin, 19, 28
Hewes
  John, 143
  Sarah, 84
Hews
  Edward, 4
Hibbs
  Amos, 108
  Jane, 99
  Nancy, 178
Hickes
  Rachel, 173
Hickman
  Henry, 115, 140
  Jane, 60
  John, 60, 100
  Joseph, 60
  Peter, 100
Hicks
  Charles, 144
  K. G., 180
  Kimble, 84
  Thomas, 68
Hide
  Philip, 35
Hieronimus
  Betsey, 60
Hiler
  Henry, 57
  Jane, 83
  Peggy, 57
  Sally, 57
  Sarah, 57
Hill
  Avelina, 110
  George, 70
  James, 64, 134
  Leithy, 110

  Mary, 168
  Nancy, 42
  Olivia, 145
Hillary
  Thomas, 130
Hilleary
  Tilghman, 139
Hilton
  Freeman, 125
Hines
  Catharine, 109
  Daniel, 109
  Elizabeth, 109
  Hester, 109
  Hugh, 135
  Linna, 109
  Mary, 109
  William, 109
Hinesling
  Dorothy, 104
  Elizabeth, 104
  Herman, 104
  Justis, 104
  Mary, 104
  William, 104
Hinksman
  Jane, 55
  Samuel, 25
Hirst
  Eli, 150, 166
  Heston, 166
  Jesse, 91, 166
  John, 32, 67
  Jonathan, 123, 150, 166, 171, 176, 177
  Mary, 32, 166
  Rebecca, 166
Hitch
  Thomas, 22
Hixon
  Andrew, 77
  Benjamin, 66, 77
  Betty, 153
  Catherine, 77, 125
  D., 151
  David, 66
  Eleanor, 182
  Elenor, 38
  Elijah, 77

Hixon
  Elizabeth, 66
  Elonar, 77
  Fleming, 153
  Flemon, 77, 89
  Jean, 77
  John, 77
  Margaret, 77, 89, 101
  Mary, 77, 125
  Noah, 77, 94, 125
  Rachel, 77
  Reuben, 50, 77
  Rheuben, 125
  Samuel, 77
  Sarah, 77
  Stephen, 77
  Stephenson, 94
  Timothy, 16, 50, 77, 89, 101
  William, 16, 66, 77
Hixson
  Benjamin, 165
  David, 165
  Eleanor, 64
  Flemon, 101
  Harriet, 162
  John, 165
  Ruth, 115
  Samuel, 64, 90, 115
  Tace, 112
  Timothy, 38, 64, 68
Hobbs
  Richard, 88
Hobson
  John, 90
Hockings
  Bridget, 167
  John, 167
  Joseph, 167
  Samuel, 167
Hodges
  Richard, 23
Hodgson
  Caroline, 177
  Sydney, 177
  William, 153
Hoe
  Alfred, 151

Hoff
  Joseph, 21
  Joshua, 140
  Silas, 140
Hoffman
  David, 156
  Eliza, 156
  Harriet, 156
  Henry, 151
  Jacob's, 156
  Jeremiah, 156
  John, 156
  Margaret, 151
  Mary, 106
  Peter, 153, 156
  Samuel, 156
Hogan
  Thomas, 3
Hoge
  Abner, 51
  Ann, 51
  David, 74
  Elizabeth, 123, 150
  George, 33
  Hannah, 136
  Isaac, 74, 123, 150
  James, 33, 91, 97, 123, 136, 144, 156
  Jesse, 74, 85, 122, 123, 124, 143
  John, 156
  Jonathan, 156
  Joshua, 74, 85, 123
  Lydia, 85
  Margary, 85
  Margery, 74
  Mary, 51, 56, 74, 85, 124, 156
  Morgan, 33
  Phebe, 123, 150
  Phila, 156
  Rachel, 123, 150
  Rebekah, 33
  Ruth, 62
  Samuel, 51, 156
  Sarah, 154
  Solomon, 20, 33, 56, 74

  Thomas, 144, 156, 163, 164, 176
  Washington, 156
  William, 33, 74, 85, 122, 123, 143, 154, 156
  Zebulon, 33
Hogen
  Thomas, 14
Hogens
  William, 17
Hogue
  Ann, 184
  Elizabeth, 34, 184
  Isaac, 35
  Jesse, 122
  Joseph, 115
  Morgan, 184
  Rachel, 173
  Sarah, 47
  William, 9, 114, 126, 143
Holding
  John, 60
Hole
  Ann, 66
  Levi, 44, 66
  Mary, 39
  Meriam, 72
  Ruth, 66
Holiday
  James, 77
Holland
  Eliener, 33
  J. B., 171
  John, 160
Holliday
  Urban, 103
Hollingsworth
  Amanda, 135
  Ann, 1
  Isaac, 1
  Jehu, 99
  John, 45, 138
  Jonah, 1
  Judith, 135
  Levi, 183
  Lydia, 1
  Phebe, 1

Index to Loudoun County Wills, 1757 - 1850

Hollingsworth
  Rachel, 1
  Unborn child, 1
Holloway
  Aaron, 107
Holmes
  Elijah, 157
  Elisha, 156
  Elizabeth, 147
  John, 15, 122, 156, 172
  Joshua, 15
  Lydia, 172
  Mary, 15
  Warner, 156
  William, 3, 15, 156
Holmns
  William, 14
Holms
  Deborah, 14
  Edward, 14
  Joseph, 14
  Joshua, 14
  Magret, 14
  Mary, 14
  Rachel, 14
  Sarah, 14
  William, 14
Holsman
  Christine, 128
Holtsman
  Margeret, 62
Homan
  Ann, 11
  Elizabeth, 47
  Hannah, 47
  Mark, 47
  Mary, 47
  Matthew, 47
  Ralph, 30
  Reuben, 47
Hon
  George, 166, 183
  John, 183
  Margaret, 166
Hooffman
  Phebe, 93
Hook
  Isaac, 31, 50

  John, 104
  Mary, 31
Hooper
  Ann, 168
  Dorcas, 104
  Mary, 104
Hooton
  Sarah, 27
Hope
  Christian, 56
  Massey, 129
Hopewell
  Ann, 15
  Hannah, 4
  John, 4
  Thomas, 4
Hophpoch
  Alice Mary, 19
  Cornelius, 19
Hopkins
  David, 76
  Gerard, 143
  James, 19
  Presly, 131
  Susannah, 76
Horseman
  Eaisas, 85
  Elender, 85
  Elizabeth, 85
  Esaias, 59, 85
  George, 85
  Helena, 26
  James, 85
  Joseph, 85
  Julia, 85
  Kitty, 85
  Sally, 85
  Stephen, 85
  William, 26, 75, 85
Hosholder
  Frederick, 100
Hoskins
  Margaret, 106
Hoskinson
  Andrew, 83, 114
  William, 107
Hospital
  Andrew, 57

Hossman
  James, 98
Hotton
  Thomas, 29
Hough. *See* Huff
  Amasa, 87, 93, 94, 95, 113
  Amos, 16, 45
  Ann, 107, 161
  Annie, 93
  Barnett, 32
  Benjamin, 87
  Bernard, 16, 146
  Edward, 107
  Eleanor, 13, 87
  Elizabeth, 86, 129, 167
  Fanny, 73
  Frances, 95
  Francis, 93
  Isaac, 65, 77, 161
  Jane, 94, 129
  Janny, 16
  Jefferson, 107
  John, 1, 5, 13, 16, 20, 45, 87, 94, 107, 172
  Jonah, 43, 45
  Joseph, 5, 16, 67, 86, 87
  Juliet, 107
  Mahlon, 45
  Mary, 28, 45, 80, 107, 154, 161
  Matlida, 95
  Nancy, 67, 87
  Peyton, 67, 86
  Philip, 177
  Rachel, 45
  Rebecca, 130
  Robert, 65, 102, 107
  Rosannah, 58
  S., 132
  Samuel, 24, 45, 86, 87, 93, 107, 119, 135, 154, 172
  Sarah, 16, 45, 107
  Thomas, 16, 86, 99

Washington, 67, 87, 95
William, 16, 41, 45, 53, 67, 86, 94, 109, 129, 130, 134, 156, 162, 164
Houghman
  Anthony, 19
  Charity, 19
Houghton
  Elijah, 42
Householder
  Adam, 28, 94, 162, 164, 169, 171
  Gideon, 162, 164, 169
  Julia, 164
Housely. *See* Owsley
Houser
  Abigail, 101
  Philip, 92, 114
Housholder
  Gideon, 140
Housley
  Ann, 79
  Moses, 79
  Points, 79
Howard
  Jacob, 135
  Mary, 90
Howel
  Hannah, 119
  Timothy, 14
Howell
  Abel, 182
  Abner, 9, 16, 182
  Andrew, 16
  Ann, 16, 39
  Benjamin, 16
  Daniel, 16
  Deborah, 39
  Elijah, 119
  Hannah, 102
  Hugh, 16
  Jesse, 182
  John, 16
  Lydda, 31
  Mahala, 156
  Mahlon, 39, 53

  Margret, 16
  Martha, 31
  Mary, 16, 53
  Phebe, 39
  Rachel, 16
  Rebecah, 53
  Reuben, 16
  Samuel, 39, 53, 102
  Thomas, 39
  Timothy, 39
  William, 16, 31, 182
Howes
  Mary, 110
Howman
  Elizabeth, 19
Howser
  John, 68
  Peggy, 68
Huddleston
  Izabel, 77
Huey
  Mary, 39
Huff
  Catharine, 97
  Elizabeth, 100, 109
  George, 88, 109
  Henry, 94, 100
  John, 8
  Phili, 182
  Philip, 177
Huffman
  Henry, 37
  John, 37, 60
  Margaret, 37
  Peter, 37
  Phebe, 163
  Phillip, 37
Huffty
  Benjamin, 47
Hughes
  Ann, 60
  Constantine, 40, 63
  Elias, 161
  Elisha, 103, 112
  Elizabeth, 12, 36
  Fanny, 141
  George, 159
  Isaac, 113
  John, 156

  Lezy, 60
  Margaret, 12
  Martha, 147, 157, 161
  Mary, 12
  Rachel, 12
  Ruth, 137
  Samuel, 103
  Theophilus, 60
  Thomas, 53, 103, 157, 161
  William, 158
Hughs
  Constantine, 54
  Isaac, 23
  Mathew, 112
  Thomas, 112
Hughy. *See* Huguley
Huguely
  James, 92
Huguley
  Abraham, 36
  Charles, 37, 46
  George, 37, 46
  Jacob, 37
  Job, 46
  John, 46
  Mary, 46
Hulls
  Elizabeth, 2
  Levan, 185
Humfrey
  Hen., 33
Hummer
  Eleanor, 120
  Francis, 120
  John, 120
  Livi, 120
  Michael, 60
  Nancy, 120
  Polly, 120
  Richard, 120
  Sarah, 120
  Washington, 120
  William, 120

Humphrey
 Abner, 28, 43, 53,
  61, 64, 76, 79,
  103, 111, 112,
  120, 134, 168
 Charles, 93, 103
 Jane, 53, 120
 Jesse, 103
 John, 28, 103, 111,
  112, 118, 120,
  131, 133
 Jonah, 103
 Joseph, 163
 Letty, 103
 Marcus, 103
 Margaret, 103
 Martha, 103
 Mary, 28, 31, 103,
  120, 134
 Morris, 103
 Phebe, 151
 Polly, 111
 Rachel, 103
 Sarah, 161
 Thomas, 28, 31, 33,
  43, 64, 72, 103,
  111, 112, 120,
  133, 134, 151,
  161, 162, 168, 169
 Urie, 103
 Ute, 103
 Willliam, 161
Humphries
 Samuel, 71, 88
 Susanna, 36, 39, 88
Hungerford
 William, 184
Hunt
 Eli, 117
 John, 107, 109
 Joseph, 109
 Major, 108
 Mary, 108, 129, 160
 Nancy, 121
 Sandy, 109
 Stephen, 22
 William, 21
Hunter
 John, 114

Nancy, 146
 William, 126
Huppoh
 Cornelius, 45
 Elsey, 45
 John, 45
 Peter, 45
Hurley
 Hannah, 21
Hurrford
 Francis, 73
Hurst
 Ann, 56
 Jemimah, 3
 Jesse, 109
 John, 14
 Thomas, 56
Huse. *See* Hughes
Hutchinson
 Isaac, 30
Hutchison
 Alexander, 143, 145,
  147, 174
 Beverly, 143, 144,
  162, 173
 Cynthiana, 142
 Elijah, 63
 Elizabeth, 30
 George, 30
 Hannah, 88
 Henry, 142, 162
 J., 147, 174
 James, 63, 143
 Jamimah, 134
 Jemima, 77
 Jer., 17, 39, 42, 49
 Jeremiah, 2, 7, 37,
  40, 45
 John, 40, 63, 143,
  144
 Joseph, 31, 55, 63,
  142
 Joshua, 46, 77
 Leah, 142
 Lemuel, 173
 Lewis, 86
 Lucinda, 143
 Lydia, 114
 Mary, 140, 142

Melvin, 143
 Nathan, 63, 88
 Peter, 24
 Reuben, 43, 63, 142
 Robert, 142
 Sampson, 63
 Sarah, 45
 Susanna, 142
 Thomas, 63, 164
 William, 63
Hutton
 John, 10
 Joseph, 10, 13
 Sarah, 10, 13
 Thomas, 10
Hychew
 Jacob, 15
 Mary, 15
 Nicholas, 15
 Sybel, 15
Hyde
 Elizabeth, 66
 Philip, 83
Hyler
 Michael, 19

—I—

Iden
 Eli, 162
 Randel, 162
 Samuel, 132, 162
 Sarah, 162
 Thomas, 162
Idon
 Catheron, 51
 Jacob, 51
 John, 51
 Samuel, 51
Iglehart
 Thomas, 174
Ingledue
 Ann, 93, 115
 Anne, 92
 Blackstone, 115
Inglidieu
 Margaret, 29

Inglish
  John, 65, 69
  Nancy, 69
Innes
  Alexander, 60
Inness
  Alexander, 184
  William, 184
Insle
  Henry, 2
  Mary, 2
  William, 2
Irey
  Jinilla, 124
  Samuel, 109
Irwin
  Elizabeth, 153
  Frances, 153
  James, 153
  Samuel, 94
Ish
  George, 151, 169
  Jacob, 65, 83, 151
  John, 151
  Lucinda, 151
  Mary, 151
  Robert, 151, 169, 170
  Susan, 169
  Susannah, 151
  William, 88, 161
  William King, 151
Israel
  Fielder, 117

—J—

Jack
  John, 24
  Nancy, 24
  Patrick, 24, 26
Jackson
  Abigil, 42
  Alexis, 1
  Alfred, 98
  Ann, 14, 42
  Asa, 141
  B., 168

  Benjamin, 72, 122, 134, 138, 140, 148
  Daniel, 27
  Ebenezer, 138
  Elizabeth, 72
  Ellen, 88
  Ephraim, 156
  Fanny, 113
  Farendo, 88
  Febe, 42
  Heneritta, 1
  Henry, 1
  James, 42
  Jane, 98
  John, 17, 42, 72, 75, 90, 101
  Lovell, 5
  Martha, 39, 42
  Mary, 42, 125, 130
  Monica, 178
  Polly, 135
  Richard, 42
  S. A., 142
  Samuel, 101
  Sarah, 42, 72, 98
  Stiles, 72
  Styles, 101
  Thomas, 14, 125
  William, 42, 125
Jacob
  Peter, 61
Jacobs
  Adam, 140
  Almira, 146
  Anne, 7
  Augustus, 146
  Caroline, 146
  Catharine, 115
  Cornelius, 146
  Elizabeth, 132, 146
  Emily, 146
  Ferdinand, 146
  Hyland, 171
  Jacob, 90
  John, 125, 171
  Lamuel, 171
  Lemuel, 146
  Matilda, 84
  Prestley, 146

  Roswell, 171
  Ryland, 171
  Sally, 84
  Thomas, 84, 179
  William, 115, 171
Jacoby
  Ann, 47
  Jacob, 47
James
  Aaron, 130
  Abel, 56
  Abigail, 130
  Anna, 119
  Anne, 33
  Benjamin, 60, 71, 130
  David, 75, 121, 130, 164
  Dean, 103, 130, 145, 151, 164
  Elias, 33, 119
  Elijah, 115, 142, 155
  Elizabeth, 130
  Ellwood, 146
  Hannah, 33
  Isaac, 33, 119
  Jacob, 42, 63
  James, 33, 119
  Jane, 121
  John, 130
  Joseph, 121
  Levi, 74, 77, 87
  Margaret, 43
  Mary, 130
  Moses, 56
  Richard, 174
  Robert, 178
  Sally, 164
  Sarah, 96, 144, 155, 174
  Smith, 134
  Susan, 130
  Susanna, 144
  Thomas, 33, 67, 99, 113, 119, 121
  William, 86, 96
Jameson
  Benjamin, 8
  John, 86

Index to Loudoun County Wills, 1757 - 1850 227

Jamison
  Robert, 13, 18
Janney
  Aaron, 120
  Abel, 1, 13, 14, 22,
    27, 34, 35, 39, 89,
    136
  Abijah, 76, 77, 87,
    107
  Alfred, 116
  Amos, 13, 14, 87,
    140
  Anna, 107
  Aquila, 29, 127
  Asa, 107, 159
  Blackstone, 29, 63,
    93, 110
  Bulah, 124
  Cosmelia, 14, 47, 78
  Daniel, 75, 107, 110,
    118, 122, 123,
    126, 133, 136,
    139, 149, 156,
    157, 163
  David, 63, 69, 107,
    183
  Eli, 36, 72, 93, 101,
    110, 137, 157,
    159, 164
  Elisha, 29, 136, 154,
    157, 176
  Eliza, 154
  Elizabeth, 38, 47,
    108, 116
  George, 136
  Grace, 87
  Hannah, 29, 38, 95,
    107
  Isaac, 36, 95
  Israel, 20, 22, 29, 37,
    38, 39, 40, 41, 43,
    63, 67, 77, 102,
    107
  Jacob, 14, 22, 24, 29,
    86, 120, 127, 168,
    171, 177
  James, 76, 107, 146,
    166, 175
  Jane, 20, 107
  Jesse, 36, 43, 76, 94
  John, 13, 27, 38, 39,
    87, 127, 150, 152,
    160, 161, 163, 177
  Jonas, 29, 50, 89, 93,
    124, 136, 154,
    158, 174
  Jonathan, 63, 75, 107
  Joseph, 1, 12, 13, 14,
    16, 20, 22, 27, 29,
    38, 39
  Lightfoot, 78
  Lott, 107
  Lydia, 93, 110, 154
  Mahlon, 5, 14, 22,
    29, 39, 41, 45, 47,
    50, 78, 97
  Maria Wilson, 172
  Mary, 5, 14, 38, 78,
    93, 102, 110, 127,
    159
  Moses, 29, 86, 124,
    149, 157
  Phineas, 107
  Pleasant, 107, 154
  Rachel, 13, 149
  Rebecca, 27, 38
  Rebeccah, 13
  Rebekah, 102
  Richard, 78, 107
  Ruth, 5, 13, 14, 136,
    154
  S. M., 171
  Samuel, 5, 13, 22,
    27, 107
  Sarah, 13, 27, 38, 78,
    86, 107, 124
  Sophia, 156
  Stacey, 36, 94
  Stephen, 113, 120,
    127
  Susanna, 38
  Thomas, 29, 39, 72,
    93
  Tomzin, 107
  William, 36, 95, 102,
    154
Janny
  Abel, 57
  Leatitia, 109
Jared
  John, 14
Jarvis
  Louisa, 147
  Washington, 134,
    142
Jeams
  Jesse, 134
  Margaret, 134
  Thomas, 134
Jeans
  Lydia, 80
Jefferson
  James, 184
  John, 183, 184
Jenings
  Edmund, 131
  James, 7, 19, 49, 158
  Nancy, 157
  Sarah, 157
  Seney, 131
Jenkin
  Isaac, 28
  Samuel, 58
Jenkins
  Alice, 47
  Alse, 110
  Amos, 25
  Athesias, 25
  Catharine, 101
  Charles, 44
  Conny, 29
  Daniel, 12
  Elijah, 109
  Elizabeth, 61, 71
  Henry, 61
  James, 11, 33
  Job, 100
  John, 44, 71, 93, 104
  Leanna, 71
  Margaret, 76
  Nancy, 33
  Priscilla, 29
  Reuben, 185
  Samuel, 109, 110
  Sarah, 101
  Simon, 104
  Stephen, 29

Jenkins
  Sylvanius, 25
  Sylvester, 44
  Thomas, 149
  William, 38, 44, 100,
    104, 120
Jenners
  Abiel, 72, 80, 99,
    102, 111, 116
  Deborah, 111
  William, 116
Jenning
  Mary, 1
  Rebeccah, 1
Jennings
  Alexander, 1
  Anna, 45
  Anne, 23
  Charles, 52
  Daniel, 23
  James, 23, 49, 52
  John, 149
  Laura, 149
  Owen, 23
  Sally, 149
  William, 149
Jett
  Catharine, 127
  Peter, 127, 164
Jewell
  Elisha, 38
  Jonathan, 26
Jinkins
  John, 12, 25
  Leana, 25
John
  Benjamin, 6
  Daniel, 6
  Dinah, 6
  Hannah, 6
  James, 5, 13
  John, 6
  Martha, 6
  Mary, 5, 6
  Sarah, 6
  Thomas, 6, 9
Johnson
  Amos, 91
  Arthur, 117
  Bayley, 7
  Caroline, 117
  Casper, 96, 102
  Charles, 117
  Eliza, 117
  Elizabeth, 117
  Evelina, 117
  George, 54
  James, 97, 115, 121
  Jeffrey, 2
  John, 7, 69, 75
  Joseph, 131, 139
  Martha, 96
  Mary, 7, 49
  Nancy, 75
  Patty, 69
  Peter, 165
  Rachel, 185
  Sarah, 69, 96
  Smith, 7
  Thomas, 117
  Tunes, 8
Johnston
  Archibald, 16
  Betty, 16
  Dennis, 16
  George, 16, 70
  Hugh, 70
  James, 70, 82, 111,
    120
  John, 70
  Margery, 70
  Peggy, 70
  Polly, 70
  Robert, 70
  Wilfrid, 16
  William, 44, 70
Joice
  George, 99
  Thomas, 107
Jolliffe
  William, 149
Jolly
  Hanna, 51
Jones
  Alford, 72
  Ann, 14, 50, 75, 88, 117
  Benjamin, 94, 110
  Edmund, 97
  Elizabeth, 3, 83
  George, 76
  Henry, 75, 88
  Horatio, 110
  Ignatius, 60, 63
  James, 10, 121
  Jane, 90
  John, 23, 83, 113,
    166, 169, 172
  Joseph, 23, 27, 64
  Joshua, 10
  Letitia, 105
  Martha, 23, 169
  Mary, 63, 105, 169
  Nancy, 88, 117
  Philip, 113
  Polly, 149
  Richard, 113
  Sarah, 53, 72, 113
  Stephen, 12
  Thomas, 53, 72, 113
  Thornton, 91
  William, 2, 4, 9, 10,
    23, 63, 83, 84,
    113, 174
Jonson
  Nancy, 103
Jordan
  Ann, 2, 83
  Catharine, 122
  Caty, 83
  George, 2
  John, 122
  Nancy, 137
  William, 83
Juray
  Abner, 60
  George, 60
  Jesse, 60
  Lewis, 60
  Mary, 60
  Rachel, 60
  Rees, 60
Jury
  Mary, 56

Index to Loudoun County Wills, 1757 - 1850   229

—K—

Kailer
  Barbara, 40
  Hannah, 40
Kalb
  Absalom, 126, 137
  Amanda, 126
  Elijah, 126, 137
  John, 91, 126
  Samuel, 126, 137
  Susanna, 137
  Susannah, 126
Karn
  Adam, 104
  Michael, 164
Karne
  Adam, 164
Kean
  Molly, 53
Keath
  Hannah, 128
  Joseph, 128
  Nancy, 128
  Price, 128
  Vincent, 128
Keen
  Ann, 15
  Elender, 17
  Elizabeth, 17
  Francis, 15
  George, 129
  James, 15
  John, 15
  Mary, 15, 17
  Nancy, 17
  Richard, 15
  Sarah, 15
Keene
  George, 63, 114
  John, 111
  Nancy, 114
  Newton, 123, 149
Kees
  Polly, 181
Keith
  Vincent, 107

Keller
  Gourley, 97
Kelley
  Edward, 65, 69
  Rebekah, 167
Kelly
  Edward, 82, 137, 185
  James, 185
  John, 35
  Joseph, 144
  Margret, 185
  Mary, 185
  Monica, 185
  Thomas, 1
Kelsie
  John, 11
Kemlar
  John, 37
  Sarah, 37
Kemp
  Daniel, 151
  Henry, 151
  Lewis, 151
  William, 151
Kendal
  Mercy, 117
Kennen
  James, 41
Kent
  Elizabeth, 71
  Elsinda, 168
  George, 168
  John, 43
  Joseph, 167
  Susannah, 43
  Thomas, 184
  William, 162
Kenworthy
  Isaac, 143
  Rebecca, 74, 143
  William, 29, 33, 123, 143
Kern
  Jacob, 60, 89
  Margaret, 166
Kerner
  Catharine, 130
Kerrick

  Anne, 164
  Phebe, 128
  Stephen, 87, 122, 123, 182, 183
  Thomas, 111, 128
Kevan
  William, 40
Kevens (Cavens)
  John, 6
Keys
  Robert, 90
Kid
  Sarah, 117
Kile
  George, 126, 127, 160
  John, 126
  Mary, 126
  Nicholas, 82
Kilgore
  George, 10, 17, 98, 184
  J. Mortimer, 157
  James, 157
Kilgour
  James, 175
  Louisa, 149
Kimbler. *See* Kemlar
Kincheloe
  Brandt, 118
  Hardwich, 118
  Hardwick, 165
  John, 118
  Mary, 165
  William, 118
Kindle
  Adam, 81
  Catherine, 81
  Sarah, 81
King
  Benjamin, 43
  Daniel, 43
  Edward, 73
  John, 4, 24, 25, 27, 34, 43, 185
  Mary, 25, 34, 77
  Osborn, 4, 25, 34, 185
  Osburn, 185

King
  Rebecca, 62
  Reuben, 185
  Sarah, 47
  Smith, 22, 25, 34, 185
  Tacey, 165
  William, 43, 153
Kirk
  Charles, 90
  Elizabeth, 83, 89
  James, 20, 21
  Josiah, 94
  Malcom, 83, 89
  Mareb, 90
  Merab, 83
  Phebe, 94
  William, 12
Kitchen
  Daniel, 32
  Margaret, 32
  Thompson, 32
  William, 32
Kitchin
  James, 26
Kitzmiller
  Archibald, 117, 135
  Elizabeth, 117
  Lydia, 117
  Martin, 117
  William, 117
Kline
  David, 142
  Elizabeth, 77, 142
  Jno. Nicholas, 142
  John, 85, 90, 142
  Lewis, 85
  Margaret, 78
  Mary, 85
  Nicholas, 142
Knight
  Priscilla, 101
  William, 120
Knott
  John, 122
  Julian, 122
  Sarah, 122
Knox
  Janet, 153
  Thomas, 153, 158, 164

—L—

Lacey
  Alexander, 51, 164
  Ann, 127
  Benjamin, 164
  Castilinia, 97
  David, 66, 97, 184
  Diadema, 97
  Elias, 46, 51, 65, 70, 75, 92, 110, 127, 164
  Elizabeth, 58
  Euphama, 51, 83
  Eyrphemia, 88
  Hulda, 83
  Huldah, 51, 145, 147, 174
  Israel, 46, 51, 57, 60, 68, 83, 92
  Joseph, 51, 78, 83
  Margarett, 86
  Mary, 164
  Matilda, 51, 83
  Meriah, 51
  Meshack, 174
  Mesheck, 51, 145, 147, 164
  Misheck, 92
  Naomi, 83, 145, 147, 174
  Niomy, 51
  Ruth, 51, 83, 145, 147, 174
  Sally, 69
  Sarah, 86, 93, 95, 97, 152
  Tacey, 51, 83, 88
  Thirza, 97
  Thomas, 86
  William, 69, 86
Lack
  William, 167
Lacock
  Jean, 21
  Nathan, 21

Lacy
  David, 66
  Elias, 50
  Mariah, 133
  Mary, 66
  Mesheck, 58
  Sally, 73
  Samuel, 66
  Sarah, 66
Lafaber
  Beckey, 68
  Fanne, 68
  Henry, 68
  Mary, 136
  Onnes, 68
  Rachel, 68
  Rosanna, 68
  Sookey, 68
  William, 68, 136
  Zilphy, 68
Lafaver
  Henry, 61
  William, 84, 92
Lafever
  Henry, 176
  John, 176
  Peter, 176
  Samuel, 176
  William, 176
Lake
  Elizabeth, 8
  John, 18
  Mary, 18
Lambag
  Rachel, 86
Lambaugh
  Thomas, 143
Lamborn
  Isaac, 113
Lambourn
  Hannah, 80
Lamm
  Ann Mary, 185
  Mary, 185
Lampart
  Fk., 38
Lane
  Aaron, 9, 36
  Anne, 9

Lane
  Carr, 9
  Catharine, 127
  Daniel, 30
  Delilah, 30
  Dewit, 127
  Enoch, 30
  Epaminondas, 127
  George, 30
  Hardage, 7, 9, 25, 36, 49, 97, 182
  Harvey, 97
  James, 3, 5, 9, 30, 36, 97, 184
  John, 30
  Joseph, 9
  Lydia, 36
  Mary, 30
  Presly, 30
  Presly Carr, 9
  Rebekah, 30
  Sally, 9, 18
  Sarah, 36, 55
  Susanna, 49
  William, 7, 9, 25, 30, 36, 39, 43, 49, 55
Lang
  Elizabeth, 153
  Peter, 39
Langley
  Alexander, 96
  John, 1
Langton
  Margaret, 117
Lanham
  Aaron, 42
  Amelia, 148
  Aquila, 42
  Bethania, 148
  Eleanor, 42
  Elizabeth, 42
  Hezekiah, 42
  Lethe, 42
  Mercy Ann, 42
  Walter, 42
  William, 170
  Zadock, 42
Lare
  John, 116

Larowe
  Isaac, 64, 82
Larrick
  Margaret, 50
Larrow
  Elizabeth, 75
Larrowe
  Isaac, 57
Lasley
  Rachel, 141
Latham
  John, 145
  Robert, 86
  Sarah, 175
Latimer
  Jacob, 85
  James, 156
  Sophia, 156
  Thomas, 100
  William, 92
Lauck
  Isaac, 173
Lawrason
  Alice, 21
  James, 21
Lawrence
  C. E., 180
  Emily, 153
  John, 180
  John E., 153
Lawson
  Randal, 184
  Thomas, 166
Lay
  Abraham, 25
  Emmanuel, 25
  George, 153
  Joseph, 25
  Marmaduke, 25
  Sarah, 4, 25
  Silvester, 4
  Stephen, 25, 47
  Sylvanus, 25, 26
Laycock
  James, 164
Layten
  Charlotte, 184
Leach
  Fielding, 174

Leachman
  George, 96
Lease
  Catherine, 40
  George, 40
  John, 40
Leath
  Elenor, 82
  Elizabeth, 82
  James, 82
  Jemimah, 82
  Joannah, 82
  Patsey, 82
  Peggy, 82
  Polly, 82
  Theodorick, 82
  William, 82
Lee
  Alexander, 116
  Alfred, 153
  Ann, 134
  Anna, 137
  Bowles, 180
  Cassius, 153
  Catherine, 134
  Charles, 153
  Daniel, 64
  Dr., 180
  Ed., 180
  Ellen, 180
  Emily, 154, 180
  Evelyn Byrd, 61
  Fanny, 68
  Flora, 153
  Francis Lightfoot, 68
  George, 61, 94, 127
  James, 64
  John, 64
  Joshua, 119
  Ludwell, 180
  Maria, 61
  Matthew, 119, 134, 158, 172
  Richard, 126, 137, 153
  Robert, 64
  Susan, 117
  Theodrick, 139
  Thomas, 61

Lee
  Thomas Ludwell, 52, 68
  William, 61
Leech
  George, 3
Legg
  Elijah, 71
  Hellen, 71
Leigh
  William, 114
Leith
  Betsey, 84
  James, 50, 84
  Mary, 50
  Patty, 84
  Peggy, 114
  Theo., 162
  Theodorck, 114
  Theodrick, 140, 147
  Wheatman, 50
  William, 50
Lemert
  Lewis, 22
Leonard
  Noble, 21
  Susannah, 76
Leslie
  Amanda, 99
  Benjamin, 99, 130, 147
  Caroline, 99
  John, 121, 129, 167
  Joseph, 99, 157
  Mary, 99
  Nancy, 99
  Samuel, 99, 130, 147, 157
  Thomas, 88, 99
Lessley
  Ann, 64
Lester
  Elizabeth, 157
  Hugh, 47
Letch
  Isaac, 14
  Jesse, 14
Levering
  Griffith, 21

Mary, 21
Septimus, 21
Thomas, 21
Lewellin
  Mary, 28
  Thomas, 5
Lewis
  Abraham, 55
  Ann, 10, 45
  Betty, 39
  Catharine, 116, 157, 165
  Catherine, 67, 71
  Charles, 40, 44, 45, 56, 59, 61, 62, 67, 71, 89, 92, 98, 100, 107, 114, 116, 118, 133, 134, 136, 143, 157, 165, 182
  Elizabeth, 71, 73, 116, 136
  Fisher, 157
  George, 6, 17, 26, 43, 45, 46, 67
  Hannah, 98
  Isaac, 55, 60
  Jacob, 55, 61
  James, 27, 45, 55, 61, 67, 71, 89, 92, 98, 116, 133, 134, 157
  Jane, 116
  Jesse, 26
  Joanna, 119
  Joel, 26, 28
  John, 7, 10, 15, 39, 45, 51, 73, 99, 116, 136, 140, 157
  Jonathan, 157, 165
  Joseph, 17, 30, 45, 55, 98, 136
  Keziah, 67
  Levi, 15
  Lewis, 67, 78, 134
  Martha, 116, 157
  Mary, 5, 67
  Nancy, 116, 157, 185
  Nathan, 18

Rachel, 67, 70
Rebecca, 39
Rebekah, 55
Samuel, 61
Sarah, 15, 49, 67, 185
Solomon, 18
Stephen, 18
Susan, 157
Susannah, 60, 99, 116
Thomas, 4, 5, 10, 11, 14, 33
Vilet, 17
Vincent, 45, 116, 157
Willam, 116
William, 10, 69, 88, 96, 98, 157
Lickey
  John, 146
  William, 121
Licky
  Conrod, 57
Lies
  Bartholeme, 18
  Catrean, 18
  Dorety, 18
  George, 18
  Hannah, 18
  John, 18
  Joseph, 18
Lifolett
  Jeremiah, 45
  Usual, 45
Likins
  James, 17
  William, 17
Lindsay
  Martha, 22
  Thomas, 22
Lindsey
  James, 56
Lingham
  Mary, 179
Linn
  James, 14
  William, 13

Index to Loudoun County Wills, 1757 - 1850

Linton
  Ann, 11, 42
  John, 7, 22, 23, 31,
    49, 92
Little
  R. H., 103
Littlejohn
  John, 36, 40, 47, 55,
    62, 71, 83, 84, 94,
    96, 184
  Monica, 20, 184
  Ruth, 158
Littler
  Sarah Ann, 108
Littleton
  Charles, 16
  Eli, 172
  Fielding, 155, 160,
    163
  Hannah, 116, 163
  Joel, 116
  John, 16, 71, 111,
    141, 163, 177
  Richard, 177
  Solomon, 47, 55, 71
  Thomas, 55, 90
  William, 1, 11, 16,
    38
Livingston
  Mary, 98
  Pleasant, 98
Lloyd
  George, 83, 98
  Joseph, 163
Locker
  Alexander, 92
  Eleanor, 92, 104
  George Lowry, 92
  Gerard, 109
  Mary, 92
  Thomas, 92
  Walter, 92
  William, 92
Lodge
  Abel, 79
  Abner, 120, 168
  Caterene, 79
  Christiana, 120
  Jacob, 79

  Jonathan, 79
  Joseph, 111, 120,
    168
  Jozabad, 16
  Jozabed, 79
  Laban, 120
  Nancy, 79
  Samuel, 120, 127,
    168
  Willam, 120
  William, 16, 79, 120,
    130, 147, 168
Logan
  Alfred, 173
  Alice, 173
  Samuel, 133, 173
  Sarah, 172
Loins
  Mary, 42
  Thomas, 42
Long
  Adam, 73
  Armistead, 58
  Barbara, 99
  Elizabeth, 52
  Jacob, 55
  James, 3
  Jane, 84
  Thomas, 3
Longbeam
  Benjamin, 170
Longley
  George, 93
  Joseph, 15
Lorentz
  Julia, 177
Losh
  Daniel, 58, 80
  Elizabeth, 58, 80
  Sebastian, 58
Losson
  Thomas, 11
Louthan
  Henry, 171
Love
  Augt., 99
  Augustine, 62, 80
  Cecelia, 153
  Eli, 91, 139, 147

  Elizabeth, 119
  Fenton, 166, 169
  Henry, 111
  James, 53, 112, 166,
    169
  Jane, 75, 98, 131,
    145
  John, 91, 119
  Leah, 107
  Lydia, 111
  Marah, 111
  Mary, 166, 169
  Nathan, 111
  Rebecca, 169
  Rebeckah, 111
  Samuel, 27, 30, 39,
    96
  Sarah, 91, 111, 119
  Susan, 166
  Susanna, 61
  Susannah, 169
  Thomas, 66, 81, 91,
    96, 107, 119
  William, 111
Lovely
  William, 113
Lovett
  Amanda, 174
  Ann, 126
  Christian, 128
  Daniel, 26, 128, 144
  David, 26, 174
  Edmund, 26, 129,
    144
  Elias, 26
  Elizabeth, 26
  James, 144
  Jonathan, 26, 29, 37,
    40, 45, 126, 160
  Joseph, 26, 53, 54,
    70, 144
  Joshua, 128
  Letisha, 26
  Lidia, 26
  Lucinda, 153
  Nancy, 37, 128
  Rachel, 128
  Sarah, 26

Lovett
  Tazewell, 174
  Thomas Alfred, 144
Low
  Elizabeth, 17
  John, 82
  Thomas, 82
Lowe
  Amanda, 174
  Amelia, 148, 154
  Edward, 154
  Landon, 174
  Mortimer, 174
  Samuel, 83
  Susannah, 174
  Tazewell, 174
Lowry
  Catharine, 64
  David, 64
  Frederick, 64
  Jacob, 64
  Lydia, 64
  Mariah, 64
  Martha, 101
  Mary, 64
  Sophiah, 64
  Thomas, 64
Loy
  Sophia, 99
Loyd
  David, 24
Lucas
  Alexander, 16
  Casander, 16
  Lindorus, 16, 64
  Ruth, 20
  Susannah, 38
Luck
  Jordan, 143
Luckett
  Alfred, 160
  Ann, 125
  Catharine, 75
  Charity, 3, 125
  Craven, 126
  David, 125, 160
  Eleanor, 125
  Elizabeth, 29, 40, 125
  F. W., 150, 169
  Francis, 70, 118, 119, 125, 126, 131, 132, 160, 171
  Henry, 160
  Horace, 160, 161
  John, 29, 36, 40, 125
  Juliett, 125
  Kelly, 125
  L-, 95
  Lawson, 29
  Lettice, 90, 98, 160
  Leven, 29, 70, 80, 90, 98, 125, 160
  Ludwell, 126, 160
  Luther, 125
  Matilda, 132, 160
  Molley, 26
  Molly Ann, 40
  Otho, 29
  Philip, 40
  Robert, 160, 161
  Samuel, 71, 80, 104, 125, 135, 147, 174, 178
  Sarah, 119, 132
  Susan, 126
  Susanna, 125
  Thomas, 125, 160
  Thomas Huxey, 29
  Virlinda, 125
  Vol, 29
  William, 3, 4, 125, 160
Lufborough
  James, 154, 167
  Nathan, 136
Luke
  Catharine, 156, 163
  Elizabeth, 41
  John, 163
  John Whalen, 163
Lumm
  John, 132
  Ruth, 128
Lunsford
  Lewis, 67
Luntz
  Jane, 169
  Lorenzo, 169
Lutsinger
  Michal, 16
  Philip, 16
  Rebecka, 16
  Sarah, 16
Lynch
  William, 170
Lyne. *See* Loins
  Mary, 77
  Robert, 77
  Sanford, 77, 86
  William, 77, 99
Lynham
  Phil., 2
Lynn
  Benson, 76
  Elizabeth, 80
  Fielding, 80
  James, 140
  John, 162
  Joseph, 162
  Luther, 162
  Maria, 162
  Mary, 11
  Michael, 159
  Pammelia, 162
  Sarah, 162
  Seymor, 162
  William, 162
Lyon
  Alexander, 112, 165
  Catharine, 165
  Jane, 112, 165
  Rebeckah, 165
Lyons
  James, 65, 168
  Peter, 166

—M—

Maccoy
  William, 1
MacDaniel
  George, 118
  John, 118
MacDanniel
  William, 68

Machlan
 Mary, 137
Mackall
 Benjamin, 35
Maclin. *See* McLin
Macrae
 Amelia, 154
Madison
 John, 126
 Rachiel, 132
Maffitt
 Sally, 110
Mageth
 John, 96
Magill
 Henry, 149, 152, 154, 167, 176
 Mary, 119
Maginnis
 Edward, 47, 115
 Jean, 47
Magruder
 George, 110
 Ninian, 42
 Peter, 110
Mains
 Archibald, 62, 66, 101, 117, 120, 133, 142
 John, 142
 Mary, 120
 William, 44, 58, 63, 120, 142
Major
 Daniel, 46
 Elijah, 46
 Elizabeth, 46
 James, 46
 Richard, 36, 45
 Sarah, 46
Majors
 Hannah, 151
Malin
 Elisha, 185
 Elizabeth, 185
Manamy
 Charles, 12
Mangold
 Valentine, 12, 13

Mankin
 Lewis, 158, 164
Manly
 John, 122
Mann
 John, 89, 102, 104, 182
Manning
 Euphemia, 97
 Nathaniel, 97
 Sally, 127
Marchant
 Mary, 141
Marcy
 Charles, 1
Mark
 John, 38
Marks
 Abel, 28, 31
 Anna, 63, 147
 David, 63
 Elisha, 8, 28, 31, 63, 67, 147
 George, 63, 72, 83, 98
 Isaak, 28
 Isaiah, 63
 John, 28, 31, 43, 63, 83
 Keziah, 139
 Kitty, 63
 Mahala, 98
 Mariah, 63
 Milly, 63
 Sarah, 63, 147
 Thomas, 28, 31, 34, 63, 139
 Uriah, 31
Marlow
 Edward, 100, 115
 George, 100, 115, 144, 158
 Henson, 115
 Thomas, 115, 141
Marlowe
 John, 179
Marmaduke
 Jesse, 70
 John, 70, 149

Olee, 70
Pressley, 70
Samson, 70
Silas, 70, 127, 149
William, 70
Marmion
 N., 131
Marsh
 James, 99
 Ruth, 99
Marshal
 James, 15
 Joseph, 5
 Rachel, 15
Marshall
 Benjamin, 170
 Frances, 53
 Jacob, 53
 James, 10, 17, 38
 John, 53, 119
 Joseph, 10, 38
 Margaret, 10
 Martha, 10
 Mary, 10
 Rachael, 10
 Racheal, 10
 Robert, 10
 Ruel, 144
 Samuel, 10, 15, 38
 Thomas, 53
 William, 38, 53, 88, 119
Martial
 Joseph, 10
Martin
 Ambrose, 48
 Andrew, 82
 Angelina, 159
 Ann, 48
 Betsey, 84
 Daniel, 48
 David, 73
 Edward, 82
 Elizabeth, 44, 82, 84, 159
 Elizabeth Murry, 159
 James, 16, 17, 19, 82, 121, 149, 159
 Jane, 48, 63

Martin
  John, 11, 54, 70, 82,
    183
  Joseph, 11, 159
  Margaret, 159
  Mary, 11, 48, 82,
    159
  Ralph, 11
  Robert, 82
  Sally, 131
  Sarah, 44, 84, 159
  Thomas, 11, 44
  Uphamma, 17
  William, 11, 16, 17,
    82, 98
Marye
  Elizabeth, 22
Mason
  Abraham, 45, 80
  Ann, 42, 66, 95
  Armistead, 80, 89,
    90, 92, 113, 169,
    179
  Armstead, 56
  Benjamin, 22, 23,
    31, 36, 39, 42
  Burgess, 42
  Catharine, 90
  Caty, 42
  Charlotte, 113, 169,
    179
  Elizabeth, 113, 179
  Emily, 90, 179
  Enoch, 123
  George, 22, 31, 42
  John, 42, 56, 80, 90,
    95, 113, 179
  Margaret, 22, 42
  Mary, 42, 56, 58, 80,
    95, 113, 179
  Richard, 80
  Sarah, 45, 80
  Stephen, 90, 179
  Stephens, 56
  Stevens, 113, 169,
    181
  Thomas, 125
  Thompson, 179

Thomson, 15, 80, 90,
  179
Westwood, 154, 181
William, 42, 113,
  138, 139, 154, 179
Masseh
  Mary, 100
Massey
  Lee, 2, 3, 9
  Lewis, 95
  Mary, 95
  Samuel, 48
Masterson
  Mary, 3
  Sarah, 12
Mateer
  James, 114
Matheny
  James, 21
Mathew
  John, 59
Mathews
  Hannah, 9
Mathias
  John, 122
Matthew
  Catherine, 124
  Hannah, 54
  Jesse, 54
  John, 54
  Jonathan, 54, 124
  Ley, 54
  Martha, 54
  Rachel, 54
  Simon, 54
  William, 54
Matthews
  Anne, 8
  Catherine, 163
  Christiana, 183
  Jesse, 163
  John, 163
  Jonathan, 163
  Mary, 163
  Rodney, 163
  Sarah, 163
  Simon, 163
  Thomas, 13
  William, 163

Matthias
  John, 83
Maulsby
  Benjamin, 147
May
  David, 133
  Elizabeth, 133
  John, 133
  Leander, 133
  William, 133
Mayhue
  Alexander, 39
  Izable, 39
  James, 39
  Moses, 39
McArter
  James, 138
  Johnathan, 114
  Jonathan, 138
  Mahlon, 138
  Mary, 138
  Moses, 138
  Rachel, 138
  Rebecca, 138
  Thomas, 138
  William, 138
McArtor
  Jonathan, 109
  Martha, 132
  Moses, 107, 109
McAtee
  Colmore, 59
McBride
  James, 59
McCabe
  Dr., 97
  George, 81, 82, 91,
    99, 112
  Henry, 21
  J. H., 109
  John, 82, 86, 88, 89,
    97, 101, 128
  Margaret, 143
  Mary, 97
  William, 39, 40
McCafferty
  Cattrehen, 18
  William, 18

Index to Loudoun County Wills, 1757 - 1850

McCamey
  Mary, 11
McCarty
  Billington, 125, 161
  Caroline, 125
  Charles, 75
  Daniel, 87
  Dennis, 16, 79, 125, 155
  Elizabeth, 174
  Emily, 113
  George, 79, 125, 170
  Henry, 132
  James, 46
  John, 1
  Jonathan, 44
  Mahala, 79
  Margaret, 125, 132, 161
  Mary, 79
  Peggy, 161
  Richard, 125, 170
  Sarah, 79
  Stephen, 170
  Thadues, 79
  William, 55, 79, 80, 87
  Winifred, 132
McCinley
  Elizabeth, 38
McClain
  Duncan, 30
  James, 52
McClean
  James, 34
McClelan
  Robert, 13
  Sarah Wilson, 13
  William, 13
McClusky
  Daniel, 65
  Rebecah, 65
  Reuben, 65
  William, 65
McConahue
  James, 18
  Jamie, 18
  Jane, 18
  John, 18
  Margaret, 18
  Mary, 18
  Samuel, 18
McConnekey
  Nancy, 91
McConneley
  Jane, 106
McCormack
  John, 62
McCormick
  James, 70
  John, 70, 71, 78, 83, 102, 108
  Martha, 70
  Mary, 108, 153, 180
  Nancy, 70
  Robert, 70
  Thomas, 108
McCowat
  Thomas, 78
McCowett
  Elizabeth, 105
McCrea
  Janey, 73
McCrony
  Sarah, 54
McCullah
  George, 76
  Jesse, 76
  Mary, 76
  Robert, 76
McCulloh
  Mary, 56
  Robert, 56
McCullough
  Clarissa, 156
  John, 156
  Mary, 156
  Susan, 156
  W. H., 146
McCutcher
  Samuel, 143
McDaniel
  Ann, 76
  Archibald, 76, 85, 109, 150
  Edward, 76
  Eleanor, 118
  Elizabeth, 174
  Fanny, 76
  James, 76, 85
  John, 118, 174
  Martin, 118
  Mary, 76
  Matilda, 76
  Nancy, 174
  Sarah, 76, 174
  Senior, 76
McDanniel
  Ann, 148
  Mary, 148
  Mason, 148
McDermot
  Stephen, 102
McDonaugh
  James, 153
McDowell
  Ann, 1
  Jean, 1
  Thomas, 1
McElroy
  Daniel, 31
  Rebekah, 31
McFadian
  Patrick, 64
McFarland
  Alfred, 151
  John, 18
McFarlin
  James, 61
  Nancy, 61
  Polly, 61
McFarling
  Elenor, 112
  James, 116
  Rachel, 134
  William, 134
McGarvick
  Israel, 162
  Polly, 162
McGaughen
  Philip, 170
McGavack
  James, 160
  Patrick, 160
  William, 160

McGeach
  Ann, 6
  Elizabeth, 6
  James, 6
  Jane, 6
  John, 6
  Joseph, 6
  Thomas, 6
  William, 6
McGeath
  Gabriel, 99
  James, 142
  Jane, 64
  John, 65, 102
  Josenah, 102
  Joshua, 64
  Polley, 64
  Thomas, 102
  William, 119
McGeth
  Betsina, 102
McGill
  Patrick, 104
McGirth
  Elizabeth, 83
McGrew
  Charles, 4
  Elizabeth, 4
  James, 4
  John, 4
  Robert, 4
McIlhaney
  Hanna, 11
  James, 11, 18, 25, 54, 59, 65, 138
  John, 11, 19, 69
  Rachel, 11
  Rosana, 11
  Thomas, 11
McIlhany
  Cecelia, 69
  Elizabeth, 69
  Hannah, 69, 73
  Harriott, 69
  James, 69, 141, 142, 149, 156, 157, 160, 175
  John, 73, 149
  Louisa, 69
  M., 159
  Mary, 69
  Mortimer, 69, 149
  Nancy, 69
  Rosanna, 69
  Taliaferro, 149
  Talliferro, 69
McIlheney
  John, 2
McIlroy
  Elizabeth, 152
McIntosh
  Thomas, 25
McIntyre
  Alexander, 16, 32
  Catherine, 32
  Charles, 32
  Christopher, 101
  Daniel, 32
  Elizabeth, 32
  Ellen, 176
  Jane, 32
  John, 32
  Lucy, 147, 176
  Mary, 101, 176
  Patrick, 32, 83, 101
  R., 147
  Robert, 32
  William, 32
McKamy
  James, 72
  John, 72
McKee
  Joseph, 13, 37
McKenna
  Anne Cecelia, 153
  J. L., 180
  James, 153
McKenny
  Jane, 70
McKim
  Agnes, 63
  Alexander, 37, 63
  Andrew, 63
  James, 37, 63, 86, 96
  Jeannet, 63
  John, 63
  Joseph, 63
  Patty, 162
  Reuhannah, 96, 102
  Robert, 63
  Samuel, 63
  William, 63, 102
McKimmie
  Elizabeth, 101
McKinley
  Daniel, 136
  Elizabeth, 115
  Hannah, 136
  Mary, 136
  Sarah, 46
  Willam, 46
McKinney
  George, 9, 49, 55, 121
  Joseph, 121
  Mary, 121
McKnight
  Benjamin, 76
  Charles, 80
  Deborah, 76
  Deliah, 76
  Eli, 76
  John, 76
  Margaret, 75, 146
  Nimrod, 76
  Peninna, 76
  Uriah, 76
  William, 76
McLaughlin
  Amos, 27
McLean
  Duncan, 33
  Mary, 33
McLin
  Mary, 162
McMachin
  Zilpah, 46
McMackin
  Alexander, 179
  Mary, 77
  William, 179
McManamy
  Ann, 73
  Catherine, 73
  Charles, 73
  Elizabeth, 73
  George, 73

Index to Loudoun County Wills, 1757 - 1850

McManamy
  Isabel, 73
  James, 73
  Jane, 73
  Margaret, 73
  Rebekah, 73
  Sarah, 73
  William, 73
McManimy
  Charles, 31
  Jane, 31
McMorris
  Sarah, 61
McMullan
  Alexander, 75
  Andrew, 75
  Archibald, 75
  Daniel, 75
  Elizabeth, 75
  Rachel, 75
  William, 75
McMullen
  Edith, 150
  George, 166
McMullin
  Andrew, 99
McNabb
  William, 126
McNathan
  James, 184
  Tabitha, 184
McNealidge
  James, 66
McNealy
  Sarah, 165
McNellage
  James, 121
  Nancy, 121
McPhersen
  Samuel, 66
McPherson
  Ann, 49
  Daniel, 49
  Isaac, 143
  James, 49
  Jesse, 49
  John, 49
  Joseph, 49
  Mary, 161

  Samuel, 62, 161
  Stephen, 49, 99
  William, 1, 49, 126
McTiney
  Francis, 72
McVay
  Margret, 91
  Patrick, 18, 19
McVeigh
  Eli, 128
  Elizabeth, 112
  Jesse, 51, 79, 106, 172
  Mary, 157
McVicker
  Ann, 69
  Esther, 69
  John, 69
Mead
  Ann, 24, 30, 72, 91
  Anne, 30
  Aquila, 129
  Aquilla, 72
  Asenath, 72
  Benjamin, 36, 40, 63, 72
  Christian, 24, 72
  Elizabeth, 91
  Ellen, 91
  Ellin, 24, 30
  Hannah, 91
  John, 72
  Joseph, 72, 91
  Lavina, 150
  Louisa, 72
  Manly, 155
  Margaret, 72, 125
  Martha, 91
  Mary, 36, 91, 155
  Phebe, 172
  Samuel, 63, 72
  Thomas, 91
  William, 2, 5, 24, 66, 91
Meade
  Sarah, 62
  William, 120
Megeach
  Anne, 2

  Elizabeth, 2
  James, 2
  Jane, 2
  John, 2
  Joseph, 2
  Mary, 2
  Thomas, 2
Megeath
  Alfred, 163
  Ann, 119
  Gabriel, 87, 163
  James, 13, 91, 151, 163
  Joseph, 158, 163, 181
  Martha, 163
  Samuel, 163, 164, 169
  William, 97
Mendenhall
  Hannah, 124
  J., 108, 116
  Jacob, 86
  Ruth, 102
Mercer
  Charles, 136, 179
  George, 168
  Henry, 79
  James, 168
  Jane, 149, 168
  John, 168, 179
  Joseph, 109
  Margaret, 168
  Mary, 149, 168
  Richard, 168
  Sophia, 168
  Thomas, 149, 168
  William, 168
  Wilson, 168
Mercer:, 149
Merchant
  Mary, 67
  Philip, 67
Meredith
  Elizabeth, 39
Merrick
  Patrick, 61
Merrill
  Ruth, 49

Merryman
  Mary, 155
Mershon
  James, 180
  Joseph, 46
  Thomas, 46
  William, 180
Metcalfe
  James, 7
  John, 7
Metthew
  Peter, 35
Metzger
  Jacob, 46
Meyer
  George, 38
  Mary, 38
Meyrick
  Griffith, 9
  Hannah, 9
  James, 9
  John, 9
Mgaha
  Benjamin, 61
Middleton
  Ann, 131
  Hannah, 5
  Jane, 5
  John, 44, 131
  Lettice, 5
  Letty, 49
  Mary, 44
  Matilda, 131
  Studley, 131
  William, 45, 123
Miers
  Phebe, 23
Milborn
  Ann, 68
  John, 68
Milbourn
  Emily, 156
  Gideon, 156
  Mary, 100
  Sarah, 100, 156
Milburn
  Elizabeth, 51
Miles
  Benjamin, 140, 159

Rhody, 78
Miley
  Benjamin, 130
  Catherine, 65
  Chrishannah, 65
  Chrisley, 65, 78
  Elizabeth, 65
  Jacob, 65
  John, 65, 130
  Nancey, 65
Milhollen
  Esther, 65
  Henry, 159
  John, 65
  Joseph, 65
  Patrick, 65, 69
Millan
  George, 164
  Hannah, 18
  Jane, 11
Milland
  Thomas, 27
Millard
  Jos., 4
Miller
  Aaron, 87
  Adam, 87
  Amy Ann, 152, 157
  Armistead, 173
  Catharine, 87
  Catherine, 6
  Christian, 13
  Daniel, 87
  Edgar, 157
  George, 61, 173
  Jacob, 87
  Jeremiah, 106
  Jesse, 87
  John, 5, 6, 27, 87, 173, 184
  Julian, 174
  Mahlon, 173
  Margaret, 102, 174
  Mary, 87, 101
  Mordecai, 157
  Moses, 87
  Peggy, 87
  Peter, 87
  Rachel, 125

Sinthy, 42
William, 87, 152, 157
Millholland
  Esther, 53
  Hetty, 53
  John, 53
  Jonathan, 53
  Mary, 53
  Patrick, 53
  Thomas, 53
Mills
  James, 137
  John, 82
  William, 104
Milner
  John, 48
Milton
  Alexander, 68, 157
  Ann Cecilia, 157
  Henry, 68
  John, 68, 69
  Peggy, 68
  Richard, 157
  Sarah, 68
Minear
  Jamima, 83
Miner
  John, 74
Mines
  John, 72, 78, 83, 110
  Martha, 148
Minnix
  Elijah, 115
Minor
  Daniel, 159
  Elizabeth, 38
  Frances, 20, 22
  Francis, 15
  George, 22
  John, 15, 20, 22, 38, 164
  Louisa Fairfax, 164
  Mary, 10
  Nancy, 93
  Nicholas, 22, 38
  Rebecca, 22, 93
  Rebekah, 93
  Robert, 159

Minor
  Spence, 22, 23, 99
  Steuart, 22
  T. J., 120
  Thomas, 22, 23, 93, 184
  William, 78
Mintur
  Duany, 173
Mitchel
  Elizabeth, 137
Mitchell
  George, 159
  Henry, 148
  Jane, 103
Mitinger
  Daniel, 18
  Jacob, 81
  Reynard, 18
  Rynart, 81
Mittinger
  Daniel, 15
Mobley
  Mary, 1, 6
  Samuel, 6
Mocaboy
  Emily, 91
Mock
  Elizabeth, 132
  George, 132
  Jacob, 132
  John Duval, 132
  Mary, 132
Moffet
  Margaret, 75
  Mary, 61
Moffett
  Benjamin, 36
  Charles, 59, 134
  David, 111
  Elenor, 134
  Elizabeth, 36, 136
  Frances, 110
  Harriet, 111
  Josiah, 27, 59, 61, 111
  Nancy, 36
  Robert, 36, 111, 162

Money
  Mary, 17
  Nicholas, 17, 26
  Racheal, 17
Monroe
  A. G., 90, 94
  Andrew, 64
  Elizabeth, 64
  George, 6
  James, 64
  Philis, 6
  Roseannah, 6
  Sarah, 6
  William, 132
Moore
  Abner, 108, 116
  Ann, 22, 108, 113
  Asa, 33, 39, 47, 48, 53, 61, 67, 68, 78, 87, 88, 100, 107, 108, 184
  Benjamin, 32, 34, 65
  Caleb, 108
  Cato, 130, 132
  Daniel, 101
  Francis, 44
  Hannah, 56, 89
  Henry, 65
  Jacob, 34, 41, 65
  James, 33, 39, 47, 48, 50, 52, 61, 68, 69, 74, 78, 84, 86, 88, 89, 94, 108, 110, 116, 184
  Jeremiah, 21, 22, 30
  John, 32, 33, 65, 101, 102, 108, 148, 164
  Joseph, 65
  Laura, 176
  Leary, 134
  Margaret, 132
  Mary, 108, 116
  Mason, 163
  Nancy, 56
  Peggy, 65
  Peter, 60, 113
  Peyton, 131
  Rebeckah, 116

  Sally, 65
  Samuel, 65, 99, 134
  Susan, 163
  Thomas, 19, 33, 108, 132
  William, 6
Morallee
  Thomas, 117, 120, 122
Moran
  Catharine, 112
  Edward, 112
  Elizabeth, 112, 165
  Gustavus, 112
  John, 73, 100, 112, 165, 171
  Mary, 73
  Richard, 112
  Samuel, 112
  Sarah, 112
  William, 112
More
  Ann, 49
  Cloe, 42
  James, 52
Morehane
  Joseph, 20, 23
Moreland
  Samuel, 169
  Sarah, 169
Moren
  Daniel, 7
  James, 7
  John, 7
  Joseph, 7
  Katy, 7
  Molly, 7
  Nancy, 7
  Peggy, 7
  Prudence, 7
Morewine
  Andrew, 68
Morgan
  Eleanor, 124
  Eliza, 108, 157
  J., 85
  Jane, 141, 167
  John, 89
  Reuben, 71

Morison
  Jane, 65
Morrallee
  John, 125
  Michael, 125
  Sarah, 170
  Thomas, 125
Morris
  Benjamin, 3
  Ede, 103
  John, 30, 182
  Mahlon, 124, 160
  Nancy, 30
  Rebecka, 3
  Samuel, 3
Morrison
  Archibald, 117
  Benjamin, 117, 141
  Charity, 117
  Edward, 117, 121, 141
  Elizabeth, 117, 141
  James, 117, 141
  Jane, 117, 141
  John, 117, 141
  Joseph, 117, 141
  Mary, 117
  Rachel, 117
  Sary, 117
Mortimer
  Bethlehem, 19
  Infamous, 19
  Sarah, 19
  William, 19
Moss
  Alfred, 159
  Carter, 110
  Elizabeth, 5, 110
  Frances, 5, 13
  Gideon, 25
  Hannah, 5
  John, 5, 8, 10, 12, 17, 20, 22, 45, 110, 160
  Milia, 52
  Robert, 110
  Spencer Aris, 23
  Thomas, 5, 37, 52, 110, 159
  William, 5, 13
Mote
  Anna, 65
Mott
  Armistead, 117, 175
  M. E., 117
  Mary, 117
  Randolph, 117
  Thomas, 106, 110, 117
Moul
  Catharine, 57
  Daniel, 57
  George, 57, 135
  Mary, 57
  Peggy, 57
  Philip, 57
  Susannah, 57
Mount
  Charity, 69, 96
  Ezekiel, 80
  John, 83, 169
  Mary, 155
  Stephen, 155
  Thomas, 143
Moxley
  Daniel, 24
  Jack, 37
  John, 59
  Joseph, 37
  Margaret, 37
  Samuel, 37
  Sary, 59
  William, 37
Moyer. *See* Meyer
Mudd
  John, 50, 87
  Patty, 87
  Walter, 87
Muir
  George, 17
  James, 17
  Jeremiah, 17
  John, 17
  Phebe, 17
  Robert, 10, 17
  Samuel, 17
Mull
  David, 41, 74, 99, 182
  George, 41, 74
  John, 41, 74
  Madlain, 41
  Margaret, 41
  Rachel, 41
Mullen
  Daniel, 96
Mullikin
  Ann, 90
  Nancy, 90
  William, 90
Murch
  Adam, 70
Murdock
  James, 32
Murpha
  Martha, 13
Murphy
  John, 90
  Michael, 26
Murray
  Catharine, 51
  E. C., 161
  Elizabeth, 174
  Samuel, 20, 24, 114
Murrey
  Catharine, 97
  Samuel, 16, 36, 87, 179, 183, 184
Murry
  Betsey, 102
  Elizabeth, 131
  John, 81
  Josiah, 180
  Samuel, 102
  Sarah, 102
Murshite
  Martha, 185
Muse
  Betsey, 94
  Edward, 94
  John, 174
  Mary, 112, 173
  Nancy, 94
  Robert, 94
  Thomas, 94, 141

Musgrove
  Emy, 21
  Gilbert, 46
Myers
  Abigail, 127
  Amelia, 112
  Andrew, 28
  Ann, 51
  Anne, 162
  Delilah, 127
  Elijah, 33, 110, 164
  Elizabeth, 112
  Hannah, 149
  Isaiah, 33
  Israel, 110
  Jacob, 127
  Jonathan, 31, 33, 52, 110
  Lambert, 52, 127
  Mahlon, 110, 162
  Mary, 23, 33, 110, 112, 127
  Sally, 52
  Sarah, 52
  Washington, 127
  William, 52, 110, 127, 160
Myre
  Jacob, 40
Myres
  Elijah, 89
  Lambert, 74
  Mary, 89
  Sally, 74
  Sarah, 74
  William, 74

—N—

Nalls
  Carr Bailey, 145, 163
Nasmith
  Margaret, 82
  Robert, 82
Natt
  Jonathan, 64
Naulton
  Catharine, 129

Neal
  Kitty, 23
  Penny, 37
  Rodham, 37
Neale
  Lettitia, 71
  Richard, 32
  Robert, 19
  Signey, 85
  Thomas, 22
  W. S., 65, 69, 89, 90, 95, 96
  William, 73, 75
Near
  John, 66
  Matilda, 126
Neece
  Devault, 52
  Gertrout, 52
Neer
  Elizabeth, 140
  George, 140
  Hannah, 131
  James, 140
  Jesse, 176
  John, 140
  Josiah, 140
  Mahaly, 140
  Matilda, 137
  Samuel, 176
  Susana, 140
Neifus
  Margaret, 54
Neilson
  William, 21, 25, 26
Nepper
  Margaret, 16
Neptune
  George, 111
  John, 19
  Ruth, 19
  Sarah, 19
Nesmith
  John, 173
Nessmith
  John, 136
  Susan, 136
Nettle
  William, 167, 173

Newell
  Sarah, 28
Newhouse
  David, 95
  Hannah, 95
  Mary, 66
Newill
  John, 29
  Margott, 28
  Rachel, 28
  Sibbel, 28
  Susanna, 28
  William, 28
Newlon
  Charles, 162
  Hannah, 153
  James, 61
  Nimrod, 168
  Polly, 168
  Rachel, 168
  Richard, 153
Newman
  Elizabeth, 35
  Frances, 180
  George, 35
  Jesse, 144
  Joseph, 35
  Nathan, 144
  Richard, 35
  Robert, 180
Newport
  Jonah, 176
  Rachel, 176
Newton
  Augustus, 147
  Frances, 147
  John, 137, 179
  Joseph, 101, 147
  Mary, 147
  Nancy, 83
  Nelly, 147
  Ruth, 79
  William, 147, 170
Nicholls
  James, 21
  Samuel, 97
Nichols
  Albert, 119
  Amer, 122

Nichols
  Amos, 102
  Ann, 74, 119, 155
  Betsy, 89
  Catharine, 174
  Charity, 90, 114, 163
  Daniel, 102
  Eli, 102
  Elizabeth, 155
  George, 119
  Hannah, 50, 122
  Harriett, 119
  Henry, 102
  Herod, 90
  Isaac, 19, 56, 76, 89,
    93, 96, 102, 114,
    118, 122, 123,
    133, 156, 171, 172
  Isach, 111
  Isaiah, 91
  Jacob, 114, 124, 155
  James, 54, 155
  Joel, 146
  John, 119, 155
  Jonah, 111, 112,
    155, 169, 171, 174
  Joseph, 133, 148,
    172
  Joshua, 133, 155,
    171, 172
  Lydia, 89, 114
  Margaret, 114, 119
  Margery, 85, 124,
    155
  Mariam, 171
  Martha, 119
  Mary, 74, 93, 114,
    119, 171, 173
  Massey, 119
  Nathan, 119, 179,
    182
  Phanny, 169
  Phebe, 114, 122,
    155, 163
  Rebecca, 102, 114,
    124, 155
  Rebeckah, 19, 109
  Samuel, 76, 96, 114,
    123, 124, 125,
    126, 155
  Sarah, 119
  Sevithen, 163
  Swethe, 114
  Swithen, 155
  Swithin, 124
  Thomas, 89, 99, 102,
    124, 129, 134,
    146, 154, 164,
    169, 172, 175
  William, 95, 114,
    119, 124, 155,
    163, 164, 172
Nicklin
  John, 46, 56
  Sarah, 45
Nickolls
  James, 27
Nickols
  Abraham, 146
  Ann, 33, 34
  Charity, 34
  George, 35, 44, 54
  Henry, 39, 40
  Isaac, 40, 56, 85, 109
  Isaiah, 34
  James, 33, 34, 35
  Jane, 146
  Lydia, 56
  Margary, 85
  Margery, 56
  Mary, 34, 109
  Nathan, 34, 35, 44,
    54, 146
  Rebecca, 85
  Rebekah, 34
  Samuel, 56, 85
  Sarah, 56
  Solomon, 34
  Susanna, 40
  William, 56, 85, 109
Nicols
  Elizabeth, 59
  Vallentine, 59
Night
  John, 55
  Mary, 55
Nisewanner
  John, 140
Niswanger
  Christian, 131
  Christopher, 65
Nitson
  Israel, 44
Nixon
  Ann, 54
  Asbury, 152
  George, 6, 35, 51,
    52, 164
  Hannah, 51
  James, 11, 116, 129
  Joanner, 52
  Joel, 73, 105, 109,
    121, 144, 151,
    152, 164, 165
  John, 51, 116, 160,
    164
  Jonah, 52, 164
  Mary, 52, 115, 116
  Nancy, 52, 89
  Rebekah, 51
  Ruth, 52
  Samuel, 116
  William, 75, 116
Noble
  Catharine, 148
  Dorothy, 148
  Elisa, 148
  Franklin, 148
  George, 148
  John, 148
  Nancy, 148
  Patsy, 148
  Peter, 148
  Sarah, 148
  Thomas, 148
  Warren, 148
  William, 148
Noding
  John, 17
  Sarah, 1
  W., 1
Noland
  Ann, 148
  Awbry, 40
  Betsy, 75

Index to Loudoun County Wills, 1757 - 1850 245

Noland
 Burr, 131, 145, 148, 163
 Catherine, 145, 148
 Dade, 75, 98
 Eleanor, 75
 Elizabeth, 131, 162, 163
 Ellen, 145
 Eneas, 26
 Francis, 75
 George, 140
 Jane, 145
 Lloyd, 75, 131, 145, 162
 Louisa, 131, 145
 Mary, 26, 98
 Nancy, 26
 Peyton, 131
 Philip, 26, 40
 Pierce, 82
 Richard, 131, 145, 148, 162
 Samuel, 75, 98, 131
 Sarah, 26
 Thomas, 26, 40, 75, 131, 136, 145, 148
 William, 74, 75, 98
Norris
 Harriet, 173
 Ignatius, 96
 Sarah, 22
Northan
 Elizabeth, 158
Norton
 Barbara, 97
 Benedict, 97
 Carolina, 97
 Edward, 1
 Elvira, 97
 Franklin, 97
 Hamilton, 97
 Hiram, 97
 Mahala, 97
 Metildia, 97
 Nathaniel, 97, 160
Norwood
 Mary, 116

Nutt
 Joseph, 93
Nutton
 Mary, 38
Nyswanger
 Catharine, 178
 Christian, 140, 149, 178
 Emily, 178
 Harriet, 178
 Henry, 178
 Jacob, 178
 James, 178
 John, 178
 Mary, 178
 Samuel, 178

—O—

O'Neal
 Ferdinando, 4
O'Mehundro
 Ann, 3
O'Neal. *See* O'Neil
 Thomas, 162
O'Neil
 Daniel, 98
 John, 98
Oatyer
 John, 136
 Peter, 136
Obrien
 Nancy, 132
Oden
 Hezekiah, 56
 James, 148, 160
 Mary, 173
 Nathaniel, 99, 134, 148, 160, 170, 173, 177
 Richard, 49
 Thomas, 37, 57, 61
Offutt
 Elizabeth, 160
 Hambleton, 120
 O., 159
 Thomas, 160
 Thornton, 131
 William, 20, 23, 39

Ogden
 Elizabeth, 99
Ogdon
 Andrew, 142
 Benjamin, 142
 Hezekiah, 142
 Nancy, 142
 Robert, 142
 William, 142
Ogelvee
 Betsey, 70
Oldaker
 Elizabeth, 28
 Henry, 28
 John, 28
Oldham
 Cyrus, 103
 Eleanor, 103
Oliham
 John, 45
Oliver
 Peter, 8
Oneal
 Margaret, 184
Oram
 Hiram, 150
 Mary, 73
Orem
 Armsistead, 140
 Enos, 140
 Henry, 140
 Jane, 140
 Lucinda, 140
 Massie, 140
 Sarah, 140
Orendorf
 Martha, 54
Orison
 Martha, 57
Orr
 Alexander, 77
 John, 11, 18, 22, 30, 77
 Susannah, 77
 William Grayson, 77
Orrison
 Ananias, 158, 160
 Jonah, 167

Osborn
　Benjamin, 21
　Craven, 64
　Hannah, 64
　Joshua, 64
　Nicholas, 12, 24, 43
　Reany, 21
　William, 36, 64
Osborne
　Abner, 28, 55
　Anthony, 57
　Mary, 55
　Nicholas, 55
　Patience, 55
　William, 26, 55
Osbourn
　John, 29
　Richard, 29
　Samuel, 29
　Sarah, 29
　William, 29
Osburn
　Abner, 26, 30, 33, 50, 174, 178
　Addison, 161, 175
　Alfred, 110
　Anna, 177
　Balaam, 132, 142, 146, 158
　Betsy, 166
　Bushrod, 177
　Craven, 99, 109, 113, 166, 174
　Hannah, 18
　Hector, 166, 175
　Herod, 166, 170, 175
　Joel, 149
　John, 177
　Jonah, 163
　Joshua, 109, 118, 119, 128, 138, 146, 148, 165, 170, 175
　Landon, 175
　Lydia, 30
　Mary, 30, 103, 142, 146
　Morris, 119
　Mortimore, 127
　Nicholas, 30, 103
　Norval, 166, 170, 175
　Patience, 150
　Phineas, 146
　Richard, 18, 148, 177
　Sally, 175
　Sarah, 166
　Tarlton, 177
　Thomas, 166
　Thompson, 175
　Turner, 109
　William, 33, 175
Osburne
　Ann, 179
　Craven, 88
　Heaton, 88
　Herod, 88
　Joshua, 88
　Landon, 88
　Norvel, 88
　Phineas, 145
　Turner, 88
　William, 25
Ott
　Nicholas, 9
Ouldaker
　Abraham, 28
　Eleanor, 28
　Enor, 28
　Henry, 28
　Isaac, 28
　Jacob, 28
　John, 28
　William, 28
Overfelt
　Benjamin, 17
Overfield
　Anna, 131
　Benjamin, 185
　Elizabeth, 46
　Hutson, 46
　John, 185
　Martin, 46, 185
　Mary, 60, 185
　Nancy, 46
　Peter, 52, 185
　Samuel, 185
　Susannah, 15
Owens
　James, 147
　John, 1, 45
　Mary, 14
　Thomas, 14
Owsley
　Ann, 80
　Moses, 80
　Thomas, 10
　William, 1
Oxley
　Aaron, 71
　Amey, 71
　Ann, 16
　Brittain, 16
　Clear, 16
　Enoch, 71
　Evrett, 103
　Francis, 71
　Henry, 10, 16, 19, 71
　Jane, 71
　Jenkin, 47
　Jeremiah, 19
　Jesse, 16, 19
　Joel, 19
　John, 19, 71
　Lewis, 71
　Mary, 19, 71
　Rachel, 16, 19
　Scintha, 71

—P—

Padgett
　Alfred, 170
Pagit
　Amy, 42
　Bayley, 134
　Frances, 42
　Francis, 42
　James, 134
　Jane, 42
　Mary, 134
　Rubin, 42
　Ruth, 42
　Timothy, 42, 63, 96, 134

Pain
  Jonathan, 54
  Nancy, 144
Painter
  Guluhnah, 76
Pairpoint
  Ann, 89
  Elizabeth, 89
  Esther, 89
Palmer
  Abel, 14, 35
  Ann, 78
  Benjamin, 145
  Cornelius, 54
  David, 14
  Edith, 145
  Elijah, 122
  Elisbeth, 14
  Elizabeth, 35, 145, 163
  Harriet, 147
  Israel, 145
  John, 14, 54
  Jonathan, 14, 21, 54
  Lidy, 21
  Priscilla, 14, 145
  Rachel, 145
  Samuel, 14, 145
  Thomas, 82
  W. C., 161
  William, 59, 82, 151, 175
Pancoast
  Ame, 66
  Ann, 56
  Elizabeth, 66
  Hannah, 66
  Israel, 66
  John, 56, 61, 82, 85, 114, 124, 180
  Joseph, 66
  Joshua, 56, 85, 114, 124, 180
  Lydia, 56, 114, 124, 180
  Priscillah, 66
  Ruth, 56, 114, 124
  Sarah, 33
  Simeon, 66
Parker
  Eliza, 45
  Hannah, 149
  Parker, 93
  Sally, 93
Parkinson
  Henrietta, 92
  William, 92
Parmer
  William, 128
Parrott
  John, 38, 40, 52
Parsons
  Jefferson, 113
  Lucy, 113
  Mary, 127
  Solomon, 127
  Ubricka, 113
Passmore
  Andrew, 94
  Benjamin, 94
  Ellis, 94
  George, 94
  John, 94
  Ruth, 94
  Sarah, 94
  William, 94
Paterson
  Janney, 21
  John, 162
Patten
  Elizabeth, 16
  John, 17
  Mary, 169
  William, 21
Patterson
  Eleanor, 84
  Elijah, 84
  Fleming, 7
  Flemon, 89
  James, 162
  Joseph, 55
  Margaret, 48
  Neil, 6
  Robert, 25
  Samuel, 9
Paul
  Edward, 45
  James, 17
  Sarah, 167
Paxon
  Amos, 61
  Elizabeth, 61
  James, 61
  John, 119
  Joseph, 61
  Nancy, 99
  Samuel, 119
  Sarah, 61
  William, 61
Paxson
  David, 169
  Elijah, 110
  Eliza, 152
  George, 169
  Griffith, 169
  Jacob, 169
  Jane, 152, 169
  Samuel, 169, 177
  Thompson, 152
  William, 75, 169
Paxton
  Sarah, 14
Payne
  Abigail, 26
  Anne, 36
  Catharina, 54
  Edmond, 82
  Edward, 27
  Elizabeth, 183
  George, 47
  Jane, 52
  John, 80
  Mary, 62
  Nancy, 144
  Sanford, 4, 26
Peacock
  Ann, 96
  Benjamin, 96
  Elijah, 158
  Hezekiah, 96
  John, 96
  Mary, 59
  Nancy, 130
  Samuel, 72, 96
  Sarah, 109
  Susannah, 96
  William, 96, 158

Peake
  Humphrey, 77
  John, 6
Pearl
  William, 32
Pearle
  Sarah, 42
Pearre
  Sally, 117
Pearson
  Christian, 5
Peck
  Asa, 147
Peckner
  Peter, 24
Peebles
  Emily, 180
Peers
  Ann, 118, 120
  Eleanor, 105, 137
  Henry, 105
  Mrs., 118
Pegg
  Catherine, 59
  Daniel, 59
  Elias, 59
  Isaac, 59
  Joseph, 59
  Nathaniel, 59
  Samuel, 59
  William, 59
Peirce
  Susannah, 170
Peirpoint
  Sam, 64
Penquite
  Ester, 48
  Jain, 48
  John, 48
  Kesiah, 127
Perdue
  Miriam, 172
Perfect
  Catharine, 36
  Christopher, 36
  Erasmus, 47
  Harriett, 83
  Jane, 36, 83
  John, 83
  Robert, 34, 36, 47, 83
  William, 83
Perril
  Charity, 8
Perry
  Benjamin, 109, 127
  Elizabeth, 12
  Mildred, 170
  Samuel, 127
  Verlinda, 127
  William, 63
Person
  Samuel, 6
Peter
  Ann, 110
  Betsy, 110
  Harriet, 110
  Mary, 110
Pettit
  Isaac, 8
  John, 8
  Margaret, 8
Pettitt
  Nancy, 170
Peugh
  Abel Marks, 138
  David, 93
  Elisha, 138
  Jonah, 138
  Leonidus, 138
  Margaret Elizabeth, 138
  Mary, 93, 138
  Rebecca, 138
  Samuel, 63, 93, 138
  Spencer, 93
  Susana, 138
  Uree, 63
  William, 93
Peyton
  Ann, 15, 21, 90, 182
  Anne, 7
  Betsy, 160
  Chandler, 41
  Craven, 7, 15, 21, 29
  Cravin, 15
  Elizabeth, 50
  Ellen, 126
  Frances, 70
  Francis, 7, 15, 21, 32, 65, 66, 70, 90
  Henry, 3
  Margaret, 7, 15, 21
  Mary, 126
  Richard, 70
  Townsend, 90
  Valentine, 15, 21, 30
  William, 7, 15, 21
Phelps
  Eli, 64
  Elisha, 64, 156
  Lucy, 64
  Mary, 156
  Polly, 64
Philips
  Benjamin, 34
  Charity, 34
  Edmond, 3
  Israel, 34
  Nancey, 34
  Nicholas, 9
  Sarah, 34
Phillips
  Asael, 20
  B., 20
  Benjamin, 20, 27, 28
  Cathrone, 5
  David, 38
  Elizabeth, 66
  Hannah, 17, 60
  Hester, 27, 28
  Hume, 20
  Israel, 27, 44
  Jenkin, 4, 17, 20, 27
  Jenkins, 5
  Joana, 4
  John, 4, 20, 27
  Mary, 5, 66, 67
  Milford, 4
  Nancy, 27
  Rachel, 152, 157
  Rhode, 20
  Samuel, 20, 28
  Sarah, 20, 27, 28, 64, 67

Phillips
  Thomas, 4, 5, 7, 27,
    44, 61, 65, 68, 69,
    78, 86, 89, 97,
    100, 101, 107,
    108, 116, 126,
    152, 157, 183, 184
  William, 66
Pickett
  William, 7
Pickins
  Robert, 75
Pidgeon
  Milly, 167
Pierce
  Eales, 60
  Elese, 17
Pierpoint
  Ann, 97
  Eli, 91, 119, 127,
    139, 147
  Esther, 33
  Obed, 49, 89
  Samuel, 91, 119, 141
Pigg
  Nathaniel, 8
Piggott
  Burr, 168
  Ebenezer, 80
  Isaac, 110, 168
  Jesse, 168
  John, 80
  Mary, 85, 168
  Nathan, 80
  Phebe, 80
  William, 80, 95, 109,
    114, 168
Pike
  Jonathan, 31, 183
Pilcher
  Edward, 43
  Moses, 43
  Sarah, 43
Pinkstone
  Athaliah, 14
  Frances, 14
  Henry, 14
Pitters
  Abraham, 15

Pitts
  Martha, 3
Plackney
  Sarah, 1
Plaster
  David, 167
  George, 167
  Henry, 137
  James, 83
  Jane, 83
  Mary, 167
  Michael, 137, 167
  Susanna, 83
Plummer
  Ursla, 86
Poland. *See* Polin
Polin
  Nathaniel, 59
  William, 59
Poling
  John, 8
  Peter, 8
  Samuel, 8, 61
Poll
  Elizabeth, 93
  Mildred, 93
  Sarah, 93
Polton
  John, 21
Pool
  Ann, 12, 35
  Benjamin, 12, 36
  Daniel, 23
  Dorothy, 23
  Elisath, 12
  Elizabeth, 23, 36, 57
  Frances Elliot, 23
  Hannah, 12, 36
  Israel, 12, 35
  Joseph, 12, 35
  Martha, 12, 36
  Mary, 12, 36
  Peggy, 135
  Rebecca, 12
  Rebekah, 35
  Sarah, 12, 36
  Thomas, 23
Poole
  Jane, 39

Poor
  J. H., 156
Pope
  John, 126
  Mary, 126
Popkin
  Catharine, 15
Popkins
  Craven, 125, 128
  John, 31
Porter
  Ann Murphy, 9
  Daniel, 9, 68
  Demsey, 9
  Edward, 2, 9
  Elias, 9, 68
  Ellender, 9
  James, 17
  Jesse, 154, 173
  John, 9, 68
  Mary, 2, 9, 14, 68
  William, 9
Poston
  Elija, 16
  Elizabeth, 58, 78
  Francis, 16
  James, 58
  Joseph, 58
  Leonard, 58, 78, 163
  Samuel, 16
  Sarah, 16
  Wilse, 78
  Wilsey, 58
Potten
  Henry, 15, 19
Pottenfield
  Adam, 91
  Catharine, 91
  Elizabeth, 91
  Henry, 91
  Jacob, 91
  Leah, 91
  Mary, 91
  Samuel, 91
Potter
  Ebenezer, 83
  Elizabeth, 83, 148,
    179
  John, 83

Potter
  Lucy, 83
  Mary, 83, 179
Potterfield
  Adam, 143
  Daniel, 104, 139
  Elizabeth, 90, 129, 143
  Jacob, 81, 90
  Mary, 143
  Samuel, 143
Potts
  Ann, 5, 153
  David, 5, 6, 22
  Edward, 6, 99, 166
  Elizabeth, 6, 24, 30, 53, 122
  Enos, 124
  Ezekiel, 4, 5, 22, 25, 30, 54, 138
  Hannah, 6
  Isaiah, 124
  Jane, 53
  John, 5, 72, 166
  Jonas, 1, 3, 5, 61, 71, 89
  Jonathan, 5, 6
  Joseph, 90
  Joshua, 124
  Lydia, 122
  Mary, 3, 5
  Nathan, 5, 24, 25, 29, 53, 54
  Rachel, 5
  Samuel, 3, 5, 6, 53
  Susanah, 5
Poulsen
  Jasper, 36
Poulson
  Isabel, 134
  Mary, 134
  Susanna, 134
Poultney
  Anthony, 1
  Elenor, 1
  John, 1
  Mary, 1
  Sarah, 1
  Susannah, 86
Poulton
  John, 34
  Martha, 34
Powell
  Albert, 109
  Alexander, 74
  Alfred, 74, 117
  Ann, 34, 50
  Betsy, 77
  Betty, 50
  Burr, 51, 73, 74, 79, 91, 98, 106, 117, 120, 148
  C. H., 117
  Catherin, 168
  Catherine, 148
  Charles, 116, 174
  Cuthbert, 74, 116, 148, 174
  Elen, 97
  Elisha, 44
  Emily, 74
  F. W., 163
  Fethy, 97
  Francis, 148
  G. Cuthbert, 160
  George, 148, 163, 175
  Gertrude, 163
  H. B., 132, 161, 171
  Hopwell, 45
  Humphrey, 145, 163, 175
  Humprhrey, 148
  John, 44, 74, 116, 156, 174, 176, 180
  Leven, 8, 16, 41, 48, 74
  Lucy, 154
  Maria, 74
  Marietta, 175
  Mary, 116
  Nancy, 93
  Peyton, 121, 140
  Robert, 44
  Sally, 74
  Sarah, 74, 119, 168
  Thomas, 74
  Virginia, 162
  W. A., 136, 139
  William, 26, 34, 42, 44, 56, 63, 74, 93, 116, 120, 131, 137, 147, 148, 163, 168
Power
  Joseph, 23, 41
  Robert, 176
  Sarah, 41
  Walter, 41, 119
Preeht
  Magdalen, 55
Presgraves
  Ann, 143
  Catherine, 71
  Elizabeth, 71
  George, 71
  John, 71, 143
  Lydia, 143
  Milly, 143
  Nancy, 71, 143
  Richard, 71, 143
  William, 71, 143
Preston
  John, 32
Pretsill
  Charity, 185
  Fredrick, 184
  Isaac, 184, 185
  John, 184
Price
  Benjamin, 57
  Evan, 8
  John, 8
  Jonathan, 6, 8, 18
  Mary, 8
  Matilda Rebecca, 179
  Oliver, 8, 15
  S. H., 177
  Samuel, 166, 177
  Sarah, 8, 9, 18, 57, 179
  Susannah, 36
  Thomas, 36
Priest
  Eleanor, 15, 19
  Samuel, 39

Index to Loudoun County Wills, 1757 - 1850

Prince
  Levy, 53
Pritchet
  Rachell, 1
Prosser
  Margaret, 151
  Mary, 169
Pryor
  William, 166
Pugh
  David, 183
  Mary, 183
  Samuel, 183
  Sarah, 183
Pullen
  Asher, 69
  Charles, 46
  Elizabeth, 32
Puller
  Mary, 100
Pullin
  Asher, 46
  Robert, 46
  William, 46
Purcel
  James, 162
  Joseph, 81
  Rachel, 169
Purcell
  Eleanor, 170
  Elizabeth, 170
  George, 170
  Jane, 170
  Mary, 170
  Samuel, 142
  Sarah, 125
  Thomas, 170
  V. V., 139
  Valentine, 118
Purdum
  Benjamin, 10, 28, 35, 41, 42, 53, 80
  Jeremiah, 10, 32, 37, 41, 50, 80
  John, 80
Pursel
  Bernard, 122, 174, 175
  Edwin, 122, 175
  Elizabeth, 29
  Enos, 122, 151, 175
  Hannah, 122, 175
  Harrison, 142
  Hector, 122, 175
  Jane, 122
  John, 111, 122, 123
  Jonah, 122, 142, 175
  Mahlon, 122, 175
  Margaret, 122, 175
  Maria, 142
  Samuel, 56, 61, 122, 174, 175
  Sarah, 29
  Volney, 142
Pursell
  Enos, 138
  Samuel, 138
Pursley
  Jonah, 135
  Maria, 135
Pursly
  Benjamin, 19
  Christan, 18
  Daniel, 19
  Deborah, 18
  Elizabeth, 18
  Henry, 19
  John, 19
  Larence, 19
  Mary, 19
  Samuel, 19
  Thomas, 18, 19
Pusey
  Joshua, 116, 154
  Mary, 116
Pyott
  Amos, 31
  John, 31
  Mary, 45

—Q—

Queen
  Abner, 63
  Elijah, 63
  Elizabeth, 63
  John, 63
  Jonah, 37, 63
  Martha, 63
  Mary, 63
  Zilpha, 63
Quick
  Gasper, 16

—R—

Race
  Elizabeth, 89
  Joab, 22
  Job, 89
Radford
  Thomas, 101
Raecner
  Susannah, 66
Ralls
  Charles, 55
  George, 55
  Jenny, 55
  John Damey, 55
Ramey
  Elizabeth, 167
  Jacob, 123, 167
  Jane, 167
  John, 31
  Lydia, 123, 167
  Nancy, 167
  Sanford, 84, 123, 141, 160, 167, 174
  William, 31
Ramy
  Sandford, 31
Rand
  Ruth, 99
Randall
  A., 168
  H. K., 168
Randle
  Jonas, 36
Rasor
  Barbery, 73
  Catherine, 73
  Christianor, 73
  David, 73
  George, 73
  Hannah, 73
  Jacob, 73
  John, 73, 100

Rasor
  Molly, 73
  Philip, 73
  Susana, 100
Ratcliffe
  Cassy, 117
Rathie
  Benjamin, 175
  Elizabeth, 137
  John, 137
Ratican
  James, 15, 19, 31, 48
  Rachel, 8
Ratluff
  Lucinda, 158
Rawlings
  Sally, 91
  Thomas, 109
  William, 152, 181
Razor
  Jacob, 104
Read
  Andrew, 2
  Ann, 2
  Barbary, 2
  Eleanor, 39
  Elizabeth, 2
  Frances, 2
  Jacob, 8
  John, 2
  Joseph, 2
  Lettice, 2
  Reuben, 2
  Ruth, 2
  Sarah, 38
  Thadeus, 2
  William, 2
Reade
  John, 27
  Reuben, 27
  William, 27
Reasnor
  Leonard, 66
Reasonor. *See* Raecner
Records
  Joseph, 23
Rector
  Harry, 26
  Peggy, 181

Redd
  Elizabeth, 72
Redman
  Agnes, 77
  Andrew, 46
  John, 41, 46
  Mary, 46
Redmond
  Andrew, 3, 70, 130
  Ann, 3, 71
  Benjamin, 70
  Elizabeth, 3
  George, 3
  Hannah, 70
  Hariot, 70
  Israel, 70
  John, 3, 70
  Margaret, 3
  Mary, 3, 130
  Nancy, 70, 130
  Sarah, 3
  Stephen, 70
  William, 3
Reece
  David, 56, 95, 106,
    112, 122, 134,
    159, 165, 169, 170
  Esther, 56
  Lewis, 56
  Polly, 56
Reed
  Andrew, 34
  Ann Grigsby, 46
  Cornelius, 34
  Elizabeth, 34, 36
  Eunus, 34
  Hannah, 108
  James, 67
  John, 46, 118
  Jonathan, 8, 34
  Joseph, 131
  Lewis, 46
  Ludwell Grigsby, 46
  Mary, 46, 69, 96
  Naomi, 63
  Naomy, 34
  Nathaniel Grigsby, 46
  Ossee, 32

Stephen, 34
  Susana, 34
Reeder
  Daniel, 8
  David, 8
  Eleanor, 8
  Elijah, 8
  Elizabeth, 8
  Gourley, 98, 118, 129
  Gourly, 107
  Jacob, 8
  Joseph, 8
  Mary, 8
  Stephen, 8
  William, 8, 98, 118
Rees
  Daniel, 99
  Edward, 34
  Elizabeth, 80
  Linney, 80
Reese
  Daniel, 97
  David, 135, 139
  Edward, 88
  Elizabeth, 141
  Joseph, 88
  Sarah, 88
  Solomon, 170
Reid
  Alfred, 84, 130
  Joseph, 24
  Polly, 65
  Rebecca, 24
Reider
  Joseph, 61
  Reigor
  John, 20
Reiley
  Elizabeth, 138
  Robert, 17
Reitchie
  Daniel, 115
Remey
  Barbara, 24
  Benjamin, 24
  Betty, 36
  Elijah, 25
  Elizabeth, 24

Index to Loudoun County Wills, 1757 - 1850

Remey
  Henry, 25
  Jacob, 18, 25, 30, 36
  James, 24
  Rebecca, 24
  William, 3
Remsburg
  Sebastian, 170
Respess
  Thomas, 16
Revely
  John, 45
Reynolds
  Elizabeth, 13, 84
  Henry, 84
  Rachel, 9
Rhodes
  Abigail, 7
  Alcinda, 113
  Alfred, 113, 178
  Ann, 7
  Anna, 105
  Effa, 113
  Elizabeth, 7, 113
  Euphamia, 178
  Eustius, 105
  George, 48, 105, 115, 152
  Hannah, 7
  John, 7, 60, 105, 184
  Joseph, 7, 24, 91
  Lydia, 113, 178
  Martha, 49
  Mary, 7, 66, 105, 184
  Moses, 5, 7
  Nancy, 113, 184
  Randall, 113
  Randolph, 84, 105
  Ruth, 105
  Samuel, 105, 113, 178
  Sarah, 105
  Tholemiah, 105, 113, 178, 184
  Thomas, 7, 24
  William, 7, 24, 48, 66, 91

Rhorbaugh
  Adam, 89
  Ann Catharine, 89
  George, 89
  Hannah, 89
Ricard
  Elizabeth, 108
Rice
  Berthamy, 184
  Bethany, 103
  Isaac, 184
  James, 184
  Jane, 184
  Jesse, 184
  John, 184
  Leonard, 184
  Rebeckah, 184
  Sampson, 184
  Susannah, 184
  William, 150, 184
Rich
  Samuel, 16, 18
Richa
  Francis, 32
Richards
  Alfred, 168
  Ann, 87, 118, 159
  Baron, 111
  Barton, 147, 153, 169
  Deborah, 76
  Elizabeth, 87, 153
  Esther, 49
  George, 106, 118, 152, 156, 159
  Hannah, 87
  Isaac, 87, 168
  Jesse, 168
  John, 87
  Leven, 168
  Lydia, 26, 153
  Mary, 87
  Pheby, 87
  Richard, 87
  Rosanah, 75
  Samuel, 87, 153
  Sarah, 87
  Thomas, 153, 168

  William, 26, 87, 118, 168
Richardson
  Daniel, 48
  Davis, 151
  James, 19
  Jamima, 38
  John, 19
  Joseph, 11
  Margaret, 115
  Mary, 3
Richart
  Magdalena, 104
Richcreek
  Gisbert, 72
  John, 72
  Philip, 72
Richey
  Isaac, 48
  Samuel, 104
Richie
  Frantz, 11
  Isaac, 48
Rickard
  Catharine, 114
  George, 131, 169
  Mary, 145
  Simon, 145
Rickart
  S., 104
Rickmyers
  Sally, 77
Riddle
  Thomas, 107
Ridenbaugh
  George, 82
  Mahala, 82, 182
  Margaret, 82
  Mary, 82
  Peter, 82
  Sarah, 82
Ridge
  Cornelius, 92
Rieley
  Joshua, 90
Rightmire
  Anna, 59
  Benjamin, 32
  James, 37

Rightmire
　Orrionehe, 21
Riley
　Joshua, 105, 108
　Lettice, 68
Rine
　George, 20
Ringgold
　Walter, 152
Ringo
　Cornelius, 20
　Margaret, 20
Ringold
　Antoinette, 128
　Tench, 128
Rinker
　Edward, 25, 81
　Henry, 25
　Sarah, 25, 81
Rion
　Dinah, 19
Ritacre
　Mary, 32
Ritaker
　Catharine, 46
Ritchardson
　Joseph, 41
Ritchie
　Catharine, 92
　Isaac, 60
　Jacob, 48
　John, 23, 92
　Mary, 92
　Thomas, 92
Riticor
　Elijah, 57, 88, 169, 170
　John, 172
　Nancy, 65
Roach
　Asa, 135
　Edmund, 53, 185
　George, 59
　Hannah, 13, 116
　James, 13, 59, 157
　John, 59
　Lucinda, 116
　Mahlon, 75, 157
　Phinehas, 157

　Richard, 34, 59, 65
　Sarah, 135
　Thomas, 136
Roal
　Joshua, 156
Roane
　Mary, 145
　S. A., 166
　W. H., 166
Robbins
　Isaac, 94
Roberson
　James, 183
Roberts
　Alice, 132
　Ann, 2
　Charles, 57
　Deborah, 124
　Elleanor, 20
　Henry, 57
　Jane, 20
　Jean, 15
　John, 2, 51
　Jonah, 106
　Joseph, 2, 183
　Joshua, 124
　Mary, 2
　Owen, 6, 8, 9, 13, 15
　Rebecca, 51
　Richard, 2
　Robert, 124
　Sarah, 109
　Stephen, 165
　Susanna, 2
　William, 2, 15, 38
Robertson
　Elizabeth, 49, 81, 142
　Hannah, 49
　Helah, 142
　Henry, 7
　Jenny, 7
　John, 81, 142
　Mary, 142
　Sarah, 142
　Seth, 142
　Susannah, 35
　Tamar, 142
　William, 35, 142

Robeson
　Ann, 8
　Sylvanus, 8
Robinett
　Allen, 6
Robinson
　John, 112
　Thomas, 12
Robison
　Elizabeth, 22
　John, 22
　Nancy, 22
　Sarah, 22
Roby
　Andrew, 167
Rodgers
　Elizabeth, 179
　Esibel, 101
　Flemon, 101
　Jane, 101
Rogers
　Asa, 131, 148, 151, 161, 172
　Dinah, 147
　Edwin, 145
　Elizabeth, 145, 153
　Elmina, 145
　Flemon, 89
　Hamilton, 86, 106, 134, 136, 147, 148, 153, 170
　Harriet, 167
　Hortensia, 167
　Hugh, 79, 91, 106, 123
　James, 89
　Joseph, 123
　Mary, 167
　Nancy, 141
　Nathaniel, 173
　Phebe, 185
　Richard, 13, 172
　Samuel, 106, 147
　Thomas, 135, 137, 143, 145, 147, 150, 151, 157, 158, 159, 160, 170
　Walter, 141, 145

Rogers
  William, 46, 161,
    162, 165, 170, 181
Roler
  Conrod, 55
  John, 55
Roller
  Conrad, 112
  Daniel, 112, 128
  David, 112
  Elizabeth, 112
  Frederick, 112
  John, 112
  Jonathan, 112
  L., 104
  Magdalena, 104
  Priscilla, 112
Rollison
  Elizabeth, 113
  Fanny, 146
  John, 113, 146
  Juliann, 113
Romine
  Abigail, 31
  Isaack, 31
  John, 31
  Peter, 17, 31
  Ruth, 29
  Sarah, 31
Roofe
  Elizabeth, 82
  John, 82
Rooles
  Candy, 131
Rooney
  Michael, 37, 46
Roots
  Nancy, 65
Roper
  Elizabeth, 36
  Ellen, 173
  James, 173
  Nancey, 36
  Thomas, 23
  Wager, 173
Ropp
  Nicholas, 153
  Samuel, 153

Rose
  Anna, 110, 159
  Christopher, 69, 154
  James, 35
  John, 71, 90, 98,
    110, 117, 131,
    154, 159
  Kitty, 105
  Robert, 154
  Silas, 64
Ross
  Armstrong, 61
  David, 61
  Elizabeth, 61
  Jane, 61
  John, 61
  Joseph, 61
  Joshua, 61
  Mary, 61
  Nancy, 61
  Rebeckah, 61
  Sarah, 61
  William, 2, 15, 61
Roszel. *See* Russell
  Anna, 136, 148
  George, 155
  Mary, 155
  Nancy, 155
  Phebe, 148, 155
  Stephen, 6, 148, 155
Roszell
  Nancy, 37
  Phebe, 37
  Sally, 37
  Sarah, 37
  Stephen, 37, 73
Rousseau
  Frances, 148
Rowan
  Emeley, 62
  George, 62, 184
  Jane, 62
  Sarah, 62
Rowen
  Sarai, 183
Rozel
  Stephen, 113
Rozsell
  Sarah, 10

Ruess
  Michael, 11
Rumsey
  Marianne, 144
Ruse
  Christeana, 102
  Christian, 102
  Frederick, 102
  Henry, 102
  Jacob, 102
  John, 102, 121, 129
  Michael, 102
  Polly, 121
  Rachel, 102
  Sarah, 121
  Solomon, 102
  Susannah, 129
Russel
  John, 170
  Robert, 41
  Samuel, 122
Russell
  Aaron, 80
  Albert, 39, 43
  Ann, 43, 81, 149
  Anthony, 3, 8, 10,
    15, 18, 170
  Catherine, 134, 158
  Charles, 113
  Charley, 123, 152
  David, 158
  Edith, 80
  Elizabeth, 40, 152,
    170
  Emily, 158, 170
  Emla, 81
  Esther, 158
  Euphamy, 102
  Francis, 18
  George, 175
  Henry, 80
  James, 80, 131, 149,
    158
  Jane, 170
  John, 81, 158
  Joseph, 80
  Joshua, 161
  Mahlon, 73, 81
  Margaret, 114, 126

Russell
  Mary, 40, 80
  Melea, 39
  Milly, 18
  Nancy, 170
  Penelope, 18
  Rachel, 80
  Robert, 48, 65, 81,
    131, 134, 184
  Sally, 170
  Samuel, 17, 65, 73,
    81, 131, 149
  Sarah, 20, 65, 73, 79,
    92, 170
  Thaddeus, 170
  Thomas, 81
  William, 9, 65, 80,
    81, 145, 160, 163,
    170
Rust
  Alfred, 130
  Elizabeth, 130
  George, 54, 64, 169
  James, 118, 175
  John, 118
  Manley, 118
  Margaret, 121
  Martha, 117
  Matthew, 121
  P. C., 165
  Peter, 121, 130, 131
  Sally, 118, 159
  Susan, 117
  Thomas, 118
  William, 33, 127
Ryan
  Phillip, 120
Rymer
  Elizabeth, 81
  Jacob, 81
  John, 81

—S—

Sackman
  Elizabeth, 161
  John, 161
Saffer
  George, 107
  Susanna, 140
  William, 140
Sagar
  Elizabeth, 145
Sagars
  George, 132
Sager
  Elizabeth, 104
  Nancy, 102
  S., 104
Said
  William, 17
Sample
  Catherine, 40
  James, 40
  Sally, 40
  Susanah, 40
Sanbower
  Adam, 104, 145
  Ann, 134, 145
  Catharine, 104
  Catherine, 134
  Christian, 104
  Elizabeth, 104
  Henry, 104
  John, 58, 104
  Julian, 145
  Magdalena, 104
  Michael, 104, 145
  Sarah, 104
  Susanna, 104
Sanders
  Aaron, 18, 46, 48,
    57, 71, 77, 95
  Ann, 150
  Barbara, 17, 46
  Benjamin, 7, 100
  Bethany, 16, 46
  Britton, 150
  Cyrus, 18, 106
  Duanna, 160
  Elizabeth, 7, 46, 100,
    160
  Emily, 106
  George, 121, 160
  Gunnel, 18
  Hamilton, 160
  Hannah, 100
  Henry, 17, 18, 46
  James, 17, 46, 100
  John, 17, 46, 106
  Mary, 46, 106
  Moses, 18, 46, 57
  Nancy, 46
  Patience, 46
  Peter, 121
  Philip, 100
  Phillip, 7
  Presley, 18, 46, 57
  Presly, 106
  Rachael, 106
  Sarah, 18, 46
  Thomas, 18, 100,
    106, 135, 151
  Washington, 100,
    121
  William, 7, 100
Sandford
  Daniel, 38
  Henry, 38
  Jeremiah, 67, 79
  Rebekah, 38
Sands
  Benjamin, 13, 19
  Edmund, 13
  Elizabeth, 81
  Esther, 53
  Gideon, 13
  Isaac, 6, 10, 13
  Jacob, 13, 57, 81
  Jonah, 116, 136,
    170, 182
  Joseph, 13
  Ruth, 171
  Sarah, 13, 136
  Stephen, 81, 93
  Thomas, 171
Sangster
  Mary, 47
Santclar
  John, 3
  Margaret, 3
Sapington
  Mary, 68
Sappington
  Edmund, 131
  John, 94
  Jonathan, 131

Mary, 131
Saunders
  Aaron, 84, 167
  Alcinda, 167
  Ann, 101
  Anna Lee, 167
  Benjamin, 167
  Catharine, 167
  Crayton, 105
  Curtis, 167
  Cyrus, 105
  Delia, 167
  Duanna, 121
  Editha, 105
  Elizabeth, 167, 173
  Evrett, 103, 105
  Evritt, 83, 138, 167
  George, 137
  Gunnell, 105, 151
  Hamilton, 121
  Henry, 105
  James, 16, 105, 167
  John, 103, 105, 121
  Mahala, 135
  Margaret, 121
  Mary, 103
  Nicholas, 121
  Philip, 167
  Polly, 44
  Presley, 103, 105, 135
  R. G., 141, 167
  Ramy, 105
  Rosabel, 167
  Susan, 167
  Susannah, 167
  Thomas, 103, 105, 107, 131, 132, 151, 167
  Washington, 167
  Westley, 121
Saurbaugh
  Elizabeth, 179
Saxton
  Elizabeth, 138
Scandrett
  Jacob, 75
Scanland
  Sophronia, 173
Scatterday
  Esther, 6
  George, 6
  John, 6, 46
Schelfield
  William, 149
Schlacht
  Rhody, 46
Schofield
  Jonathan, 65
Schooley
  Aaron, 86
  Ann, 30
  Charles, 168
  Dorothy, 30
  Eli, 115
  Elisha, 84
  Eliza, 168
  Elizabeth, 86, 149, 168
  Enoch, 115
  Ephraim, 174
  Hannah, 40
  Henry, 137
  Isaac, 93
  J. P., 147
  James, 137
  Jesse, 30
  John, 23, 30, 84, 86, 89, 115, 137, 174
  Jonas, 166, 178
  Jonathan, 168
  Mahlon, 137
  Mary, 84
  Presley, 172
  Reuben, 53, 65, 69, 84, 97, 113, 115
  Reubin, 137
  Richard, 137
  Samuel, 23, 30
  Sarah, 23, 110, 137
  Tacy, 110
  William, 23, 84, 93, 128, 137
Schoolley
  Onnes, 68
Schryock
  Elizabeth, 135
  George, 135
  Michael, 134
  Nancy, 135
  Samuel, 135
  Susanna, 135
Schwenk
  George, 38
Scott
  Anna, 111
  Elizabeth, 22, 51, 102, 111
  George, 168
  Hannah, 15, 51, 111
  Isaac, 111
  Jacob, 111
  James, 23
  Joseph, 10, 15, 111
  Margaret, 14
  Martha, 15
  Merab, 51
  Peggy, 23
  Rachel, 23
  Rebecca, 111
  Robert, 12, 14, 15, 22
  Samuel, 10, 14, 15, 20, 22, 23, 92
  Stephen, 51, 111
  Susannah, 14, 22
  Thomas, 15, 73
  William, 15, 55
Sealock
  Thomas, 55
Sears
  Charles Lee, 25
  Elizabeth, 25
  William, 183
Seaton
  Hiram, 84, 96, 176
  James, 176
  John, 176
  Margary, 96
  Nancy, 176
  Robert, 176
  Townshend, 176
  William, 91, 96, 123, 176
Seeders
  Sarah, 153
  William, 153

Selden
  Eleanor, 158
  Eliza, 158
  John, 158
  Mary, 139
  Wilson, 139, 158, 180
Self
  Athesias, 26
  Charnock, 20
  Elizabeth, 20, 44
  Joseph, 20
  Presley, 20, 26, 44, 45
  Thomas, 20
Selfe
  Nancy, 43
Semple
  Sarah, 39
Settle
  Ann, 77
  Daniel, 56, 116
  Dorcas, 56
  Elizabeth, 56, 112
  Henry, 56, 59
  Isaac, 112
  Ishmael, 60
  Jane, 77
  Mary, 56, 112
  Newman, 56, 116
  Reuben, 56, 60
  Susannah, 56, 116
  Thomas, 180
Seward
  Anne, 3
  Nicholas, 3
Seybold
  Alice, 32
  Hannah, 32
  Hester, 32
  Isaac, 32
  James, 32
  Jesper, 32, 33
  Jesse, 32
  John, 32
  Rebakah, 32
  Robert, 32
  Silas, 32

Shadburn
  Amos, 52
Shafer
  Jacob, 115
Shaffer
  Christiana, 127
  Conrad, 100
  Elizabeth, 100, 127, 139
  George, 127
  Henry, 127
  Jacob, 100, 141
  John, 100
  Lucinda, 127
  Magdelena, 100
  Michael, 127
  Phillip, 43
  Polly, 127
  Solomon, 127, 139
  William, 100
Shaftoe
  James, 51
Shanks
  Susannah, 71
Sharp
  Jacob, 45
  Jeptha, 129
  Sarah, 128
Sharpe
  Elizabeth, 23
Shaver
  Jacob, 28
  John, 72
  Polly, 73
Shaw
  Amos, 182
  Eliza, 115
  John, 115, 122
  Mary, 115
  Rebecca, 115
  Sidney, 115
  Susan, 115
Shawen
  Cornelius, 99
  D., 119
  David, 99, 102, 159
  George, 99, 125
  Mary, 99
  William, 123

Sheark
  Michael, 48
Shearman
  Susan, 51
Sheid
  George, 98
  James, 69, 98
  John, 98
  Martinah, 98
  Rebecca, 98
  Sarah, 98
  William, 98
Shelton
  Elizabeth, 44
Sheperd
  William, 23
Shepherd
  Ann, 154
  Catherine, 118
  Charles, 71
  Edward, 111
  Eleanor, 71
  Elizabeth, 71
  Fanny, 71
  Francis, 169
  Jacob, 169
  James, 71
  Jane, 169
  John, 71
  Jonathan, 111
  Kitty, 71
  Leven, 71
  Melville, 169
  Nancy, 71, 169
  Polly, 71
  Thomas, 118, 154
  William, 29, 111
Shermindine
  Ann, 83
  James, 83
Shield
  Alfred, 164
  Catherine, 163
Shields
  Alfred, 132
  Joseph, 33, 63
Shipman
  Stephen, 31
Shively

Index to Loudoun County Wills, 1757 - 1850

George, 59, 71, 88
Jacob, 55
Rebeccah, 88
Sarah, 76
Shockheart
  George, 24
Shoemaker
  Abraham, 102
  Anna, 69
  Catharine, 90
  Charlotta, 87
  Christiana, 69
  Daniel, 69, 101
  George, 11, 23, 69, 139
  Jacob, 23, 139
  John, 69
  Joseph, 69
  Judith, 70
  Mary, 139
  Naylor, 154
  Pamelia, 140
  Peggy, 87
  Sarah, 70
  Simon, 70, 90, 139
  Sollomon, 69
Sholders
  Conrod, 5
Shomaker
  Jacob, 41
Shore
  Michael, 11, 21
Short
  Alice, 28
  Catharine, 35
  Cornelia, 166, 177
  George, 166
  Henry, 64
  Jacob, 35
  John, 35, 155
  Rebekah, 28
  Robert, 28, 52
  Sarah, 28
  Susan, 166
  Susannah, 28
Shorts
  Alice, 54
Shoulders
  Conrod, 5

Shover
  Adam, 9, 32, 43, 48, 58, 70, 104, 124
  Charlotte, 104
  Elizabeth, 104
  George, 104
  John, 70, 104
  Magdalena, 104
  Mary, 179
  Simon, 104, 112, 179
  Sophia, 179
  Susan, 145
  Susanna, 104
Shreve
  Abner, 36
  Anne, 36
  B., 141
  Benjamin, 2, 22, 36, 54, 135, 179
  Catherine, 2
  David, 2
  Elizabeth, 2
  Elizabeth (Hulls), 2
  James, 2, 9
  Joshua, 36
  Mary, 2
  Massey, 9
  Samuel, 9
  Sarah, 2
  William, 2, 36, 44
Shrieves
  Mary, 45
Shrigley
  Lawrence, 13
Shriver
  Jacob, 140, 144
Shry
  Elizabeth, 185
Shults
  Elizabeth, 62
Shumaker
  Catharine, 129
  Daniel, 74
  Elizabeth, 62
  George, 62
  Jacob, 62, 159
  Simon, 62, 74, 116

Shumate
  M. C., 160
  Maria, 142
  Murphey, 135
  Taliafarro, 136
Shutt
  Caroline, 166, 175
  Jacob, 175
Siddall
  Isaac, 53
Siddle
  Sarah, 61
  William, 61
Silcott
  Barsheba, 116
  Jacob, 98, 107, 108, 132
  Jesse, 63, 156
  Mesheck, 156
  Mortimer, 156
  William, 84
Sim
  Catharine, 52
  Thomas, 52, 56, 60
Simmonds
  Frances, 17
Simms
  Charity, 157
  Charles, 25, 157
  James, 157
  John, 157
Simond
  Thomas, 1
Simpson
  Catharine, 98
  Eliza, 169
  Elizabeth, 151, 161
  Emily, 161
  French, 83, 113, 169
  Gilbert, 4
  Hendley, 83, 125
  Henson, 79, 80, 83, 87
  James, 83, 87, 176
  John, 55, 83, 102, 146, 161, 167, 169, 176
  Mary, 55, 83, 169
  Matilda, 180

Simpson
  Nancy, 185
  R. T., 148
  Samuel, 83, 172
  Susannah, 172
  William, 55, 83, 128
Sinckler
  Alexander, 2
  Elizabeth, 2
  George, 2
  Hester, 2
  Isaac, 2
  John, 2
  Mary, 2
  Robert, 2
  Wayman, 2
Sinclair
  George, 74
  James, 150, 169, 171
  Jane, 138
  John, 29, 55, 96,
    131, 132, 140,
    154, 167, 172, 184
  Leanna, 142
  Leannah, 136
  Milly, 172 .
  Rachel, 49
  Samuel, 29
Singleton
  Joshua, 54
  Mary, 180
  Washington, 180
Sinkins
  Elizabeth, 48
Sinkler
  Sarah, 1
Sipher
  Susanna, 186
Skillman
  Abraham, 136
  Alcinda, 151
  Lucinda, 179
  William, 151
Skilman
  Abraham, 121, 172
  Catharine, 15
  James, 172
  John, 15, 49
  Marcus, 172

Maria, 172
Martha, 172
Violinda, 83
Skinner
  Alexander, 90
  Ann, 90
  Cornelius, 70, 136
  Elizabeth, 90
  Francis, 90
  Gabriel, 90, 131
  Isaac, 136, 173
  Jacob, 183
  James, 136, 173
  Jane, 91
  John, 136, 173, 177
  Martha, 136
  Mary, 90
  Nathan, 137, 148
  Nathaniel, 136, 148,
    151, 173
  Peggy, 46
  Phineas, 13
  Phoeby, 91
  Rebecah, 91
  Rebecca, 183
  Richard, 13, 70
  Robert, 90
  Samuel, 82, 90, 148
  Sarah, 90, 179
  Sucky, 183
  Usher, 183
  William, 136
Skiver
  Delilah, 124
Slater. *See* Statzer
  Catherine, 123
  Christena, 123
  Elizabeth, 94
  Jacob, 123
  Samuel, 103, 123
  William, 123, 166
Slates
  Adam, 128
  Connard, 128
  Frederick, 112, 128
  John, 128
Slatser
  Jacob, 23

Slaughter
  Gabriel, 126
Sloan
  Rachel, 45
Slocombe
  Robert, 16
Smale
  John, 170
  Simon, 125, 170
Smalley
  Andrew, 15, 21
  Cathrine, 21
  David, 21
  Ezekiel, 21
  Isaac, 21
  Joshua, 21
  Susannah, 21
  William, 21, 96
Smallwood
  Bayn, 61
  Jane, 154
  John, 139
  Leaven, 67
Smarr
  Andrew, 42
  Ann, 42
  Charles, 42
  Elizabeth, 42
  Fanny, 42
  George, 42
  John, 42
  Peril, 42
  Reuben, 42
  Robert, 42
  Samuel, 42
  Sarah, 42
  Susan, 161
  William, 179
Smidley
  Mathias, 35
Smith
  Abraham, 28, 157
  Alexander, 142
  Alice, 25, 49, 66
  Allice, 18
  Amos, 107
  Ann, 25, 66, 72, 86
  Barbarah, 72
  Benjamin, 162

Index to Loudoun County Wills, 1757 - 1850   261

Smith
  Catharine, 47, 74
  Catherine, 62, 72
  Charles, 38, 83, 86, 185
  Charlotte, 105
  Clator, 38
  Clement, 152
  Conner, 38
  D. G., 170
  Daniel, 18, 150
  David, 25, 66, 72, 91, 92, 105, 124, 125, 150, 176
  Edward, 183
  Eleanor, 9
  Elenor, 182
  Elizabeth, 18, 62, 113, 182
  Emala, 86
  F. W., 117
  Fleet, 71, 77
  Frederick, 47, 48, 52, 55, 58, 186
  George, 25, 36, 38, 62, 66, 71, 74, 78, 81, 83, 84, 104, 180
  Gideon, 26
  Hannah, 22, 63, 74, 78, 84
  Henry, 25, 120
  Hugh, 98, 106, 111, 185
  Jacob, 62, 72, 107, 108
  James, 18, 61, 107, 145, 148, 163
  Jane, 36
  Jean, 18
  Jemima, 26
  Job, 169
  Jobe, 178
  John, 9, 25, 47, 81, 107, 138, 152, 153, 154, 158, 170, 182
  Jonas, 154
  Joseph, 61, 133
  Keren, 36
  Kezia, 107
  Lucy, 151
  Lydia, 36, 62
  Margaret, 182
  Maria, 142
  Marion, 162
  Martha, 66, 150
  Mary, 18, 25, 34, 47, 62, 72, 74, 84, 107, 109, 132, 142
  Minor, 18
  Nancy, 38
  Nathaniel, 38
  Pusey, 185
  Rachel, 62, 107
  Ralph, 67
  Richard, 19, 128, 152, 168
  Sally, 47
  Samuel, 25, 62, 70, 89, 107, 108
  Sarah, 25, 32, 62, 65, 66, 72, 74, 83, 84, 137, 138, 141
  Seth, 70, 79, 89, 95, 107, 108, 114, 115, 116, 118, 129, 132, 133, 147, 153, 165, 169, 170, 177
  Susanna, 47
  Susannah, 62
  Sybilla, 47
  T. W., 131
  Temple, 183
  Thomas, 25, 29, 66
  W., 70
  Walter, 152
  Weedon, 32, 68, 83
  William, 3, 6, 9, 14, 17, 18, 25, 26, 28, 30, 39, 50, 53, 64, 66, 74, 81, 99, 119, 154
  Winifred, 38, 86
  Winneford, 185
  Withers, 36
Smitley
  Mathias, 47, 55, 62, 70, 81
Smitly
  Mathias, 24
Smoot
  George, 159
Snedeker
  Garrat, 8
Sneed
  Achilles, 126
Snider
  Catherine, 185
  Henry, 185
  Jacob, 185
  Peter, 185
  William, 185
Snoke
  Elizabeth, 186
Snyder
  Elizabeth, 55, 120
Sockman
  Sarah, 127
Solomon
  Henrietta, 113
Soop
  John, 35
Sorrell
  Elizabeth, 13
  John, 13, 23
  Martha, 3, 13
  Thomas, 3, 13
Sothard
  Larance, 4
Sotherd
  Sarah, 4
  William, 4
Souder
  Anthony, 58, 140
  Elizabeth, 140
  Jacob, 58
  John, 140, 177
  Margaret, 58, 109
  Mary, 123, 140
  Michael, 58, 109, 140
  Peter, 140
  Philip, 58, 109
  Rachel, 140
  Susana, 58, 140

Sowers
  B. W., 105
Speaker
  Ann, 50
Speck
  Catherine, 80
  Margaret, 80
Speckt
  Andrew, 58
  Peggy, 58
  Rosanna, 58
Spencer
  Hannah, 67
  Jasper, 101
  John, 3, 45, 67
  Margaret, 67
  Mary, 67
  Nathan, 22, 50, 56, 67
  Rachel, 67
  Samuel, 67
  Sarah, 67, 85, 124, 155
  William, 67, 124, 155
Spinks
  John, 144
Spoon
  Elizabeth, 35
  Joseph, 58
  widow, 57
Spring
  Andrew, 79, 113
  Casper, 113, 169
  David, 113
  Elizabeth, 123
  Jacob, 113
  John, 113
  Joseph, 113
  Lydia, 166
  Michael, 113
Sprote
  L. W., 153
Spurr
  Frances, 31
  James, 1
  Judath, 1
  Richard, 1, 12, 16, 31

Squires
  Ann, 19
  Asa, 60
  Elizabeth, 33
  Henson, 155
  John, 155
  Nancy, 155
  Sally, 19
  Thomas, 19, 155
St. Clair
  Alexander, 105
Stadley
  Elizabeth, 61
Stalcup
  Rebecca, 61
Stanard
  Robert, 168
Stanhope
  William, 11, 22, 44, 45
Stark
  Elizabeth, 10
  John, 10
  Nancy, 10
  Siner, 10
  Susanna, 10
  William, 1, 10
Starkey
  Elizabeth, 66
  Eppha, 66
  Jacob, 66
  Jane, 66
  John, 67
Starks
  Elizabeth, 53
States
  Elizabeth, 102
  Frederick, 62, 101
Statler
  John, 129
Statzer
  Catherine, 58
  John, 58
Steel
  John, 58
Steer
  Ann, 53
  Benjamin, 28, 45, 53, 97

Beulah, 166
  Elizabeth, 97, 161
  Hannah, 53
  Isaac, 48, 50, 53, 90, 97, 110, 124, 159, 161
  J. H., 161
  James, 174
  Jane, 74
  John, 48, 53, 74
  Jonah, 149, 161, 163
  Joseph, 48, 53, 87, 97, 149, 161, 166
  Mary, 53, 149
  Rachel, 161
  Samuel, 157
  Sarah, 108, 116
  Thomas, 53
  William, 97, 130, 149, 157, 161
Steere
  Isaac, 57, 73, 95, 115, 185
  James, 2
  John, 55
  Rebekah, 115
Steers
  Hannah, 60
  Isaac, 60
  Joseph, 60
  Mary, 60
  Thomas, 60
Steiner
  William, 151
Stenchecun
  Rebecka, 159
Stenson
  Prudence, 181
  Stephen, 181
Stephens. *See* Stevens
  Ann, 25, 34
  Anne, 184
  Benjamin, 47
  Edward, 12
  Eleanor, 25, 27, 34
  Elizabeth, 25, 34
  Else, 12
  Ephraim, 12
  George, 47

Stephens
  Giles, 12
  Hannah, 47
  Henry, 47
  Hezekiah, 47
  James, 12, 47
  John, 85
  Joseph, 4, 25, 34
  Leven, 84
  Lewis, 184
  Mary, 85
  Richard, 27, 34
  Robert, 27, 34
  Thomas, 12, 84, 85
  William, 47
  Zachariah, 47
Stephenson
  James, 134
  Jane, 45
  Thomas, 45
  W. A., 173
  William, 45
Stetz
  Margaret, 55
Stevens. *See* Stephens
  Alice, 19
  Ann, 53, 142
  Eleanor, 95, 108
  Ezekiah, 53
  Fanny, 53
  Hannabel, 142
  Hannah, 13, 19
  Henry, 53, 71, 95, 108
  James, 19, 47, 53
  John, 76, 142
  Joseph, 53
  Margaritt, 53
  Rebecky, 53
  Robert, 13, 142
  Rosamond, 142
  Sally, 142
  Thomas, 76, 142
Stevenson
  Betsy, 55
Stevins
  Eleanor, 71
Stewart
  Henrey, 134

Stiffle(r)
  Christener, 32
  Martin, 32
Stock
  Christena, 178
Stocks
  William, 81
Stokey
  Nehemiah, 66
Stone
  Daniel, 67, 69, 86, 94, 96, 108, 130
  Jane, 47
  Sarah, 86
  William, 96, 102, 140
Stoneburner
  Adam, 182
  Betsey, 73
  Catharine, 166
  Frederick, 104
  J. C., 177
  John, 58
Stonestreet
  Augustus, 75
  Basil, 53, 75
  Benjamin, 75
  Elizabeth, 75
  Sarah, 75
  Thomas, 102
Stouseberger
  John, 53, 79, 185
Stousenberger
  John, 75
Stoutseberger
  Jacob, 143
  John, 94, 100, 143
  Margarett, 143
  Samuel, 143
Stoutsenberger
  Albert, 170
  Elvina, 170
  Jacob, 170
  Mary, 170
  Samuel, 170
Stoven
  Charles, 157
Stover
  Edwin, 164

Stovin
  Charles, 74, 112
  John Lewis, 112
Stowers
  Mrs., 148
Strauther
  Sally, 135
Streets
  Margaret, 57
Stribling
  Cecelia, 149
  Francis, 104
Stringfellow
  Benjamin, 176
Strington
  Dorcas, 125
Striplin
  Mary, 21
  William, 21
Strite
  Abraham, 180
Strother
  James, 100
Stroud
  Ann, 3
  George, 3
  James, 3
  Samuel, 3
  Susanah, 3
Stroupe
  Mary, 24
  Milcher, 24
Strup
  M., 185
Stuart
  Anne, 77
Stuck
  Elizabeth, 166, 177
  Ferdinando, 123, 166, 177
  Jane, 177
  Lydia, 166, 177
  Mary, 166, 177
  Nancy, 166, 177
  Peter, 166, 177
Stull
  John, 152

Stump
  Beckey, 65
  C., 45
  Eleanor, 99
  Elizabeth, 1
  Jacob, 45
  Jane, 1
  Joseph, 99
  Peter, 46, 65
  Polly, 65
  Sarah, 99
  Thomas, 1, 99
Suddarth
  Lawrence, 182
  Mary, 182
  Owen, 182
  William, 182
Suddith
  William, 85
Suffron
  Mary, 121
Sugars
  Joseph, 142
Sullivan
  Eliza, 146
  Elizabeth, 82
  John, 82, 146
  Murtho, 59, 82
  Samuel, 82
  William, 82
Summers
  Francis, 55
  George, 25, 30, 36, 55, 71, 182
  Henry, 85, 183
  Jacob, 134, 140
  Margaret, 37
  Mary, 71
  Polly, 36
  Richard, 93
  William, 78, 146
Surghnor
  Betsy, 165
  John, 134, 165
  Sally, 165
Suter
  Alexander, 152
Sutherland
  Alexander, 46, 53
  Anne, 46
  Nancy, 53
  Thomas, 53
Sutton
  Elijah, 92
  Mary, 10
Swain
  Joseph, 7
Swank
  Catharine, 112
Swann
  Robert, 149
  Thomas, 83, 128, 149
  William, 149
  Wilson, 149
Swart
  Adrein, 32
  Alexander, 126
  Amelia, 180
  Barnet, 180
  Burr, 180
  Charles, 180
  Elizabeth, 48, 172, 179
  Fayette, 180
  James, 179, 180, 185
  John, 18, 48, 172
  Maria, 172
  Mary, 46
  Samuel, 180
  Simon, 56
  William, 91, 151, 185
Swarts
  Mary, 57, 75
Swearingen
  Julia, 97
Swick
  Anthony, 16
Swink
  Adam, 22
  Jane, 22
  Rachel, 22
Switser
  Jacob, 4
Sword
  Ann, 83
  John, 83

Urriah, 83
Sybold
  James, 28
Sypherd
  George, 104
  Matthew, 124
  Sarah, 134, 145

—T—

Tablor
  Ann, 179
Tailor
  Elizabeth, 146
Talbert
  Anne, 20
  Benjamin, 20
  Frances, 20
  John, 20
  William, 20
Talbot
  Barbara, 25
  Benjamin, 25
  Hannah Neale, 25
  Henry, 25
  Mary, 25
Talbott
  Ann, 86
  Anne, 48
  Elisha, 48
  Elizabeth, 48, 78, 86
  Jane, 74
  Jesse, 48
  John, 48
  Joseph, 39, 48, 73, 77, 78, 80, 82, 89, 116
  Mary, 48
  Rebekah, 48
  Samuel, 48
  Sarah, 48
  Susannah, 48
Talbut
  Anne, 5
  Henry, 183
  Hugh, 183
Talbutt
  Hannah, 25, 34

Index to Loudoun County Wills, 1757 - 1850 265

Tallieferro
  John, 27
Tar
  Aaron, 130
Tarbert
  Elizabeth, 67
  James, 68
  Samuel, 67
  Thomas, 67
Tarel
  William, 30
Tate
  Edith, 85, 114, 124
  Levi, 85, 114
Tavender
  Ann, 87
  George, 51
  Miriam, 109
  Patty, 51
  Richard, 81
  Susannah, 31
Tavener
  Betsy, 116
  Eli, 116
  George, 116
  Hiram, 116
  Isaac, 116
  James, 116
  Jonah, 116
  Joseph, 116
  Lott, 168
  Mary, 116
  Phebe, 168
  Richard, 116
  Tabitha, 116
Tavenner. *See* Tavender
  Ann, 124, 155, 174
  Benjamin, 144
  Catharine, 144
  Charles, 170
  Eli, 144
  Elizabeth, 144, 170
  George, 92, 155, 183
  Hannah, 174
  James, 155
  John, 134, 174
  Jonah, 155, 172, 176
  Jonathan, 137, 155
  Joseph, 91, 174

Levi, 174
Louisa, 170
Mahlon, 174
Mariam, 171
Mary, 144, 174
Nancy, 170
Richard, 124, 135,
  144, 155
Samuel, 155
Sarah, 137, 144, 172
Susan, 174
Thomas, 102
William, 144, 155,
  174
Tavenor
  George, 97
Taverner
  George, 14, 23
Taverns
  George, 14
Taylor
  Agnes, 84
  Alfred, 110
  Alice, 73, 84
  Amy, 108
  Benjamin, 51, 126,
    141, 145, 156,
    157, 161, 164,
    167, 176
  Bernard, 48, 50, 54,
    62, 66, 72, 76, 77,
    89, 91, 92, 94,
    102, 107, 124,
    136, 150, 162, 172
  Charles, 145, 176
  Charlotte, 109
  Christian, 144
  Craven, 33
  Cynthia, 33
  David, 179
  Elizabeth, 33, 56
  George, 23, 33, 172
  Griffin, 118
  Hannah, 122
  Henry, 10, 46, 56,
    95, 107, 118, 124,
    125, 132, 164,
    172, 174
  Jack, 33

James, 107, 171
Jane, 147
Jesse, 45, 68
Jessey, 46
John, 6, 7, 10, 15,
  21, 46, 56, 68, 70,
  107, 110
Jonathan, 48, 68, 93,
  107, 136, 154,
  168, 172, 176
Joseph, 46, 53, 95,
  109, 128, 139, 145
Joshua, 10, 162
Leatitia, 145
Lewis, 175
Lucy, 107
Lydia, 95
Mahlon, 74, 80, 95,
  109, 122, 141,
  145, 154, 162, 168
Mandly, 33
Margaret, 56, 107
Mary, 46, 100, 109,
  145
Matthew, 56
Molly, 56
Nancy, 172
Nicholas, 56
Patty, 23
Polly, 73
R. I., 125
Rachel, 46
Richard, 168
Robert, 110, 179
Ruth, 95, 141
Samuel, 68, 141
Sarah, 32, 46, 172
Stacy, 40, 44, 49, 56,
  59, 61, 64, 88, 91,
  94, 103, 109, 122,
  134, 141
Stephen, 33
Susan, 118
Susannah, 10, 56,
  132
Thomas, 41, 46, 69
Timothy, 44, 99,
  141, 145, 149, 176
Walter, 56

Taylor
  William, 10, 20, 32,
    33, 48, 54, 143,
    145, 179
  Yardley, 99, 122,
    123, 124, 136,
    150, 154, 166,
    168, 172, 176
  Yardly, 93, 95
Tebbs
  A. S., 141
  A. Sidney, 171, 176
  Algernon, 167
  Foushee, 134
  Hannah Sim, 143
  Julia, 141
  Margaret, 118
  Willoughby, 55
Templar
  William, 67
Templer
  John, 89
  William, 89, 128
Tenly
  Patrick, 29
Tharp
  Polly, 140
Thatcher
  Albine, 59
  Alice, 88
  Ann, 21
  Bartholomew, 21
  Calvin, 59, 88
  John, 21, 35
  Jonah, 59
  Joshua, 183
  Katharine, 21
  Mary, 59, 161
  Nancy, 59
  Rachel, 21
  Richard, 21, 35, 39, 59
  Silvester, 183
  Stephen, 21, 88
  William, 59
Thomas
  Amet, 10
  Amy, 5
  Ann, 1

  Benjamin, 39
  Catharine, 40
  Catherine, 39
  Daniel, 173
  David, 1, 31, 35, 36, 44, 50
  Elizabeth, 1, 50, 51, 170
  Ellen, 173
  Emmet, 12
  Evan, 1, 8, 51
  George, 44, 90
  Griffith, 51
  Hannah, 24, 30
  Hariet, 169
  Herod, 90
  Jacob, 51
  James, 1
  Jefferson, 113
  Jesse, 50
  John, 16, 22, 29, 39, 76, 101, 173
  Joseph, 6, 24, 39, 50, 51, 86, 119, 120, 175
  Leonard, 20, 39
  Lloyd, 74
  Maria, 173
  Martha, 24, 44, 50
  Mary, 24, 114, 173, 183
  Matilda, 50
  Maziah, 173
  Mo., 25
  Moses, 183
  Nancy, 82, 173
  Nathaniel, 173
  Owen, 33, 43, 44, 50
  Philip, 31, 44, 50, 76, 80, 88, 113, 119
  Phineas, 51
  Robert, 40
  Ruth, 50
  Sally, 175
  Sarah, 50
  Susannah, 50
  Ubricka, 113
  William, 12, 183

Thompkins
  James, 40
  Marcia, 40
Thompson
  Amos, 6, 61, 62
  Andrew, 37
  Ann, 174
  Asa, 62, 67
  Betsy, 65
  Betzey, 41
  Edward, 12
  Eleanor, 65
  Eunice, 62
  Isaac, 37
  Israel, 3, 6, 9, 11, 12, 18, 20, 41, 48, 65, 68, 86
  James, 172
  Jane, 61, 62, 67
  John, 62, 172
  Jonah, 41, 65, 69, 75, 163
  Lomax, 37
  Margaret, 98
  Mary, 62
  Nancy, 41, 65, 86
  Penelope, 37
  Phoebe, 62
  Pleasant, 41, 65
  Rebecca, 62
  Rev. Mr., 6
  Sally, 41, 65, 68, 75
  Samuel, 41, 75
  Sarah, 41, 62, 68, 86, 163
Thomson
  Jonah, 46
  Mary, 69
  Thomas, 37
Thorn
  Humphrey, 9
Thornton
  Anthony, 27
  Benjamin, 27
  Catharine, 27
  Charles, 122
  John, 27
  Mary, 122
  Sarah, 122

Index to Loudoun County Wills, 1757 - 1850

Thornton
  Seth, 27
  William, 27
Thrailkill
  John, 28
Thrasher
  Luther, 166
Thrashere
  John, 145
Thrift
  Ann, 11
  William, 59, 61, 112, 167
Tillett
  Edward, 47, 67, 115, 126
  Effey, 87
  Eleanor, 148
  Eliza, 97
  Elizabeth, 47, 67
  Giles, 47, 87, 135
  Hannah, 111
  Honor, 135
  Honour, 87
  James, 47
  Jane, 148
  John Love, 148
  Mahala, 87
  Margarett, 87
  Nancy, 87, 135
  Samuel, 47, 87, 135, 148
  Sarah, 87
Tilman
  Sarah, 42
Timms
  Betsey, 143
  Henry, 143
  Jane, 143
  Jesse, 135, 143
  John, 68, 143
  Joseph, 71
  Milly, 71
  William, 118
Tippet
  Charles, 159
Tippett
  Elizabeth, 138

Titherex
  Catey, 36
  George, 36
  Polly, 36
Titus
  Jane, 111
  John, 131
  Tunis, 178
Tobin
  Esther, 11, 12
  George, 12
  James, 12, 59
  Joseph, 12
  Lydia, 12
  Mary, 12
  Naomy, 12
  Robert, 12
  Rosannah, 12
  Ruth, 12
  Thomas, 12
Tobit
  Hannah, 21, 36
  John, 36
Todd
  John, 38
  Mary, 38
  Rebeckah, 38
  Robert, 38
  Samuel, 38
Todhunter
  Isaac, 10
  John, 10
  Margaret, 10
Tolee
  Stephen, 19
Toll
  Betsey, 98
  Emily, 80
  Jonathan, 98
Tolles
  Marey, 78
Tomkins
  Asahel, 184
  Benjamin, 183
  Betsey, 183
  Jonah, 184
  Marcy, 183
  Nancy, 183
  Polly, 183

Tomlinson
  Elizabeth, 50
  Mary, 50
  Sarah, 50
  Thomas, 50
  William, 50
Tompson
  Benjamin, 180
  Daniel, 180
  French, 180
Torreyson
  Lidia, 140
Torrison
  Catharine, 155
  Lewis, 155
  William, 151
Torryson
  Lewis, 157
Towberman
  Peter, 57
Towner
  Benjamin, 55
  Fanny, 55
  John, 55
Toy
  Mary, 36
Tracey
  Everit, 146
Trahern
  Isaac's heirs, 142
  Israel, 142
  James, 22, 35, 40, 142
  Rebeccah, 22
  Samuel, 142
  Sarah, 22, 142
  Thomas, 137, 142
  William, 22
Trammel
  Jemima, 4
Trammell
  Garard, 11
  Garr, 11
Trayhern
  Dinah, 50
Trayhorn
  Asa, 88
  Enos, 88
  Isaac, 88

Trayhorn
　Israel, 88
　James, 88
　Jesse, 88
　Samuel, 88
　Thomas, 88
Treebe
　John, 11
Tribby
　Asahel, 75, 81
　Elizabeth, 75, 127
　George, 75
　James, 112
　John, 112
　Jonathan, 75
　Joseph, 69, 70, 75
　Josiah, 73
　Louisa, 75
　Mary, 111, 112
　Ruth, 75
　Sarah, 75
　Thomas, 54, 111, 112
Triplet
　Mary, 171
Triplett
　Daniel, 105
　Elizabeth, 17, 132
　Enoch, 44, 132
　Francis, 105
　Gordan, 177
　James, 73, 127, 132
　Jesse, 132
　John, 105
　Katharine, 73
　Lucinda, 73
　Martha, 64, 73
　Mary, 132, 177
　Nancy, 105
　Nathaniel, 105
　Philip, 73
　Reuben, 73, 129, 132
　Samuel, 27
　Sarah, 177
　Simon, 11, 27, 37, 50, 64, 69, 73, 129
　Thomas, 105, 132
　Uriel, 177
　William, 73, 105

Trittipo
　William, 132
Troutman
　Peter, 94
Trussel
　John, 33
Tucker
　Ann, 25
　Christopher, 65
　Mary, 25
Turley
　Alexander, 133
　Ann, 22
　Charles, 22, 30, 133
　Ignatius, 37
　John, 30, 37, 54, 68
　Lawson, 85
　Sarah, 37
Turner
　Anne, 7
　Betty, 49
　Eusebia, 161
　Fielding, 7, 40
　Frances, 110
　George, 151
　James, 84
　Jesse, 166
　John, 40
　Lewis, 7, 40
　Major, 40
　Mary, 132, 161
　Mimy, 71
　Sally, 84
　Samuel, 166, 173
　Thomas, 84
　William, 14, 40
　Winifred, 40
Turnipseed
　Alcinda, 178
Tushtimer
　Jacob, 52
Tutt
　Ann, 95
　Ann Mason, 179
　Charles, 57, 95
　Eliza, 120
Twiddy
　George, 19

Tygert
　Anne, 165
Tyler
　Anne, 6
　Benjamin, 6
　Charles, 6
　Edmund, 110
　Esther, 64
　James, 64
　John, 3, 6, 29, 32, 33, 51, 65, 76, 83, 88
　Letty, 83
　Spence, 6
　Susanna, 6
　William, 6, 23
Tytus
　Francis, 135

—U—

Ullem
　Andrew, 94
　Jacob, 94
　John, 94
　Peggy, 94
Unglesbee
　John, 131
　Thomas, 131
Updike
　Amon, 52
　Amos, 145
　Barsina, 130, 147
　Daniel, 52
　Edon, 145
　Elizabeth, 52
　Jane, 52
　John, 14, 52, 145
　Nancy, 145
　Peggy, 145
　Phebe, 52, 145
　Rufus, 52, 145
　Sally, 145
　Samuel, 52, 145
　Sarah, 52
Upp
　John, 106
　Sarah, 51

Urton
 Besheba, 163
 Jane, 175
 Norman, 163

—V—

Vail
 Nancy, 141
 Nathan, 141
Van Buskirk
 Ann, 179
Vance
 Agnes, 48
Vanderen
 Barnard, 24, 29
Vandevander
 Cornelius, 167
 Isaac, 13
Vandevanter
 A. M., 157, 159, 177
 Albert, 137
 Ann, 142
 Anne, 120
 Armstead, 158
 Cecelia, 171
 Cornelius, 57, 136
 Elizabeth, 120, 142
 Fenton, 137
 Gabriel, 121, 124,
  136, 142, 159, 177
 Isaac, 57, 73, 124,
  136, 167, 177, 184
 James, 136, 167
 John, 57, 64, 73,
  136, 184
 Joseph, 57, 95, 101,
  136, 149, 184
 Mary, 57, 120, 136,
  142, 149, 150, 167
 Pleasant, 68
 Sarah, 57
 Washington, 168
 William, 136
Vandeventer
 Gabriel, 134
 Isaac, 127, 133
Vandiver
 Amenthia, 3

Ann, 3
Edward, 3
George, 3
Sarah, 3, 11
Tobitha, 3
Vanhorn
 Ann, 92
 Chilton, 92
 George, 92
 John, 37
 Sarah, 92
Vanhorne
 Elizabeth, 45
Vanpelt
 John, 42
 Richard, 81
Vansickle
 Emanuel, 156
 Esther, 54
 Mahala, 156
 Philip, 54
 William, 156
Vansickler
 Emanuel, 181
 Hester, 172
 John, 172
 Philip, 85, 172
Vansikle
 Gilbert, 13
Vanvacter
 Solomon, 147, 175
Varnes
 John, 185
Vaugh
 Kizziah, 71
Veal
 E. C., 158
Veale. *See* Darne
 Amos, 38
 Charles, 38
 Elizabeth, 37
 John, 37, 38, 103,
  112, 164
 Linny, 85
 Lydia, 37, 38
 Peggy, 38
 Polly, 38
 Thomas, 37, 38, 103,
  112

William, 38, 92, 103
Vere
 John, 185
Vermilion
 Jane, 132
Vermillion
 Benjamin, 158
 Maria, 158
Vernon
 Daniel, 97, 111
 Hester, 111
 Isaiah, 111
 James, 99
 John, 50, 75, 99, 111
 Phebe, 99
 Rebeckah, 109
 Ruth, 1
Verts
 Jacob, 104
 William, 169
Vestel
 John, 6
Vickers
 Abraham, 118
 Anna, 118
 Rosanah, 138
Vietch
 Jemimah, 86
Vincel
 George, 139
 John, 139, 159
 Mary, 139, 159
 Philip, 139
 Solomon, 139, 143
Vincell
 Adam, 37
Vines
 Ann, 3
Vinner. *See* Winner
 John, 69
Vinsel
 George, 81
Violet
 Ashford, 132
 James, 133
 John, 132
 Phebe, 132
 William, 133

Violett
  Ashford, 127
  Benjamin, 84
  Edward, 114
  Elijah, 84, 127
  James, 84, 127
  Jamimah, 84
  Jemima, 84, 114, 127
  John, 84, 127
  Juliet, 84
  Mary, 127
  Phebe, 127
  Sampson, 84
  Sarah, 114
  William, 127
Virts
  Edw., 180
  Peter, 132
Virtz
  Adam, 102
  Barbary, 102
  Betey, 102
  Caty, 102
  Christiana, 102
  Elizabeth, 102
  Henry, 102
  John, 102
  Peter, 102
  William, 102
Vollmer
  Margaret, 101

—W—

Wade. *See* Waid
  Hannah, 173
  James, 183
  Jesse, 183
  John, 173
  Mary, 183
  Robert, 41, 121
Wager
  Gerard, 131
Waggoner
  Mary, 49
Waid
  Robert, 78

Walker
  Benjamin, 92, 99, 147
  Craven, 129
  Garret, 92
  Garrett, 99, 158
  George, 91
  Isaac, 22, 102, 108, 111, 113, 116, 124, 132, 149, 168
  John, 18
  Martha, 120
  Mary, 158, 179
  Nathan, 154
  Ruth, 99, 158
  Suyntha, 102
  Thornton, 137, 142, 153
  William, 92
Wallace
  Elizabeth, 154
Wallentine
  Catharine, 33
  Elizabeth, 34
  George, 33
  Mary, 34
Walraven
  Josiah, 165
  Lydia, 165
Walrond
  William, 29
Walrund
  Elizabeth, 42
Walsh
  Elizabeth, 115
  George, 115
  Thomas, 115
Walter
  John, 170
Walters
  Dinah, 89, 102
  George, 89
  Isaac, 89, 102
  James, 89, 164
  Mahlon, 89, 102
  Mary, 115
  Sarah, 122
Waltman
  Armistead, 174

Caroline, 174
  David, 101, 108
  Elisebeth, 101, 108
  Emanuel, 23, 100, 166
  George, 23
  Jacob, 23, 82, 89, 101, 108, 174
  John, 101, 108
  Joseph, 101
  Margarita, 23
  Mariah, 108
  Mary, 174
  Mereah, 101
  Michael, 23
  Milton, 174
  Mortimer, 174
  Samuel, 23, 101, 108
  Sary, 179
  William, 23
Walton
  Mary, 48
  Nicholas, 48
  Sarah, 48
Wanger
  Abraham, 4
War
  John, 132
Ward
  Anne, 27
  Elisabeth, 172
  Elizabeth, 47
  Emily, 172
  Lawrence, 22
  Mary, 176
  William, 176
Warfield
  Alexander, 117
  Charles, 117
  David, 117
  Dennis, 117
  Lott, 117
Warford
  Abraham, 55
  Catharine, 55
  Elijah, 78
  Hannah, 55
  James, 78
  Job, 26

Warford
  John, 46, 78
  Lydia, 78
  Mary, 78
  Samuel, 78
  Sarah, 55
  Theodocia, 55
  William, 55
Warner
  Acinda, 144
  Caty, 71
  Leonard, 121
  Sarah, 69
Washington
  Bushrod, 52
  Dorothia, 52
  Elizabeth, 110
  Mildred, 52
  Sarah, 177
Waterman
  A. G., 106, 118
  Augustus, 161
Waters
  Barbara, 180
  Benjamin, 159
  Catharine, 180
  Dorothy, 159
  Elizabeth, 109
  Jacob, 108, 140, 180
  Levi, 180
  Patty, 70
  Plummer, 131
  Susannah, 178
Wathen
  Isaac, 101
Watkins
  Benjamin, 70
  Christian, 63
  Ebenezer, 63
  Leonard, 125
  Sarah, 93
Watson
  Lemuel, 152
  Susannah, 27
  Thomas, 13, 23, 80, 103
  Weldon, 27
  William, 103

Watt
  Duanna, 156
  John, 131, 156
Watter
  John, 185
Watters
  Mahlon, 93
Wattkins
  James, 29
Watton. *See* Walton
Watts
  Thomas, 53
Waugh
  A. P., 152
  Alexander, 54
  Lemuel, 106
  Mary, 90
  Susannah, 54
Wayland
  Sarah, 173
Weadon
  Jane, 42
  John, 153, 161, 175
Weagley
  George, 78
Wealty
  Elizabeth, 130
Wean
  Sarah, 123
Weatherby
  Matthew, 102
Weatherley
  Jane, 79
Webber
  Harriet, 127
Webster
  Anna, 129
  Mary, 143
Weeden
  Josiah, 41
Weedon
  James, 88
  Sarah, 151
Weeks
  Clarissa, 153
  James, 148
Weisel
  Frederick, 3

Weist
  John, 99
Welch
  Jamimah, 14
  Silvester, 14
Weldon
  Nancy, 123
  W. S., 88
Wells
  Jacob, 9
  Noah, 62
  Sally, 62
  Samuel, 62
Welsh
  James, 169
Wenner
  Elizabeth, 108
  Elsebeth, 101
  Emanuel, 101
  John, 101, 108
  Jonathan, 134, 145, 151, 177
  Lydia, 177
  Sarah, 166, 177
  William, 64, 104
Wertenbaker
  Sarah, 173
West
  Ann, 3, 7, 15, 29
  Cato, 2, 7
  Charles, 2, 7, 15, 29
  Elenor, 78
  Elizabeth, 7, 15, 29
  George, 6
  John, 7, 43, 45, 67
  Joseph, 45, 139
  Margaret, 182
  Mary, 2, 7, 184
  Norman, 97
  Thomas, 7, 15, 29
  Uree, 103
  W., 2, 3, 5
  William, 2, 3, 7
Wetsel
  Mary, 129
Whaley
  Amelia, 49
  Ann, 25
  Barbara, 30

Whaley
  Benjamin, 24, 25
  Charles, 25
  Elijah, 25
  Elizabeth, 25
  George, 25
  Gilson, 25, 30
  Henry, 25
  James, 24, 25, 49, 52
  John, 25, 30
  Lettice, 52
  Levy, 49
  Mereman, 49
  Penelope, 25, 34, 49
  Rebecca, 25
  Sarah, 49
  Vincent, 49
  William, 25, 30, 31, 34, 49, 149
  Winnafred, 49
Wharton
  Catherine, 181
Whealer
  Mary, 32
Wheatly
  Margaret, 83
Wheeler
  Elizabeth, 97
  Mary, 178
Whelan
  Catharine, 182
  Catherine, 60
  James, 60, 182
  Judith, 60, 182
  Margaret, 60, 182
  Timothy, 60, 182
  Winnifred, 60, 182
Wherry
  Elizabeth, 110, 136
  Mary, 136
Whitacre
  Abner, 77, 133
  Alice, 77, 128, 133
  Amos, 77, 134
  Ann, 53
  Benjamin, 26, 77
  Caleb, 26, 36, 128
  Ed, 44
  Elizabeth, 26
  Enuck, 26
  George, 26
  Hannah, 134, 147
  John, 40, 77, 114, 134
  Joseph, 26
  Joshua, 26
  Lydia, 129
  Martha, 26, 44
  Neomy, 26
  Phebe, 128
  Robert, 26
  Ruth, 26, 133
  Tamer, 133
  Thomas, 133
  Thornton, 133
White
  Adin, 167
  Agnes, 90, 157
  Albina, 130, 147
  Ann, 36, 87, 95
  B., 118
  Benjamin, 35, 73, 87, 95, 144
  Benniah, 103, 149
  Christeana, 125
  Daniel, 35, 52, 57, 87
  Eden, 144
  Edon, 144
  Eli, 103
  Elizabeth, 51, 87, 107, 130, 144, 147
  George, 167
  Hannah, 144
  James, 73, 77, 90, 116, 149, 157
  Jane, 116
  John, 69, 75, 90, 93, 95, 99, 138
  Josabed, 107
  Joseph, 35, 51, 57, 90, 96
  Josiah, 18, 19, 72, 90, 99, 107, 167
  Josibed, 95
  Jozabed, 93
  Levi, 86, 87
  Louisa, 144
  Margaret, 73, 93, 95, 125
  Mary, 144, 156, 167
  Maryann, 125
  Nancy, 144, 149, 157
  Polly, 69
  Rachel, 72, 107, 130, 147
  Rebecca, 144
  Rebekah, 35
  Richard, 35, 144, 167
  Robert, 59, 77, 90, 134, 149, 157
  Samuel, 35
  Sarah, 51, 93, 95
  Susanna, 79
  Theodore, 93
  Thomas, 37, 41, 72, 76, 90, 116, 121, 129, 138, 149, 158, 160
  Washington, 107, 130, 147
  William, 35, 87, 107, 116
Whitely
  William, 6
Whiteman
  Sarah, 141
Whitmore
  Catherine, 119
  George, 119
  Michael, 119
  Polly, 118
Wiard
  Michael, 151
Wiatt
  Jacob, 43, 81
  Mary, 81
Wiest
  Catharine, 99
Wigginton
  Benjamin, 4, 17
  Eleanor, 17
  Elenor, 17
  Elizabeth, 17
  Ellison, 19
  Henry, 17

Index to Loudoun County Wills, 1757 - 1850

Wigginton
- James, 4, 35
- John, 4
- Presley, 144, 158
- Roger, 12, 17
- Sarah, 4
- Spencer, 19
- William, 17, 19

Wikmen
- William, 9

Wilcoxan
- Levi, 85

Wildman
- Aaron, 115
- Abraham, 36, 124
- Anna, 124
- Elenor, 115, 182
- Elizabeth, 58, 115
- Enos, 100, 115
- Grace, 58
- Hannah, 116
- Jacob, 2, 3, 58, 115
- Jair, 51
- James, 58, 115
- Jane, 100
- John, 58, 115, 179, 182
- Joseph, 58, 115, 179
- Juannah, 115
- Juliann, 115
- Leatitia, 95
- Letitia, 36
- Marcy, 58
- Martin, 179
- Mary, 58
- Millary, 115
- Nancy, 115
- Polly, 68
- Rachel, 58
- Rebecca, 97
- Sarah, 58, 115

Wiley
- Garitson, 135
- William, 162

Wilkenson
- Anna, 129
- Hannah, 129
- John, 129
- Joseph, 129
- Mary, 129

Wilkinson
- Eleanor, 173
- George, 46
- Israel, 90
- Jesse, 50
- Joseph, 50
- Macha, 90
- Rachel, 50
- Thomas, 85

Wilkison
- Elizabeth, 115
- William, 115

Wilks
- Samuel, 14, 34

Willcoxson
- Agnes, 4
- Elizabeth, 4
- John:, 4
- Mary, 4

Willett
- Elizabeth, 178
- George, 178
- Sarah, 170

William
- Joseph, 152

Williams
- Abner, 28, 50, 51, 80, 143, 149
- Agathy, 26
- Ann, 40
- Daniel, 29
- Eleazer, 50
- Elijah, 16
- Elizabeth, 28, 64
- Enos, 45, 53, 57
- Hannah, 28, 57, 64, 147
- Henry, 28
- Isaac, 171
- Israel, 64
- J., 48, 50, 53, 85
- James, 45, 128
- Jane, 68
- Jenkins, 31
- Jeremiah, 23
- Jinkin, 45
- John, 6, 15, 28, 43, 51, 74, 75, 78, 80, 86, 87, 89, 93, 95, 97, 102, 113, 116, 124, 132, 143, 149
- Joseph, 45
- Joshua, 26
- Jude(y), 54
- Levi, 72
- Lydia, 75, 86, 124
- Margrate, 45
- Martha, 147
- Notley, 10, 72, 128
- Original, 1
- Presly, 94
- Rachel, 149
- Rebecca, 80, 143
- Rehoboth, 28
- Richard, 9, 45, 57
- Samuel, 72
- Sarah, 152, 157
- Susanna, 43
- Sydnor, 147
- Thomas, 12, 68, 157
- Unce, 28
- Uriah, 31, 59
- Walter, 10
- William, 11, 28, 39, 74, 149
- Willis, 152
- Wilson, 113
- Zachariah, 130

Williamson
- Jesse, 129
- Nancy, 42

Willis
- Nicholas, 97

Willson
- Alexander, 38, 182
- Asa, 67
- Cathrine, 15
- David, 12
- Ebenezer, 67
- Elenor, 38
- Elizabeth, 15, 38, 182
- George, 15
- Hannah, 67
- James, 38, 182

Willson
  Jane, 67
  John, 18, 67
  Joseph, 15
  Margaret, 15
  Nancy, 67
  Samuel, 67
  Thomas, 67
  William, 38, 182
Wilson
  Anna, 110
  Charlotte, 159
  Elizabeth, 91, 137, 172
  Fanny, 127
  Hannah, 153
  Henry, 31, 77, 84, 91
  James, 21, 148
  Jane, 106
  John, 31, 83, 95, 101, 105, 106, 110, 116, 136, 141, 146, 158, 164, 174, 182
  Julia, 138, 154
  Juliet, 148
  Kezia, 31
  Levi, 71
  Lydia, 127
  Mahlon, 95
  Maria, 31, 78, 91
  Martha, 51
  Mary, 21, 31, 150, 158
  Milly, 159
  Nelson, 148
  Norvil, 159
  Presley, 123
  Richard, 127
  Robert, 183
  Russel, 2
  Tamer, 114
  Thomas, 153
  William, 164, 172
Wince
  Catherine, 127
  Philip, 127
Wincel
  George, 129
  Philip, 176
Winder
  Adah, 127
  William, 51
Windgrove
  Elizabeth, 66
  John, 66
  Nancy, 66
Windsor
  Richard, 129
  Thomas, 129
Wine
  Ann, 164
  Catharine, 109
  Christian, 55
  Daniel, 109, 130
  George, 109
  Jacob, 109
  John, 109
Winegardner
  Harbard, 19
  Henry, 19
  Levi, 135
Winifred
  Mary. {Rev., 156
Winlock
  Effy, 55
  Joseph, 55
Winner
  John, 69
Winsell
  George, 115
Winser
  John, 4
Wintzel
  Adam, 11
  Elizabeth, 11
Wirnald
  Rachel, 115
Wirts
  Anna Mary, 47
  Catharine, 47
  Christina, 48
  Henry, 124
  Jacob, 47, 124
  John, 48, 124, 176
  Louinda, 124
  Mary, 124
  Michael, 48
  Peter, 47, 124
  Susannah, 124
  William, 47, 124
Wirtz
  Peter, 140
  William, 139
Wise
  George, 147
  Joseph, 140
Wisheart
  Henry, 14
Wissinger
  Peggy, 100
Wolcard
  William, 71
Wolf
  Ann, 165
  John, 24
  Mary, 75
Wolfinger
  Jacob, 180
Wolforde
  George, 139
Wolikin
  Judy, 128
Wollard
  Joseph, 71
  Mary, 71
Wood
  Joseph, 80, 110, 159, 162
  Lashley, 19
  Lidia, 159
  Lydia, 137, 161
  Mary, 22
  Milley, 22
  William, 161
Woodard
  Jamima, 64
  Octavia, 155
Wooddy
  David, 105
  Elizabeth, 105
  James, 105, 139
  John, 105
  Mary, 105
  Ruth, 105
  William, 105

Woodey
  Elizabeth, 84
Woodford
  Elizabeth, 127
  William, 60
Woodward
  Jane, 12
  Jesse, 12
  Prudence, 12, 41
  Sarah, 12
Woofter
  Betsey, 83
  James, 66
  John, 67
  Jonathan, 67
  Mary, 66
  Priscilla, 67
  Sebastian, 66
  Susanna, 67
Wooleard
  William, 59
Woolford
  Jane, 130
Woollard
  Ann, 32
  Elender, 32
  Elizabeth, 32
  Isaac, 32
  Jean, 32
  John, 32
  Joseph, 32
  Mary, 32
  William, 32
Wornal
  John, 146
Wornall
  Edey, 25
  Elizabeth, 25
  James, 25, 91
  Mary, 91
  Roby, 25
  Thomas, 25
  William, 91
Wornel
  Agnes, 140
  Charlotte, 140
  Elizabeth, 140
  James, 140
  John, 140
Wornell
  John, 105
Worsley
  Eliza, 133
  Elizabeth, 133
  Frances, 133
  Jane, 133
  John, 105, 133
  Mary, 133
  William, 133, 173
Worthington
  Cassandra, 166
  Elizabeth, 64, 88, 109, 166, 175
  Harriet, 166
  Joseph, 166, 175
  Joshua, 109, 175
  Lucy, 166
  Nancy, 166
  Sarah, 166
Wren
  James, 62
  Jane, 62
  Margaret, 62
  Mary, 78, 84
  Patsy, 119
  Sanford, 78
  Sarah, 149
  Thomas, 120
  Travis, 62
  William, 20, 62, 78, 84
Wrenn
  Elizabeth, 171
Wright
  Alfred, 137
  Anthony, 96
  Aron, 162
  C. F., 177
  Catharine, 163
  Charles, 132, 137
  Charlotte, 174
  Daniel, 96
  Edward, 163
  Effy, 162
  Elizabeth, 96, 163, 175
  Ellen, 175
  John, 96, 133, 147, 163
  Joseph, 160, 162, 163
  Jotham, 142, 147
  Julius, 163
  Lewis, 163
  Margaret, 41
  Martha, 24, 30
  Mary, 1, 132, 137, 147, 163
  Moses, 96
  Nancy, 160, 162, 163, 174
  Patterson, 96, 160, 162
  Robert, 41, 96, 175
  Samuel, 52, 68, 96, 160
  Sarah, 175
  Sarah Ann, 163
  W. G., 121
  William, 24, 68, 96, 138, 160, 162
Wunder
  H. S., 152
  Thomas, 183
Wyatt
  Abner, 11
  Edward, 11
  John, 11
  Margaret, 11
  Reuben, 11
  Ruth, 11
  Thomas, 11
  William, 117
Wyckoff
  Nicholas, 14
Wycoff
  Cornelius, 56
Wyer
  Uriah, 56
Wykoff
  Abraham, 70
  Cornelius, 70
  Isaac, 70
  Margaret, 70
  Nicholas, 70
  Peter, 70

Wynkoop
  William, 169
Wynn
  Jesse, 80
  John, 131
  Mary, 131
  Robert, 28, 41, 48, 51
  Susanna, 131
  Ulysses, 131

—Y—

Yakey
  John, 169
  Martin, 169
  Simon, 143, 169
Yates
  Alice, 2
  Benjamin, 2
  Hannah, 2
  Isaac, 2
  Jane, 2
  Joseph, 2
  Mary, 27

  Providence, 2
  Robert, 2
  Sarah, 79, 86
  William, 2
Yeaca
  Catharine, 79
  Elizabeth, 79
  Jacob, 79
  Martin, 79
  Mary, 79
  Peter, 79
  Simon, 79
Yeakey
  Barbara, 176
Yeates
  Benjamin, 17
  George, 17
  Johanna, 17
  Joshua, 17
  Samuel, 17
Yeco
  Simon, 75

Yoe
  William, 67

Young
  Abner, 120
  Archibald, 76
  David, 92, 124, 155
  Effee, 103
  Elizabeth, 85, 124, 155
  Emily, 166, 175
  Israel, 114
  John, 85, 146
  Rebecca, 163
  Samuel, 88
  Thomas, 166
  William, 163

—Z—

Zimmerman
  Eliza, 150, 177
  Elizabeth, 154, 172
  Henry, 177
  Samuel, 172

www.ingramcontent.com/pod-product-compliance
Lightning Source LLC
Chambersburg PA
CBHW071700160426
43195CB00012B/1533